# Contents

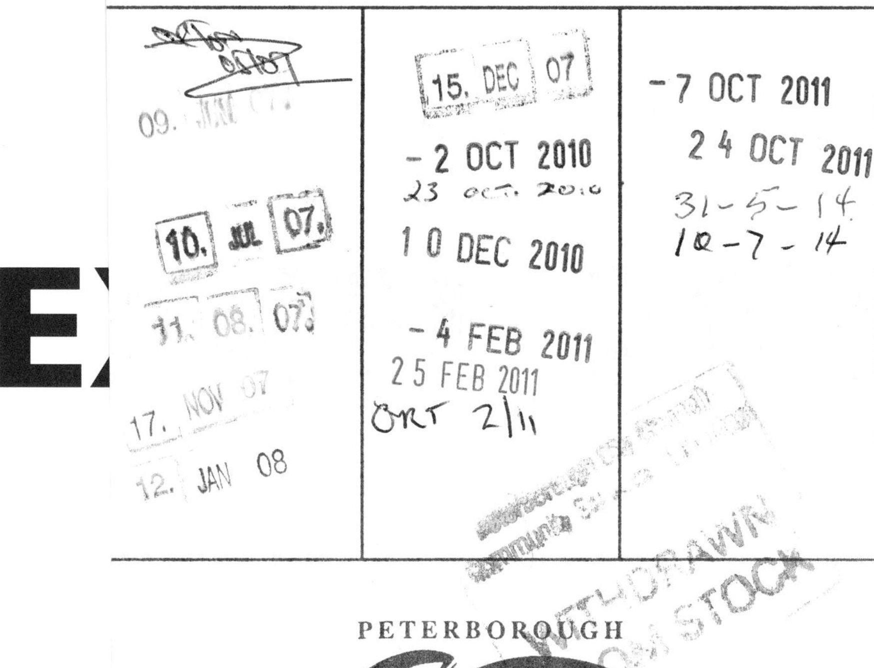

In easy steps is an imprint of Computer Step
Southfield Road · Southam
Warwickshire CV47 0FB · United Kingdom
www.ineasysteps.com









Printed and bound in the United Kingdom

ISBN-13 978-1-84078-317-9
ISBN-10 1-84078-317-6

# 1 Introduction

*This chapter shows how the spreadsheet, the electronic counterpart of the paper ledger, has evolved in Excel, taking advantage of the features in the associated Microsoft Office System and the supporting Windows systems (Vista and XP).*

# The Spreadsheet Concept

Spreadsheets, in the guise of the accountant's ledger sheet, have been in use for many, many years. They consisted of paper forms with a two-dimensional grid of rows and columns, often on extra-large paper, for example forming two pages of a ledger book (hence the term spreadsheet). They were typically employed by accountants to prepare budget or financial statements. Each row would represent a different item, with each column showing the value or amount for that item over a given time period. For example, a forecast for 30% margin and 10% growth might show:

**Don't forget**

Ledger sheets predate computers and hand calculators and have been in use for literally hundreds of years.

| | | | | | | |
|---|---|---|---|---|---|---|
| Margin % | 30 | | | | | |
| Growth % | 10 | | | | | |
| | | | | Profit Forecast | | |
| | | January | February | March | April | May |
| Cost of Goods | | 6,000 | 6,600 | 7,260 | 7,986 | 8,785 |
| Sales | | 7,800 | 8,580 | 9,438 | 10,382 | 11,420 |
| Profit | | 1,800 | 1,980 | 2,178 | 2,396 | 2,635 |
| Total Profit | | 1,800 | 3,780 | 5,958 | 8,354 | 10,989 |

Any changes to the basic figures would mean that all the values would have to be recalculated and transcribed to another ledger sheet to show the effect, e.g. for 20% margin and 60% growth:

| | | | | | | |
|---|---|---|---|---|---|---|
| Margin % | 20 | | | | | |
| Growth % | 60 | | | | | |
| | | | | Profit Forecast | | |
| | | January | February | March | April | May |
| Cost of Goods | | 6,000 | 9,600 | 15,360 | 24,576 | 39,322 |
| Sales | | 7,200 | 11,520 | 18,432 | 29,491 | 47,186 |
| Profit | | 1,200 | 1,920 | 3,072 | 4,915 | 7,864 |
| Total Profit | | 1,200 | 3,120 | 6,192 | 11,107 | 18,972 |

To make another change, for example to show 10% margin and 200% growth, would involve a completely new set of calculations. And each time, there would be the possibility of a calculation or transcription error creeping in.

**Don't forget**

The first spreadsheet application was VisiCorp's VisiCalc (visible calculator). Numerous competitive programs appeared, but market leadership was taken first by Lotus 123, and now by Microsoft Excel.

With the advent of the personal computer, a new approach became possible. Applications were developed to simulate the operation of the financial ledger sheet, but the boxes (known as cells) that formed the rows and columns could store text, numbers or a calculation formula based on the contents of other cells. The spreadsheet looked the same, since it was the results that were displayed rather than the formulas themselves. However, when the contents of a cell were changed in the spreadsheet, all the cells whose values depended on that cell were automatically recalculated.

This new approach allowed a vast improvement in productivity for activities such as forecasting. In the example shown above, you'd set up the initial spreadsheet using formulas, rather than calculating the individual cell values. Your spreadsheet might contain a set of values and formulas, for example:

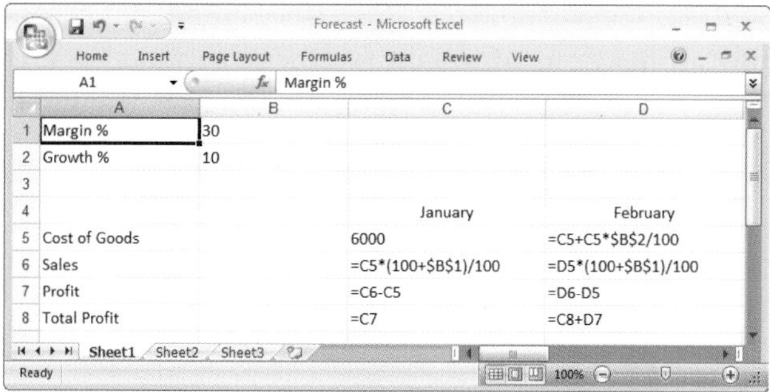

| | A | B | C | D |
|---|---|---|---|---|
| 1 | Margin % | 30 | | |
| 2 | Growth % | 10 | | |
| 3 | | | | |
| 4 | | | January | February |
| 5 | Cost of Goods | | 6000 | =C5+C5*$B$2/100 |
| 6 | Sales | | =C5*(100+$B$1)/100 | =D5*(100+$B$1)/100 |
| 7 | Profit | | =C6-C5 | =D6-D5 |
| 8 | Total Profit | | =C7 | =C8+D7 |

The = sign signifies to Excel that what follows is a formula and must be calculated.

However, what would normally be displayed is the actual values that the formulas compute, based on the contents of other cells:

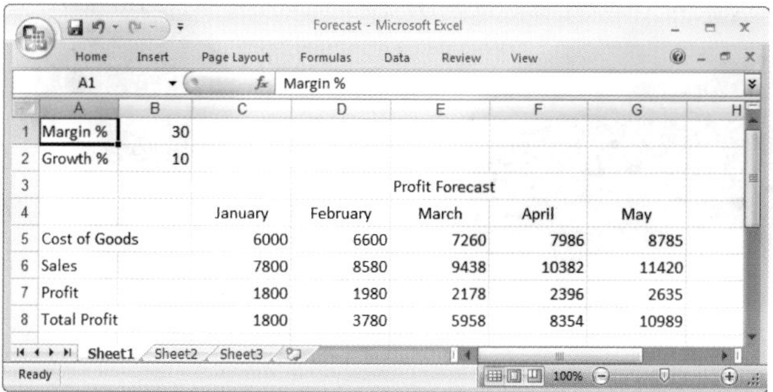

| | A | B | C | D | E | F | G |
|---|---|---|---|---|---|---|---|
| 1 | Margin % | 30 | | | | | |
| 2 | Growth % | 10 | | | | | |
| 3 | | | | | Profit Forecast | | |
| 4 | | | January | February | March | April | May |
| 5 | Cost of Goods | | 6000 | 6600 | 7260 | 7986 | 8785 |
| 6 | Sales | | 7800 | 8580 | 9438 | 10382 | 11420 |
| 7 | Profit | | 1800 | 1980 | 2178 | 2396 | 2635 |
| 8 | Total Profit | | 1800 | 3780 | 5958 | 8354 | 10989 |

When you want to see the effect of changes, e.g. different values for margin and growth, you change just those items, and instantly see the effect as the values calculated by the formulas are adjusted.

The capabilities of the spreadsheet applications have evolved, and the use of spreadsheets has extended far beyond the original financial planning and reporting. They can handle any activity that involves arrays of values interrelated by formulas, for example grading examination scores, interpreting experimental data, or keeping track of assets and inventories. In fact, the newest spreadsheet applications seem to support just about any requirement you can imagine.

Sets of predefined functions were added, plus support for writing small programs or macros to manipulate the data. Further developments incorporated graphs, images and audio.

# Microsoft Excel

VisiCalc and Lotus 123 were MS-DOS programs, subject to its command-line interface, but Microsoft Excel was developed for Windows. It was the first spreadsheet program to allow users to control the visual aspects of the spreadsheet (fonts, character attributes and cell appearance). It introduced intelligent cell recomputation, where only cells dependent on the cell being modified are updated (previous spreadsheet programs recomputed everything all the time, or waited for a specific Recalc command).

Later versions of Excel were shipped as part of the bundled Microsoft Office suite of applications, which included programs such as Microsoft Word and Microsoft PowerPoint.

Versions of Excel for Microsoft Windows and Office include:

| | | |
|---|---|---|
| 1987 | Excel 2.0 | Windows |
| 1990 | Excel 3.0 | Windows |
| 1992 | Excel 4.0 | Windows |
| 1993 | Excel 5.0 | Windows |
| 1995 | Excel 7.0 | Office 95 |
| 1997 | Excel 8.0 | Office 97 |
| 1999 | Excel 9.0 | Office 2000 |
| 2001 | Excel 10.0 | Office XP |
| 2003 | Excel 11.0 | Office 2003 |
| 2007 | Excel 12.0 | Office 2007 |

The newer versions of Excel provide many enhancements to the user interface, and incorporate connections with Microsoft Office and other applications. The basis of the program, however, remains the same. It still consists of a large array of cells organized into rows and columns, and containing data values or formulas with relative or absolute references to other cells. This means that many of the techniques and recommendations included in this book will be applicable, whichever version of Excel you may be using, or even if you are using a spreadsheet from another family of products, though of course the specifics of the instructions may need to be adjusted.

**Don't forget**

Microsoft Multiplan, the predecessor of Excel, was an MS-DOS program. There were also Apple Mac versions of Excel, starting with Excel 1.0.

**Don't forget**

Originally, the program was referred to by the full name Microsoft Excel, since the name Excel belonged to a financial software program. However, Microsoft now owns that trademark, so this distinction is no longer necessary.

# Microsoft Office 2007

Microsoft Office 2007 is part of the 2007 Microsoft Office System, which also includes Microsoft Office servers, services and Web access programs. It replaces the previous version, Microsoft Office 2003, and is shipped in eight different editions:

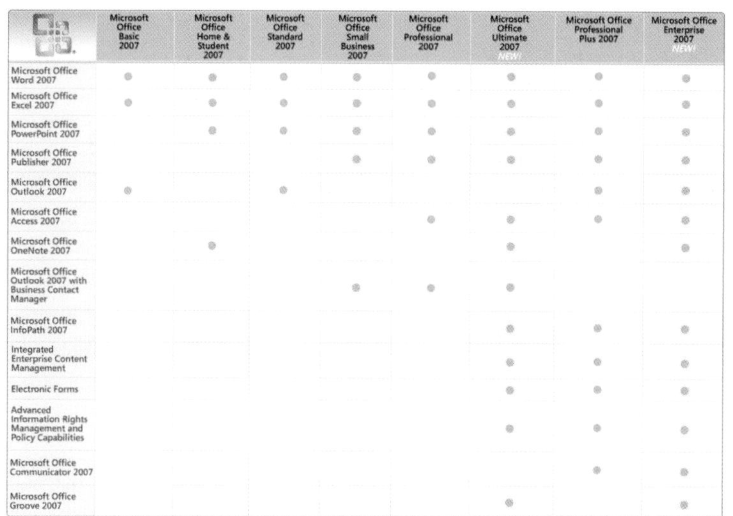

| | Microsoft Office Basic 2007 | Microsoft Office Home & Student 2007 | Microsoft Office Standard 2007 | Microsoft Office Small Business 2007 | Microsoft Office Professional 2007 | Microsoft Office Ultimate 2007 NEW! | Microsoft Office Professional Plus 2007 | Microsoft Office Enterprise 2007 NEW! |
|---|---|---|---|---|---|---|---|---|
| Microsoft Office Word 2007 | ● | ● | ● | ● | ● | ● | ● | ● |
| Microsoft Office Excel 2007 | ● | ● | ● | ● | ● | ● | ● | ● |
| Microsoft Office PowerPoint 2007 | | ● | ● | ● | ● | ● | ● | ● |
| Microsoft Office Publisher 2007 | | | | ● | ● | ● | ● | ● |
| Microsoft Office Outlook 2007 | ● | | ● | | | | ● | ● |
| Microsoft Office Access 2007 | | | | | ● | ● | ● | ● |
| Microsoft Office OneNote 2007 | | ● | | | | ● | | ● |
| Microsoft Office Outlook 2007 with Business Contact Manager | | | | ● | ● | ● | | |
| Microsoft Office InfoPath 2007 | | | | | | ● | ● | ● |
| Integrated Enterprise Content Management | | | | | | ● | ● | ● |
| Electronic Forms | | | | | | ● | ● | ● |
| Advanced Information Rights Management and Policy Capabilities | | | | | | ● | ● | ● |
| Microsoft Office Communicator 2007 | | | | | | | ● | ● |
| Microsoft Office Groove 2007 | | | | | | ● | | ● |

All these editions include Microsoft Excel, and this application is also available as a separate, stand-alone product.

Excel (along with Word, PowerPoint, Access and Outlook) incorporates the new result-oriented user interface, with the Ribbon, the Office button, Galleries, Live Preview and other features. It also uses the new Microsoft Office file format, OpenXML, as the default file format.

The file format is based on XML and uses ZIP compression, so files will be up to 75% smaller than those in the previous Microsoft Office file formats.

There's enhanced Help in Office 2007, with the User Assistance System that replaces the Office Assistants. In the new system, Super Tooltips explain what each button does, and how each function performs.

Other shared Office features include the Document Theme, which defines colors, fonts and graphic effects for a spreadsheet or other Office document, and collaboration services for sharing spreadsheets and documents with other users.

**Hot tip**

You may sometimes see this product referred to as Office 12, since this is the internal numbering system used by Microsoft development teams.

**Don't forget**

Excel 2007 also supports the XPS (Extended Paper Specification) and the Adobe PDF (Portable Document Format) file formats. A separate download is required for these formats.

# What's New in Excel 2007

**Don't forget**

A spreadsheet in Excel contains multiple sheets, each of which is known as a Worksheet. The set of worksheets in the Excel file forms a Workbook.

In addition to the new features of Microsoft Office 2007 that are shared with the other Office applications, Microsoft Excel has its own exclusive new features. These include:

1. Worksheets can have up to 1,048,576 rows and 16,384 columns, rather than the previous limits of 65,536 by 256

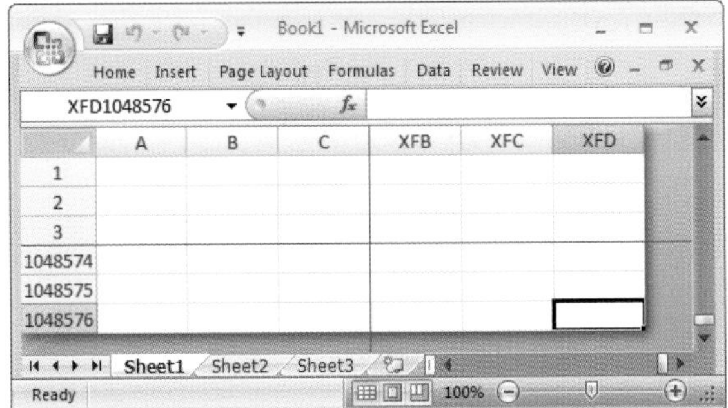


2. Color Scales, Icon Sets and Data Bars apply conditional formatting, based on values of cells in a group

3. Page Layout view allows you to create and update spreadsheets as they will appear when printed

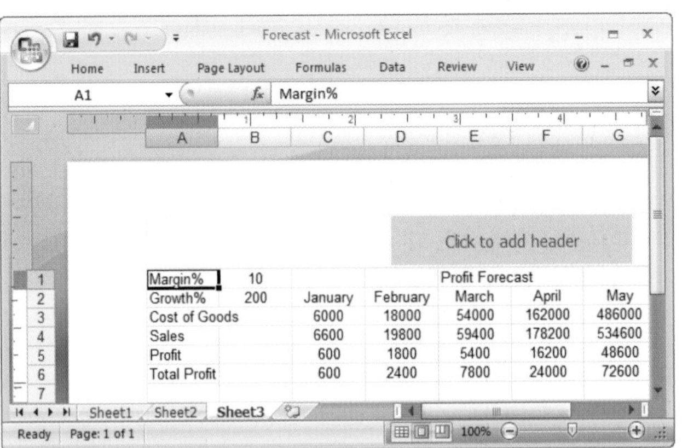


4. The new charting engine supports advanced formatting, including 3D rendering, transparencies and shadows, and will highlight trends in the data.

# System Requirements

To install and run Excel 2007, your computer should match or better the minimum hardware and operating system requirements for Office 2007. If you are upgrading to Office 2007 from Office 2003, the hardware should already meet the requirements, though you may need to upgrade your operating system. For an upgrade from Office 2000 or Office XP, you will need to check that both hardware and operating system meet the minimum specifications for Office 2007, which include:

| | |
|---|---|
| Operating system | Windows XP SP2, Windows Server 2003 or Windows Vista |
| Processor speed: | 500 MHz or higher |
| Memory | 256 MB or higher |
| Devices | DVD drive |
| Hard disk | 2 GB available space for installation |
| Monitor | 800x600 minimum resolution (1024x768 or higher recommended) |
| Internet connection | Broadband connection recommended for download and product activation |

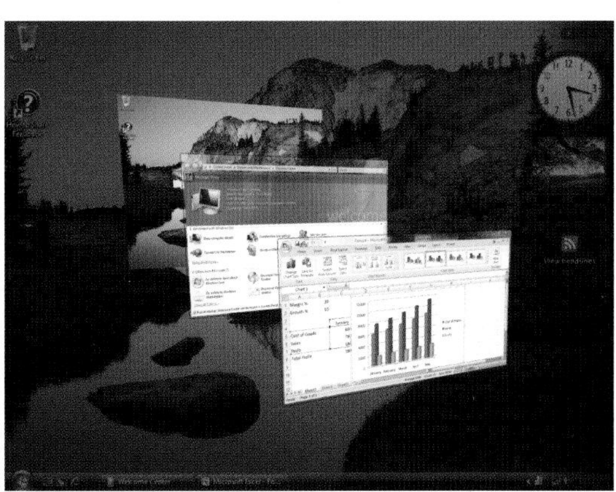

Don't forget

These are minimum requirements. You may need other components to use some of the features in Excel (e.g. a sound card and speakers to handle audio clips).

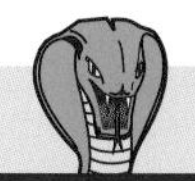

Beware

Your computer must also meet the hardware requirements for your chosen operating system. These may exceed the minimum specifications for Office 2007, especially with advanced systems such as Windows Vista Aero.

## Additional Software Requirements

If you have another computer that is still running Office 2000, Office XP or Office 2003, and you need to work with Excel files that are in the Office 2007 format, you must download the Office 2007 Compatibility Pack from www.microsoft.com/downloads.

# The Office 2007 Ribbon

The menus and toolbars that were used in previous versions of Excel used a top-down approach that made it difficult to find the appropriate tools. These have been replaced by the Ribbon. With this, commands are organized in logical groups under command tabs. These include the Home, Insert, Page Layout, Formulas, Data and Review tabs, and they follow the order in which tasks are normally performed. When you click any of these tabs, the corresponding commands are displayed in the Ribbon.

Hot tip

Other Office 2007 programs that use the Ribbon include Access, PowerPoint, Word and some parts of Outlook.

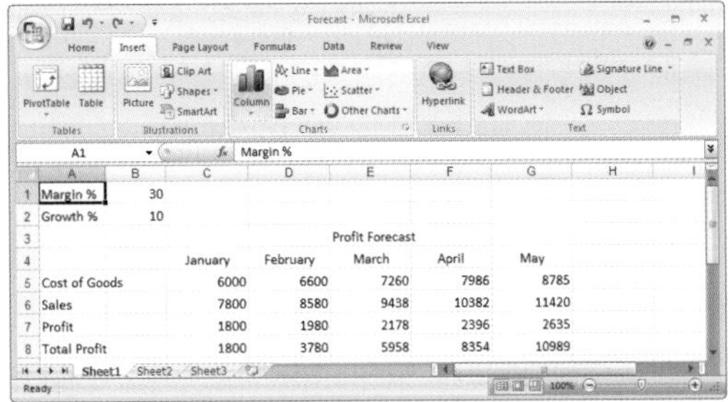


The Ribbon may also include contextual command tabs, which appear when you perform a specific task. For example, if you select some data and then click the Column button in Charts, the chart tool tabs Design, Layout and Format will be displayed.

Don't forget

The File menu is replaced by the Office button, positioned to the left of the Command tab line. This provides general document file functions (see page 18).

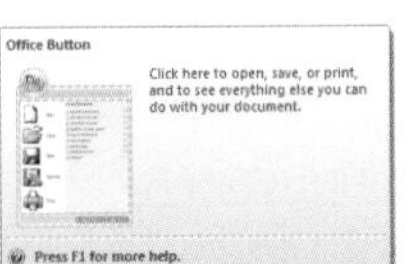


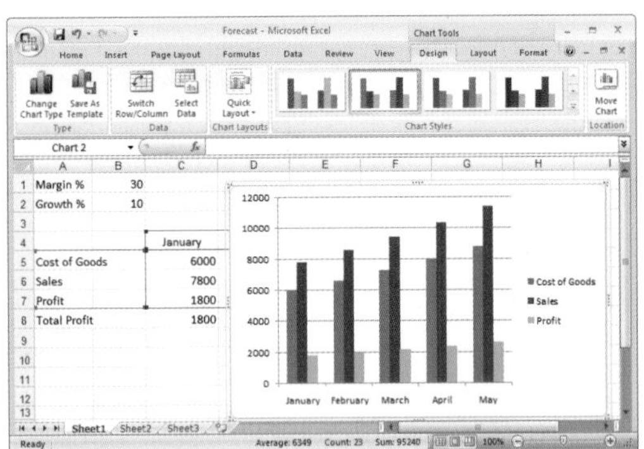


You can access the commands on the Ribbon using shortcut keys, even when the Ribbon has been minimized (see page 118).

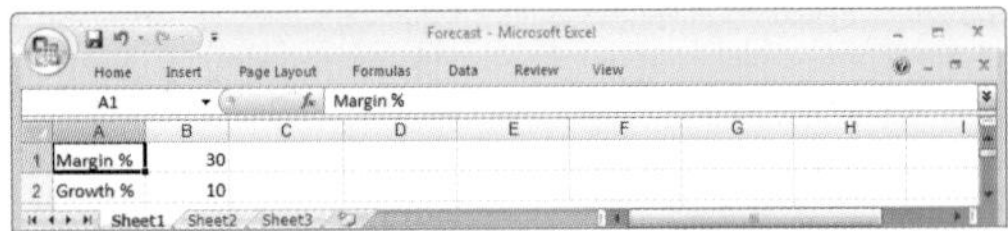

# Start Excel under XP

To start Excel 2007 when it is installed under Windows XP:

1. Click the Start button, then click All Programs and then click Microsoft Office

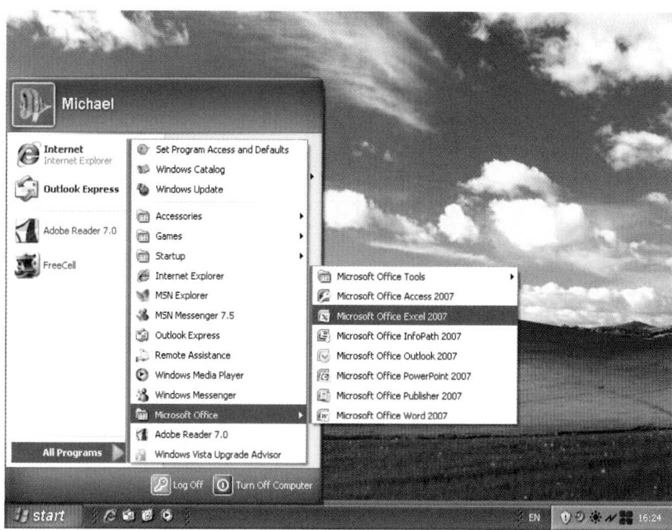


2. Click the Microsoft Office Excel 2007 entry

The next time you want to run Excel, you will find its entry in the list of recently used programs.

To ensure that Excel is always available on the main Start Menu list:

1. Right-click the Excel entry and select Pin to Start menu

2. An entry for Excel will be added above the line, in the top section of the Start menu

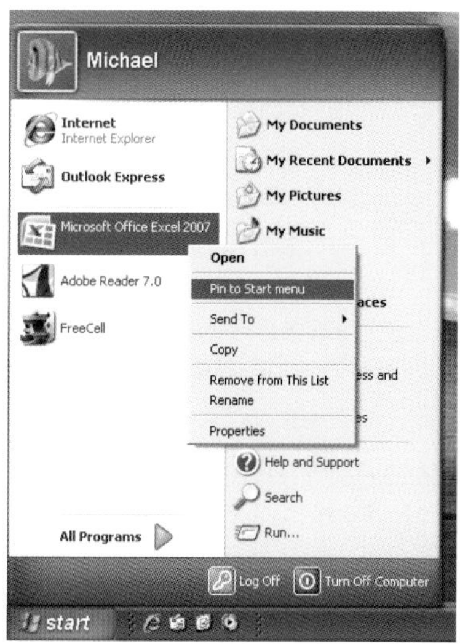

# Start Excel under Vista

With Excel installed under Windows Vista, you will use the new style of Start menu to begin running Excel 2007.

1. Click the Start button (with the Windows logo) and move the mouse pointer over the All Programs entry

2. When the program list appears, click Microsoft Office and select Microsoft Office Excel 2007

Excel will be added to the list of recently used programs.

3. Right-click the Excel entry and select Pin to Start Menu to add it to the fixed list of programs, above the line on the Start menu

4. Alternatively, you can select Add to Quick Launch, to put the Excel entry there

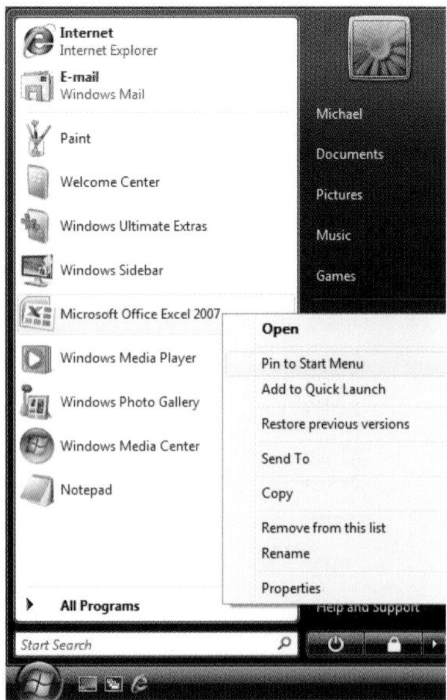

# Activation

When you start Excel for the first time after installation, you will be prompted for the Product Key, if you have not already entered this during Setup. When you enter the key, the Activation Wizard will start up.

If you are connected to the Internet, the Wizard contacts the Microsoft licensing servers to validate your product key and activate your program.

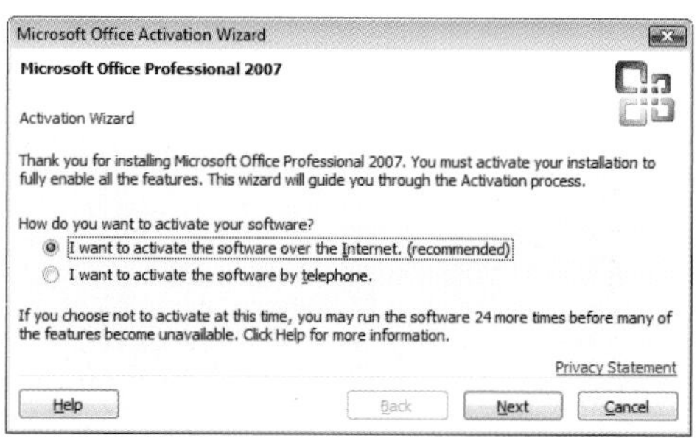


Once this is completed, you are given the chance to register for free online services from Microsoft, such as the Office Live subscription.

1. Click Go to Office Online

2. Click the button, and provide your details, to set up your personalized interface to http://office.microsoft.com/

## Hot tip

Activation is Microsoft's anti-piracy procedure, designed to verify that software products are legitimately licensed.

## Don't forget

Microsoft Office Live is a hosted service that can provide you with a free domain name, a website and email accounts.

## ...cont'd

If you do not have an Internet connection available, telephone the Activation Center using the number provided by the Activation Wizard, and activate your product with the help of the customer service representative.

If you chose to cancel the Activation Wizard the first time you started the application, you can initiate activation at a more convenient time.

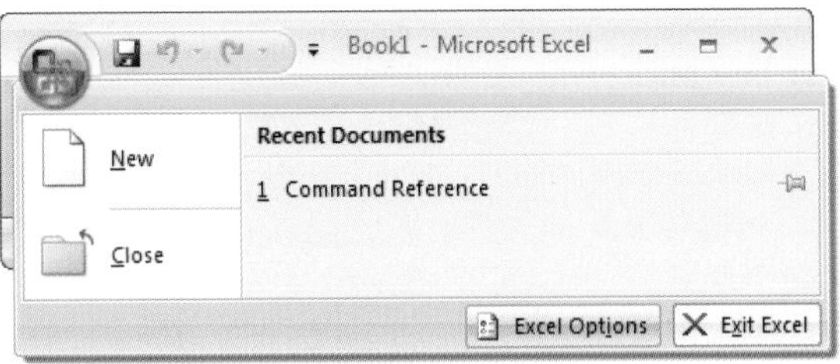

**Beware**

You can run Excel up to 25 times, but after that it acts as a viewer only, without the ability to create or modify spreadsheets, until you do enter the product key and activate the product.

1. Click the Microsoft Office button, and then click the Excel Options button

2. Click Resources, click Activate, and follow the Activation Wizard prompts

If your software has already been activated, you will receive a notification message.

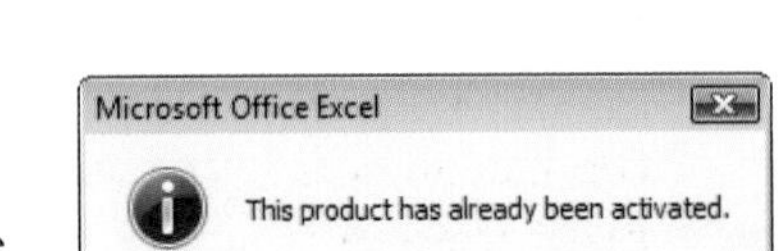

# Excel Command Reference

The new user interface may be very logical and intuitive, but if you are used to a previous release of Excel you may have trouble finding a particular command. If so, you'll be able to locate the equivalent command in Excel 2007 using the Excel 2003 command reference guide.

1. Start Excel and click the Excel Help button, or press the F1 key

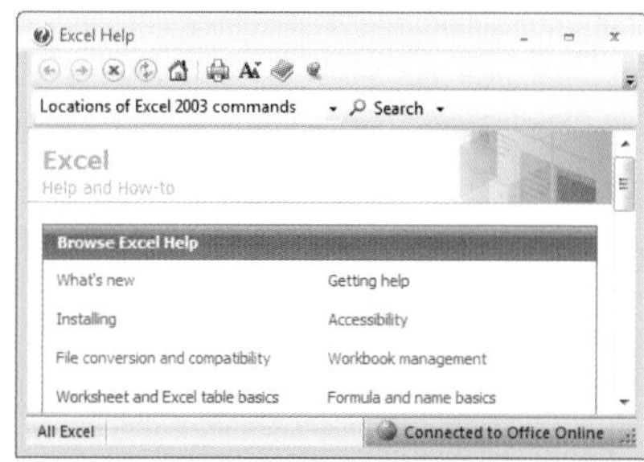


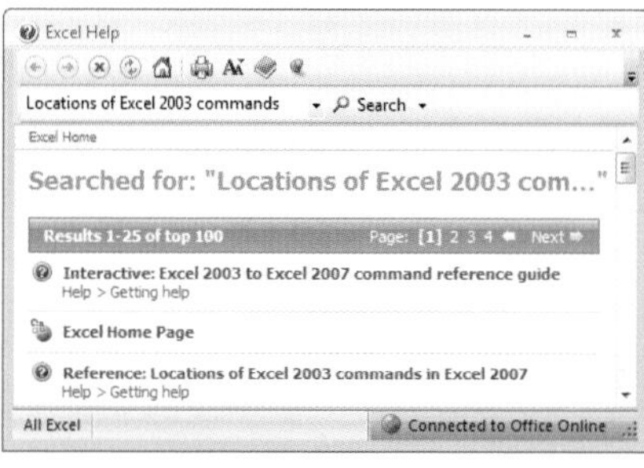


2. Search for the topic Locations of Excel 2003 Commands

3. Select the Reference entry; then scroll down and click the link for the Excel Ribbon Mapping Workbook

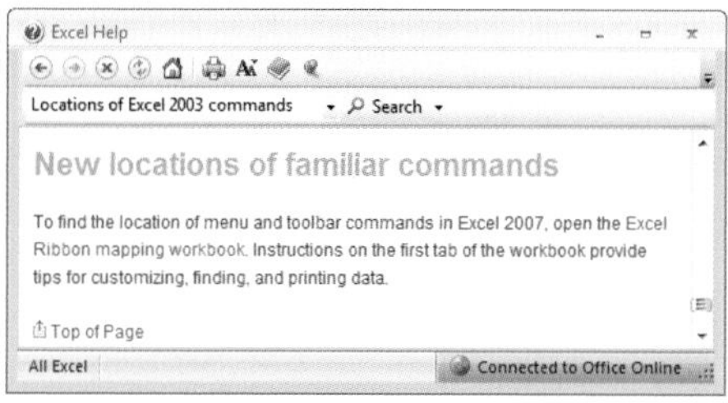


4. Select Save to download the workbook file to your disk drive. Select the Documents folder, to make it easier to locate the workbook.

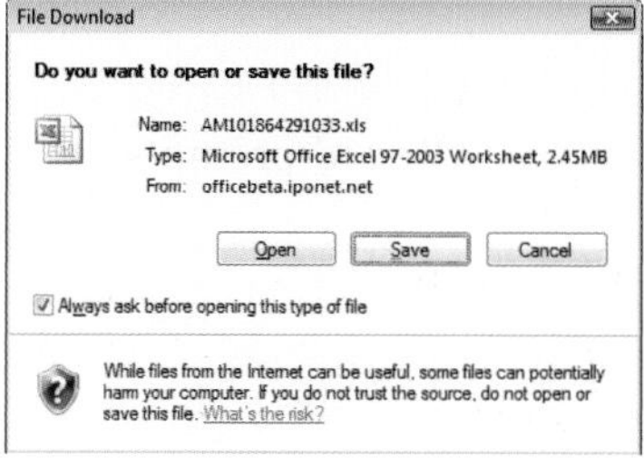


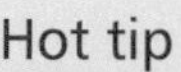

You should enable the option to show content from Office Online, to get the latest version of the reference. See page 35 for more information about using Microsoft Office Excel Help.

You could open the workbook immediately, but it is better to save it to disk so that it is available the next time you are looking for a command.

## ...cont'd

**Don't forget**

There are more than forty worksheets in the Command Reference. To list them, right-click the Worksheet scroll bar. Click More Sheets, if the menu or toolbar you want isn't shown.

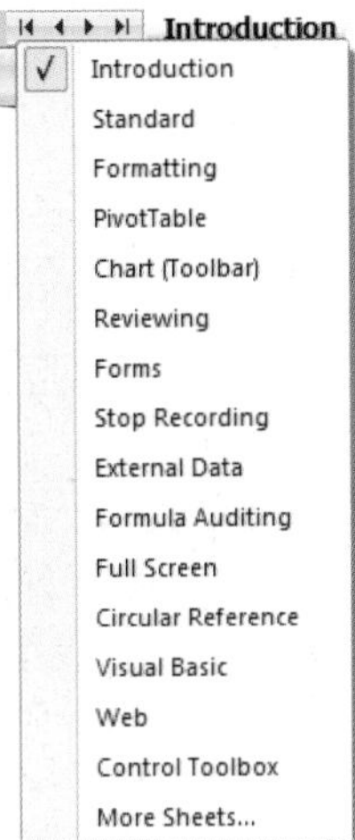


5. Click the Office button, select Open, and then locate and select the downloaded file and press the Open button

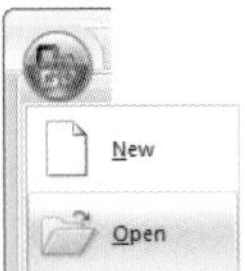


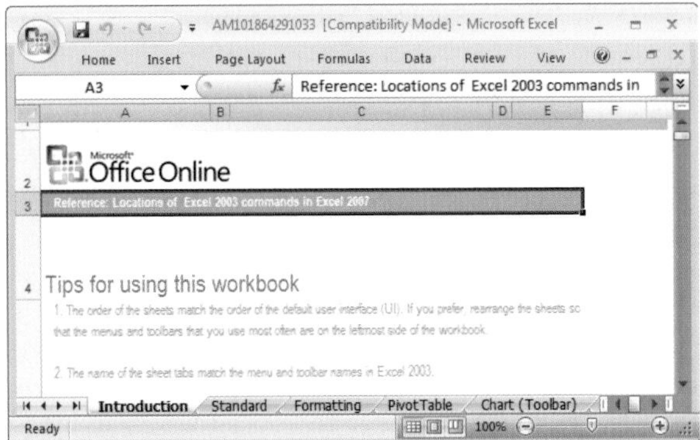


There is a worksheet for each of the menu and toolbar names from Excel 2003. For example, the File worksheet lists the commands now located via the Office button.

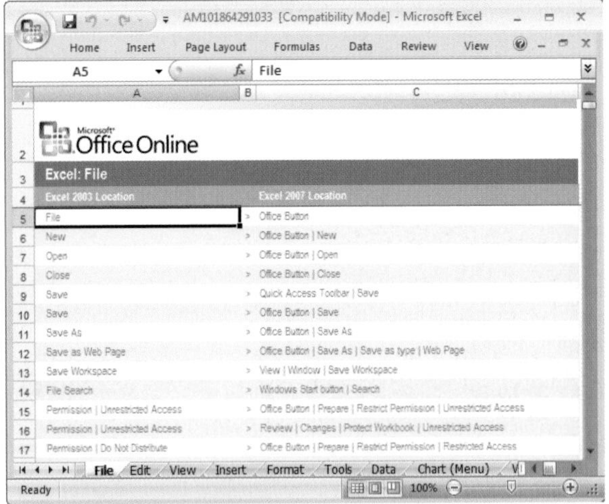


6. To search for a specific command, click the Home tab and click Find & Select, and then Find

7. Type the command name you wish to locate. Options must be set to search within Workbook, not just Sheet

Copy & Paste

# 2 Begin with Excel

*We start with a simple workbook to show what's involved in entering, modifying and formatting data, and performing calculations. This includes ways in which Excel helps to minimize the effort. We cover printing, look at Excel Help, and discuss the various file formats associated with Excel.*

# The Excel Window

Workbook is the term that Microsoft uses for an Excel spreadsheet.

When you start Excel it displays the Excel window with a blank workbook called Book1.

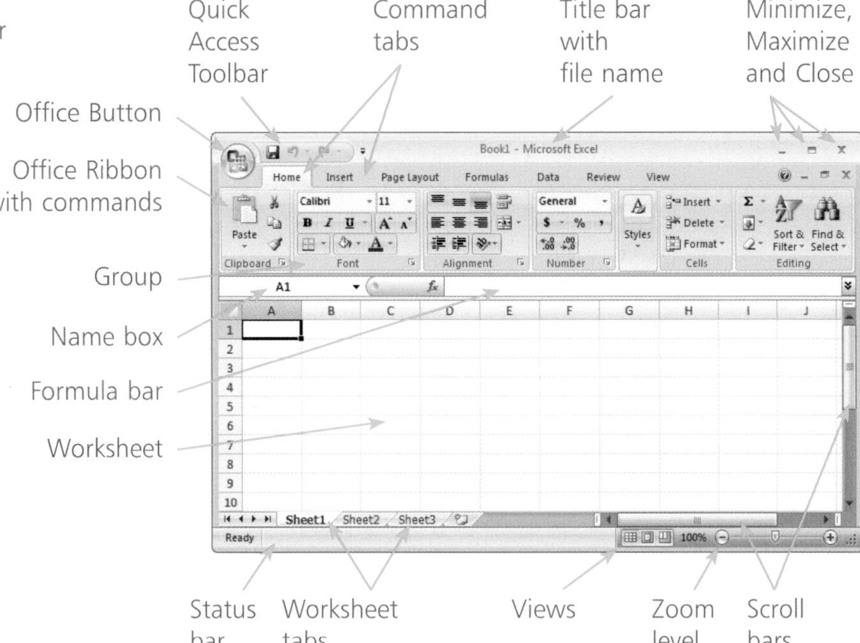

Hot tip

The Home tab contains all the commands required for basic worksheet activities, in the Clipboard, Font, Alignment, Number, Cells and Editing groups.

1. Move the mouse over a command icon in one of the groups (e.g. in Alignment on the Home tab) to see the command description

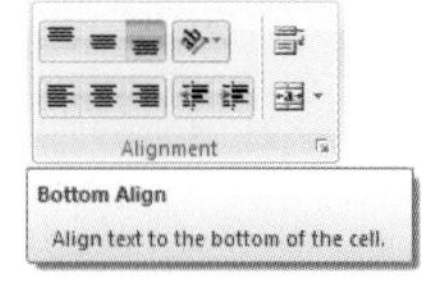


2. Click the down-arrow next to a command (e.g. Orientation) to see additional related commands

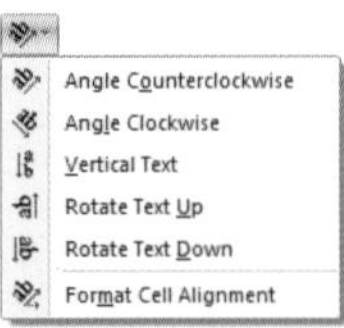


3. Click the arrow next to a group name (e.g. Alignment) to see the associated dialog box

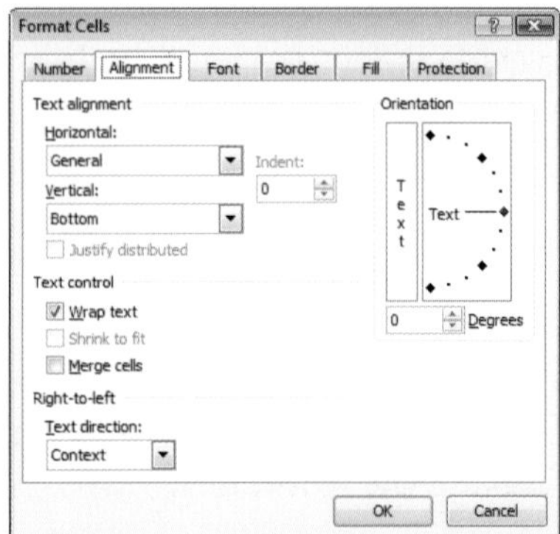

By default, Excel provides three separate arrays of data (known as worksheets) in the workbook. These are named Sheet1, Sheet2 and Sheet3. Each worksheet is the equivalent of a full spreadsheet, and has the potential for up to 1,048,576 x 16,384 cells arranged in rows and columns.

The rows are numbered 1, 2, 3 and onwards, up to a maximum of 1,048,576. The columns are lettered as A to Z, AA to ZZ, and then AAA to XFD. This gives a maximum of 16,384 columns. The combination gives a unique reference for each cell, from A1 right up to XFD1048576.

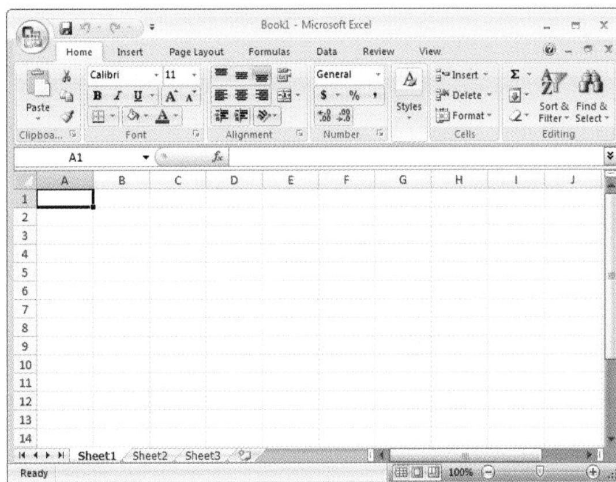

Only a very few of these cells will be visible at any time, but any part of the worksheet can be displayed on the screen, which acts as a rectangular porthole onto the whole worksheet.

Use the scroll bars to reposition the screen view, or type a cell reference into the name box, e.g. ZZ255.

See page 44 for other ways to navigate through the worksheet.

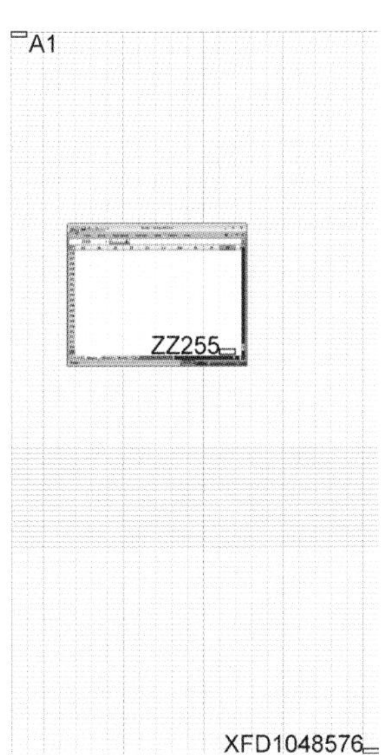

## Hot tip

One worksheet is usually all that you need to create a spreadsheet, but it can sometimes be convenient to organize the data into several worksheets.

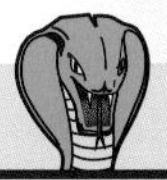

## Beware

These are the theoretical limits for worksheets. For very large numbers of records, a database program may be a more suitable choice.

## Don't forget

The actual number of cells shown depends on your screen resolution, the cell size and the mode of display (e.g. with the Ribbon minimized, or full screen view).

# Create a Workbook

We will start by creating a simple personal budget workbook, to illustrate the processes involved in creating and updating your Excel spreadsheet.

1. With Excel open, the blank workbook Book1 is displayed. This can be used as the basis for your new workbook

2. If you need to create a new, empty spreadsheet, click the Home button and select New. Choose the Blank Template, click the Blank Workbook icon, and press the Create button. A new workbook will be opened, called Book2 (or whatever is the next sequential number)

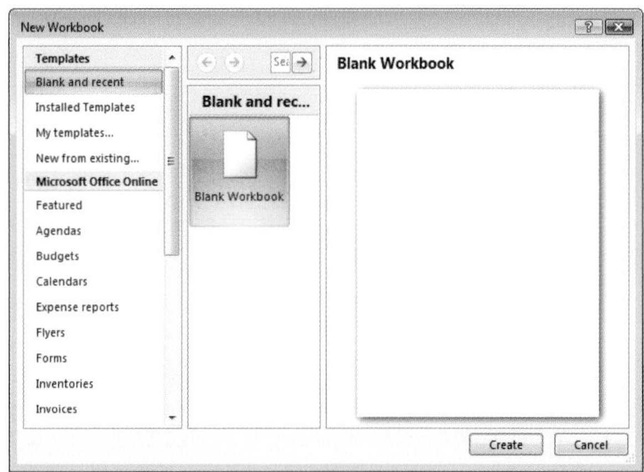


Hot tip

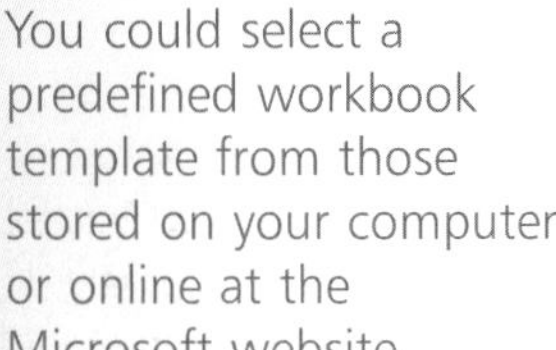

You could select a predefined workbook template from those stored on your computer or online at the Microsoft website.

3. Type the spreadsheet title My Personal Budget in cell A1, and press the down-arrow or the Enter key, to go to cell A2 (or just click cell A2 to select it)

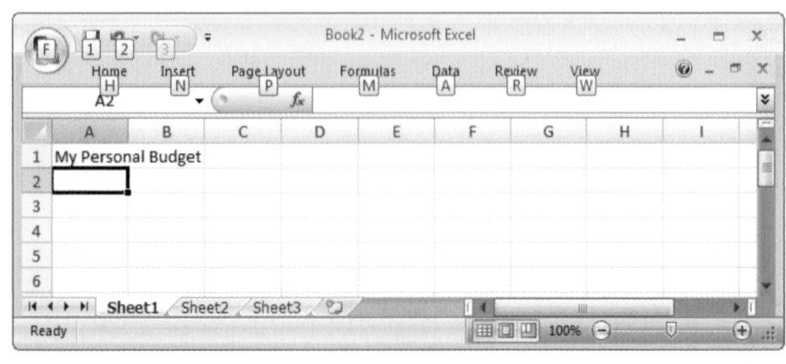

Don't forget

Text is automatically aligned to the left of the cell and numbers are aligned to the right.

# Add Data to the Worksheet

1. Continue to add text to the cells in column A, pressing the down-arrow or Enter to move down after each, to create these labels in cells A2 to A13:

   Income
   Salary
   Interest/dividend
   Total income
   Expenses
   Mortgage/rent
   Utilities
   Groceries
   Transport
   Insurance
   Total expenses
   Savings/shortage

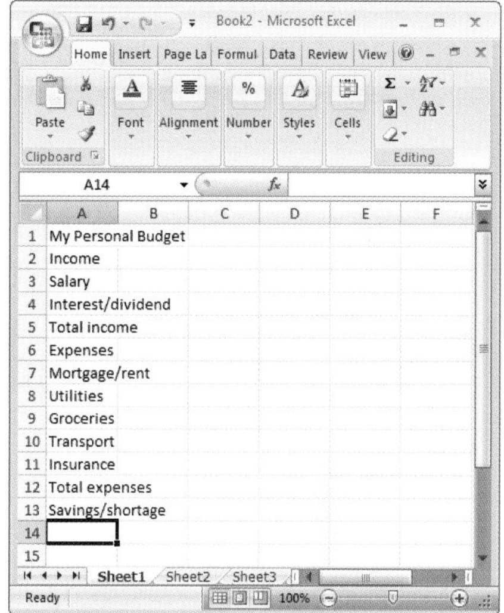


2. Click the Office button and select Save (or press the Ctrl+S keyboard shortcut)

3. To save the workbook in the Documents folder, type a file name, e.g. My Personal Budget, and press the Save button

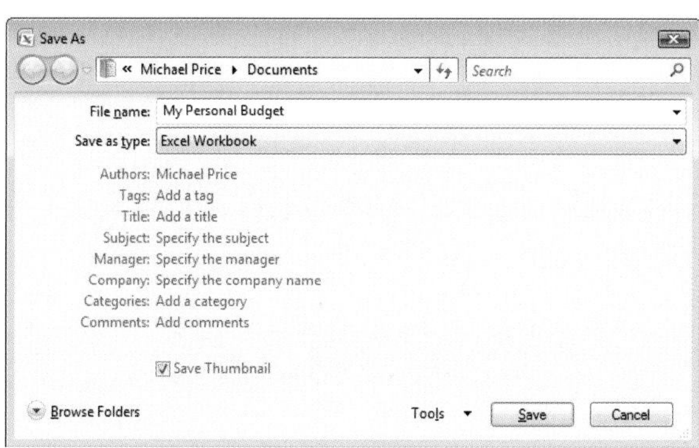
Save As
« Michael Price ▸ Documents
Search
File name: My Personal Budget
Save as type: Excel Workbook
Authors: Michael Price
Tags: Add a tag
Title: Add a title
Subject: Specify the subject
Manager: Specify the manager
Company: Specify the company name
Categories: Add a category
Comments: Add comments
☑ Save Thumbnail
Browse Folders
Tools
Save
Cancel

Note that you can add information to classify the document, such as Tag words, Title or Subject. If you create numerous documents, these details can help you sort your documents and workbooks, and locate particular documents more easily.

**Hot tip**

If the text is already available in another document, you can copy and paste the information, to save typing.

**Beware**

Save the workbook regularly while creating or updating spreadsheets, or you run the risk of losing the work you've done if a problem arises with the system.

# Build the Worksheet

We want to fill in the columns of data for each month of the year, but first we need an extra row after the title, for the column headings. To add a row to the worksheet:

1. Select the row (click the row number) above which you want to insert another row, e.g. select row 2

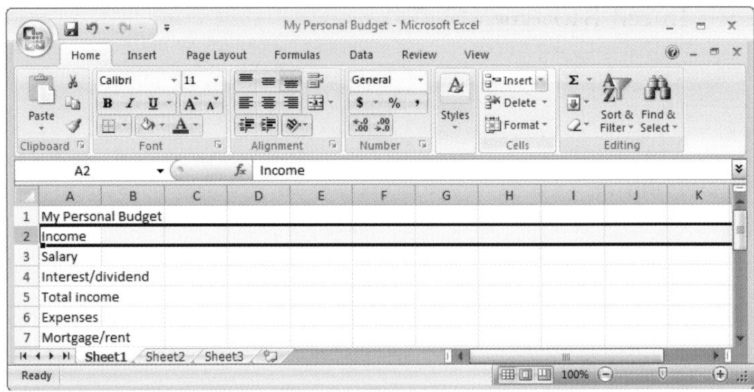

2. Click the Home tab and then, in the Cells group, click the arrow next to Insert and click Insert Sheet Rows

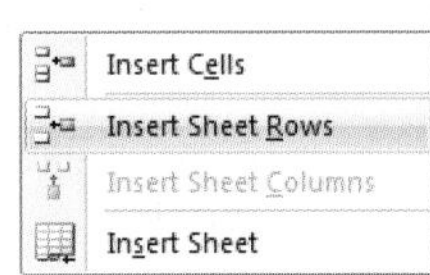


3. Click cell B2 in the new row and type January; then press Enter twice

4. Type 3950 in cell B4, press Enter, type 755 in cell B5 and press Enter again

5. In cell B6 type = and click B4, type + and click B5 (to get =B4+B5); then press Enter to see the total displayed in B6

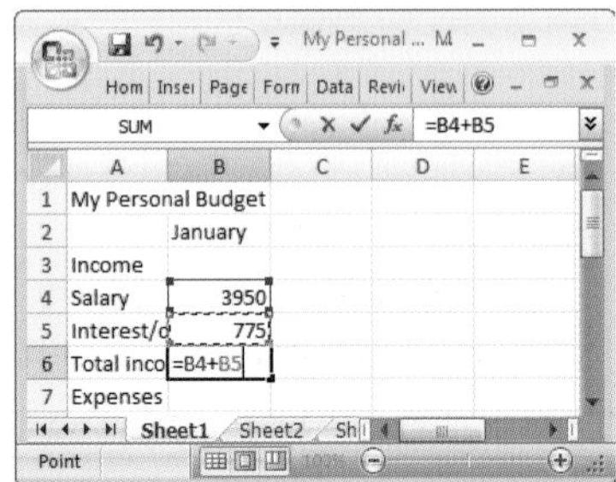

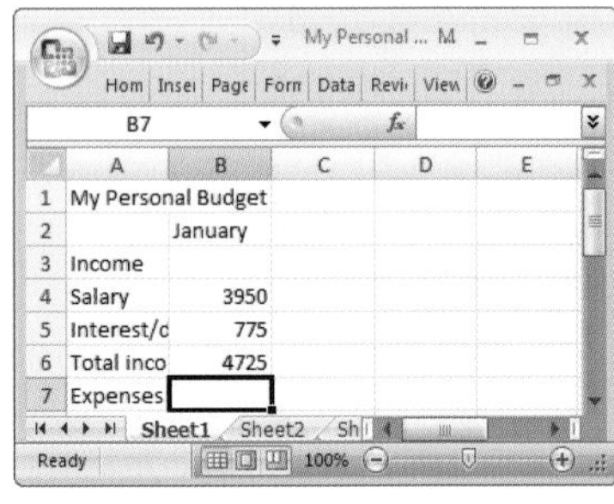

## Hot tip

To insert multiple rows, select a block of as many as you need and click Insert; the new rows will be inserted above the selection. Use a similar procedure to insert columns.

## Don't forget

The = signifies that what follows is a formula. This creates a formula in cell C6 to specify that Total income = Salary plus Interest/dividend. Excel automatically calculates the result and displays that in cell C6. If you select the cell and look in the Formula bar, you'll see the formula.

6. Click cell B8 and then type the values 2250, 425, 1150, 350 and 450 (pressing the down-arrow or Enter after each)

7. In cell B13 type =SUM( and then click B8, type a period, click B12, type ) and press Enter, and then click B13 to see the Formula bar contents

## Don't forget

You can click B13 and then click the AutoSum button in the Editing group on the Home tab. This automatically sums the adjacent cells, in this case the five cells above, giving =SUM(B8:B12). See page 68 for more details of AutoSum.

Some of the labels in column A appear truncated. The full label is still recorded, but the part that overlapped column B cannot be displayed if the adjacent cell is occupied.

To change the column width to fit the contents

1. Select the column (click the letter heading)

2. On the Home tab, in the Cells group, select Format

3. Under Cell Size, select AutoFit Column Width

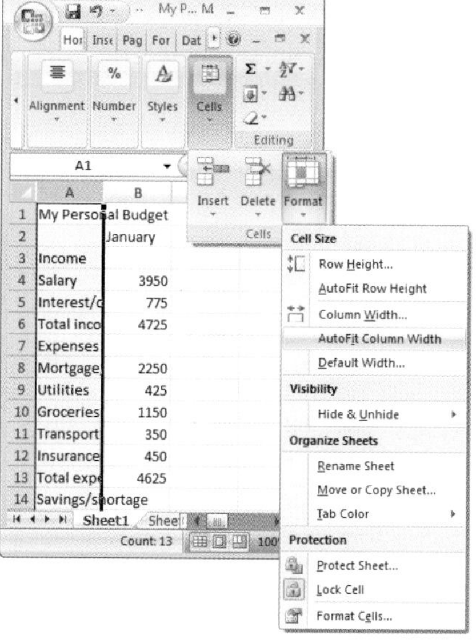


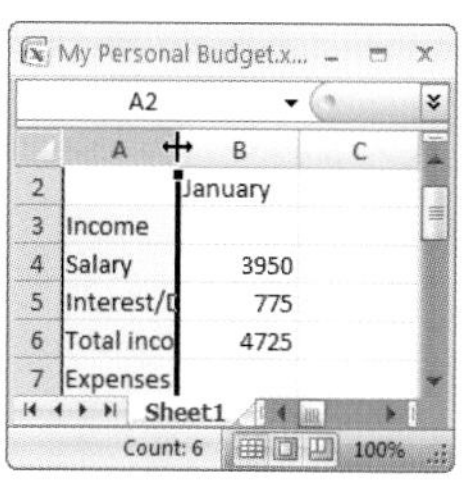

4. Alternatively, move the mouse pointer over the column boundary and double-click to Autofit to contents, or drag to widen manually

## Don't forget

Column width is measured in characters (assuming a standard font). The default is 8.43, but you can set any value from 0 to 255.

## Hot tip

To change a group of columns, select the first, hold down Shift and select the last. For non-adjacent columns, select the first, hold down Ctrl and click other columns.

# Fill Cells

We've typed January, but the rest of the monthly headings can be automatically completed, using the Fill handle.

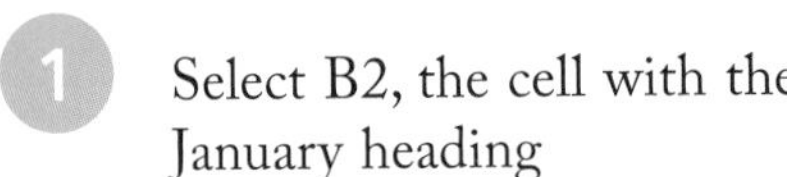

1. Select B2, the cell with the January heading

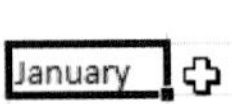


2. Move the mouse over the Fill handle

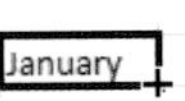


3. Click and drag to adjacent cells

4. Release the mouse button when you have sufficient cells

5. Change the fill options when necessary, to copy cell contents or to fill with or without formatting

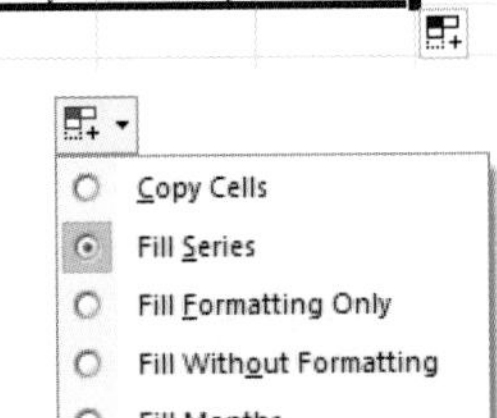


Excel understands a variety of entry types. If you start with Jan, rather than January, you'll fill adjacent cells with Feb, Mar, Apr etc.

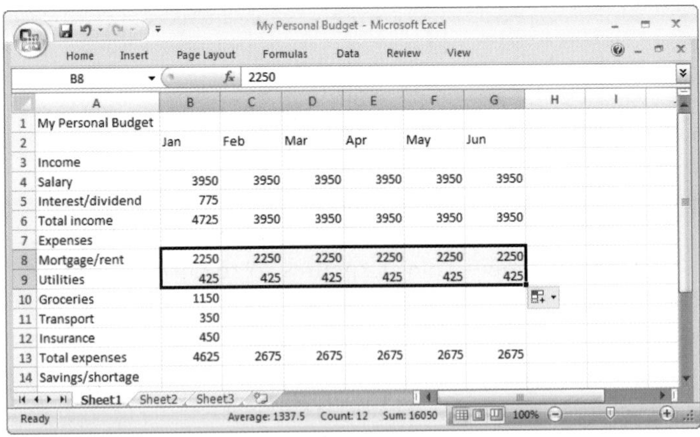


| | A | B | C | D | E | F | G |
|---|---|---|---|---|---|---|---|
| 1 | My Personal Budget | | | | | | |
| 2 | | Jan | Feb | Mar | Apr | May | Jun |
| 3 | Income | | | | | | |
| 4 | Salary | 3950 | 3950 | 3950 | 3950 | 3950 | 3950 |
| 5 | Interest/dividend | 775 | | | | | |
| 6 | Total income | 4725 | 3950 | 3950 | 3950 | 3950 | 3950 |
| 7 | Expenses | | | | | | |
| 8 | Mortgage/rent | 2250 | 2250 | 2250 | 2250 | 2250 | 2250 |
| 9 | Utilities | 425 | 425 | 425 | 425 | 425 | 425 |
| 10 | Groceries | 1150 | | | | | |
| 11 | Transport | 350 | | | | | |
| 12 | Insurance | 450 | | | | | |
| 13 | Total expenses | 4625 | 2675 | 2675 | 2675 | 2675 | 2675 |
| 14 | Savings/shortage | | | | | | |

1. Select cell B4 and fill cells C4:G4 with a copy of B4. Repeat for B6 to C6:G6 and B13 to C13:G13. Select the block of cells B8:B9, and fill cells C8:G9

## Hot tip

Use the Fill handle to copy cells or replicate a formula, or expand a series, depending on the cell contents. For example, type 1 and 2 in adjacent cells, select both and use Fill to create a full list of numbers.

## Don't forget

Formulas are adjusted to show the column change, e.g. =B4+B5 will become =C4+C5, =D4+D5 etc. See page 61 for more details on this effect, which is called relative addressing.

# Complete the Worksheet

1. Select cell H2 and type Period as the heading

2. Select cell H4, click AutoSum in Editing on the Home tab, and press Enter

3. Select cell H4 and fill cells H5:H14; then select cell H7 and press Delete (no total needed in this cell)

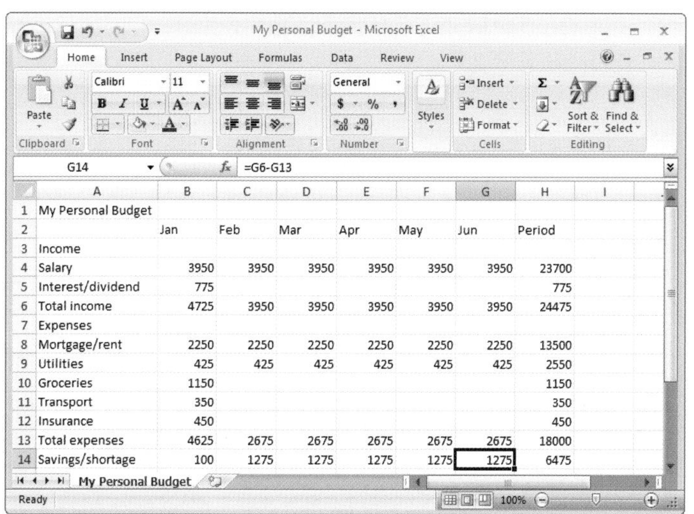


| | A | B | C | D | E | F | G | H |
|---|---|---|---|---|---|---|---|---|
| 1 | My Personal Budget | | | | | | | |
| 2 | | Jan | Feb | Mar | Apr | May | Jun | Period |
| 3 | Income | | | | | | | |
| 4 | Salary | 3950 | 3950 | 3950 | 3950 | 3950 | 3950 | 23700 |
| 5 | Interest/dividend | 775 | | | | | | 775 |
| 6 | Total income | 4725 | 3950 | 3950 | 3950 | 3950 | 3950 | 24475 |
| 7 | Expenses | | | | | | | |
| 8 | Mortgage/rent | 2250 | 2250 | 2250 | 2250 | 2250 | 2250 | 13500 |
| 9 | Utilities | 425 | 425 | 425 | 425 | 425 | 425 | 2550 |
| 10 | Groceries | 1150 | | | | | | 1150 |
| 11 | Transport | 350 | | | | | | 350 |
| 12 | Insurance | 450 | | | | | | 450 |
| 13 | Total expenses | 4625 | 2675 | 2675 | 2675 | 2675 | 2675 | 18000 |
| 14 | Savings/shortage | 100 | 1275 | 1275 | 1275 | 1275 | 1275 | 6475 |

4. Select cell B14, type =B6-B13 and then press Enter (you can type the whole formula, or select the individual cells)

5. Select cell B14; then drag and fill to copy the formula for Total Income - Total Expenses to the cells C14:G14

Since only one worksheet is needed:

1. Right-click the Sheet2 tab and select Delete, and repeat for the Sheet3 tab

2. Right-click the Sheet1 tab, select Rename, type My Personal Budget and then press Enter

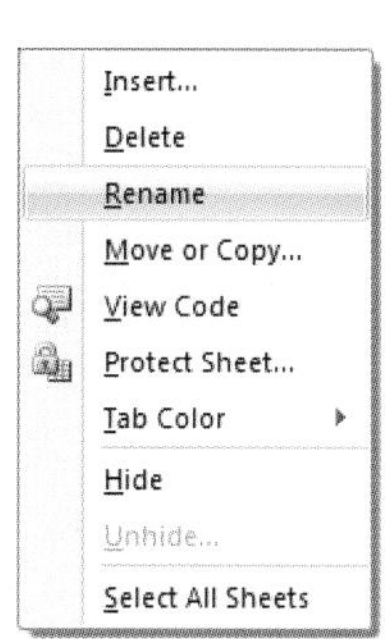

## Hot tip

It is sometimes more efficient to fill a whole range of cells, and then clear the ones that are not necessary.

## Don't forget

The worksheet is now ready for monthly income and expense figures to be entered, with updated totals for the period displayed.

# Format the Text

Although not essential for the actual functioning, formatting the text can make it easier to handle the workbook, and make prints more readable.

There are numerous changes that you could make, but at this stage we will just make some changes to font size and styles, and to the text placement.

11
8 9 10 11 12 14 16 18 20 22 24 26 28 36 48 72

1. Click cell A3, press Ctrl and click cells A7, A13 and A14, and then click the arrow next to Font Size (in the Home tab Font group) and click 14; then click Bold

2. Click the column label cell B2, press Shift and click cell H2, and then select font size 14, Bold for cells B2:H2, and select Align Text Right in the Home, Alignment group

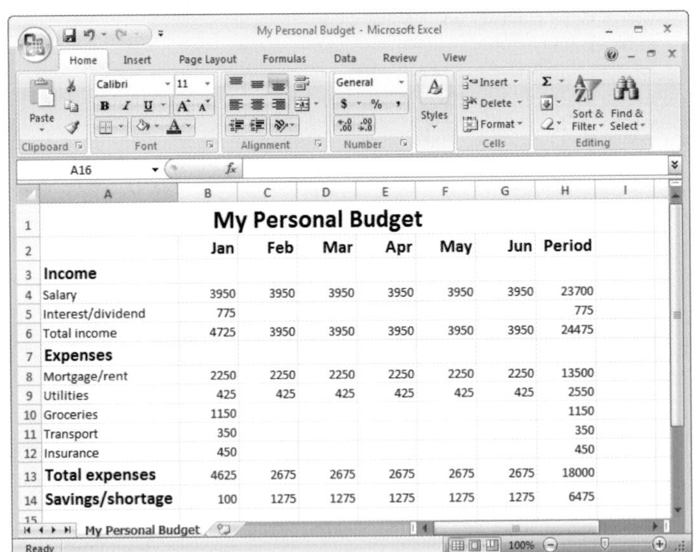

| | A | B | C | D | E | F | G | H |
|---|---|---|---|---|---|---|---|---|
| 1 | | My Personal Budget | | | | | | |
| 2 | | Jan | Feb | Mar | Apr | May | Jun | Period |
| 3 | Income | | | | | | | |
| 4 | Salary | 3950 | 3950 | 3950 | 3950 | 3950 | 3950 | 23700 |
| 5 | Interest/dividend | 775 | | | | | | 775 |
| 6 | Total income | 4725 | 3950 | 3950 | 3950 | 3950 | 3950 | 24475 |
| 7 | Expenses | | | | | | | |
| 8 | Mortgage/rent | 2250 | 2250 | 2250 | 2250 | 2250 | 2250 | 13500 |
| 9 | Utilities | 425 | 425 | 425 | 425 | 425 | 425 | 2550 |
| 10 | Groceries | 1150 | | | | | | 1150 |
| 11 | Transport | 350 | | | | | | 350 |
| 12 | Insurance | 450 | | | | | | 450 |
| 13 | Total expenses | 4625 | 2675 | 2675 | 2675 | 2675 | 2675 | 18000 |
| 14 | Savings/shortage | 100 | 1275 | 1275 | 1275 | 1275 | 1275 | 6475 |

3. Select the range of cells A1 to H1, then on the Home tab select Merge and Center in the Home, Alignment group, and then select font size 20, Bold, for the workbook title

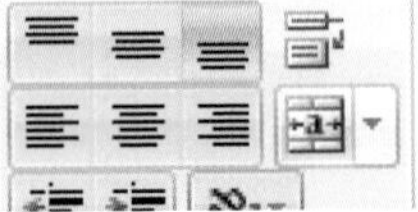

## Hot tip

The worksheet changes momentarily, as you move over the font sizes, showing you how the change would affect the appearance.

## Don't forget

Whenever you make changes, save the workbook to disk, so that the changes won't be lost.

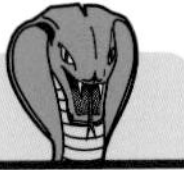

## Beware

You may need to reapply AutoFit when you make changes to the font size and style for labels.

# Number Formats

To apply a specific format to numbers in your worksheet:

1. Select the cells that you wish to reformat, and click the down-arrow in the Number Format box

| | | | | | | |
|---|---|---|---|---|---|---|
| 3950 | 3950 | 3950 | 3950 | 3950 | 3950 | 23700 |
| 775 | 567.75 | | | | | 1342.75 |
| 4725 | 4517.75 | 3950 | 3950 | 3950 | 3950 | 25042.75 |
| | | | | | | |
| 2250 | 2250 | 2250 | 2250 | 2250 | 2250 | 13500 |
| 425 | 425.04 | 425 | 425 | 425 | 425 | 2550.04 |
| 1150 | 1124.9 | | | | | 2274.9 |
| 350 | 437.5 | | | | | 787.5 |
| 450 | 450 | | | | | 900 |
| 4625 | 4687.44 | 2675 | 2675 | 2675 | 2675 | 20012.44 |
| 100 | -169.69 | 1275 | 1275 | 1275 | 1275 | 5030.31 |

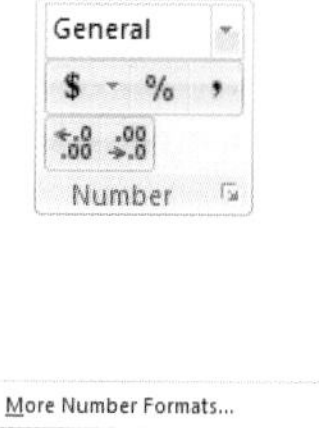


More Number Formats...

2. Select More Number Formats and then choose, for example, Number, 2 decimal places, and Red for negative numbers

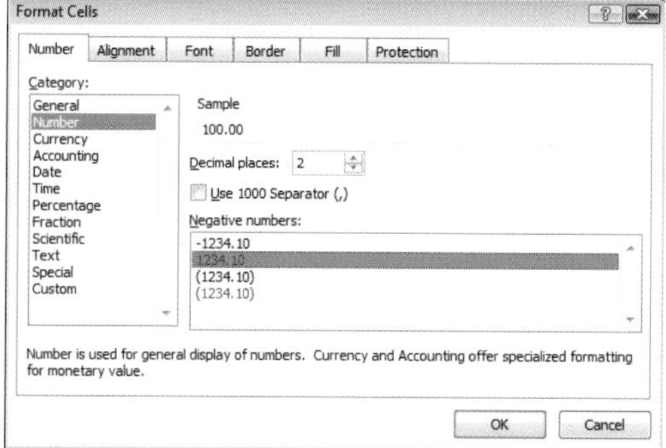


3. Click OK to apply the format to the selection

4. Change the column widths if required, to display the full numbers (see page 27)

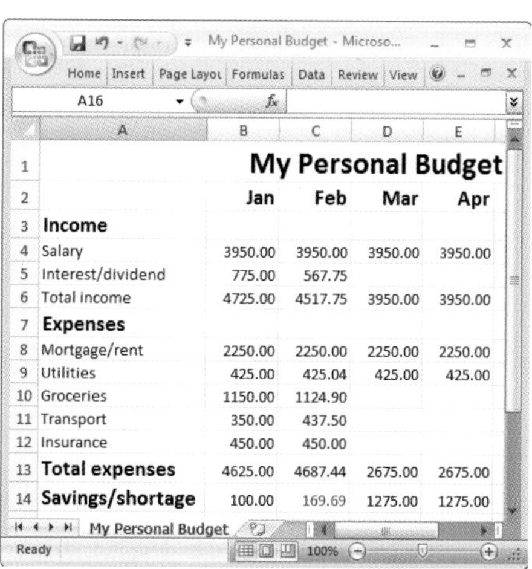

| | A | B | C | D | E |
|---|---|---|---|---|---|
| 1 | | My Personal Budget | | | |
| 2 | | Jan | Feb | Mar | Apr |
| 3 | **Income** | | | | |
| 4 | Salary | 3950.00 | 3950.00 | 3950.00 | 3950.00 |
| 5 | Interest/dividend | 775.00 | 567.75 | | |
| 6 | Total income | 4725.00 | 4517.75 | 3950.00 | 3950.00 |
| 7 | **Expenses** | | | | |
| 8 | Mortgage/rent | 2250.00 | 2250.00 | 2250.00 | 2250.00 |
| 9 | Utilities | 425.00 | 425.04 | 425.00 | 425.00 |
| 10 | Groceries | 1150.00 | 1124.90 | | |
| 11 | Transport | 350.00 | 437.50 | | |
| 12 | Insurance | 450.00 | 450.00 | | |
| 13 | **Total expenses** | 4625.00 | 4687.44 | 2675.00 | 2675.00 |
| 14 | **Savings/shortage** | 100.00 | 169.69 | 1275.00 | 1275.00 |

**Don't forget**

The General format isn't consistent. Decimal places vary, and Excel may apply rounding, to fit numbers in if the column is narrow.

| | |
|---|---|
| 3950 | 3950 |
| 567.8 | 567.75 |
| 4518 | 4517.75 |
| | |
| 2250 | 2250 |
| 425 | 425.04 |
| 1125 | 1124.9 |
| 437.5 | 437.5 |
| 450 | 450 |
| 4687 | 4687.44 |
| -170 | -169.69 |

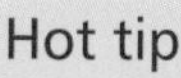

**Hot tip**

See page 58 for details of the various types of formats available for numbers in cells.

# Print the Worksheet

## Hot tip

If you want just part of the data in the worksheet, select the range of cells before starting Print.

1 Open the workbook, and select the worksheet you want to print (if there's more than one)

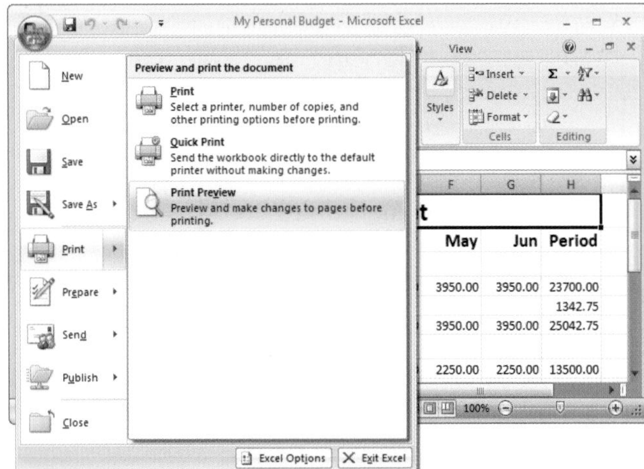


## Don't forget

Press the Zoom button to toggle between the close-up view and the full-page views.

2 Press the Office button and then click the arrow next to the Print button, and select the Print Preview entry

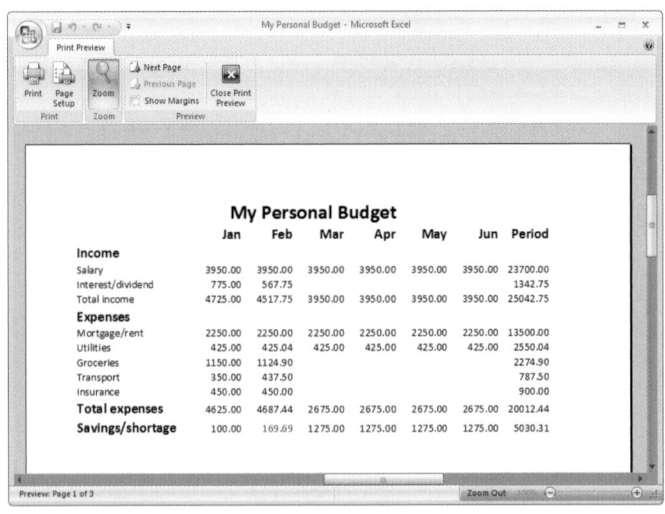


**My Personal Budget**

| | Jan | Feb | Mar | Apr | May | Jun | Period |
|---|---|---|---|---|---|---|---|
| **Income** | | | | | | | |
| Salary | 3950.00 | 3950.00 | 3950.00 | 3950.00 | 3950.00 | 3950.00 | 23700.00 |
| Interest/dividend | 775.00 | 567.75 | | | | | 1342.75 |
| Total income | 4725.00 | 4517.75 | 3950.00 | 3950.00 | 3950.00 | 3950.00 | 25042.75 |
| **Expenses** | | | | | | | |
| Mortgage/rent | 2250.00 | 2250.00 | 2250.00 | 2250.00 | 2250.00 | 2250.00 | 13500.00 |
| Utilities | 425.00 | 425.04 | 425.00 | 425.00 | 425.00 | 425.00 | 2550.04 |
| Groceries | 1150.00 | 1124.90 | | | | | 2274.90 |
| Transport | 350.00 | 437.50 | | | | | 787.50 |
| Insurance | 450.00 | 450.00 | | | | | 900.00 |
| **Total expenses** | 4625.00 | 4687.44 | 2675.00 | 2675.00 | 2675.00 | 2675.00 | 20012.44 |
| **Savings/shortage** | 100.00 | 169.69 | 1275.00 | 1275.00 | 1275.00 | 1275.00 | 5030.31 |

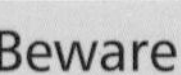

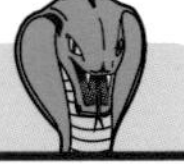

## Beware

Excel will select a print area that includes all cells that appear to have data in them (including blanks). If you scroll past the end of the data and accidently click a key or the spacebar, Excel may select a larger print area than you anticipate.

3 Check to see exactly what data will be printed, especially if there are more pages than you were expecting

4 Press the Print button in Preview to display the Print dialog

5 Change the printer if desired, and set the page range and number of copies

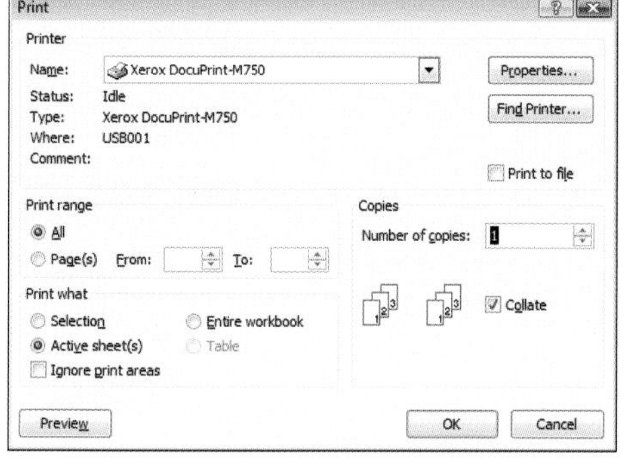


6 Under “Print what”, choose to print the selection, the active sheet or sheets, or the entire workbook

You can preset the area that will be printed:

1 Select the range of cells that you normally want printed

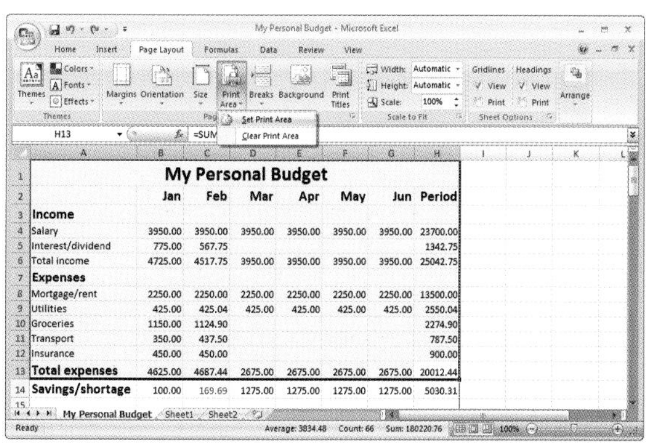

| My Personal Budget | Jan | Feb | Mar | Apr | May | Jun | Period |
|---|---|---|---|---|---|---|---|
| **Income** | | | | | | | |
| Salary | 3950.00 | 3950.00 | 3950.00 | 3950.00 | 3950.00 | 3950.00 | 23700.00 |
| Interest/dividend | 775.00 | 567.75 | | | | | 1342.75 |
| Total income | 4725.00 | 4517.75 | 3950.00 | 3950.00 | 3950.00 | 3950.00 | 25042.75 |
| **Expenses** | | | | | | | |
| Mortgage/rent | 2250.00 | 2250.00 | 2250.00 | 2250.00 | 2250.00 | 2250.00 | 13500.00 |
| Utilities | 425.00 | 425.04 | 425.00 | 425.00 | 425.00 | 425.00 | 2550.04 |
| Groceries | 1150.00 | 1124.90 | | | | | 2274.90 |
| Transport | 350.00 | 437.50 | | | | | 787.50 |
| Insurance | 450.00 | 450.00 | | | | | 900.00 |
| **Total expenses** | 4625.00 | 4687.44 | 2675.00 | 2675.00 | 2675.00 | 2675.00 | 20012.44 |
| **Savings/shortage** | 100.00 | 169.69 | 1275.00 | 1275.00 | 1275.00 | 1275.00 | 5030.31 |



2 Select the Page Layout tab, click the Print Area button in the Page Setup group, and select Set Print Area

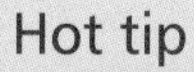

## Hot tip

You could click Print from the Office button menu (or press Ctrl+P) to go directly to Print, bypassing Print Preview.

## Don’t forget

If there is a print area defined, Excel will print only that part of the worksheet. If you don’t want to limit the print this time, select “Ignore print areas”.

## Hot tip

If you are sure that the default print settings are what you require, you can click the Office button and choose Quick Print to start the print immediately.

# Insert, Copy and Paste

You can rearrange the contents of the worksheet or add new data by inserting rows or columns and copying cells. For example, to add an additional 6 months of information:

1. Click in column H, press Shift and click in column M

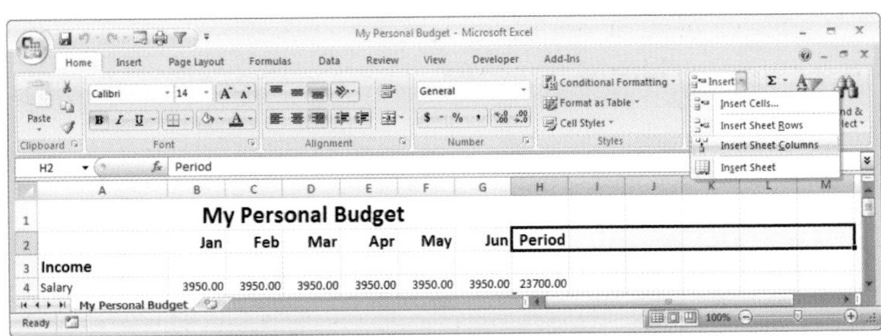

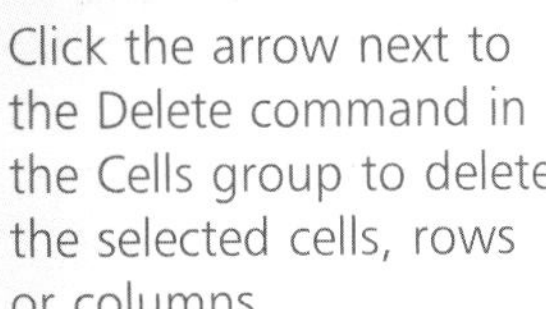

**Don't forget**

Click the arrow next to the Delete command in the Cells group to delete the selected cells, rows or columns.

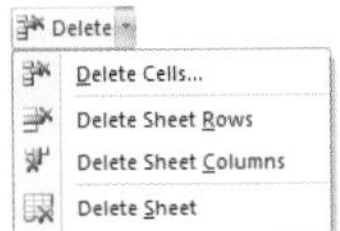


2. Select the Home tab; then in the Cells group click the arrow next to Insert and choose Insert Sheet Columns

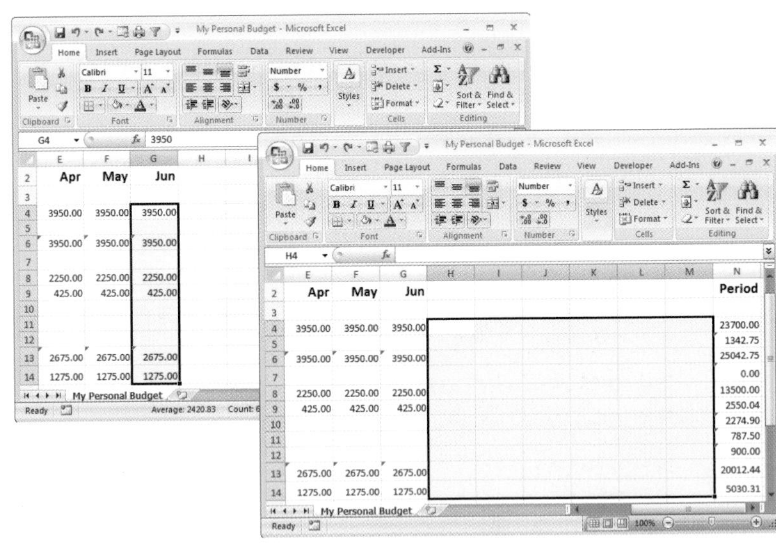



**Hot tip**

Select the existing month headers and use the Fill handle (see page 28) to extend the headers through to Dec.

3. Select the range G4:G14, click the Copy button, select the range H4:M14 and click the Paste button

4. Change the formula in cell N4 from =SUM(B4:H4) to =SUM(B4:M4), and copy the formula into cells N5:N14

**Don't forget**

Select the Cut button, click the new location and select the Paste button, to move the contents of cells.

# Excel Help

Previous versions of Office had a Help menu on the Menu bar, but in Office 2007 applications such as Excel the main entry point to Help is the small question-mark icon on the right of the window, below the Minimize/Maximize/Close buttons. Selecting this (or pressing the F1 key) displays the main browser-style Help window, at the Home page with the top-level list of contents.

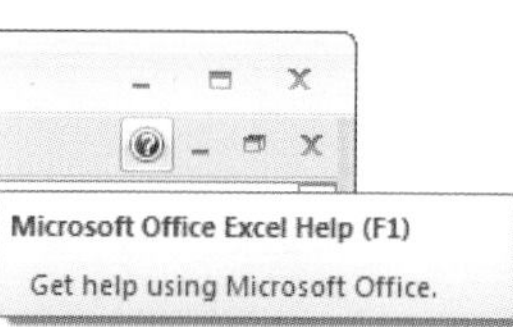


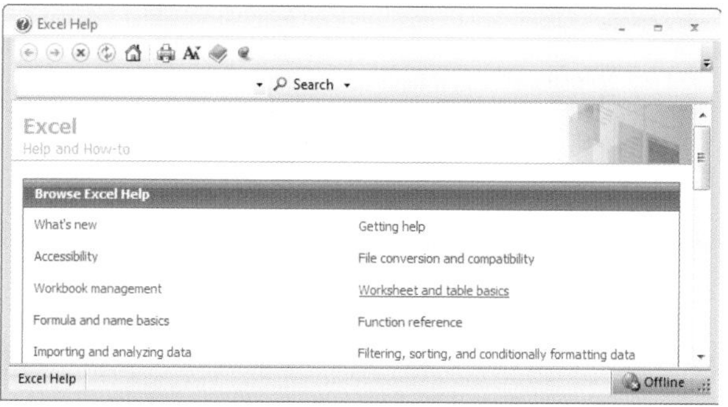


For more specific help, type keywords into the search box and press the Search button, to list related articles in blocks of 25.

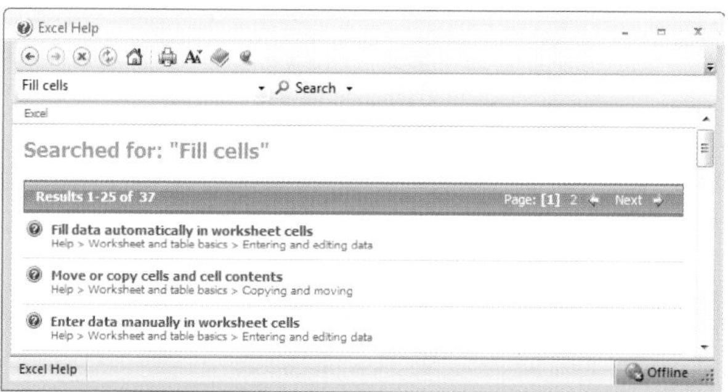


Click the button at the bottom-right of the Help window, and you can choose to show content from the computer only or from the Office Online website. If you have an always-on connection to the Internet, choose the Office Online option and the button changes accordingly.

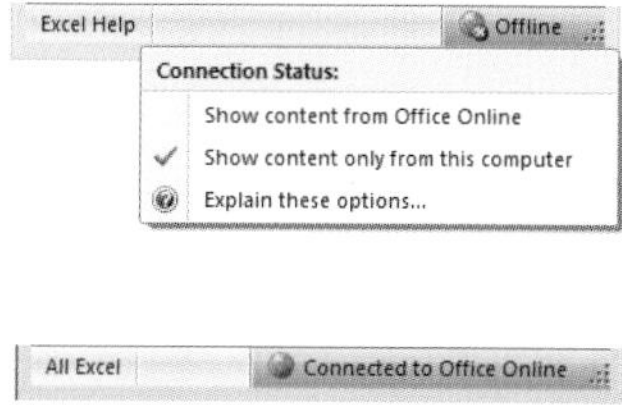

## Hot tip

To browse Excel Help using a hierarchical list, click the Table of Contents button on the Help toolbar.

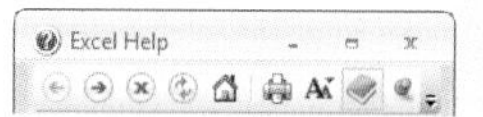

## Don't forget

You can click the arrow next to the Search button, and change the scope of the search for online or offline help.

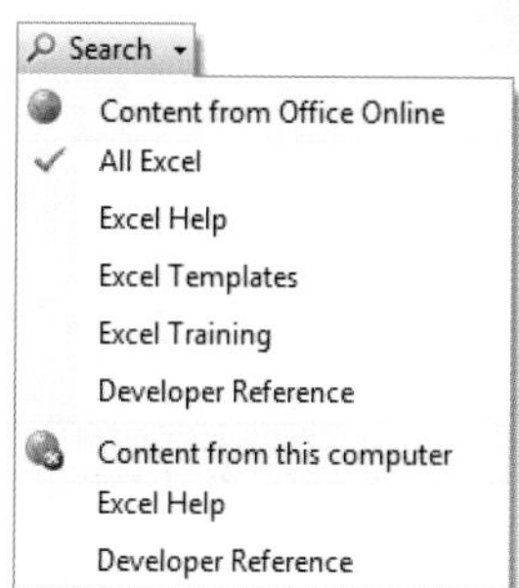

# Contextual Help

You do not always need to search for help – you can get specific information on a particular command or operation.

Some tooltips have just a brief description, plus a keyboard shortcut where appropriate. Other tooltips are more expansive.

1. Open a command tab and move the mouse pointer over a command in one of the groups, to reveal the tooltip

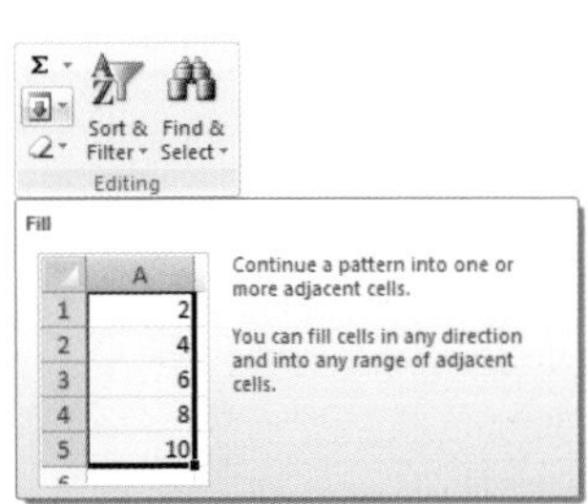


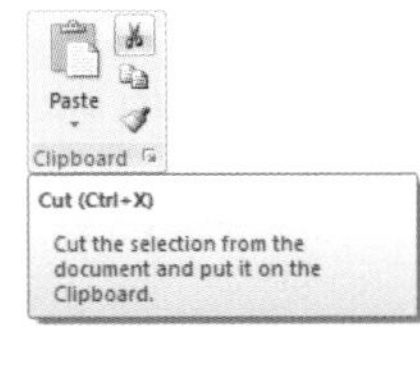


2. If you see the Help icon at the foot of the tooltip, press F1 (with the tooltip still visible) to see the relevant article

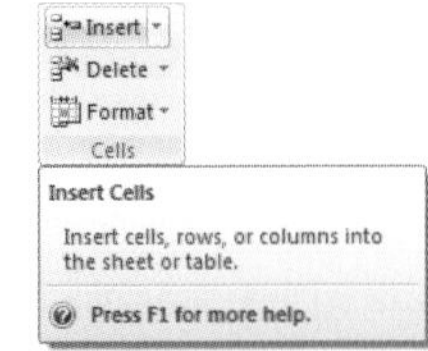




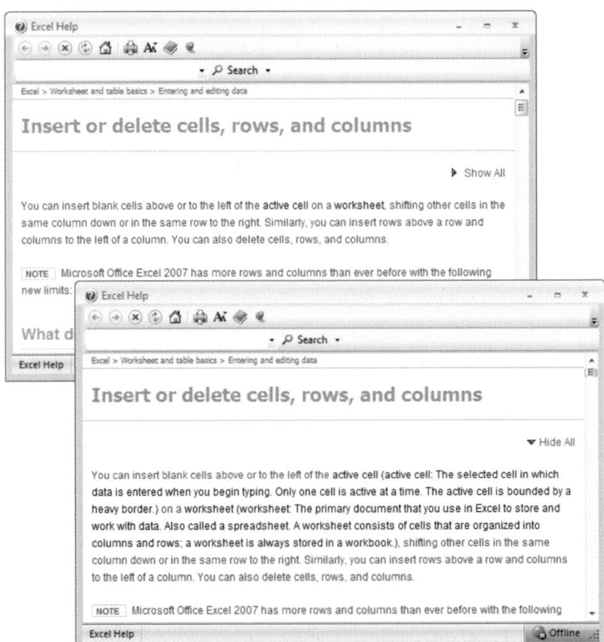

You can still use the Search box to locate additional articles on the topic of interest.

3. Click Show All to expand the text and include the definitions for particular terms within the article

# Excel File Formats

When you create a workbook in Excel 2007 and save it (see page 25), it uses the default file type .xlsx. To save your workbook in the format used by previous versions of Excel:

1. Click the Office button, move the mouse over the Save As button, and select the Excel 97–2003 file format

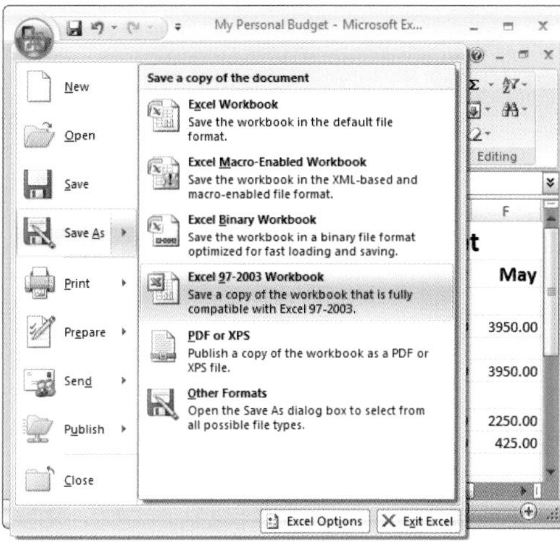


2. Change the file name if desired and click the Save button

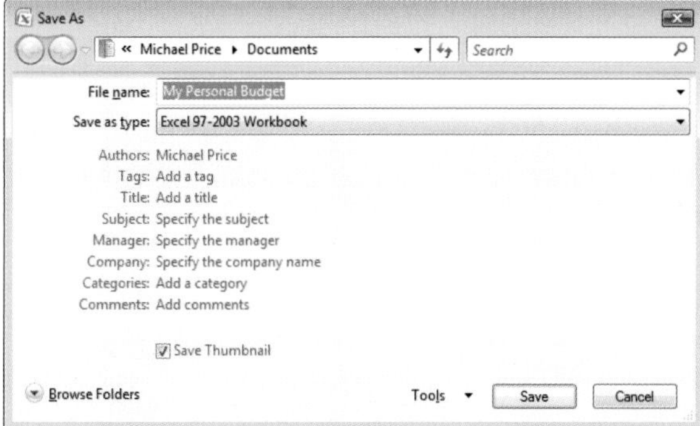


3. If you retained the original file name, you'll have two files of the same name but different types

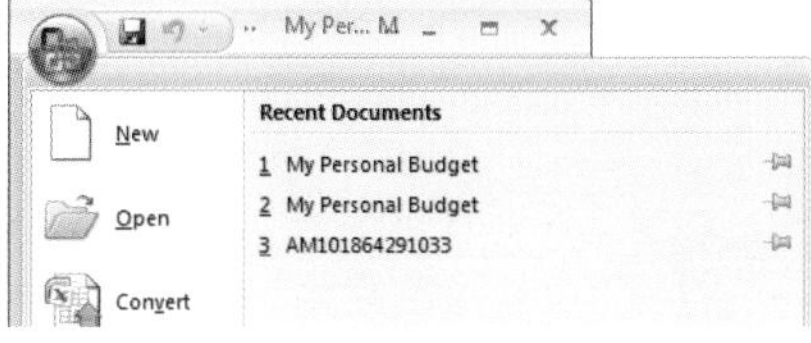

## Hot tip

If you open and modify a workbook created in an earlier version of Excel, it will remain as file type .xls unless you choose to save it in the Excel 2007 file format.

## Hot tip

To see file types, open Folder Options from the Windows Control Panel, and clear the box "Hide extensions for known file types".

Recent Documents

1 My Personal Budget.xls
2 My Personal Budget.xlsx
3 AM101864291033.xls

## ...cont'd

You can save your workbooks in a variety of other file formats, which will make it easier to share information with others who may not have the same applications software.

### Hot tip

You can also display the Save As dialog by pressing F12, or by selecting Other Formats from the Save As list on the Office button.

1. Click the Office button then click the Save As button

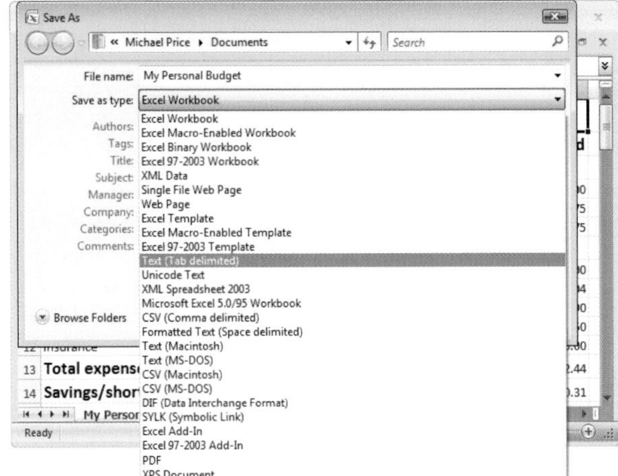


2. Click the Save As Type box to list the file types supported, and select the format you want to use

The Text (Tab delimited) format or the CSV (Comma delimited) formats are often used, since most applications will support these formats. All text and number formatting will be removed, and only the current worksheet is saved. If there's more than one worksheet in your workbook, you'll need to save each one to a separate file.

### Don't forget

You must use negative signs or brackets rather than the red color code, since colors will be removed from the data when the text files are created.

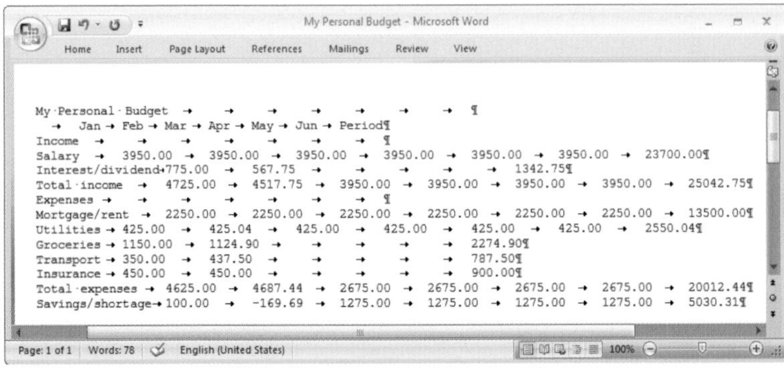

# 3 Manage Data

*This chapter introduces navigation tools, commands and facilities to enable you to find your way around and work with large spreadsheets. It shows how existing data can be imported into Excel to avoid having to retype information.*

# Use Existing Data

If the information you want to add to a workbook already exists in another application, you may be able to import it into Excel and use it without having to retype the data, as long as you can prepare it in a suitable file format.

To identify the file types that can be opened directly in Excel:

1. Select the Office button and click Open (or press Ctrl+O)

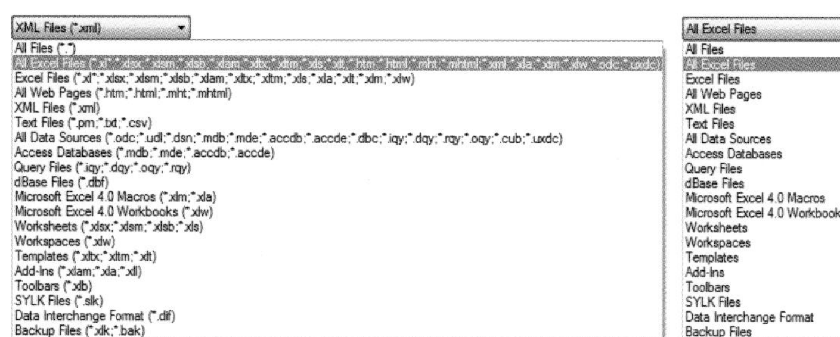


2. Click the file type box, alongside the file name box

3. Identify a file type supported by the other application (e.g. Text or CSV) and then click Cancel

4. Extract data from the other application as that file type

For example, you might have a large number of MP3 tracks, created by transferring your CD collection to the hard drive.

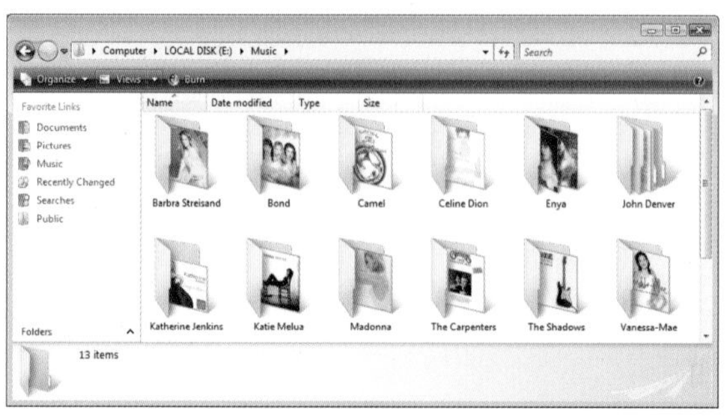


Each file stores particulars of the music it contains, including title, album, artist, composer, recording date, quality (the bit rate used

## Hot tip

If you clear the box "Hide extensions for known file types" in Windows Folder Options, you'll see the full details for the supported file types.

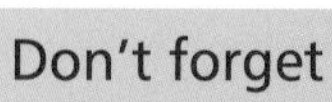

## Don't forget

Details of the music are downloaded from the Internet when you transfer the tracks to the hard disk using an application such as Windows Media Player. It also records the settings used for the conversion to MP3.

for conversion), genre etc. These are held in the form of MP3 tags, and an application such as MP3 Tag Tools can scan the files and extract the tags, allowing you to make changes or corrections.

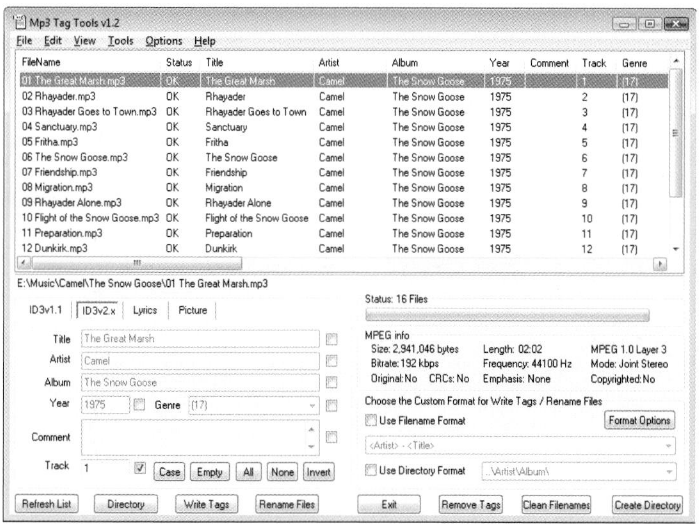

This is just an illustration of how you might extract data from an existing application. Whatever the contents, most applications provide a method for exporting data, usually to a text file format.

You can scan many files at once, and then Export the tags. This will generate a tab-delimited text file, with data fields enclosed in quotation marks, and paragraph marks between lines.

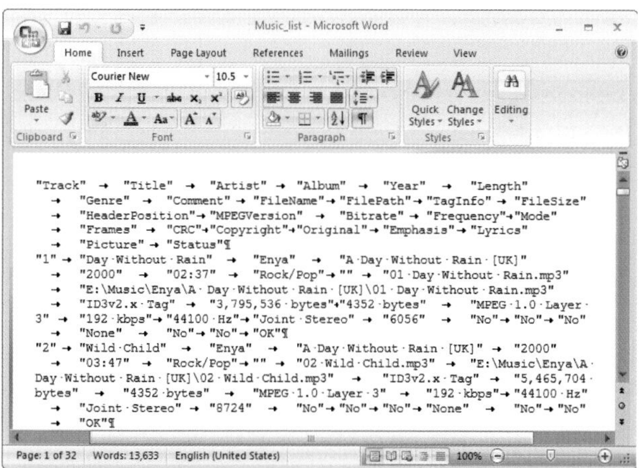

## Hot tip

Empty data items (null values) are represented by a pair of adjacent quotation marks, set between two tab marks. Track lengths are shown as times (mm:ss).

→ "Yes" → "" → "03:37"¶

The first line gives field names for data items, and each subsequent line relates to one MP3 file (usually one track of an album), with values for all data items in the same sequence as the field names.

# Import Data

1. Select Open from the Office button, change the file type to Text, select the data file you exported, and click Open

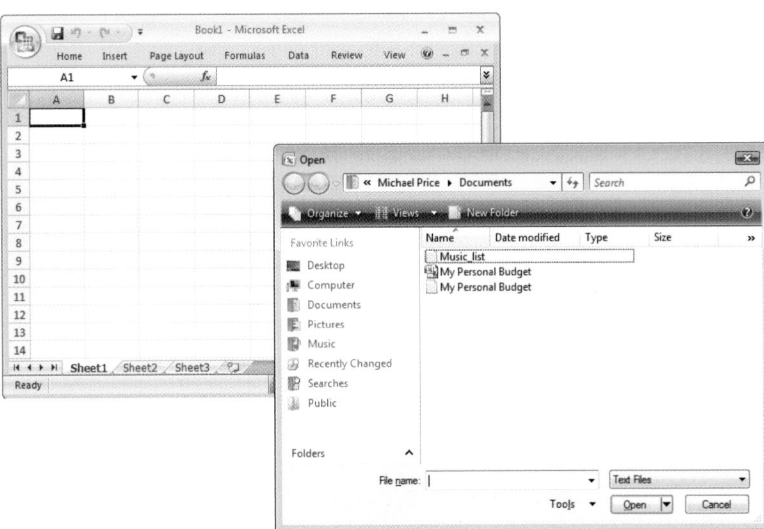


## Hot tip

Select the file type that you used to export data from the application, and follow the prompts. This example shows the process for text files.



2. This launches the Text Import Wizard, which assesses your file and chooses the appropriate settings

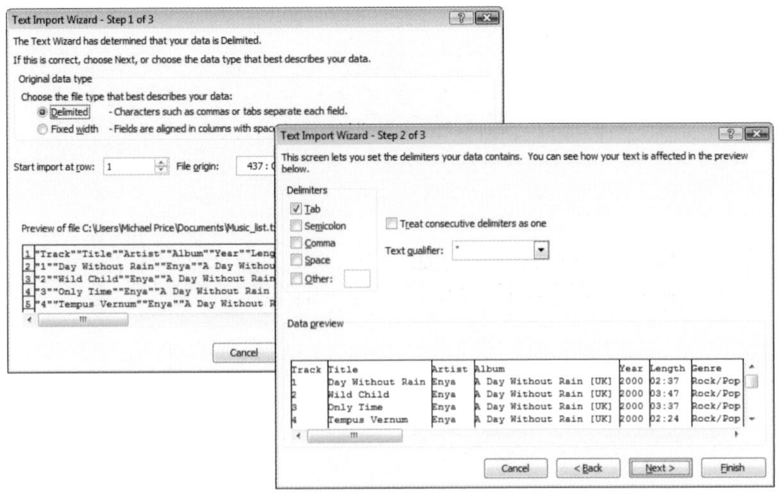


## Don't forget

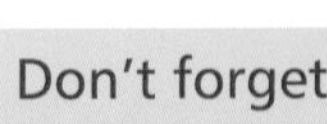

Check the settings applied by the import wizard, and make any changes that are required for your particular files.

3. Adjust the delimiters and the text qualifier for your file if any changes are needed, and preview the effect

4 Review each column, and decide whether you want to skip that data item, change the format or accept the suggestion

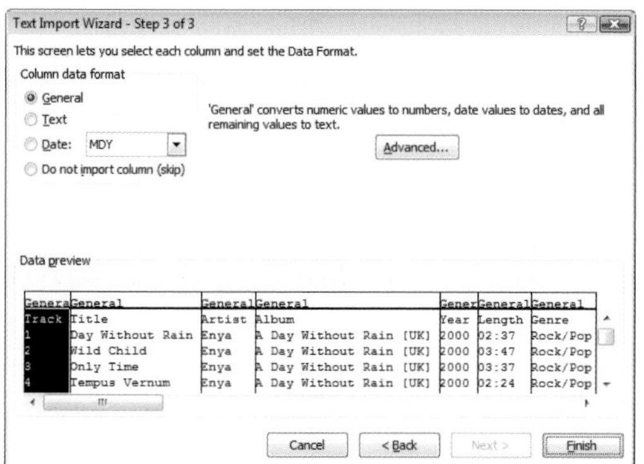

## Don't forget

The General data format is the most flexible, since it interprets numerical values as dates, leaving all other values as text.

5 Click the Finish button to load the data into your Excel worksheet, with lines as rows, and data items as columns

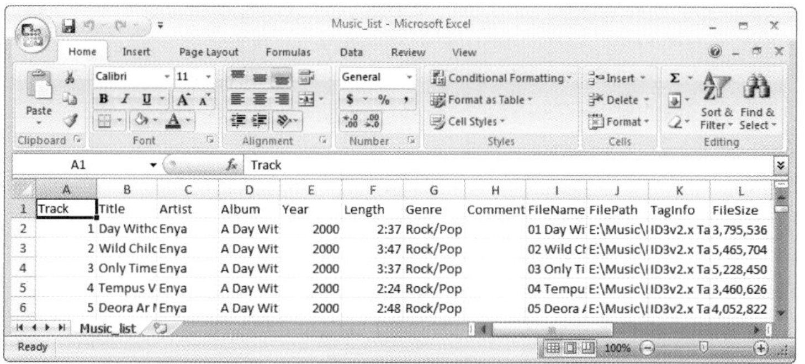


6 Select Save As from the Office button, change the file type to Excel Workbook and press the Save button

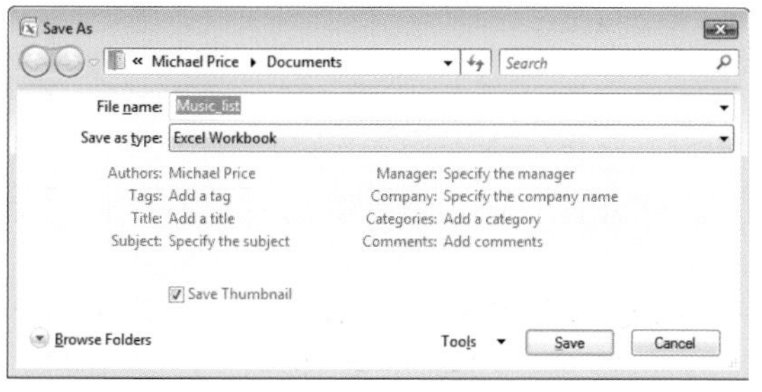


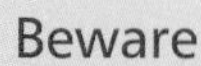
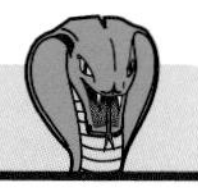

## Beware

The worksheet will be saved as a text file and will overwrite your original import file, unless you save the worksheet as an Excel Workbook or another file type.

# Navigate the Worksheet

If you've transferred information from an existing application and find yourself with some rather large worksheets, you'll welcome the variety of ways Excel provides to move around the worksheet.

## Arrow keys

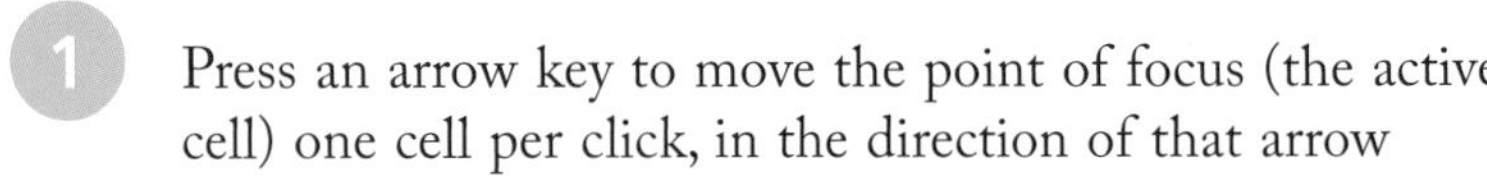

1. Press an arrow key to move the point of focus (the active cell) one cell per click, in the direction of that arrow

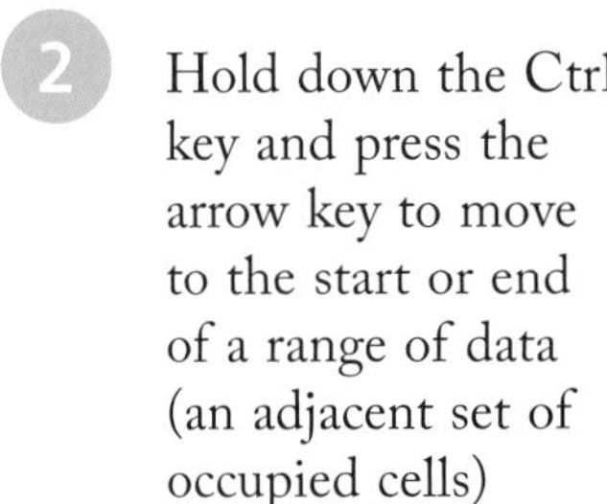

2. Hold down the Ctrl key and press the arrow key to move to the start or end of a range of data (an adjacent set of occupied cells)

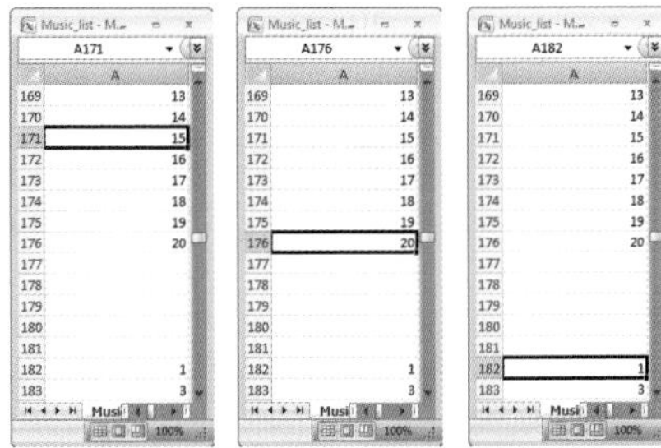

3. To select cells while scrolling to the start or end of a range, hold down the Ctrl and Shift keys and press the arrow key

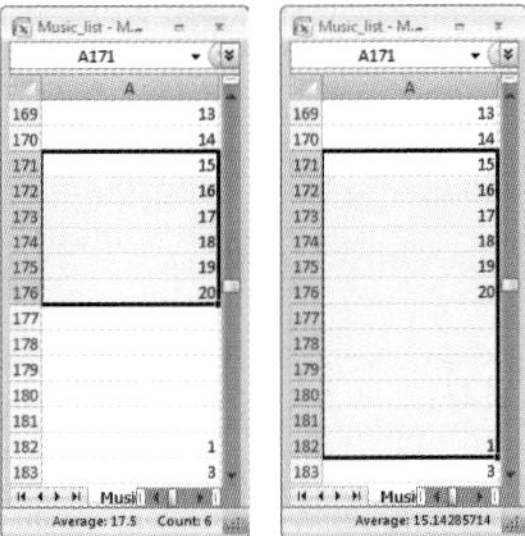

4. Press Ctrl+Shift+Arrow again to extend the selection

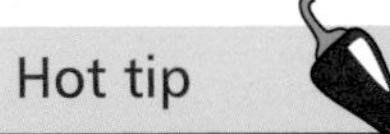


Ctrl+Arrow takes you to the edge of the worksheet, if the active cell is the last occupied cell in the direction of the arrow.

## Scroll Lock

If you press the Scroll Lock button to turn on scroll locking, this will change the actions performed by the arrow keys.

1. The arrow key now moves the window view up or down one row, or sideways one column, depending which arrow key you use (the location of the active cell is not changed)

2. Press Ctrl+Arrow key to shift the view vertically by the depth of the window, or horizontally by the width of the window, depending on the arrow key

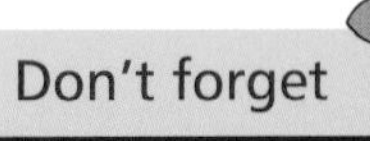


When the Scroll Lock is selected, the words Scroll Lock are displayed on the status bar, and the Scroll Lock light on the keyboard is turned on

## Scroll Bars

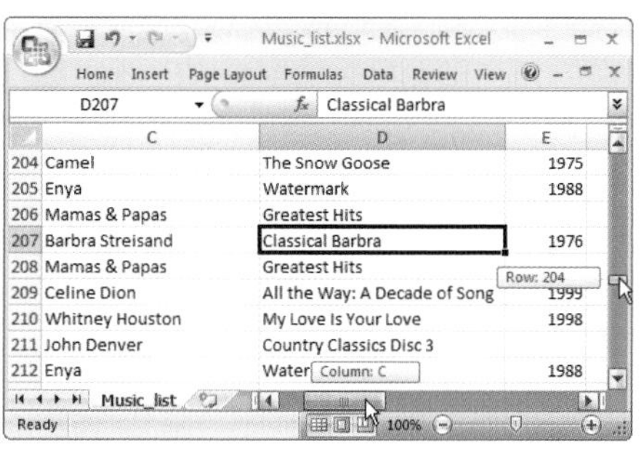


1. Click the vertical scroll arrows to move one row up or down

2. Click above or below the scroll box to move a window's depth up or down

3. Click the horizontal scroll arrows to move one column to the left or right

4. Click to the left or right of the horizontal scroll box, to move a window width left or right

5. Click one of the scroll boxes, and Excel displays the row number or column letter as you drag the box

### Don't forget

The sizes of the scroll boxes are based on the ratios of visible data to total data, and their positions are the relative vertical and horizontal locations of the visible area within the worksheet.

## Split View

You can split the window, so that you can scroll separate parts of the worksheet in two or four panes independently.

1. Hover over the split box on the vertical scroll bar or the horizontal scroll bar

2. When the pointer becomes a double-headed arrow, click it to display the split bar, and drag this over the worksheet to where you want the split

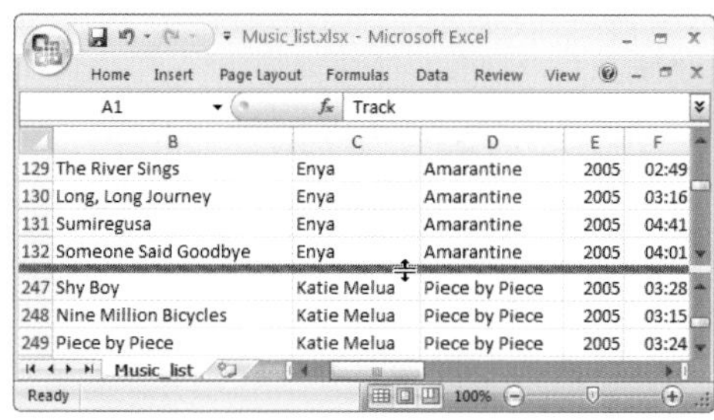


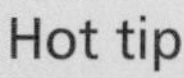

### Hot tip

To remove either the horizontal or the vertical split bar, you just double-click on the bar.

# Scroll with Wheel Mouse

1. Rotate the wheel forward or back to scroll a few lines at a time

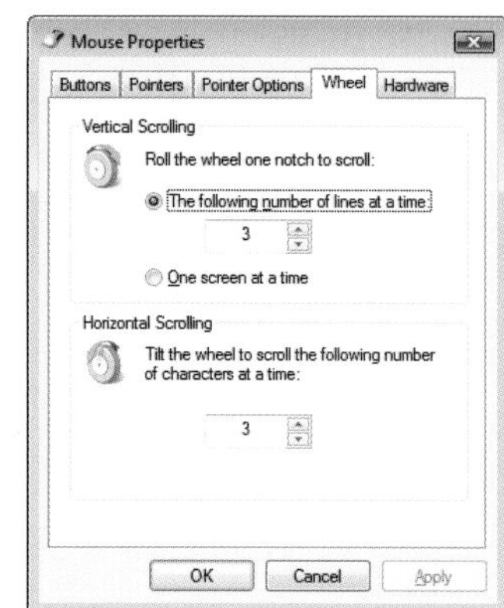


2. To change the amount scrolled, open Control Panel and select Mouse; then click the Wheel tab and change the number of lines or choose "One screen at a time"

The Wheel Mouse properties in Windows Vista also allow horizontal scrolling if the wheel can be tilted left or right.

## Continuous Scroll

1. Hold down the wheel button, and drag the pointer away from the origin mark in the direction you want to scroll.

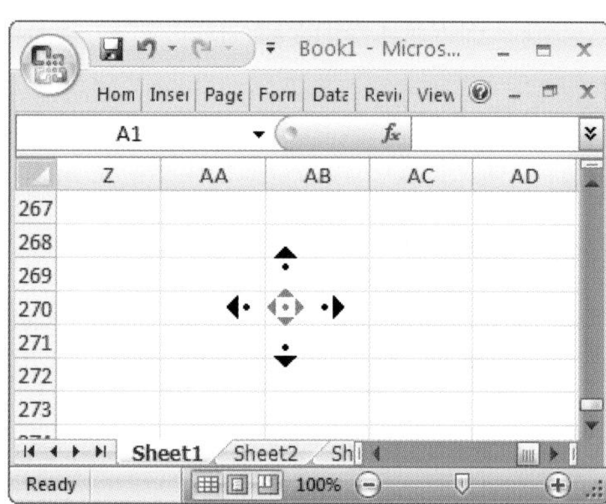


2. Release the wheel when you reach the required position

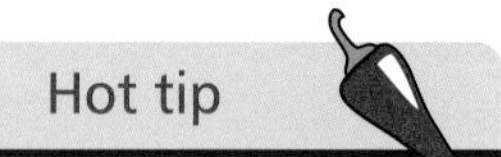


Move the pointer away from the origin mark to speed up scrolling. Move the pointer closer to the origin mark to slow down scrolling.

## Hands-Free Scroll

1. To scroll automatically, click and release the wheel button, and then move the mouse in the required direction

2. The further away from the origin mark you place the mouse pointer, the faster the scrolling

3. To slow down scrolling, move the mouse pointer back, closer to the origin mark

4. To stop automatic scrolling, click any mouse button

# Navigate with Keystrokes

The use of the arrow keys for navigation is covered on page 44. Here are some additional keyboard shorts.

## End Key

With Scroll Lock off, press End and then press one of the arrow keys to move to the edge of the data region

With Scroll Lock on, press End to move to the cell in the lower-right corner of the window

Ctrl+End moves to the last used cell (end of lowest used row)

Ctrl+Shift+End extends the selection to the last used cell

## Home Key

With Scroll Lock off, press Home to move to the beginning of the current row

With Scroll Lock on, press Home to move to the cell in the upper-left corner of the window

Ctrl+Home moves to the beginning of the worksheet

Ctrl+Shift+Home extends the selection to the beginning

## Page Down Key

Page Down moves one screen down in the worksheet

Alt+Page Down moves one screen to the right

Ctrl+Page Down moves to the next sheet in the workbook

Ctrl+Shift+Page Down selects the current and the next sheet

## Page Up Key

Page Up moves one screen up in the worksheet

Alt+Page Up moves one screen to the left

Ctrl+Page Up moves to the previous sheet in the workbook

Ctrl+Shift+Page Up selects the current and the previous sheet

## Tab Key

Tab moves one cell to the right in the worksheet

Shift+Tab moves to the previous cell in the worksheet

**Don't forget**

If you are entering or changing data using the keyboard, you might prefer to stay on the keyboard and use these additional shortcuts to navigate the worksheet, rather than using the mouse.

# Sort Rows

If you are looking for particular information, and don't know exactly where it appears in the worksheet, you can use Excel commands to help locate the items.

Click the column that contains the information, and select Sort & Filter from the Home tab, Editing group

Custom Sort allows you to sort the worksheet by several fields, for example Artists and Albums.

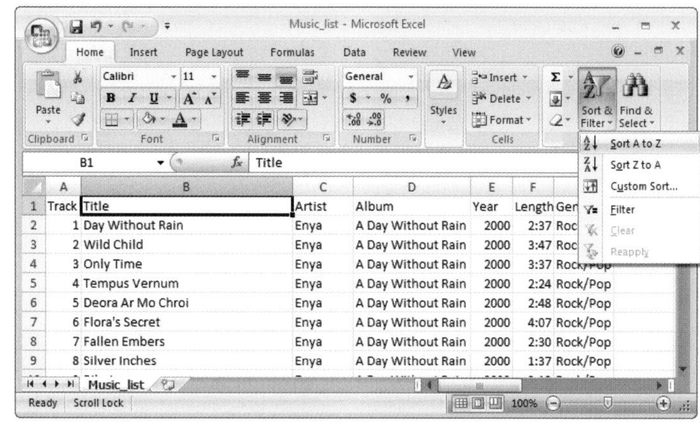




2 Choose Sort A to Z (or Sort Z to A if the required information would be towards the end of the list)

## Hot tip

Excel will sort the rows of data, using the column selected, so all the related data will stay together.

Excel provides a more structured way of handling a range of data such as this, with the Excel Table – see page 72.

3 Scroll through the list (using the navigation techniques described on pages 44–45) to locate the relevant entries

4 If you wish to preserve the original sequence of rows, respond No to the Save message, when you close the workbook

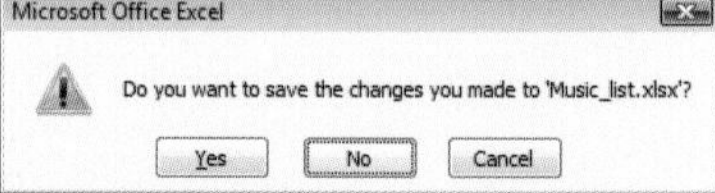

# Find Entries

If you'd rather not change the sequence of the rows, you can use the Find command to locate appropriate entries.

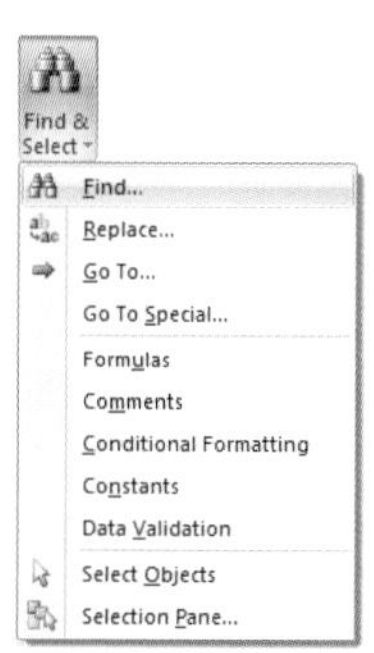


1. Click the column with the information, choose Find & Select from the Editing group on the Home tab, and then click Find (or press Ctrl+F)

2. Click the Options button if necessary (Excel remembers the last setting)

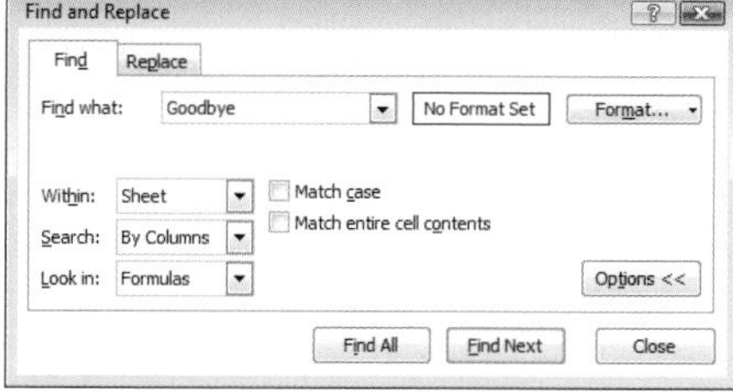


3. Specify a word or phrase, select the options to search within the worksheet and in the Column, and then click Find Next

4. Repeat Find Next to locate subsequent matching entries

5. You can click Find All to get a list of the cell addresses of the matching entries

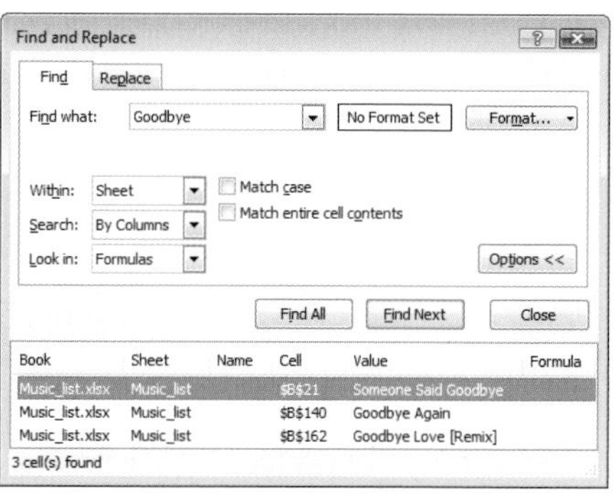

Select all the cells in the column, and the search will be restricted to that part of the worksheet.

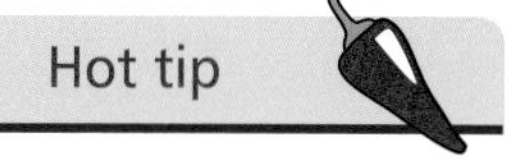


You can include case in the check, and you can require a full match with the entire cell contents.

# Filter Information

The Filter part of the Sort & Filter command can be very helpful in assessing the information that you have imported, because it allows you to concentrate on particular sections of the data.

1. Select all the data (for example, click in the data region, press Ctrl+End, and then press Shift+Ctrl+Home)

2. Select Sort & Filter from the Home tab, Editing group and then click the Filter command

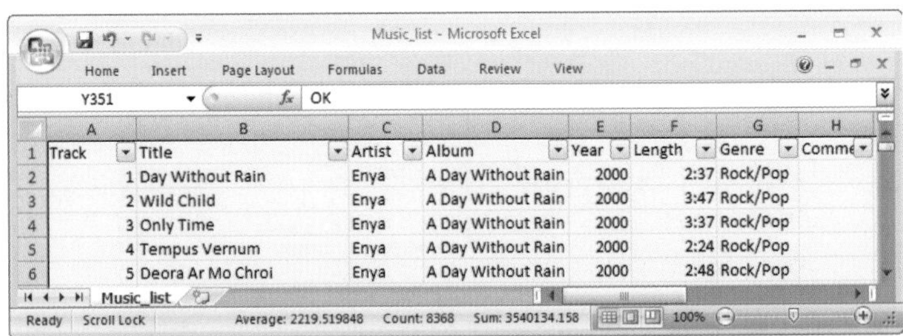

3. Click the arrow box in the column heading, to display the unique values

4. Clear the boxes for unwanted values, to leave only those you want to view

5. Click the OK button to display the entries that contain those values (e.g. tracks with guest artists specified)

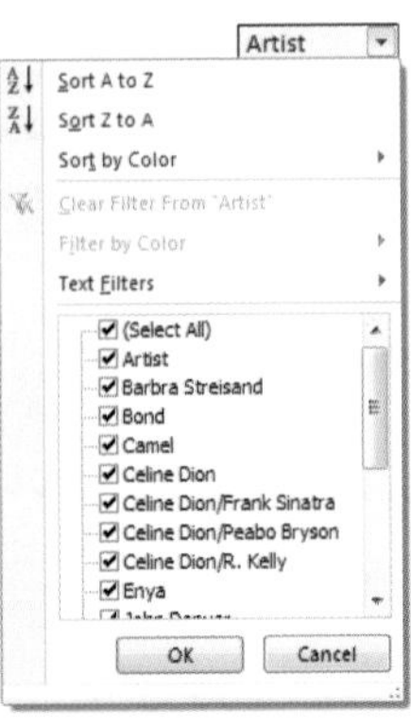

If you want just a few entries, clear the (Select All) box, which clears all the boxes; then reselect just the ones you want.

6 Make the changes that are required (e.g. copy guest artists to the Comments field, leaving just the main artist)

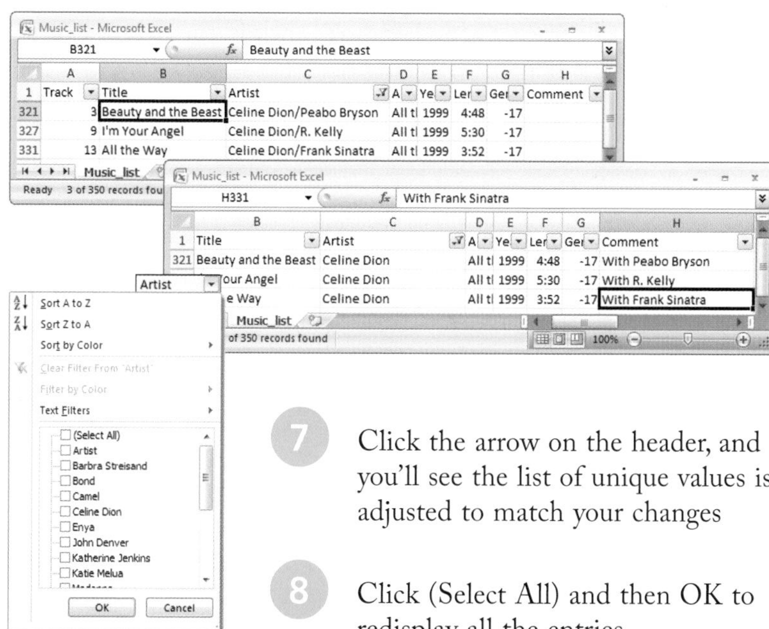


7 Click the arrow on the header, and you'll see the list of unique values is adjusted to match your changes

8 Click (Select All) and then OK to redisplay all the entries

You can filter for blank entries, to identify cells with missing data.

1 Click the arrow for Track, click (Select All) to clear the box, then select (Blanks) and click OK

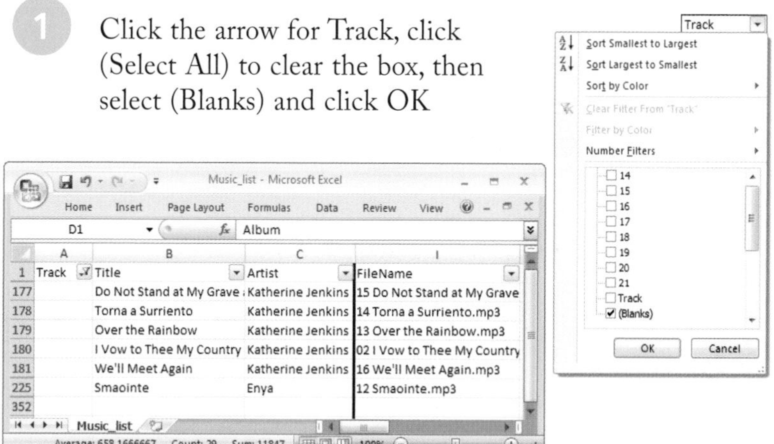


2 You can then correct the missing entries, in this case by copying the track numbers from the FileName column

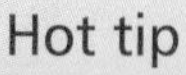

**Hot tip**

Having consistent values for the entries makes it much easier to sort and organize your information.

**Don't forget**

To remove the filters, reselect the Filter command from the Home tab, Editing group. This will redisplay all of the entries.

**Hot tip**

In this view of the worksheet, columns D to H are hidden (see page 55) to make it easier to view the relevant sections of the data.

# Remove Duplicate Entries

## Hot tip

Sorting (see page 48) may help you spot repeated entries, caused for example when some data gets imported twice, but Excel offers a more systematic method.

## Don't forget

You will be permanently deleting data, so you should make a copy of the workbook before removing duplicate values.

## Beware

Duplicate values are based on the displayed value, not on the stored value, so differences in format will make the entry appear unique.

A duplicate entry is where all values in the row are an exact match for all the values in another row.

To find and remove duplicate values

1. Select the range of cells.

2. Select the Data tab; then from the Data Tools group, click Remove Duplicates

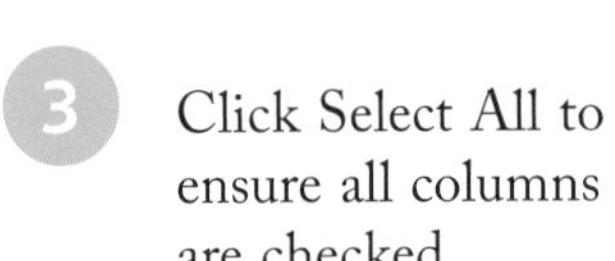

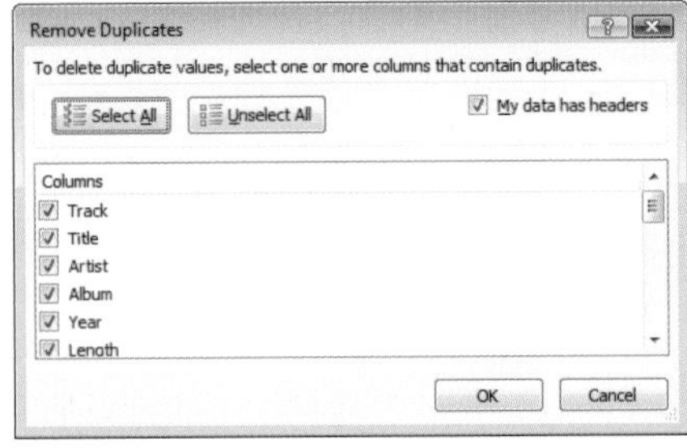


3. Click Select All to ensure all columns are checked

4. Clear the box for "My data has headers", if you suspect these may be repeated

5. Click OK, to detect and delete the duplicates

A message is displayed indicating how many duplicate values were removed and how many unique values remain

6. Click OK

# Check Spelling

A spelling check is sometimes a useful way to assess the contents of some sections of your worksheet.

1. Select the relevant parts: for example, click one column, press and hold Ctrl, and then click more columns

2. Select the Review tab, and click the Spelling command in the Proofing group (or press F7)

3. Click Change All if the word being corrected is likely to appear more than once

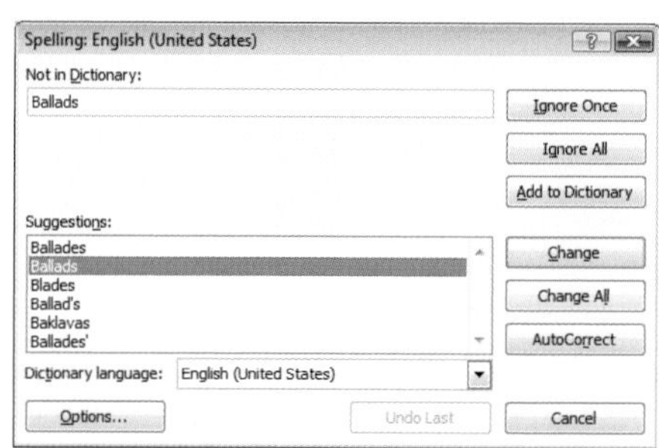

4. Click Ignore All if there are spelling warnings for valid terms or foreign words

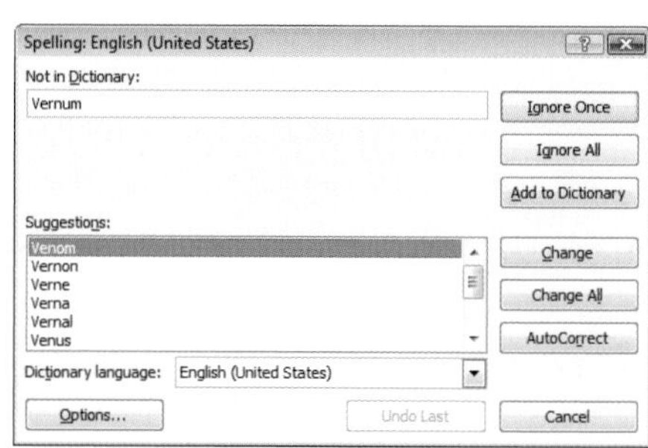

5. Click OK when the spelling check completes

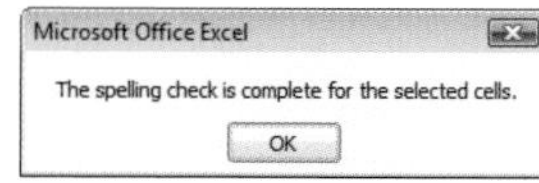

Choose columns of data that are suitable for spell-checking.

# Freeze Headers and Labels

When you navigate a worksheet, column headings and row labels will move off screen, making it more difficult to identify the data elements. To keep these visible, start by clicking on the worksheet.

1. Click the cell below the headings and to the right of the labels (e.g. with one row and one column, choose cell B2)

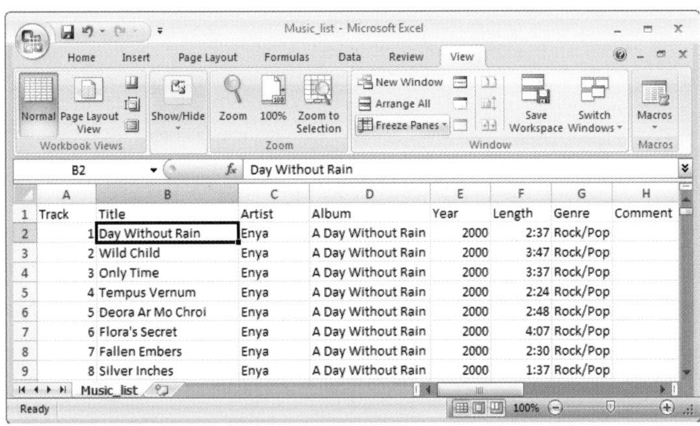


**Hot tip**

There are predefined options for a single heading row, or a single label column.

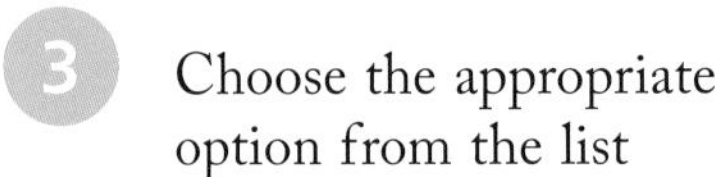

2. Select the View tab and click the Freeze Panes command from the Window group

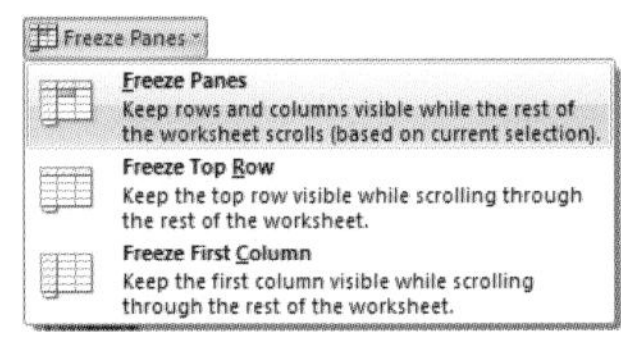


3. Choose the appropriate option from the list

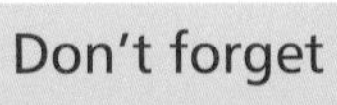

**Don't forget**

You can now scroll down, and the headings stay visible. Similarly, if you scroll across, the row labels now stay visible.

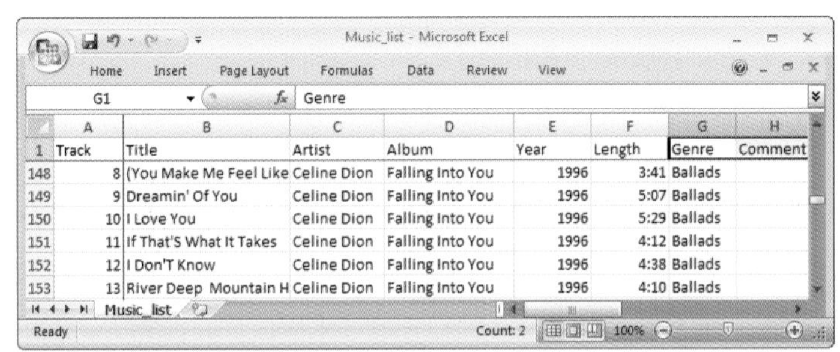


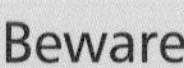

**Beware**

You must unfreeze panes before you sort your worksheet (see page 48).

4. The first entry for the Freeze Panes command changes to the undo option Unfreeze Panes

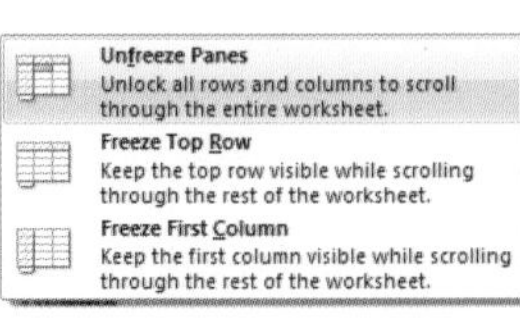

# Hide Columns or Rows

To make it easier to view particular portions of the worksheet, you can tell Excel not to display certain columns or rows

1. Select the columns or rows that you want to hide. For example, to select non-adjacent columns, select the first column, hold down Ctrl and select subsequent columns

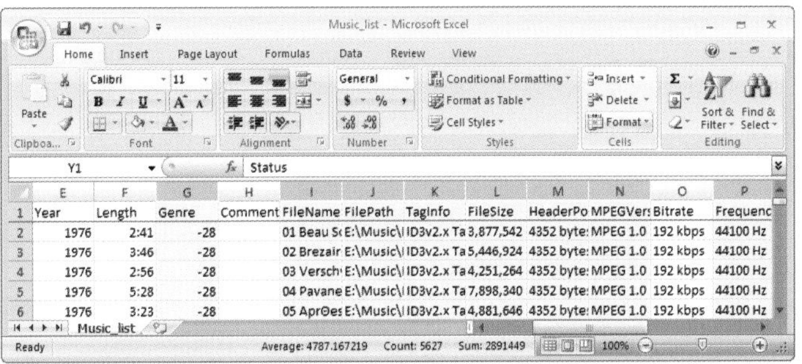


2. Select the Home tab, and click the Format command from the Cells group

3. In the Visibility section, click Hide & Unhide, and then click Hide Rows or Hide Columns, as appropriate

Format
Cell Size
Row Height...
AutoFit Row Height
Column Width...
AutoFit Column Width
Default Width...
Visibility
Hide & Unhide
Hide Rows
Hide Columns
Hide Sheet
Unhide Rows
Unhide Columns
Unhide Sheet...
Organize Sheets
Rename Sheet
Move or Copy Sheet...
Tab Color
Protection
Protect Sheet...
Lock Cell
Format Cells...

To display hidden rows or columns:

1. Select the rows above and below hidden rows, or select the columns either side of hidden columns

2. Select Unhide Columns or Unhide Rows from the Hide & Unhide menu, in the Visibility section as shown above

**Hot tip**

You cannot cancel the selection of a cell or range of cells in a non-adjacent selection without canceling the entire selection.

**Don't forget**

A column or row also becomes hidden if you change its column width or row height to zero. The Unhide command will reveal columns and rows hidden this way.

**Hot tip**

You can also right-click selected rows or columns and then click Hide or Unhide.

# Protect a Worksheet

## Don't forget

Once you've set up your worksheet the way you want it, you can lock it to protect it from being accidentally changed.

## Beware

Although it does offer a password option, this command is really only suitable for avoiding accidental damage, not preventing deliberate changes.

## Hot tip

When you protect the sheet, the command changes to Unprotect Sheet, to allow you to reverse the process.

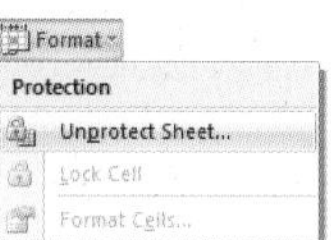


1. Select any columns (e.g. Comments) that you might want to update

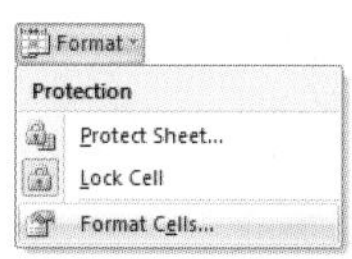


2. On the Home tab, select Format from the Cells group, and click Format cells

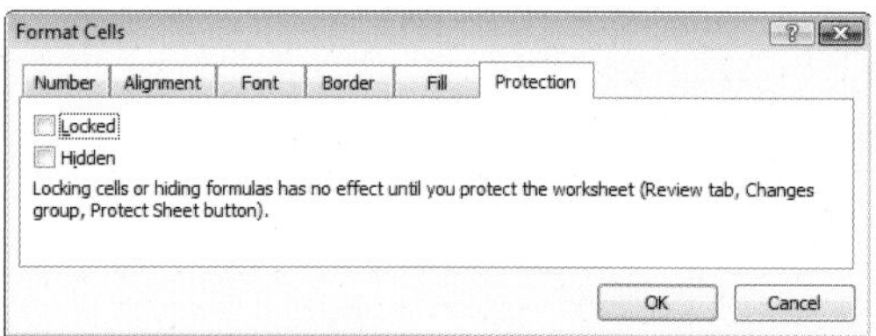


3. Select the Protection tab; then clear the Locked box, and the Lock Text box also, if this is displayed

4. To protect the remaining part of the worksheet, select Format again and this time select Protect Sheet

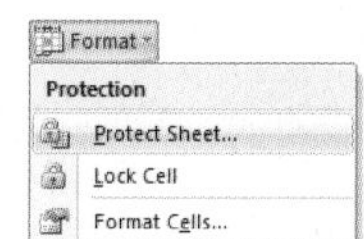


5. Ensure that all users are allowed to select locked and unlocked cells and then click OK

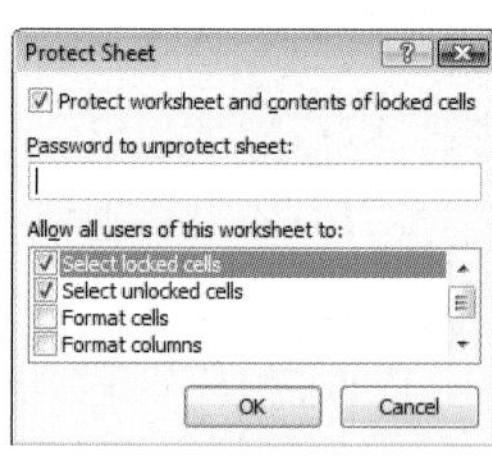


6. You can edit cells in the chosen columns, but will get an error message if you try to edit any other cells

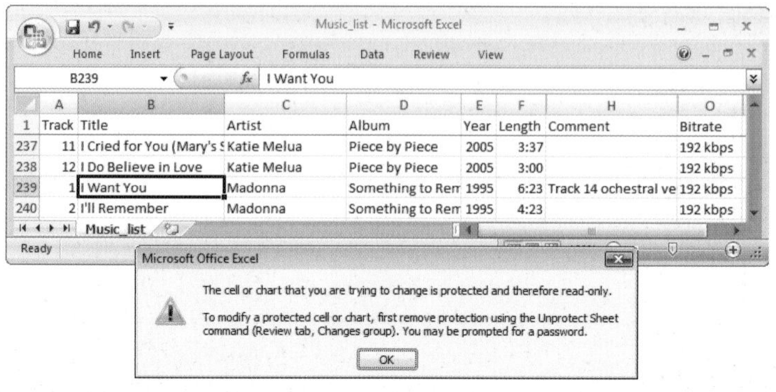

# 4 Formulas and Functions

*Various formats for numbers are explained and options for referencing cell locations are reviewed. These provide the basis for an introduction to functions and formulas, beginning with operators and calculation sequence, and including formula errors and cell comments.*

# Number Formats

The cells in the worksheet contain values in the form of numbers or text characters. The associated cell formats control how the contents are displayed.

**Don't forget**

The values can be typed directly into the cells, imported from another application (see page 42) or created by a formula.

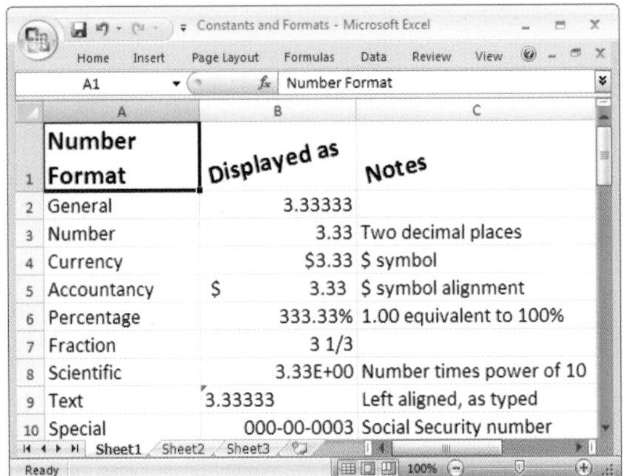

| | A | B | C |
|---|---|---|---|
| 1 | Number Format | Displayed as | Notes |
| 2 | General | 3.33333 | |
| 3 | Number | 3.33 | Two decimal places |
| 4 | Currency | $3.33 | $ symbol |
| 5 | Accountancy | $ 3.33 | $ symbol alignment |
| 6 | Percentage | 333.33% | 1.00 equivalent to 100% |
| 7 | Fraction | 3 1/3 | |
| 8 | Scientific | 3.33E+00 | Number times power of 10 |
| 9 | Text | 3.33333 | Left aligned, as typed |
| 10 | Special | 000-00-0003 | Social Security number |

Cells B2 to B10 all contain the same value (3.33333) but each cell has a different format, which changes the way that the number appears on the worksheet. To set the number format:

**Hot tip**

The Special format is for structured numbers, e.g. zip or postal codes, telephone numbers and social security numbers.

1. Select the cell or cells; then click the Home tab, select Format in the Cells group, and choose Format Cells

2. Select the Number tab and choose the category to see how the contents would appear, and to select attributes such as decimal places and the appearance of negative numbers

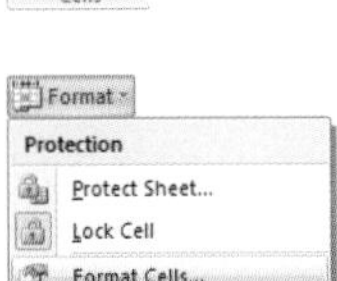


**Don't forget**

The default is General, which is based on the cell contents. Use Number when you need decimal places and Currency or Accounting for money amounts.

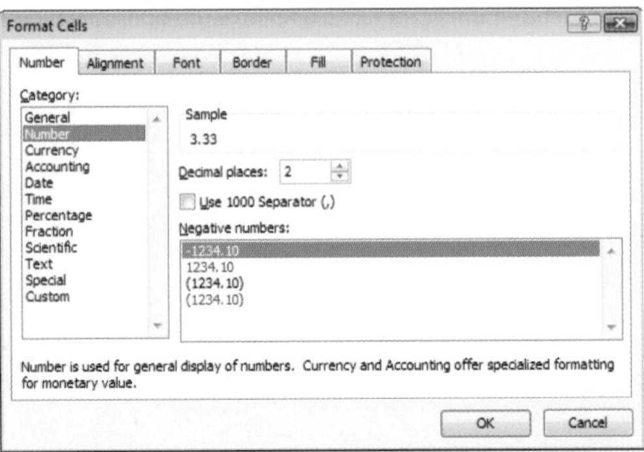

Date and Time are also number formats, but in this case the number is taken as the days since a base point in time.

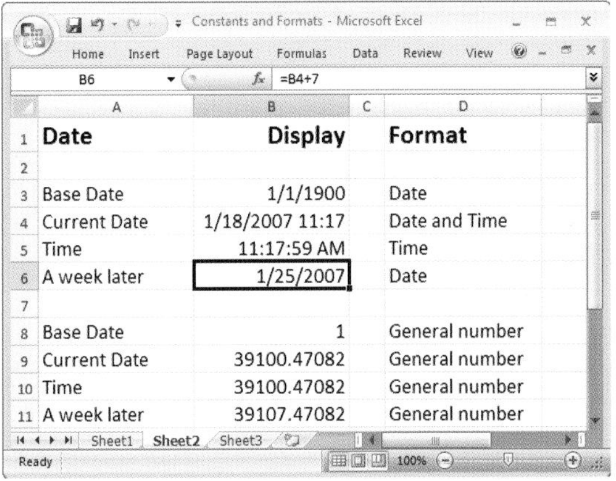


**Don't forget**

Because dates and times are stored as numbers, you can use them in formulas and calculations.

Cells B3 to B6 are formatted as dates or times. The same numbers are shown in cells B8 to B11, formated as General. This shows that day 1 is January 1st, 1900 and day 39100 is January 18th 2007, while day 39107 is a week later. Decimals indicate part days.

To set or change the date or time format:

1. Open Format Cells, select the Number tab, and click Date or Time to see the list of format options

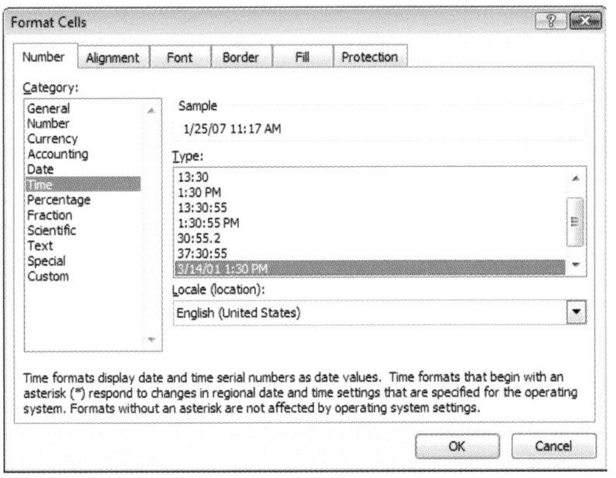


2. Choose a format option and click OK, or click Custom to see other time and date formatting options

**Don't forget**

Some of the formats depend on the specific country and location defined in the Windows regional options, found in the Control Panel.

# Text Formats

Excel recognizes cells containing text, such as header and label cells, and gives them the General format, with default text format settings (left-aligned, and using the standard font).

To change the format for such cells:

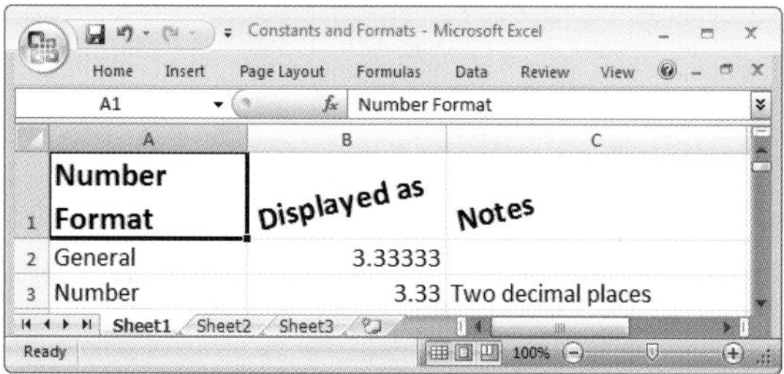

1. Select the cells and open Format Cells, select the Font tab and choose the font, style, size and color

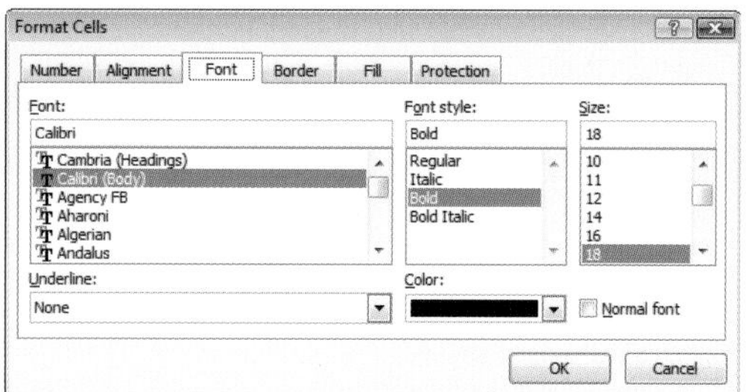


Hot tip

See page 30 for more examples of setting text format options for font and alignment, including the Merge Cells option.

Don't forget

The text in cell A1, as shown above, uses the Wrap Text option to keep the text within the column width. Cells B1 and C1 illustrate the use of Orientation to fit the headings into the cells.

2. Select the Alignment tab and change the text controls, alignment or orientation settings

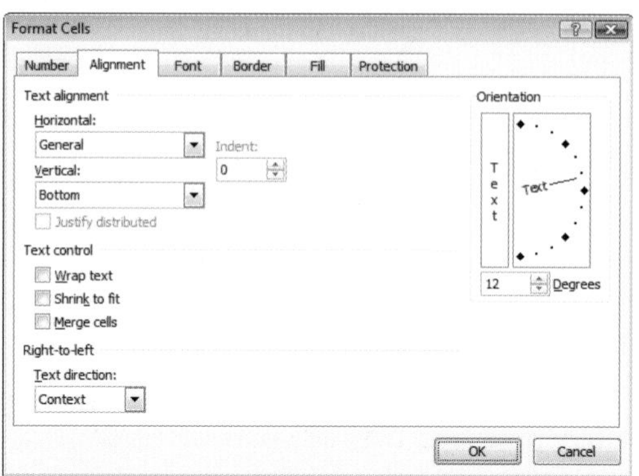

# Relative References

A cell could contain a formula rather than an actual value. Excel performs the calculation that the formula represents, and displays the result as the value for that cell. For example:

In this worksheet, cell D3 shows the amount spent on DVDs (price times quantity) calculated as =B3*C3.

| | A | B | C | D | E |
|---|---|---|---|---|---|
| 1 | **Invoice** | | | | |
| 2 | **Product** | **Price** | **Quantity** | **Amount** | |
| 3 | DVDs | 12.95 | 5 | 64.75 | |
| 4 | Notepads | 2.45 | 4 | 9.80 | |
| 5 | Books | 7.99 | 3 | 23.97 | |
| 6 | | | | 98.52 | |
| 7 | Sales tax | 7.50% | | 7.39 | |
| 8 | Shipping | | | 4.95 | |
| 9 | Total Cost | | | 110.86 | |

The formulas for D4 and D5 are created by copying and pasting D3. The cell references in the formula are relative to the position of the cell containing them, and are automatically updated for the new location.

A cell reference in this form is know as a **relative reference**, and this is the normal type of reference used in worksheets.

| | A | B | C | D | E |
|---|---|---|---|---|---|
| 1 | **Invoice** | | | | |
| 2 | **Product** | **Price** | **Quantity** | **Amount** | |
| 3 | DVDs | 12.95 | 5 | =B3*C3 | |
| 4 | Notepads | 2.45 | 4 | =B4*C4 | |
| 5 | Books | 7.99 | 3 | =B5*C5 | |
| 6 | | | | =D3+D4+D5 | |
| 7 | Sales tax | 0.075 | | =D6*B7 | |
| 8 | Shipping | | | 4.95 | |
| 9 | Total Cost | | | =D6+D7+D8 | |

The results of formulas can be used in other formulas, so the total in cell D6 is calculated as =D3+D4+D5.

The sales tax in cell D7 is calculated as =D6*B7. Note that B7 is displayed as a value of 7.5%, the cell format being Percentage. The actual value stored in the cell is 0.075.

The worksheet could have used a constant value instead, such as =D5*7.5/100 or =D5*7.5%. However, having the value stored in a cell makes it easier to adapt the worksheet when rates change. It also helps when the value is used more than once.

The shipping cost in cell D8 is a stored constant.

The final calculation in the worksheet is the total cost in cell D9, which is calculated as =D6+D7+D8.

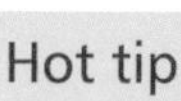


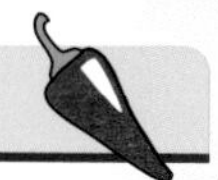

The cells hold formulas as stored values, but it is the results that normally get displayed. To switch between results and formulas, press Ctrl+` (the grave accent key). The top illustration here shows values and the lower one displays formulas.

## Don't forget

The value B7 is a relative cell reference like the others, but this may not be the best option. See page 62 for the alternative.

# Absolute References

Assume that calculation of the sales tax per line item is required. The value in cell E3 for the DVDs product would be =D3*B7.

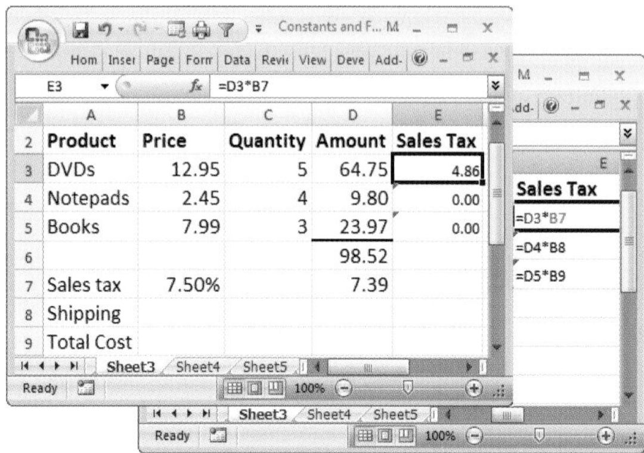


You might be tempted to copy this formula down into cells E4 and E5, but as you see here the results would be incorrect, giving zero values because the **relative reference** B7 would be incremented to B8 and then B9, both of which are empty cells.

The answer is to fix the reference to B7 so that it doesn't change when the formula is copied. To indicate this, you edit the formula to place a $ symbol in front of the row and column addresses.

Don't forget

To fix the column, place $ before the column letter. Likewise, to fix the row, put $ before the row number. The other part of the reference will change when the formula is copied.

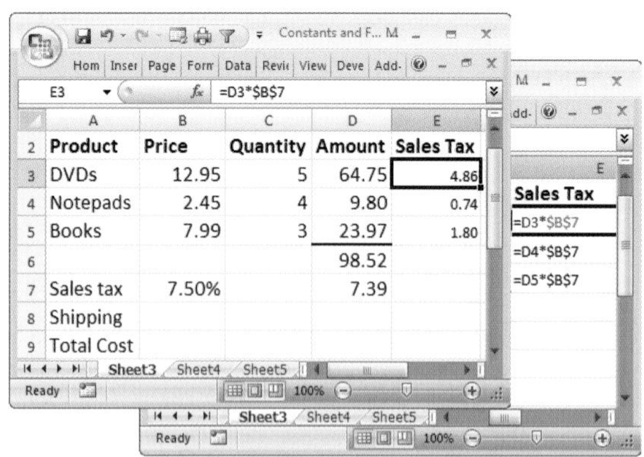


Copy this formula down into cells E4 and E5, and the reference $B$7 doesn't change, so the results are correct. This form of cell reference is known as an **absolute reference**.

A cell reference with only part of the address fixed, such as $D3 or D$3, is known as a **mixed reference**.

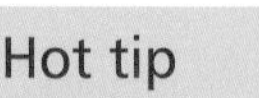

Hot tip

Select a cell reference in a formula and press F4 to cycle between relative, absolute and mixed cell references.

# Name References

Names provide a different way of referring to cells in formulas. To create a name for a cell or cell range:

1. Select the cell or the group of cells you want to name

2. Click the Name box, on the left of the Formula bar

3. Type the name that you'll be using to refer to the selection and press Enter

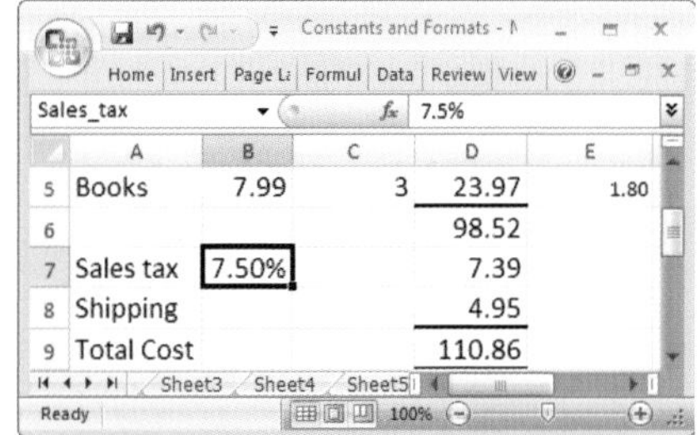


4. Click the Formulas tab and select the Name Manager in the Defined Names group, to view names in the workbook

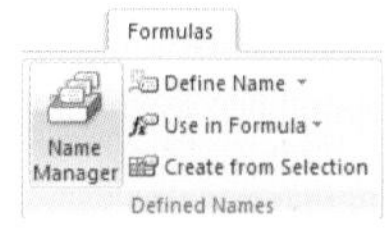


Names create absolute references to cells or ranges in the current worksheet. They can be used in formulas, and when these are copied the references will not be incremented.

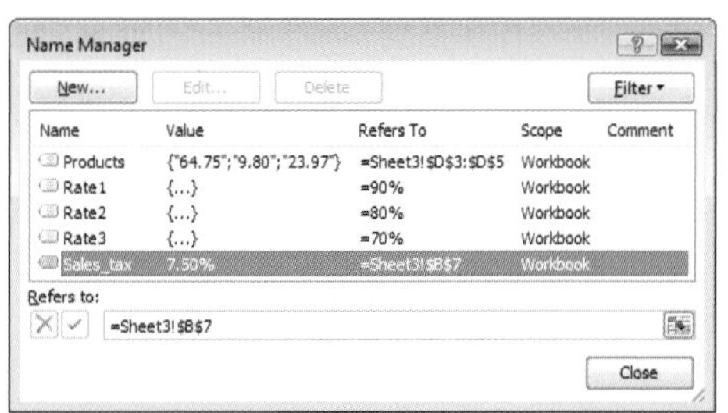


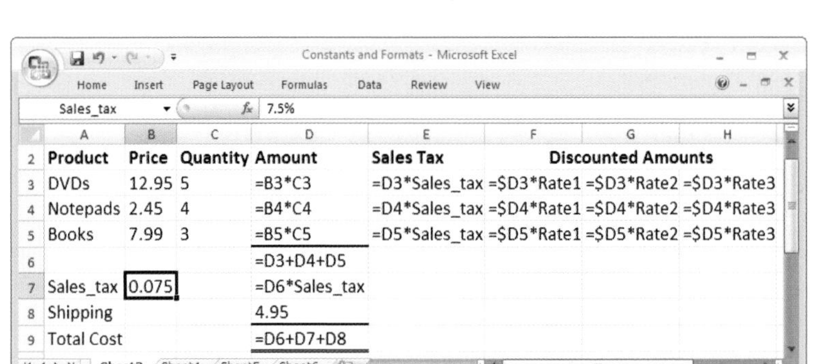


| | A | B | C | D | E | F | G | H |
|---|---|---|---|---|---|---|---|---|
| 2 | Product | Price | Quantity | Amount | Sales Tax | | Discounted Amounts | |
| 3 | DVDs | 12.95 | 5 | =B3*C3 | =D3*Sales_tax | =$D3*Rate1 | =$D3*Rate2 | =$D3*Rate3 |
| 4 | Notepads | 2.45 | 4 | =B4*C4 | =D4*Sales_tax | =$D4*Rate1 | =$D4*Rate2 | =$D4*Rate3 |
| 5 | Books | 7.99 | 3 | =B5*C5 | =D5*Sales_tax | =$D5*Rate1 | =$D5*Rate2 | =$D5*Rate3 |
| 6 | | | | =D3+D4+D5 | | | | |
| 7 | Sales_tax | 0.075 | | =D6*Sales_tax | | | | |
| 8 | Shipping | | | 4.95 | | | | |
| 9 | Total Cost | | | =D6+D7+D8 | | | | |

You cannot use a name such as R1, since that is an actual cell reference. You must specify a non-ambiguous name, such as Rate1.

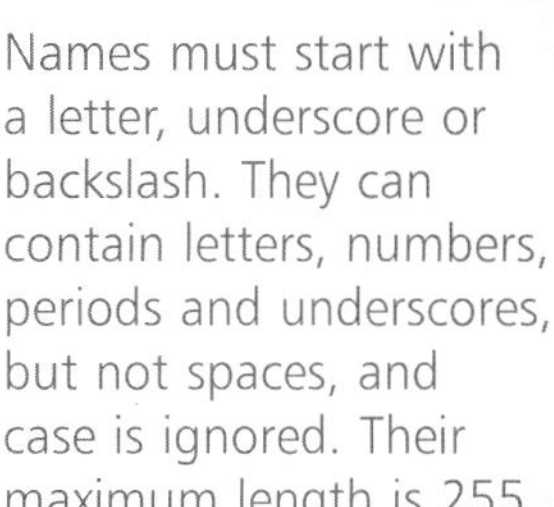

**Don't forget**

Names must start with a letter, underscore or backslash. They can contain letters, numbers, periods and underscores, but not spaces, and case is ignored. Their maximum length is 255 characters.

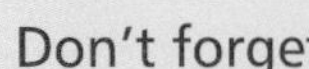

**Don't forget**

Names can be defined for a cell, for a range or group of cells, or for constants and functions.

# Operators

The formulas shown so far have used several operators (+, *, %) but there are many other operators you might use, in a number of categories, including the following:

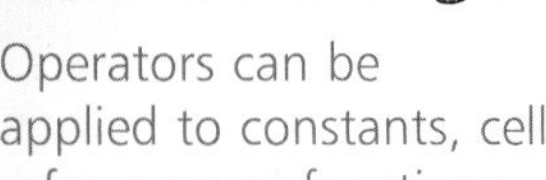

Don't forget

Operators can be applied to constants, cell references or functions.

| Category | Meaning | Examples |
|---|---|---|
| **Arithmetic** | | |
| + (plus sign) | Addition | A7+B5 |
| - (minus sign) | Subtraction<br>Negation | C6-20<br>-C3 |
| * (asterisk) | Multiplication | C5*C6 |
| / (forward slash) | Division | C6/D3 |
| % (percent sign) | Percent | 20% |
| ^ (caret) | Exponentiation or Power | D3^2 |
| **Comparison** | | |
| = (equal) | Equal to | A1=B1 |
| > (greater than) | Greater than | A1>B1 |
| < (less than) | Less than | A1<B1 |
| >= (greater than with equal) | Greater than or equal | A1>=B1 |
| <= (less than with equal) | Less than or equal | A1<=B1 |
| <> (not equal) | Not equal | A1<>B1 |
| **Text** | | |
| & (ampersand) | Connect/join | "ABCDE"&"FGHI" |
| **Reference** | | |
| : (colon) | Range | B5:B15 |
| , (comma) | Union | SUM(B5:B15,D5:D15) |
| (space) | Intersection | B2:D6 C4:F8 |

Don't forget

The result of any of these comparisons will be a logical value, either True or False.

Hot tip

The Intersection of two ranges is a reference to all the cells that are common between the two ranges.

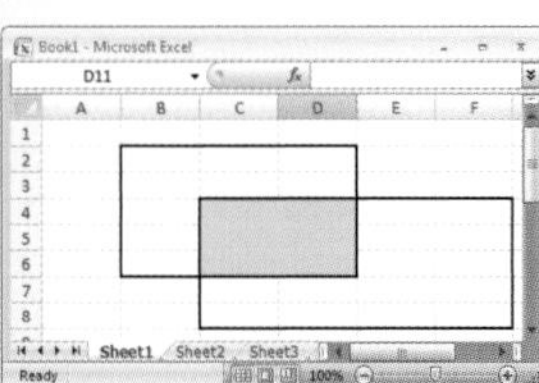

# Calculation Sequence

The order in which a calculation is performed may affect the result. As an example, the calculation 6+4*2 could be interpreted in two different ways. If the addition is performed first this would give 10*2, which equals 20. However, if the multiplication is performed first the calculation becomes 6+8, which equals 14.

To avoid any ambiguity in calculations, Excel evaluates formulas by applying the operators in a specific order. This is known as **operator precedence**. The sequence is as follows:

| | | |
|---|---|---|
| 1 | : ␣ , | colon single-space comma |
| 2 | – | negation |
| 3 | % | percentage |
| 4 | ^ | exponentiation |
| 5 | * / | multiplication division |
| 6 | + - | addition subtraction |
| 7 | & | concatenation |
| 8 | = <> <= >= <> | comparison |

When the formula has several operators with the same precedence, for example multiplication and division, Excel evaluates the operators from left to right.

These are some example formulas that illustrate the effect of operator precedence on the calculation result:

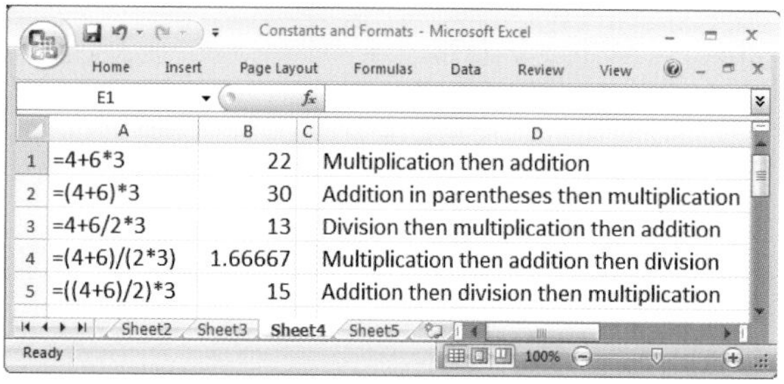

Constants and Formats - Microsoft Excel

| | A | B | C | D |
|---|---|---|---|---|
| 1 | =4+6*3 | 22 | | Multiplication then addition |
| 2 | =(4+6)*3 | 30 | | Addition in parentheses then multiplication |
| 3 | =4+6/2*3 | 13 | | Division then multiplication then addition |
| 4 | =(4+6)/(2*3) | 1.66667 | | Multiplication then addition then division |
| 5 | =((4+6)/2)*3 | 15 | | Addition then division then multiplication |

You can use parentheses to change the order of evaluation, since expressions within parentheses will be evaluated first. If there are parentheses within parentheses (nested), Excel will evaluate the expression in the innermost pair of parentheses first, and work out towards the outermost.

**Don't forget**

Operator precedence is a mathematical concept used by all programming languages and applications such as spreadsheet programs that include computation.

# Functions

Functions are predefined formulas that perform calculations based on specific values, called arguments, provided in the required sequence. The function begins with the function name, followed by an opening parenthesis, the arguments for the function separated by commas, and a closing parenthesis. They are used for many types of calculation, ranging from simple to highly complex.

If you are unsure which function is appropriate for the task, Excel will help you search for the most appropriate. To select a function in the Invoice worksheet:

1. Click the cell where you want to use a function as the formula, for example the total amount cell D6

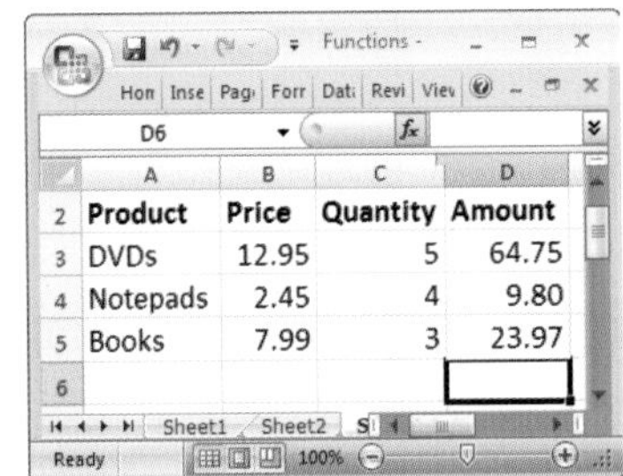


2. Click Insert Function on the Formula bar

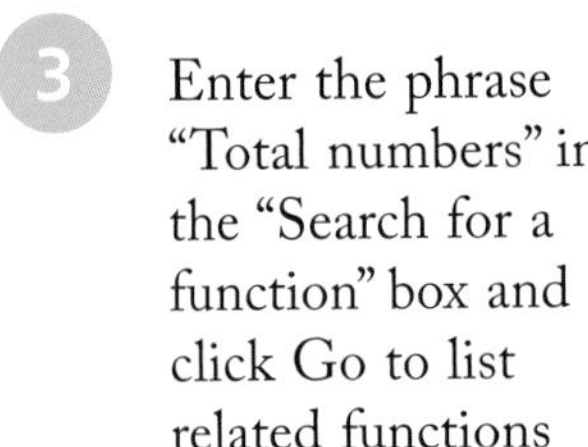

3. Enter the phrase "Total numbers" in the "Search for a function" box and click Go to list related functions

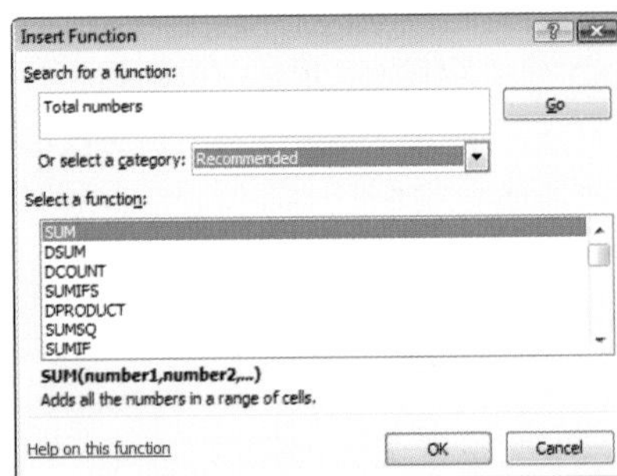


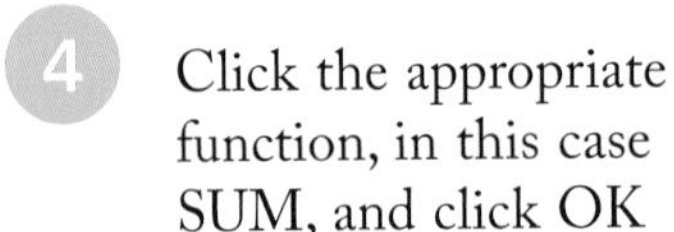

4. Click the appropriate function, in this case SUM, and click OK

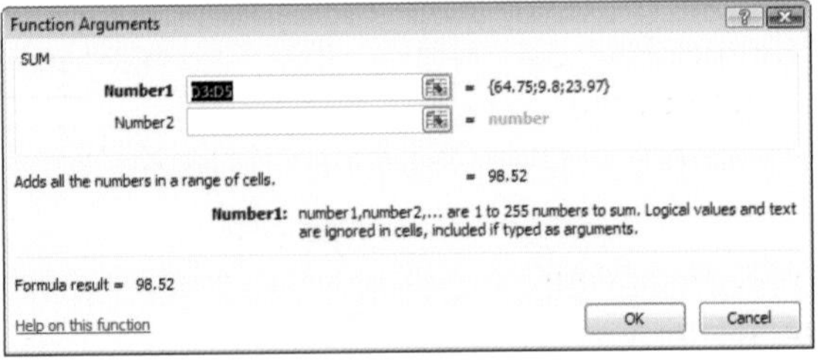


5. Check the suggested arguments, in this case the range D3:D5, see the result this gives, and click OK if this is what you are expecting

**Hot tip**

Arguments can be numbers, text, cell references or logical values (i.e. True or False).

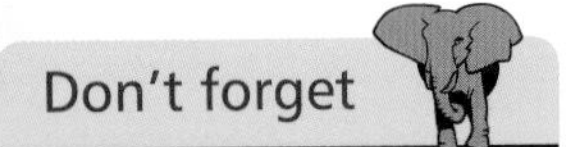

**Don't forget**

You can also find a function by browsing. Select a category.

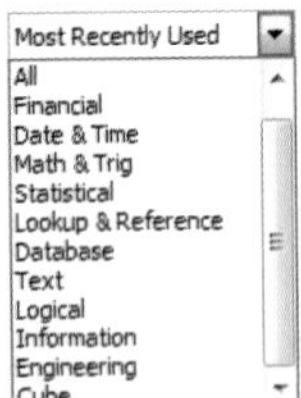


**Hot tip**

To select or change the arguments, click the Collapse Dialog button, select the cells on the worksheet, and then press the Expand Dialog button.

## Autocomplete

Even when you know the function needed, Excel will help you set it up, to help avoid possible syntax and typing errors.

1. Click the worksheet cell, and begin typing the function, for example click the total cost cell D9, and type =s

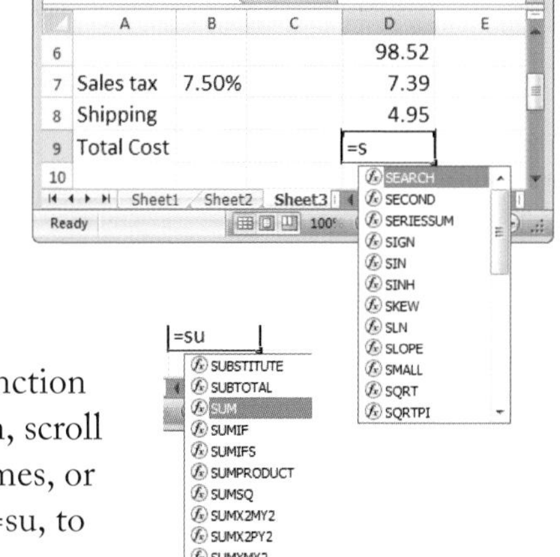

2. Excel lists functions that match so far, so you can select a function and see its description, scroll down to see more names, or continue typing, e.g. =su, to narrow the list

3. When you find the function required, double-click the name and then enter the arguments required

4. For example, click D6, press period and click D8.

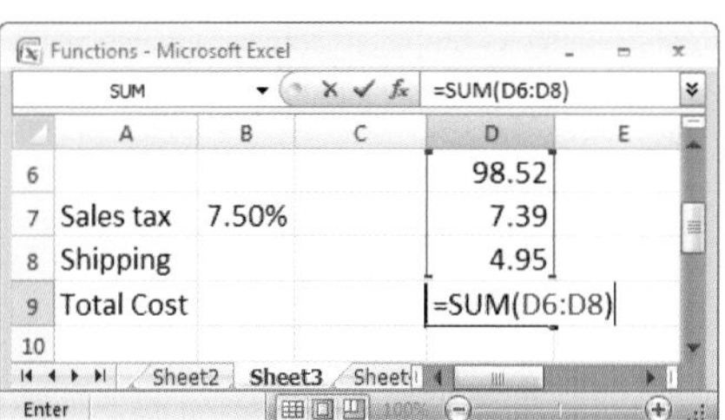

5. Type the closing parenthesis, and then press Enter

6. The formula with the function is stored in the cell and the result will be displayed

### Hot tip

Click on the function name in the prompt to display help for that function.

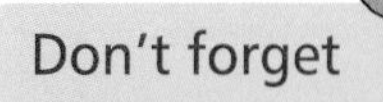

### Don't forget

Type the range name if you have already defined the required cells (see page 63).

# AutoSum

**Hot tip**

All the cells up or across to the first non-numeric or empty cell are included in the total.

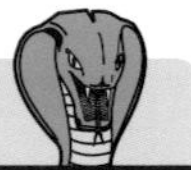

**Beware**

Autosum will add columns, if possible, rather than rows. With only one or two rows, Autosum will total the current row. With more rows above the formula cell, Autosum will total the column by default.

**Hot tip**

In either case, you can click the arrow next to AutoSum, and select from the list of functions offered.

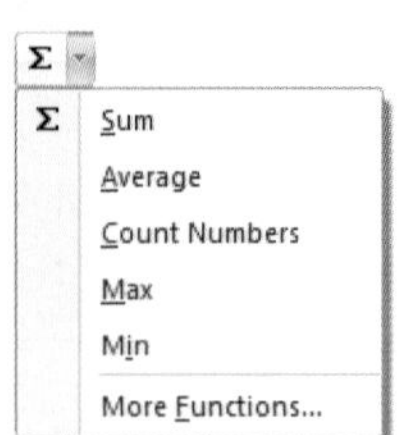


1. Select the cell below a column of numbers or to the right of a row of numbers

2. To total the numbers, click AutoSum in the Editing group on the Home tab

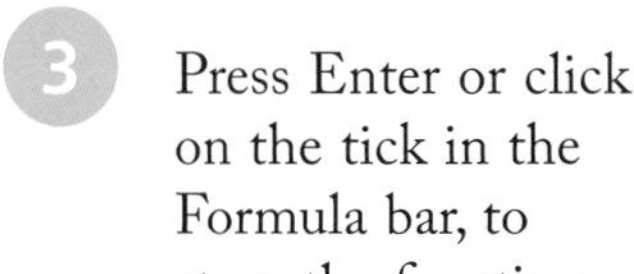

3. Press Enter or click on the tick in the Formula bar, to store the function

## Select and AutoSum

When you have multiple rows or columns, or the numbers aren't separated from others by blank cells, you need to preselect the cells.

1. Select a block of numbers with empty cells below and/or to the right of the cells

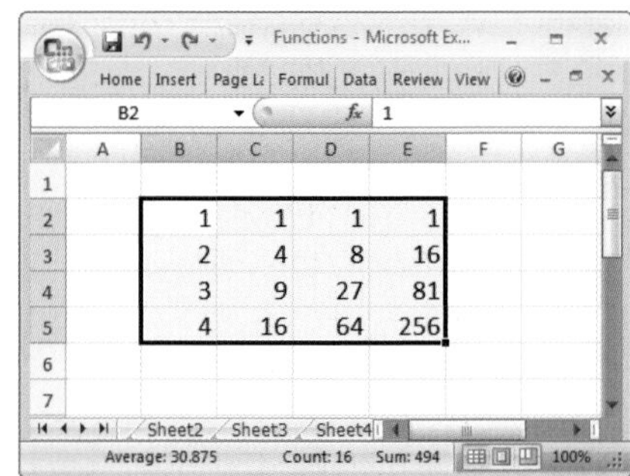

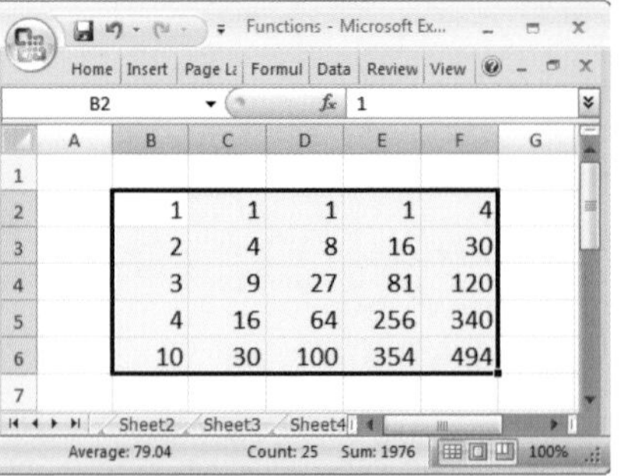

2. Click AutoSum to total the columns and/or the rows (there is no need to press Enter)

The same AutoSum option is also provided in the Function Library group on the Formulas tab, along with links to various sets of functions.

# Formula Errors

Excel helps you to avoid some of the more common errors when you are entering a formula.

1. When you type a name, Excel outlines the associated cell or range, so you can confirm that it is the correct selection

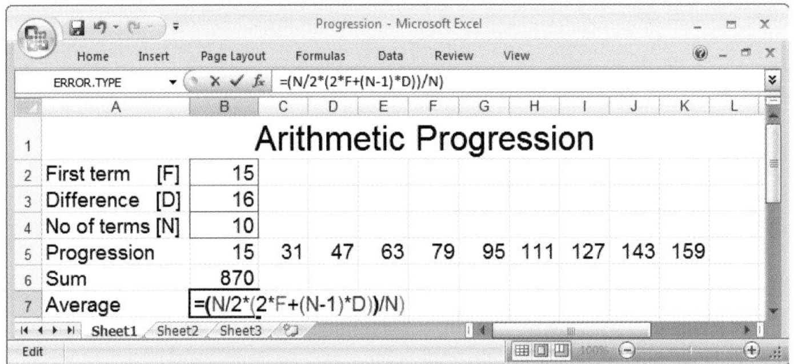


=(N/2*(2*F+(N-1)*D))/N)

2. With nested functions, Excel colors the parentheses, to help you ensure they are in matching open/close pairs

3. If you do make an error, such as an extraneous parenthesis, it is often detected and corrected.

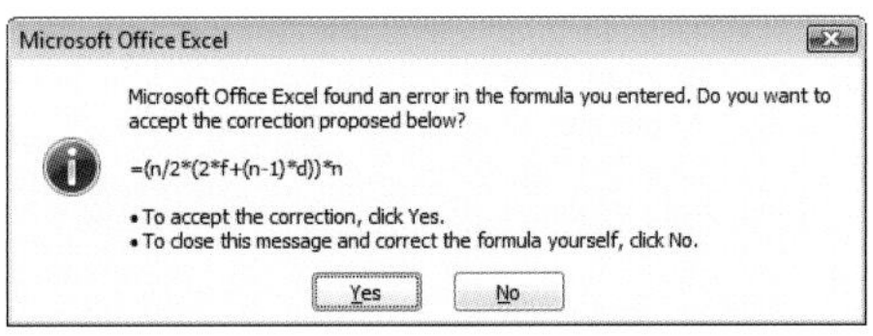


4. If the result overflows the available space, Excel displays hash signs

5. There's a similar display for other errors, but in addition a green flash shows in the top left-hand corner of the cell.

6. Click the green flash, then the information icon and finally the Help entry, for more details of the error

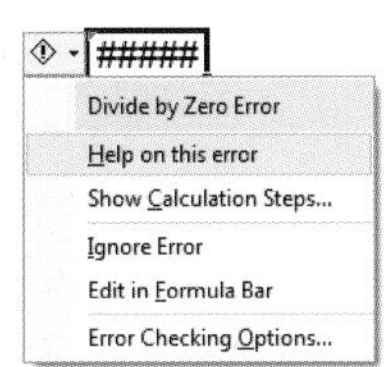


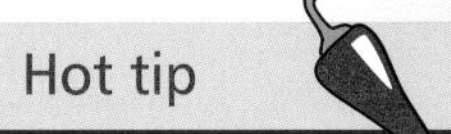

In this example F, D and N are defined names.

This totals and averages the terms in a number series, with formulas that have several levels of parentheses.

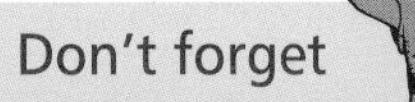

Other common errors that are displayed this way include #NAME? (name not recognized) and #REF! (invalid reference).

# Add Comments

Hot tip

When there are comments in your worksheets, you can print them as displayed on the sheet, or at the end of the sheet.

You can add notes to a cell, perhaps to explain the way in which a particular formula operates.

1. Click the cell where the comment is meant to appear

2. Select the Review tab, and click New Comment in the Comments group

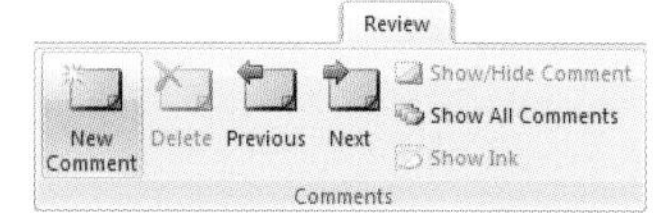


3. Your user name is shown, but you can delete this if you wish, and then add your comments

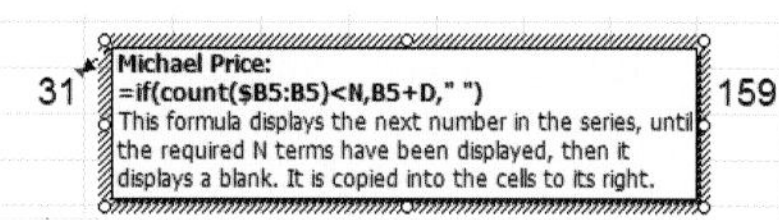


4. Format the text if desired, and then click outside the comment box to finish

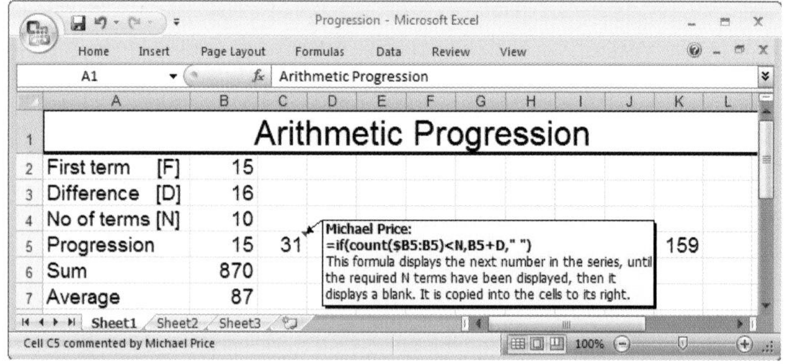


5. The presence of a comment is indicated by the red flash at the top right of the cell, and the comment box appears when you move the mouse over the cell

6. The Edit Comment command replaces New Comment when the selected cell contains an existing comment

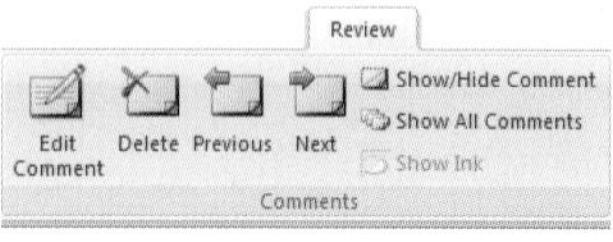

# 5 Excel Tables

*The Excel table structure helps you to keep sets of data separate, so that you don't accidentally change other data when you are inserting or deleting rows and columns. There are other benefits also, such as structured cell references and automatic filters, sorts and subtotals.*

# Create an Excel Table

To make it easier to manage and analyze a group of related data, you can turn a range of cells into an Excel Table. The range should contain no empty rows or empty columns.

To illustrate this feature, a table is used to interpret the genre (music classification) codes contained in the MP3 tags for music files (see page 40). This field usually appears as a genre code such as (2) for country music, or (4) for disco.

You can find a table of genre codes and meanings on the web page www.true-audio.com/ID3#Genres:

Hot tip

In an Excel Table, the rows and columns are managed independently from the data in other rows and columns on the worksheet. In previous releases of Excel, this feature was called an Excel list.

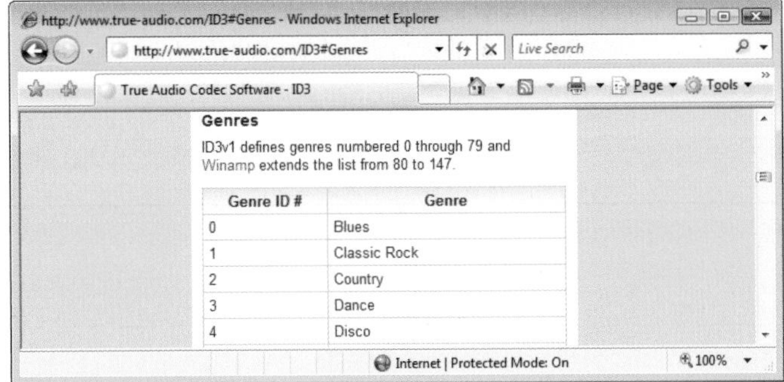

Beware

The genre code is contained in brackets, and the value will therefore be treated as a negative number when the data is imported to an Excel worksheet.

1. Select the table in Internet Explorer, and press Ctrl+C

2. Open the Music_List worksheet and locate an empty column beyond the existing data (leave some extra empty columns)

3. Select the first cell in the column and then press Ctrl+V to copy the Internet table of codes into the worksheet

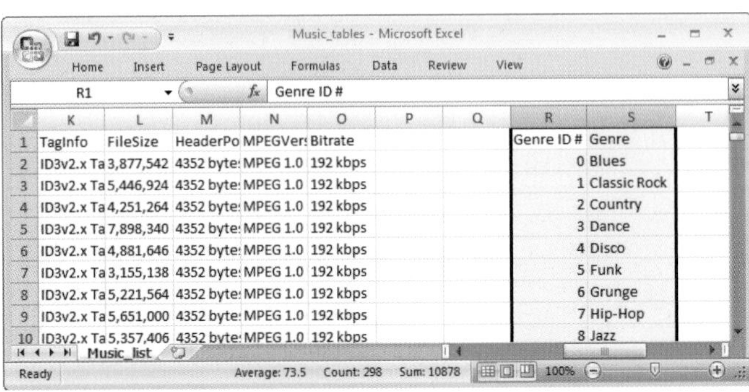

4 With the data selected, click the Insert tab, and then click Table in the Tables group

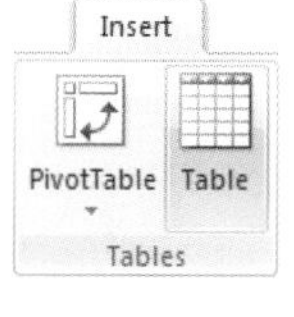


5 Check that the appropriate range of data is selected

6 If the first row has names, click "My table has headers"; otherwise let Excel generate default headers

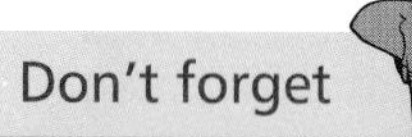

**Don't forget**

It may be best to remove worksheet protection, and unfreeze panes, before you insert the new data.

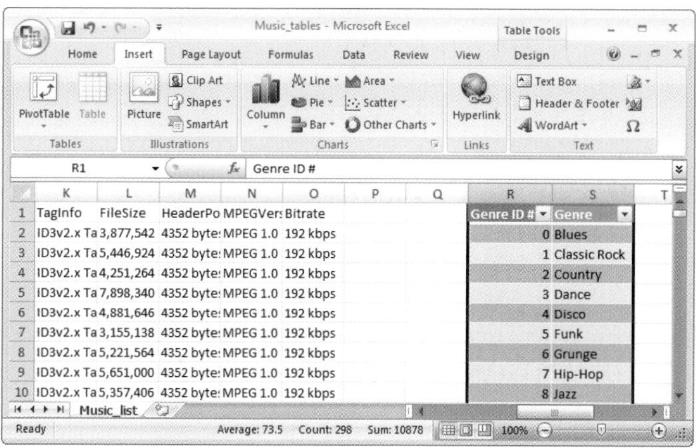

**Don't forget**

If you click in the table, the context-sensitive Table Tools and Design tabs are displayed, so that you can customize or edit the table.

The table is given the default banding style, and Filter boxes are automatically added in the header row of each column, allowing you to sort or filter the contents.

The table will be given a default name such as Table1. To change this name:

1 Click in the table, and click the Design tab

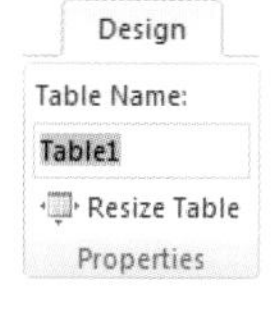


2 Click the Table Name box in the Properties group to highlight the name

3 Type the new name for the table and press Enter to apply the change (and update any references to the old table name)

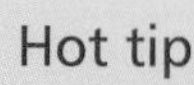

**Hot tip**

You can also change the names of tables using the Name Manager on the Formulas tab (see page 63).

# Edit Tables

Hot tip

You can insert more than one table in the same worksheet, and work with each of them independently.

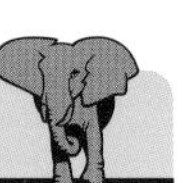

Don't forget

Click adjacent cells to delete more than one column or row in the table at a time.

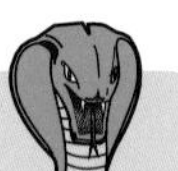

Beware

Don't click the Delete button itself, or you will delete the cells, rather than display the menu. If you do delete cells, press the Undo button on the Quick Access Toolbar.

1. Select the Music data, click Table on the Insert tab to create a table, and change its name to Music

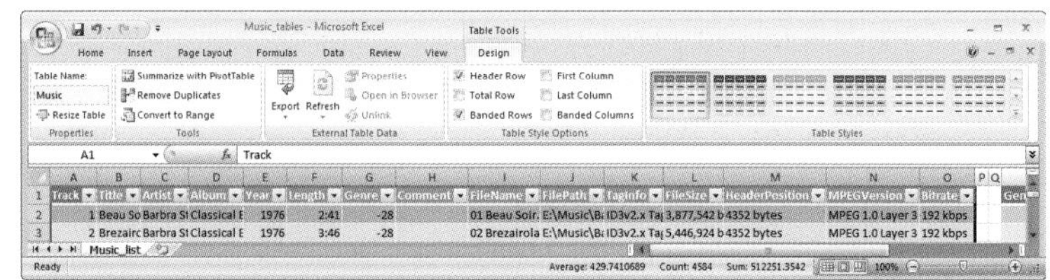

2. Click any column in the Music table that is not required; then select the Home tab, click the arrow next to Delete in the Cells group and choose Delete Table Columns

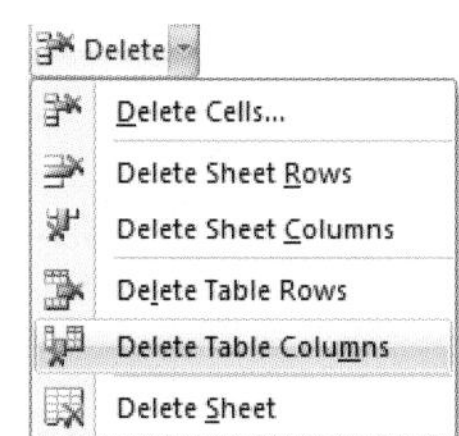


3. Go to the end of the Codes table, click in the last cell and press Tab to add a row

4. Type an entry such as 148, New; then add another row with 149, New and another with 150, Other

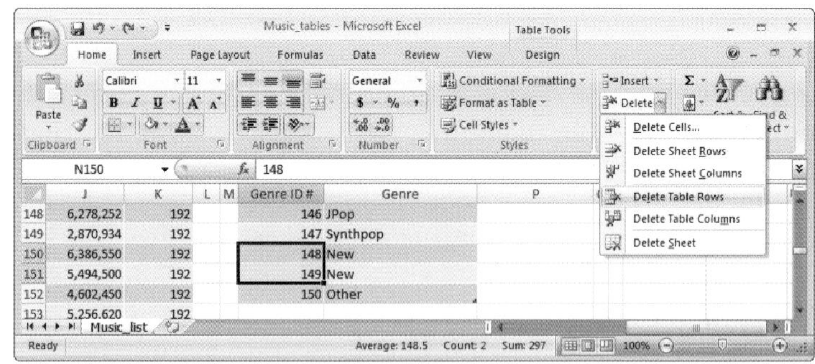


5. Select the cells with values 148 and 149 then select the Home tab, and choose Delete, Table Rows.

Inserting or deleting rows and columns in one table will not affect the other tables in the worksheet.

# Table Styles

The Design tab provides options to change the formatting of the rows and columns in the table.

1. Select First Column or Last Column in the Type Style Options group, to apply special styles to those columns

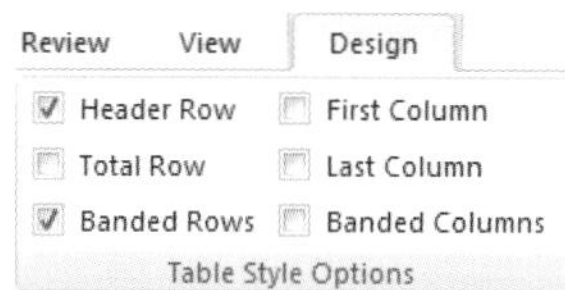


2. Click the Quick Styles button in the Table Styles group to view the full list of styles

3. A styles selection bar will be displayed if there's room, and you can scroll the styles, or press the More button to show the full list

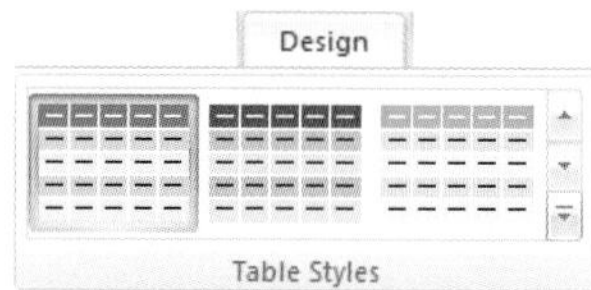


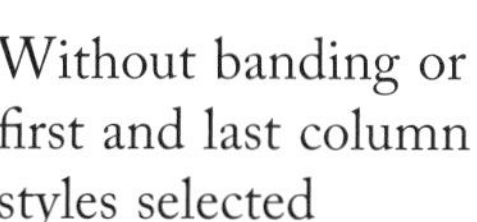

Without banding or first and last column styles selected

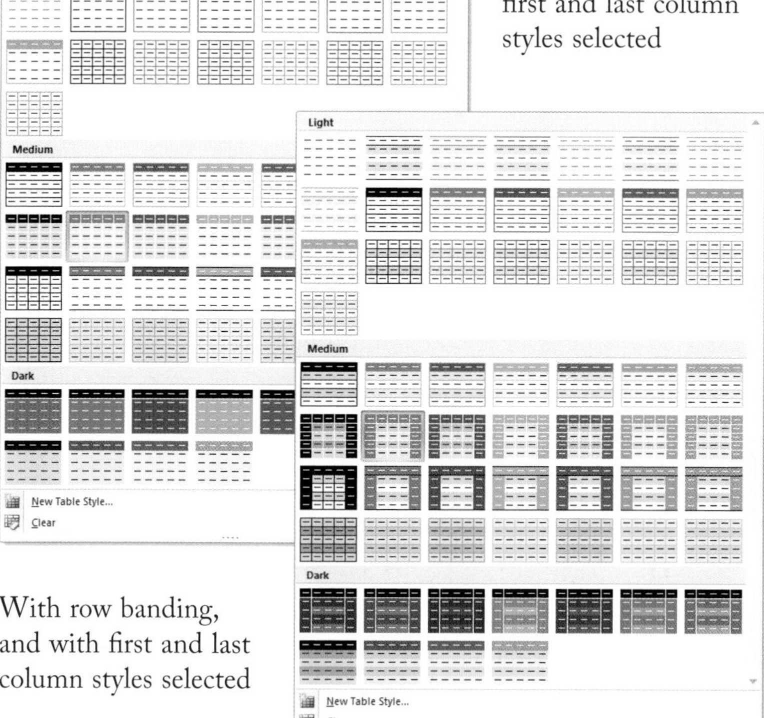


With row banding, and with first and last column styles selected

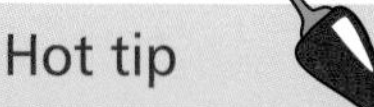


Styles are grouped into light, medium and dark sets, with additional effects for end columns and for banding.

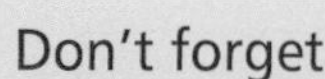

Move the mouse pointer over any one of the style options, and the table will immediately illustrate the effects that would be applied if you selected that option.

# Table Totals

You can add a Totals row at the end of the table, and display the totals for columns (or use another function appropriate to the type of information stored in the column).

1 Click in the table, select the Design tab and click the Total Row box in the Table Style Options group

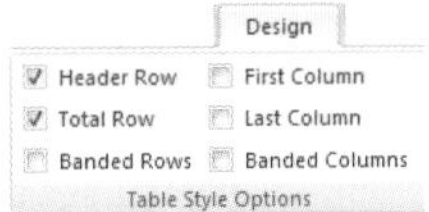

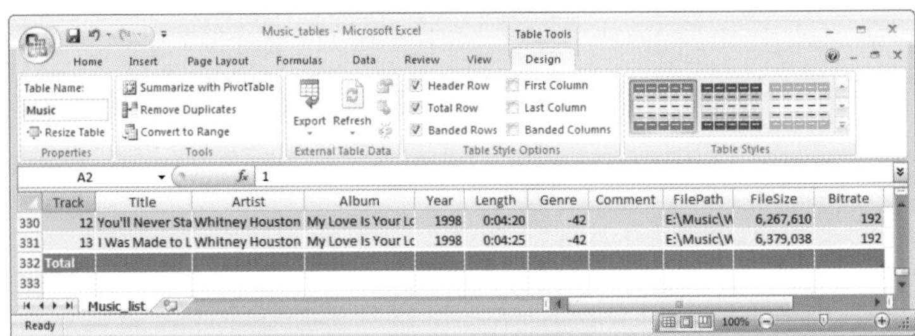

2 The Totals row is added as the last row of the table, and you can choose which cells should have a calculated value

3 For example, click the Total cell for the Length column, click the arrow, and select the Sum function, as these values are times

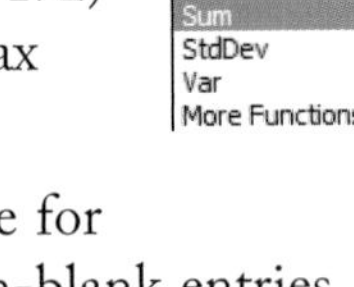


4 For Bitrate (with values such as 128, 160 or 192) the relevant function might be Min or Max

5 For FileSize perhaps Average is best, while for Titles and Comments, you can Count non-blank entries

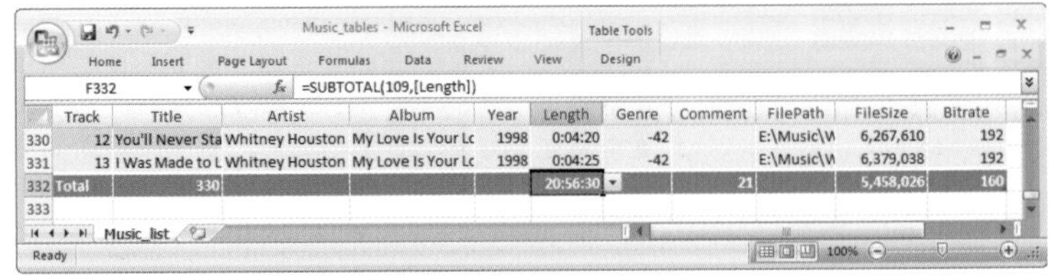

In these cases the Subtotal function is inserted, with a function number indicating the operation selected from the list. The choice of More Functions allows any Excel functions to be used.



## Hot tip

These are the function numbers used by the Subtotal function:

| Number | Function |
|---|---|
| 101 | AVERAGE |
| 102 | COUNT |
| 103 | COUNTA |
| 104 | MAX |
| 105 | MIN |
| 106 | PRODUCT |
| 107 | STDEV |
| 108 | STDEVP |
| 109 | SUM |
| 110 | VAR |

The functions also use structured references to the table (see page 78).

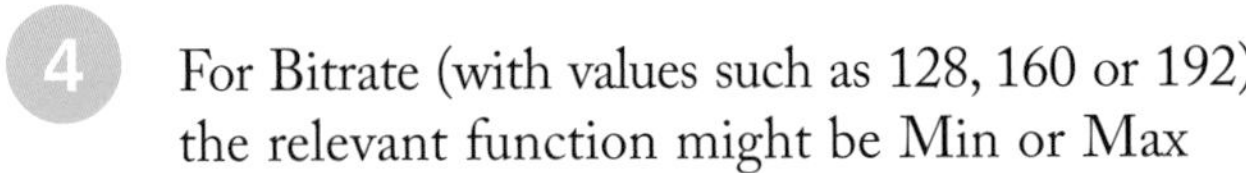

# Count Unique Entries

For Artist and Album, the ideal would be to count all unique entries, to give the numbers of individual artists and albums stored in the table. Here is one way to do this:

1. Click in the Total cell for the Artist column and begin typing the function =sum(1/countif(

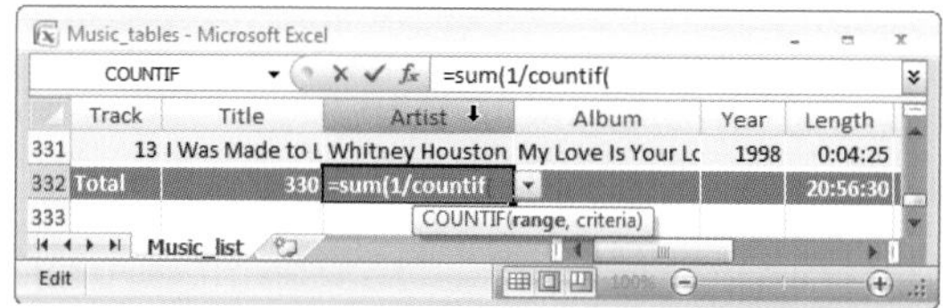


2. Click the Artist header to extend the formula

3. Type a comma, click the Artist header again, and then type two closing parentheses

4. This is an array formula, so press Shift+Ctrl+Enter (rather than Enter) and the count will be displayed

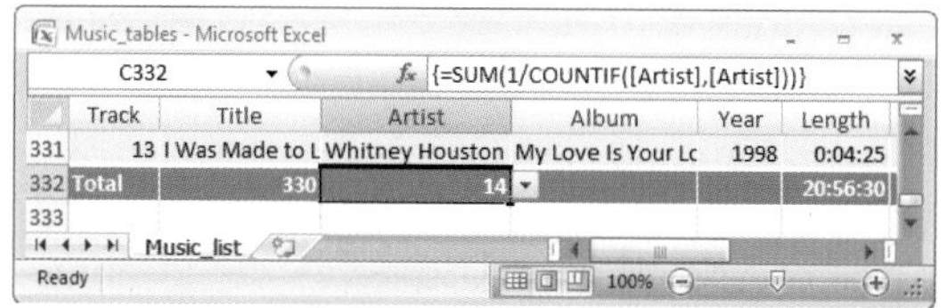

## Hot tip

This calculates the frequency for each entry, inverts these counts, and sums the resulting fractions. For example, if an entry appears three times you get 1/3 + 1/3 + 1/3 for that entry, giving a count of 1. Each unique entry adds another 1.

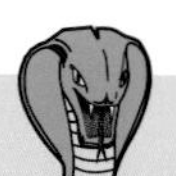

## Beware

This method of counting the number of duplicate entries assumes that there are no empty cells in the range being checked.

## Don't forget

Use a similar formula to count the number of unique entries in the Album column.

# Structured References

Hot tip

The use of structured references in formulas is more efficient than using full column references (e.g. $F:$F), dynamic ranges or arrays.

Beware

You should avoid the use of special characters such as space, tab, line feed, comma, colon, period, bracket, quote mark or ampersand in your table and column names.

The formulas shown for the totals illustrate the use of structured references. These allow you to refer to the contents of a table using meaningful names, without having to be concerned about the specific row numbers and column letters, or changes that are caused when rows and columns are added or deleted. The structured references use the table name and column specifiers:

| | | |
|---|---|---|
| =Music | The table data | A2: K331 |
| =Music[Length] | All the data in the Length column | F2:F331 |

You can add a special item specifier, to refer to particular parts:

| | | |
|---|---|---|
| =Music[#All] | The entire table, with headers, data and totals | A1:K332 |
| =Music[#Data] | The table data | A2:K331 |
| =Music[#Headers] | The header row | A1:K1 |
| =Music[#Totals] | The totals row | A332:K332 |
| =Music[[#This Row],[Length]] | The nth cell in the named column (where n is the active row (e.g. 12)) | F12 |

For formulas within the table, such as subtotals on the Totals row, you can leave off the table name. This forms an unqualified structured reference, e.g. [Bitrate]. However, outside the table you need the fully qualified structured reference, e.g. Music[Bitrate].

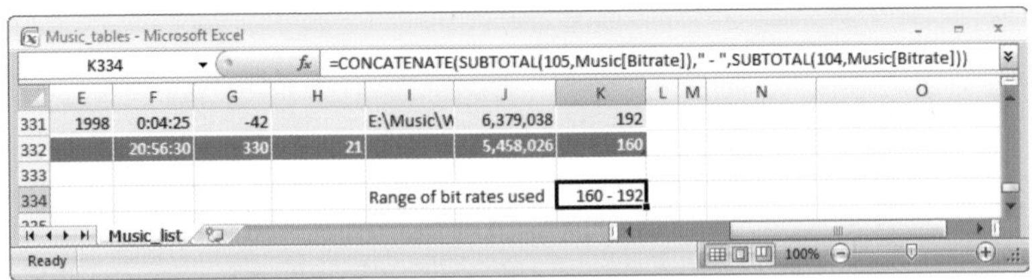


This formula includes two subtotal functions (see page 76) to obtain the minimum and the maximum values from the Bitrate column. The results are separated by a hyphen, and the three items are concatenated (joined) to form a single text string. This is displayed in the cell K334 which contains the formula.

# Calculated Columns

You can add a calculated column to an Excel table. This uses a single formula that adjusts for each row, automatically expanding to include additional rows.

Start by inserting a new column in the table.

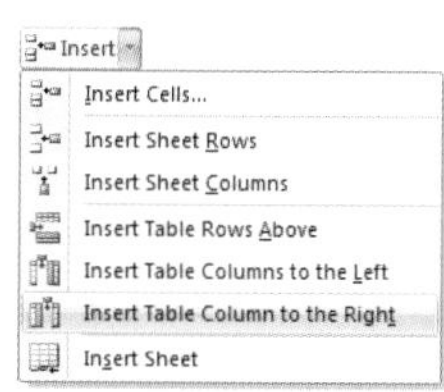


1. Click the end column (Bitrate), select the Home tab, and click the arrow next to Insert, which is found in the Cells group

2. Click Insert Table Columns to the Right, and then rename the new column as Style (i.e. music style)

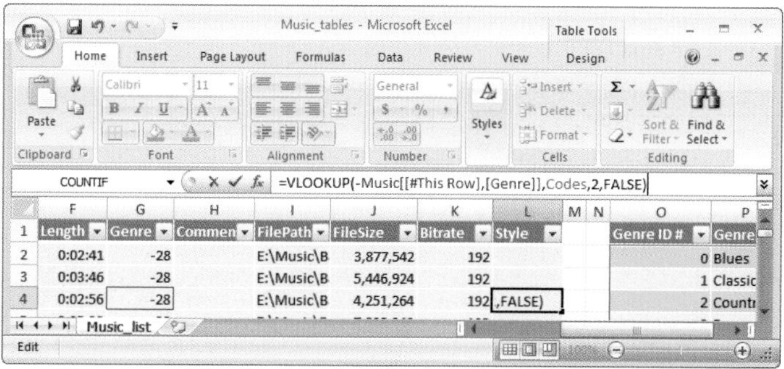


3. Click anywhere in the Style column and type a formula

The formula that you type is automatically filled into all cells of the column, above as well as below the active cell.

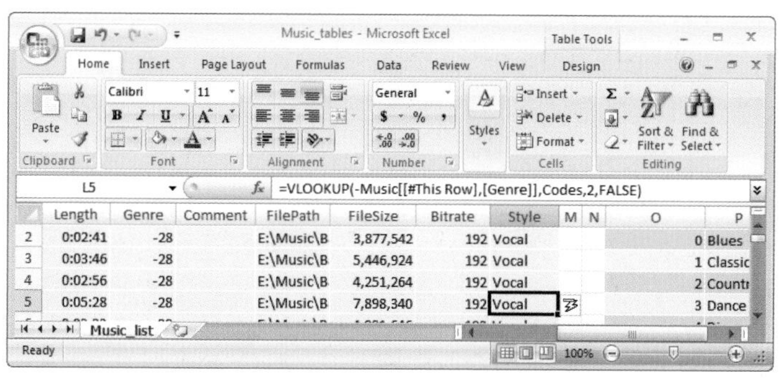

## Don't forget

You need to enter the formula only once, and you won't need to use the Fill or Copy command when the table grows.

## Hot tip

The formula in this example is a vertical table lookup. It matches the value from the Genre column with an entry in the first column of the Codes table. It copies the associated text from the second column into the Styles column. See page 90 for an example of an hlookup (a horizontal lookup).

# Insert Rows

Beware

Adding empty rows may cause temporary errors in formulas that need data in all cells, as illustrated here. The problems will be resolved as soon as the data gets added.

1. Scroll to the last cell in the table, press Tab to add a new row, and you'll see that the new formula is replicated

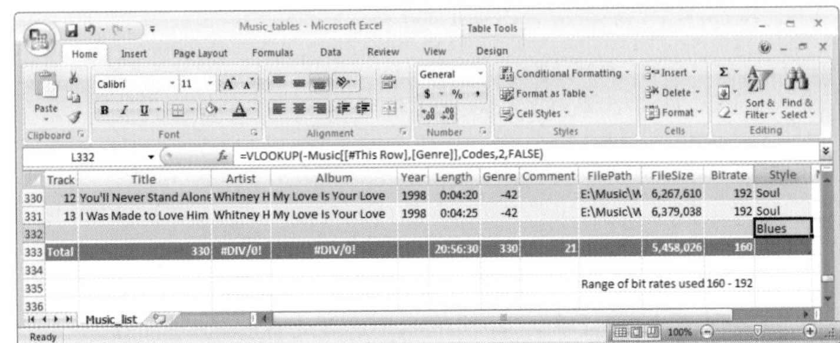


2. To add more data from a text file (see page 42), click a cell in an empty part of the worksheet, select the Home tab and From Text (in the Get External Data group)

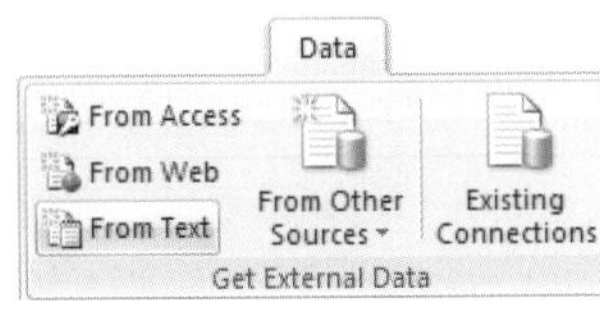


3. Locate and double-click the data file, and use the Text Import Wizard to specify the structure of the data file

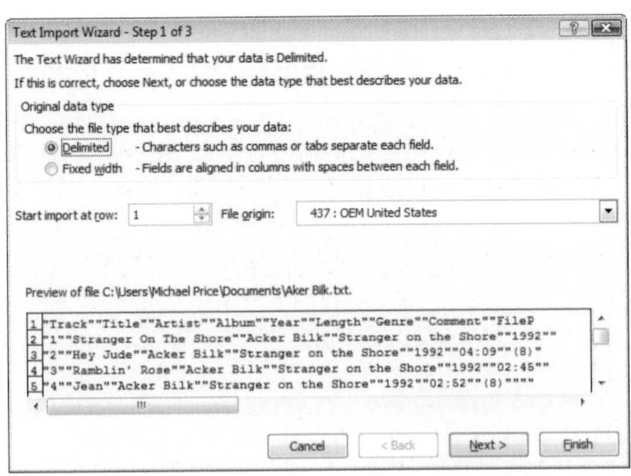

Hot tip

You cannot import data directly from an external source into the table, so you must use another part of the worksheet as an interim.

4. Confirm the temporary location for the data in the worksheet

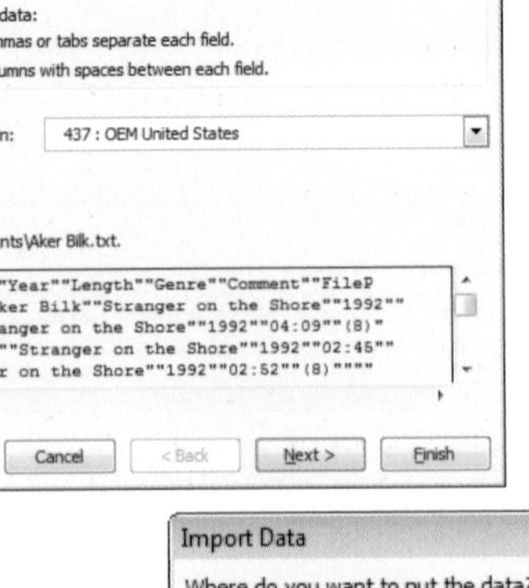

5. Highlight the new data (excluding the header row), select the Home tab and click Copy from the Clipboard group

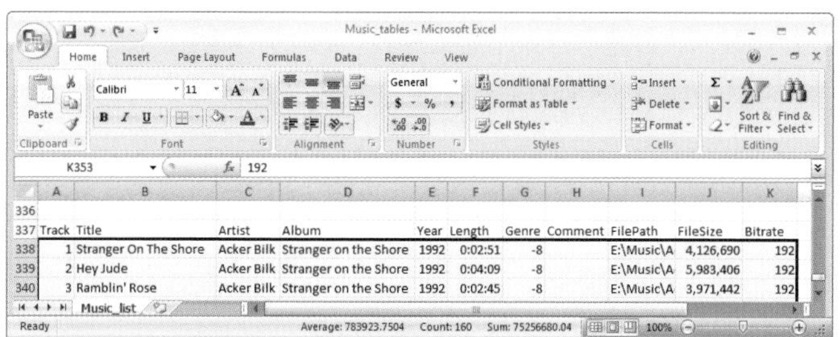

6. Click the first cell in the new row at the end of the table; then select Paste from the Clipboard group

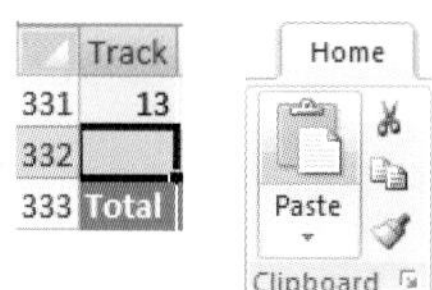


7. Additional rows are inserted into the table to accommodate the new data records

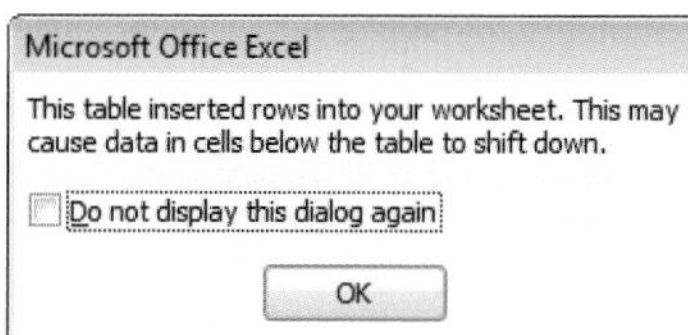


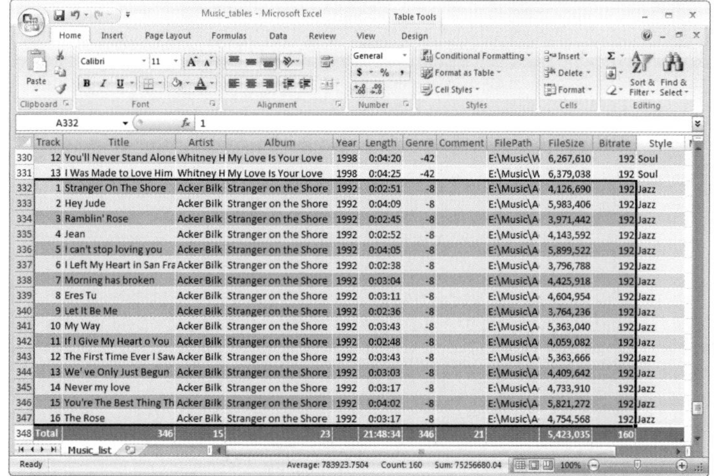

8. The data is inserted into the extended table, and the formulas and totals are recalculated

## Hot tip

You can type new rows directly into the table, pressing tab at the end of each row ready to enter the next row.

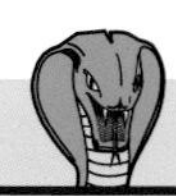

## Beware

Adding new rows or columns to the table causes worksheet data outside the table to be shifted. You should check for potential problems in data that is not in a defined table.

## Don't forget

When the rows have been inserted, you can delete the temporary data stored in the worksheet below the table.

# Custom Sort

When new rows are inserted, it may be appropriate to sort the table, to position the new rows where they belong.

1. Click in the table, select the Home tab, click Sort & Filter in the Editing group and select Custom Sort

   Or

   Click in the table, select the Data tab, and click Sort in the Sort & Filter group

2. The first time, there are no criteria defined, so click the arrow in "Sort by" to add a header, e.g. Artist

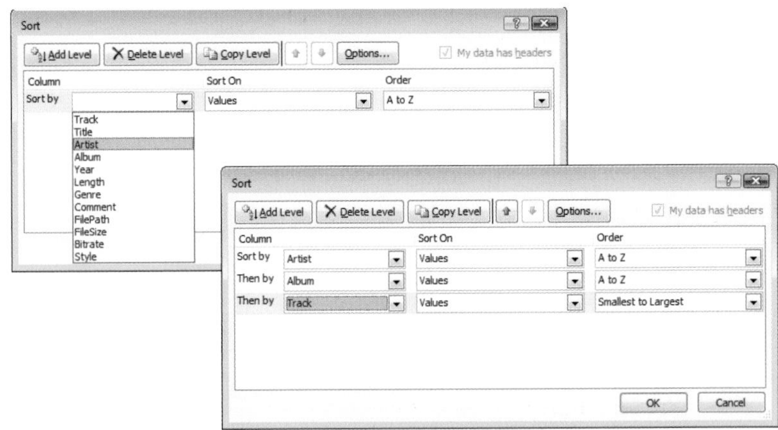

3. Click the Add Level button, choose a second header (e.g. Album), and then add a third level (Track), and click OK

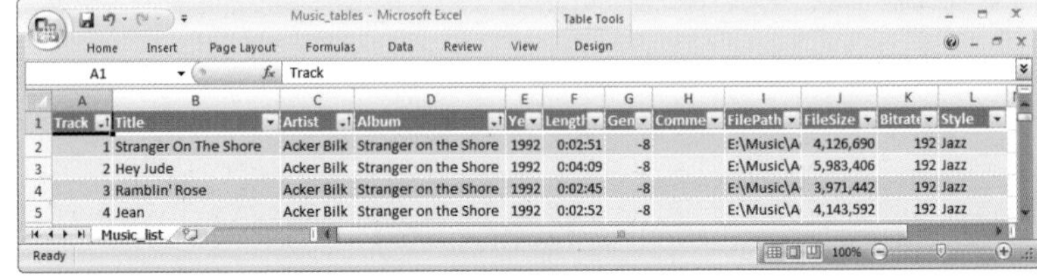

The sorting criteria used for each table will be saved when the workbook is saved, so it is easy to re-sort in the same way after future updates and modifications. The Filter box icon is modified to show that sorting is in effect.

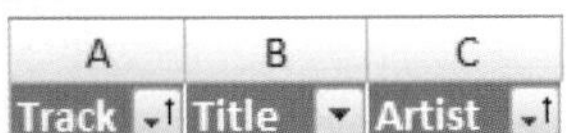

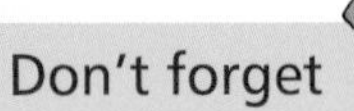

By default columns with text values are sorted A to Z, while columns with number values are sorted smallest to largest.

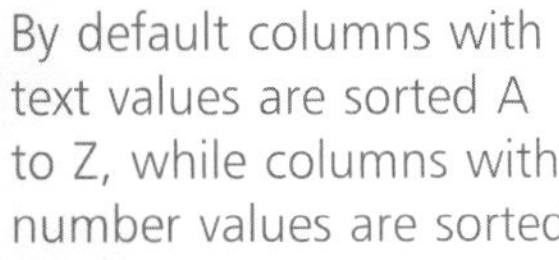

# Print a Table

You can print a table without having to select the print area explicitly (see page 32).

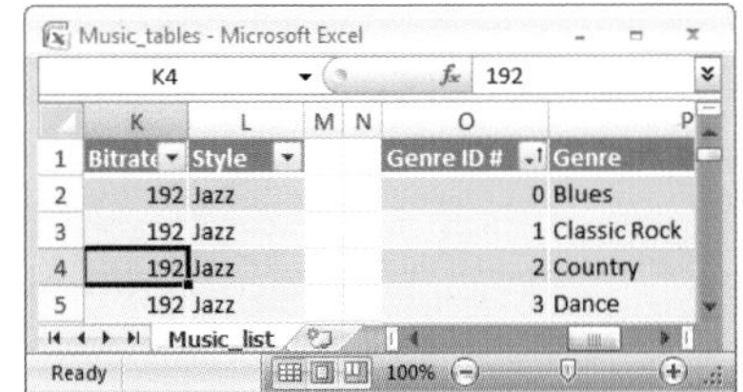


1. Select any cell within the table to activate that table

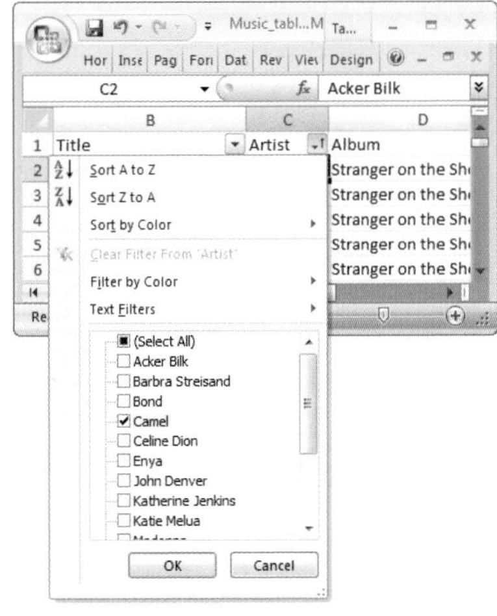


2. To print a subset of the table, use the Filter boxes to restrict the data displayed, e.g. choosing a specific Artist

3. Press the Office button and then select Print (or press the Ctrl+P shortcut)

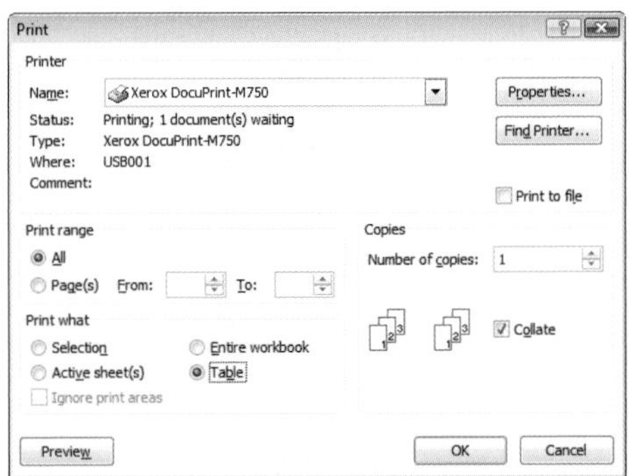


4. Under "Print what", click the Table button

5. Click the Preview button to see what data will be printed

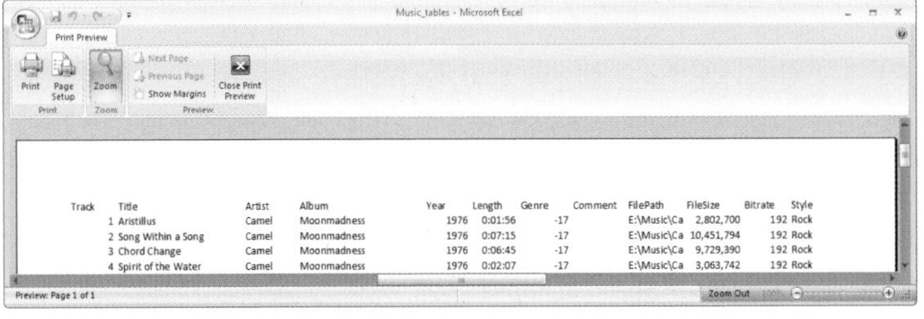


## Hot tip

You may wish to change to a different table style that is more suitable for printing (or select None for a plain effect).

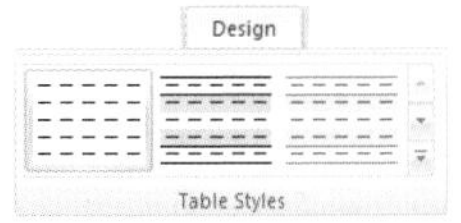


## Don't forget

When you apply filters to the table, only the data that is still displayed will be included in the print.

## Beware

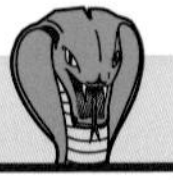

Subtotals will be adjusted to match the filtered results. However, some formulas on the Totals row may continue to refer to the whole of the table contents.

# Summarize a Table

You can summarize the data using the PivotTable feature. See page 165 for another example.

1. Click in the table, select the Insert tab, and then click the PivotTable button in the Tables group

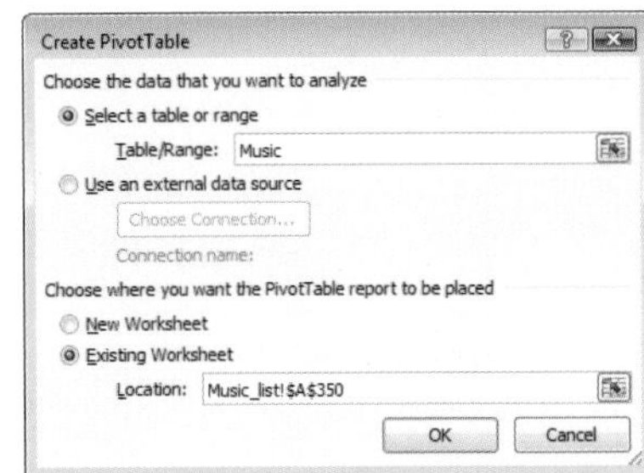


2. Choose the location for the PivotTable report, either a new worksheet or an empty portion of the current worksheet, and then click OK

3. An empty PivotTable report is added at the location specified

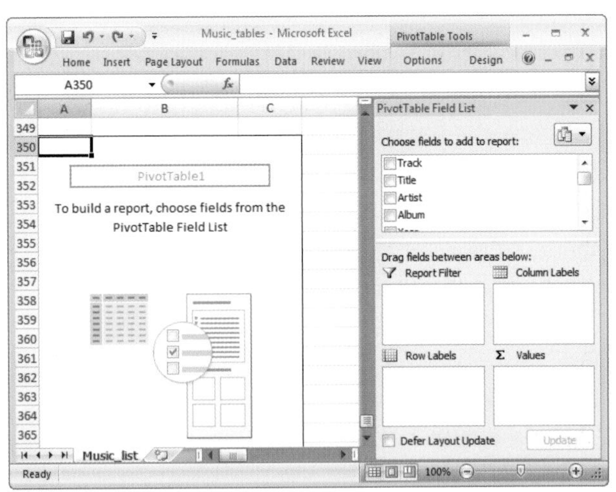


4. Click the boxes to select fields from the Field List (for example Artist, Album, Track and Length)

5. Rearrange the fields by clicking and dragging, or right-click a name and select in which area it should appear

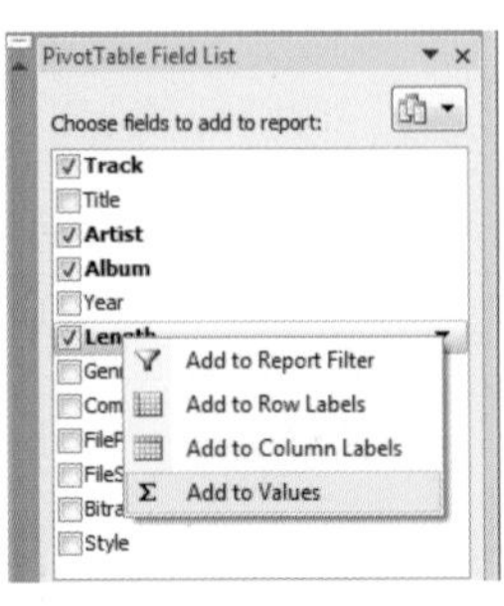

Click the Collapse Dialog box, select the first cell of the location, and then click the Expand Dialog box.

By default, text fields are added to the Row Labels area, and fields containing numbers are added to the Values area.

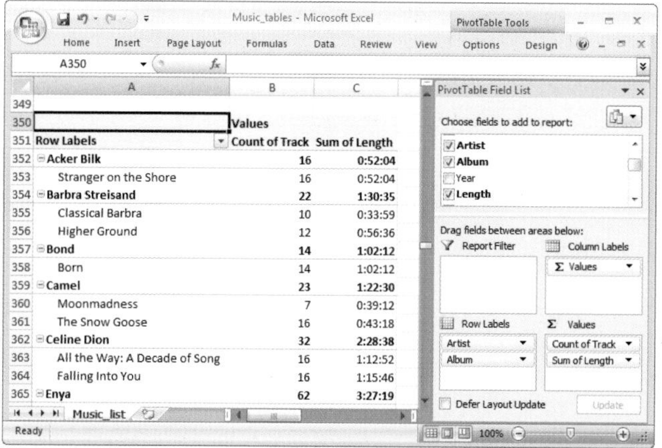

6 Click a numeric field in the Values list to reposition, move to a different area, or change value field settings

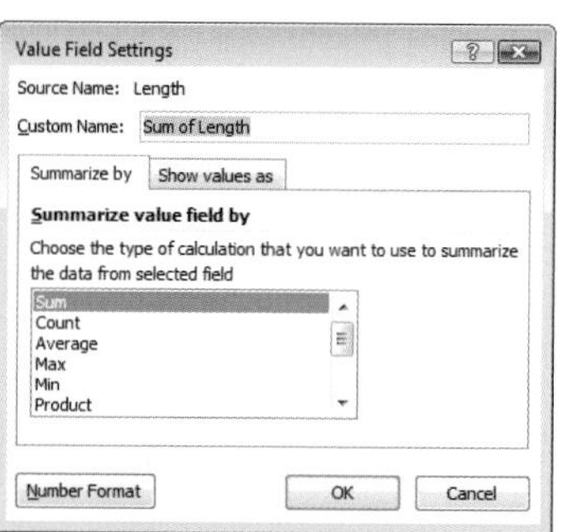

7 Choose how to summarize the values (e.g. sum, count or average them)

8 Click the Number Format button to change the way that a numeric value is displayed

9 When you select PivotTable, Design and Options commands will be added to the Ribbon

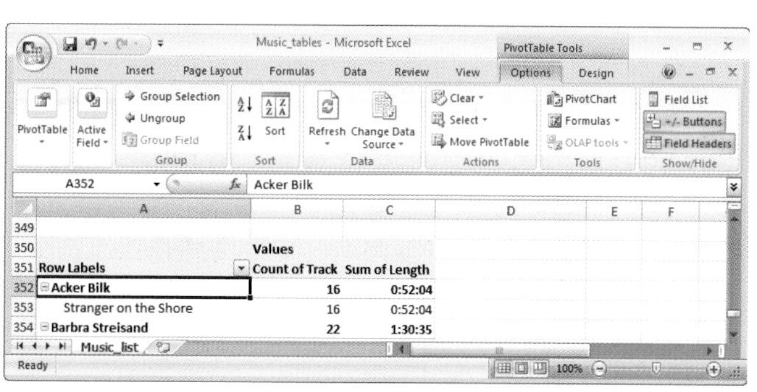

## Don't forget

When you click a field name that has text values, you can select Field Settings, which displays appropriate options.

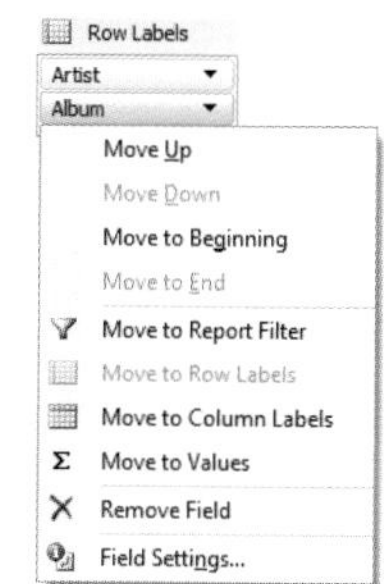

## Hot tip

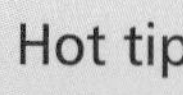

Click the Field List toggle command in the Show/Hide group to hide or reveal the field list. From here you can also collapse or expand the report details.

# Convert to a Range

**Hot tip**

If you have just created a table from a range of data (see page 72), you can switch back to the range form by clicking Undo on the Quick Access toolbar.

**Don't forget**

To remove the table style from the cells, select all the data, click the Home tab, click the down-arrow next to Cell Styles in the Styles group, and choose the Normal style.

You can turn an Excel table back into a range of data.

1. Click in the table to display the Table Tools entry on the ribbon

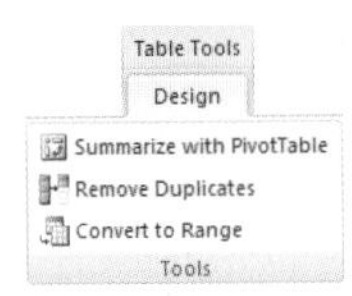


2. Select the Design tab, and click Convert to Range in the Tools group

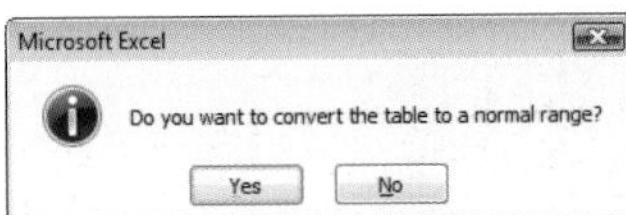


3. Click Yes to confirm that you do want to convert the table to a data range

4. The cell styles will be preserved, but the filter boxes will be removed from the headers

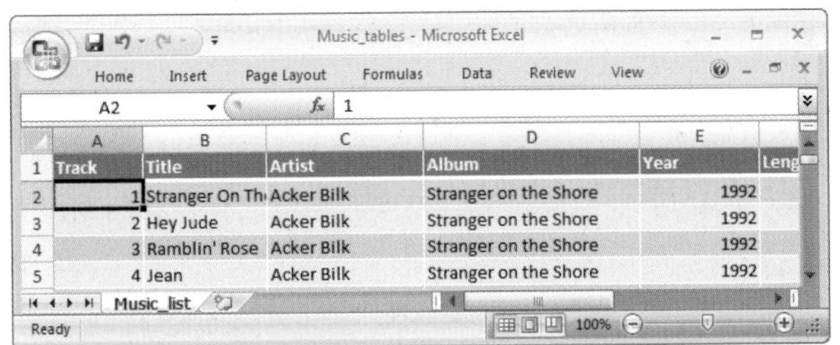


5. The Totals row will still appear, but all references will now be standard $A$1-style absolute cell references

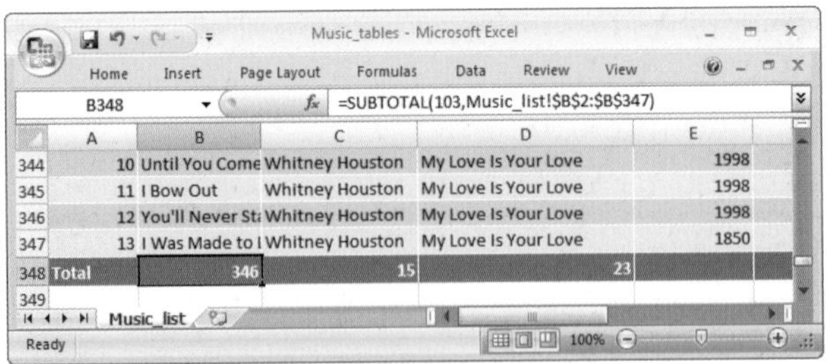


6. If you convert the range into a table again, you will need to recreate the structured reference formulas for the Totals row and the calculated columns

# 6 Advanced Functions

*There is a large library of functions. To help locate the ones you want, related functions are grouped by category, and there's a Recently Used list. More functions are provided via Excel Add-ins. With nested functions in your formulas, use the Evaluate command to see how they work.*

# Function Library

1 Select the Formulas tab to see the Function Library group

The Function Library contains over 320 functions, so categories are used to organize them, and there's also a search facility.

This starts with the Insert Function command, which allows you to enter keywords to search for a function (see page 66), or you can select from one of the categories.

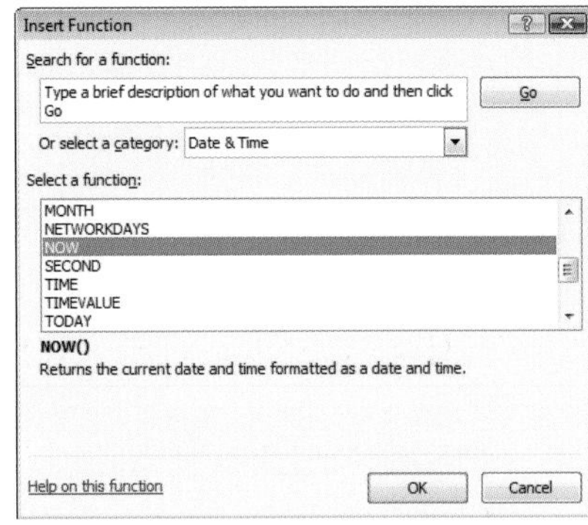


It provides the syntax and a brief description for any function that you select, plus a link to more detailed help on that function.

Click a Category command for an alphabetical list of the names of the functions that are included

The categories and the numbers of functions included in each are:

| | | | |
|---|---|---|---|
| AutoSum | 5 | Lookup & Ref | 18 |
| Recently Used | 10 | Math & Trig | 60 |
| Financial | 53 | Other Statistical | 83 |
| Logical | 7 | Other Engineering | 39 |
| Text | 24 | Other Cube | 7 |
| Date & Time | 20 | Other Information | 17 |

## AutoSum

AutoSum (introduced on page 68) provides quick access to functions (Sum, Average, Count, Min and Max) that are quite possibly the most frequently used functions in most workbooks.

AutoSum and Recently Used are the only categories that include duplicates of functions.

## Recently Used

Recently Used remembers the functions you last used, allowing you to make repeated use of functions with the minimum of fuss, and without having to remember their particular categories.

# Logical Functions

Sometimes the value for one cell depends on the value in another cell. For example, test scores could be used to set grade levels.

1. The formula in C2 is =B2>=50 and gives the result True or False, depending on the value in B2

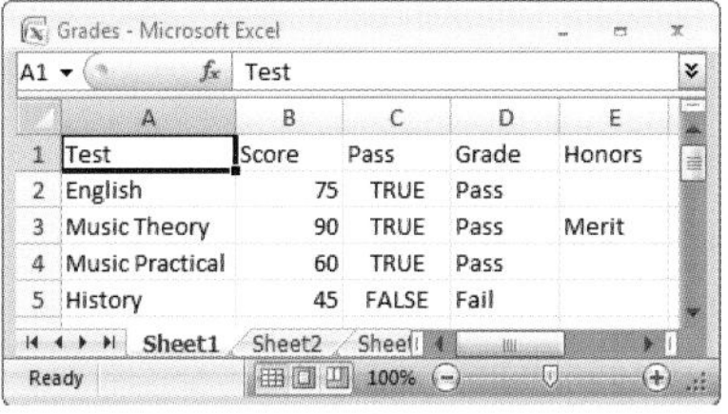


2. To display the more meaningful Pass or Fail, you'd use an IF formula such as in D2, with =IF(B2>=50,"Pass","Fail")

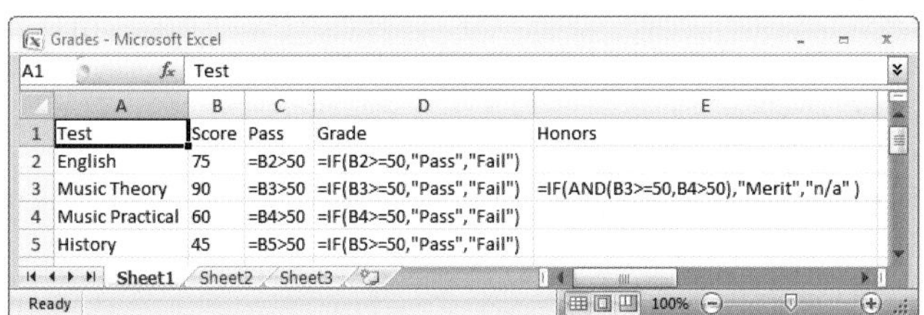


3. Sometimes you need to check two conditions, e.g. in the E3 formula =IF(AND(B3>=50,B4>=50),"Merit","n/a")

The IF functions can be nested, with the False value being replaced by another IF function, to make a further test.

1. This formula gives the country code if the name matches, or goes on to test for the next country name in the list

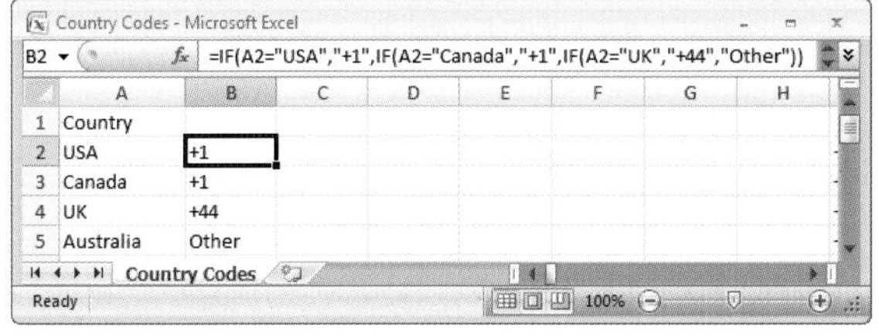


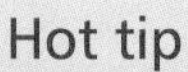

Comparisons (e.g. using the <, = or > operators) that are either True or False are the basis of logical functions.

## Don't forget

The AND function includes a set of logical tests, all of which must be True to give a True result.

## Hot tip

You could use an OR function for the first two countries here, since a match for either would give the same code.

# Lookup/Reference Functions

If you have a number of items to check against, set up a list.

**Hot tip**

You can have up to 64 levels of nesting, but long IF formulas can be awkward to type in. A better alternative may be a Lookup function.

1. This example uses a list of country names (in alphabetical order) with their country codes, stored in rows D1:IF2

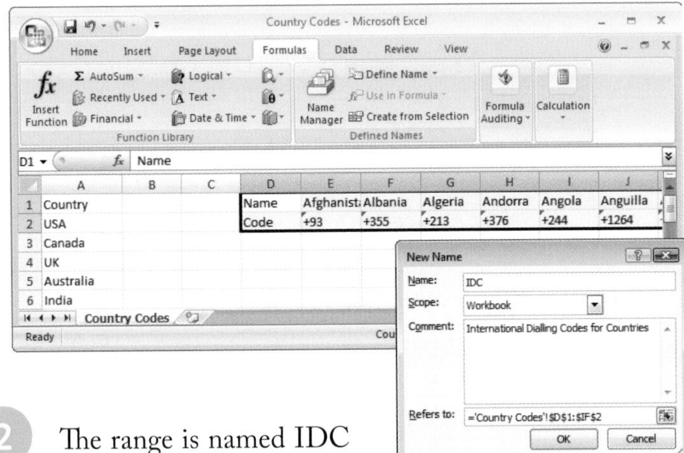


2. The range is named IDC

3. The lookup function requires the value, the lookup range and the row number for the result (in this case row 2)

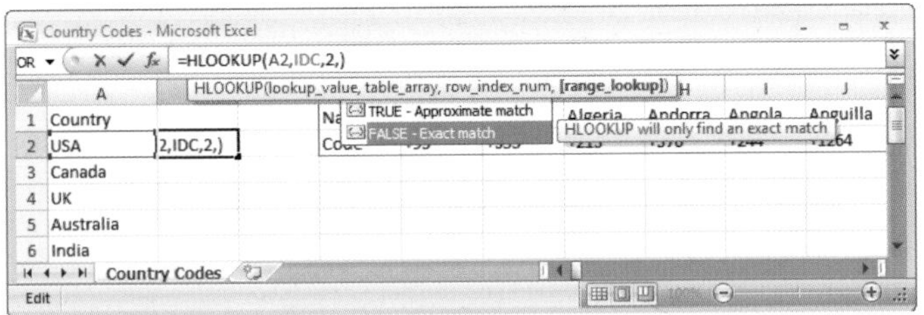

**Don't forget**

For range_lookup, you specify a logical value of True to get close matches, or False to allow exact matches only.

4. Copy the formula down to check other country names

5. A mistype of Andorra results in N/A, indicating that no match could be found

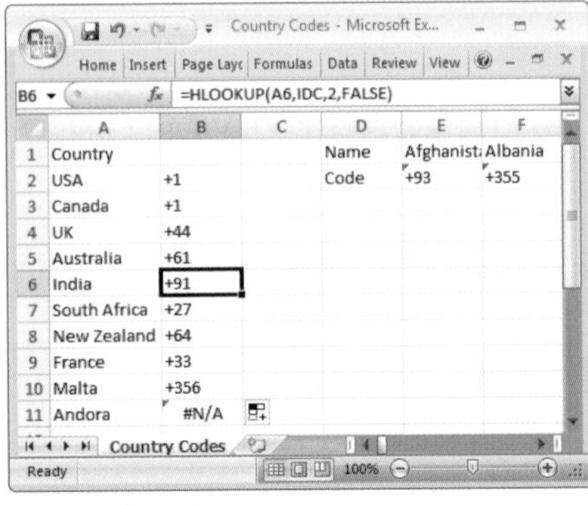

To reverse the process, and replace a number by a text value, you could use the CHOOSE function. For example:

1. To convert the value in cell B2 into a Rank, enter =CHOOSE(B2,"First","Second","Third","Fourth","Fifth")

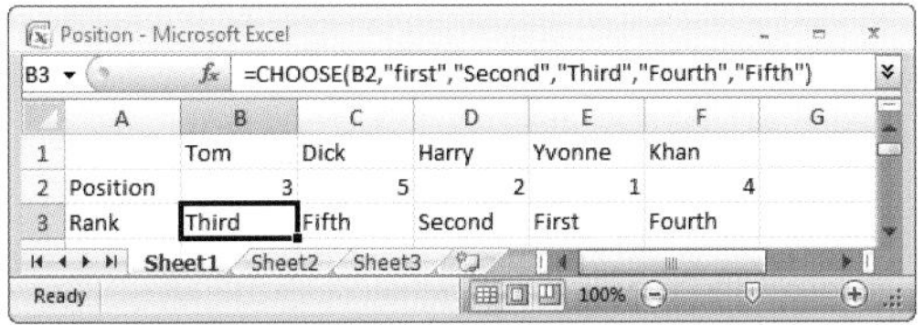


| | A | B | C | D | E | F | G |
|---|---|---|---|---|---|---|---|
| 1 | | Tom | Dick | Harry | Yvonne | Khan | |
| 2 | Position | 3 | 5 | 2 | 1 | 4 | |
| 3 | Rank | Third | Fifth | Second | First | Fourth | |

2. Copy the formula across to rank cells C2 to F2

3. To apply a suffix to the position value, use the formula =B2&CHOOSE(B2,"st","nd","rd","th","th")

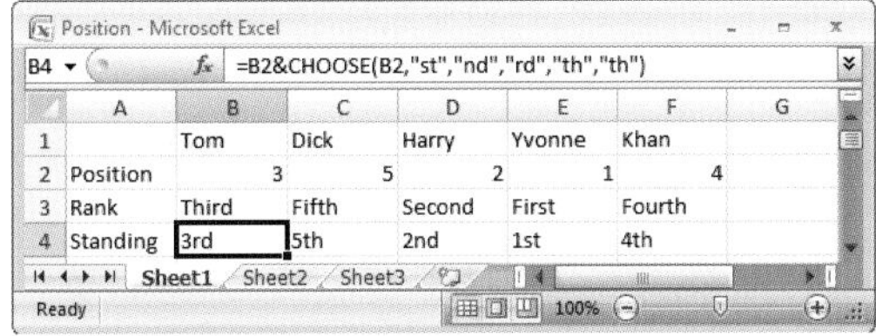


| | A | B | C | D | E | F | G |
|---|---|---|---|---|---|---|---|
| 1 | | Tom | Dick | Harry | Yvonne | Khan | |
| 2 | Position | 3 | 5 | 2 | 1 | 4 | |
| 3 | Rank | Third | Fifth | Second | First | Fourth | |
| 4 | Standing | 3rd | 5th | 2nd | 1st | 4th | |

4. Copy the formula across to rank cells C2 to F2

You can store the values in a range of cells, but you must list the relevant cells individually.

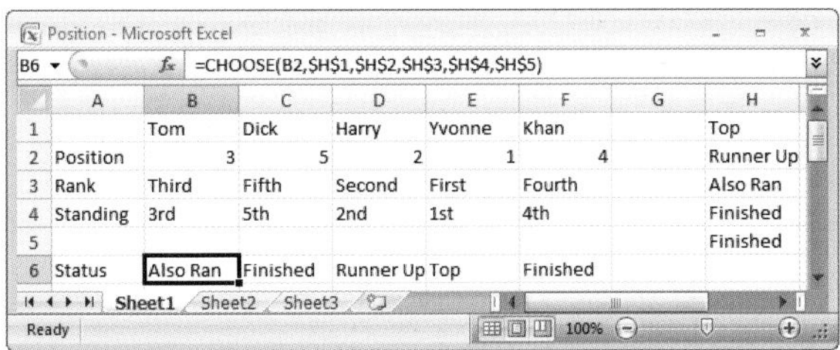


| | A | B | C | D | E | F | G | H |
|---|---|---|---|---|---|---|---|---|
| 1 | | Tom | Dick | Harry | Yvonne | Khan | | Top |
| 2 | Position | 3 | 5 | 2 | 1 | 4 | | Runner Up |
| 3 | Rank | Third | Fifth | Second | First | Fourth | | Also Ran |
| 4 | Standing | 3rd | 5th | 2nd | 1st | 4th | | Finished |
| 5 | | | | | | | | Finished |
| 6 | Status | Also Ran | Finished | Runner Up | Top | Finished | | |

You should use absolute cell references for the list of values, so that you can copy the formula without changing the references.

**Hot tip**

The contents of B2 are used as an index to select from the list of 5 values provided. A maximum of 254 values could be used.

**Hot tip**

Here the suffix chosen from the list is appended to the index number.

**Beware**

Index values outside the range provided (in these examples 1–5) will cause a #Value! error.

# Financial Functions

Excel includes specialized functions for dealing with investments, securities, loans and other financial transactions.

For example, to calculate the monthly payments required for a mortgage, you'd use the PMT function. Assume a purchase price of $250,000, interest at 6% per annum, and a 30-year period.

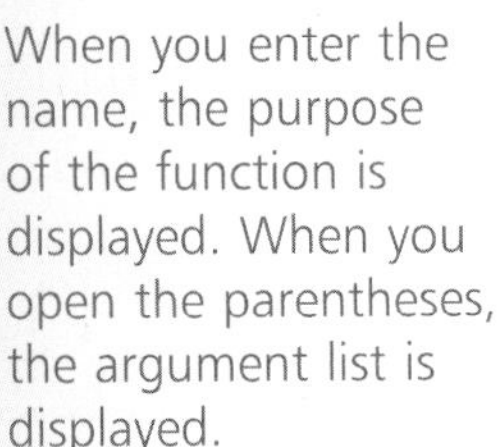

**Hot tip**

When you enter the name, the purpose of the function is displayed. When you open the parentheses, the argument list is displayed.

1. Enter the initial information into a worksheet; then for the payment begin typing the function =PMT(

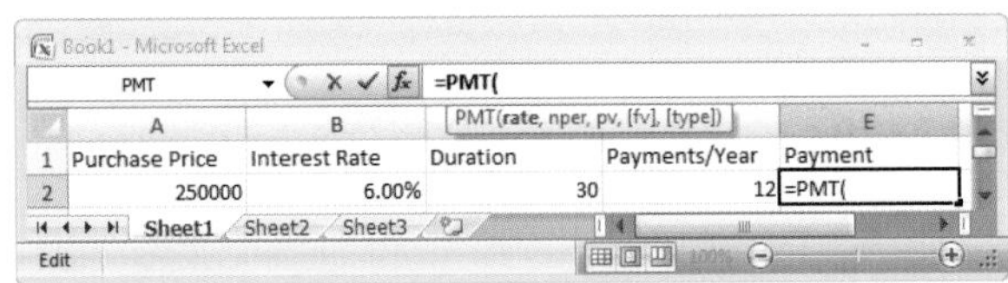

**Don't forget**

As you select each argument box the requirements are described, and you can use the Collapse and Expand buttons to select values from the worksheet.

2. Click the Insert Function button to display the input form for the function arguments

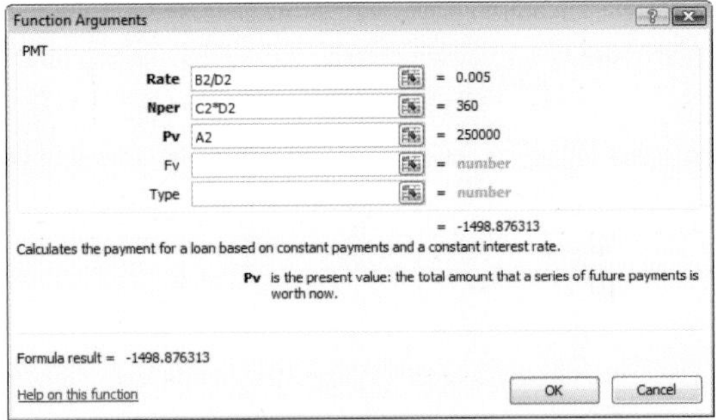


3. Click the Rate box and enter the interest rate per payment period (i.e. 6%/12 or B2/D2)

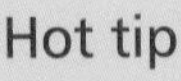

**Hot tip**

The amount is shown as a negative number, because it is a payment.

4. Click the Nper box and enter 30*12 or C2*D2; then click the PV box and enter $250,000 or A2; then click OK

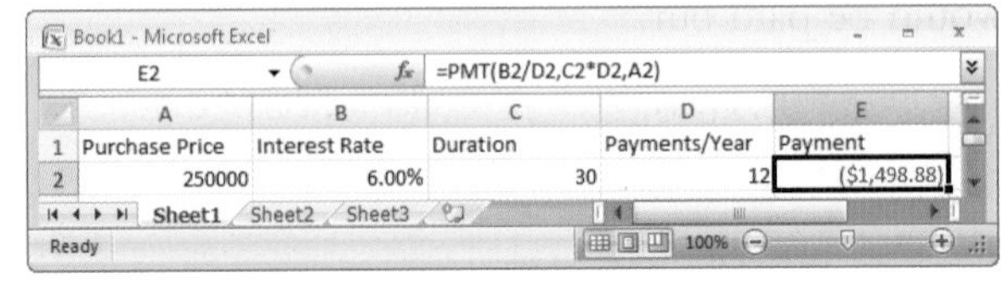

Perhaps you'd like to know what would happen if you paid the mortgage off over a shorter period.

1. Select the existing values and calculation and drag down using the Fill handle to replicate into three more rows

Book1 - Microsoft Excel

E5 =PMT(B5/D5,C5*D5,A5)

| | A | B | C | D | E |
|---|---|---|---|---|---|
| 1 | Purchase Price | Interest Rate | Duration | Payments/Year | Payment |
| 2 | 250000 | 6.00% | 30 | 12 | ($1,498.88) |
| 3 | 250000 | 6.00% | 25 | 12 | ($1,610.75) |
| 4 | 250000 | 6.00% | 20 | 12 | ($1,791.08) |
| 5 | 250000 | 6.00% | 15 | 12 | ($2,109.64) |

2. Change the duration to 25, 20 and 15 years on successive rows, and observe the revised monthly payments required

3. Add a column to show total interest paid, and enter the cumulative interest function =CUMIPMT(

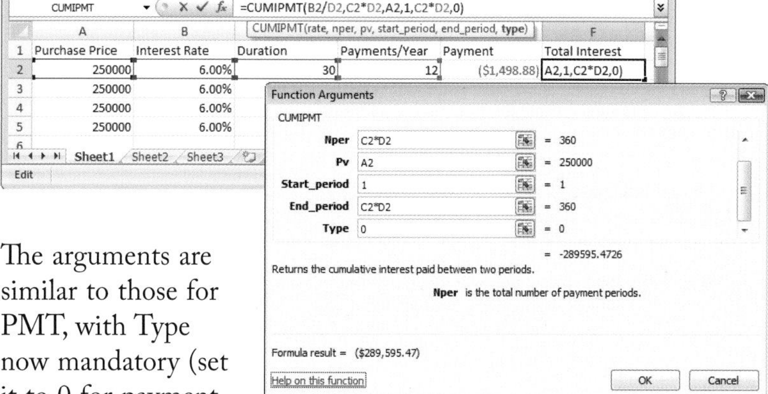


The arguments are similar to those for PMT, with Type now mandatory (set it to 0 for payment at end of month). The result shows how much interest would be paid out.

Copy the formula down to see the figures for the other loan durations.

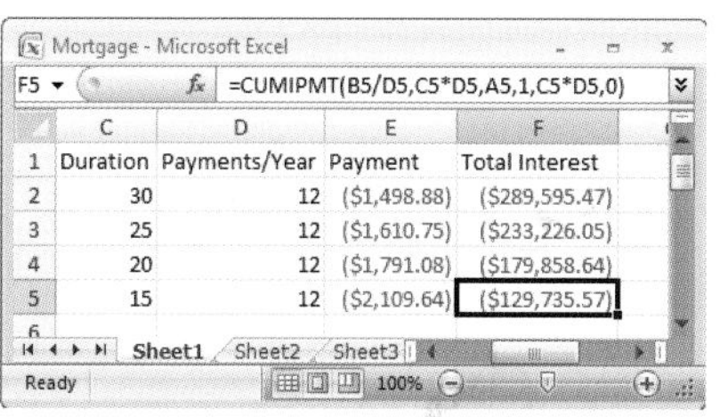
Mortgage - Microsoft Excel

F5 =CUMIPMT(B5/D5,C5*D5,A5,1,C5*D5,0)

| | C | D | E | F |
|---|---|---|---|---|
| 1 | Duration | Payments/Year | Payment | Total Interest |
| 2 | 30 | 12 | ($1,498.88) | ($289,595.47) |
| 3 | 25 | 12 | ($1,610.75) | ($233,226.05) |
| 4 | 20 | 12 | ($1,791.08) | ($179,858.64) |
| 5 | 15 | 12 | ($2,109.64) | ($129,735.57) |

**Don't forget**

You could type a new value into the Duration cell, and see the new payment. However, copying the rows makes it easier to compare the different options.

**Hot tip**

You can calculate the interest over any part of the loan, but putting the first and last payments gives the total interest over the whole period of the loan.

# Date & Time Functions

Date and time values (see page 59) are numbers, and count the days since the starting point (usually January 1st, 1900). However, they can be displayed in various date or time formats.

Hot tip

Excel also supports the 1904 date system, the default for Apple Mac computers, where a date value of 1 is taken as January 2nd, 1904.

1. The whole-number portion of the value converts into month, day and year (with account taken for leap years)

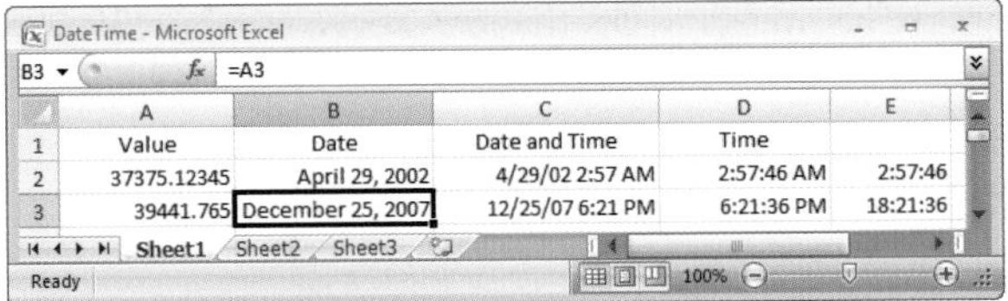

| | A | B | C | D | E |
|---|---|---|---|---|---|
| 1 | Value | Date | Date and Time | Time | |
| 2 | 37375.12345 | April 29, 2002 | 4/29/02 2:57 AM | 2:57:46 AM | 2:57:46 |
| 3 | 39441.765 | December 25, 2007 | 12/25/07 6:21 PM | 6:21:36 PM | 18:21:36 |

Don't forget

In the example, the value of the date is displayed, to illustrate the operations. You type the date, e.g. as 4/12/2007, and Excel automatically converts it into a number value and stores it in the cell. The cell format controls what's displayed.

2. The decimal portion indicates the time of day, so .123 is 2:57, and .765 is 6:21PM (or 18:21 on the 24-hour clock)

## Date and Time Calculations

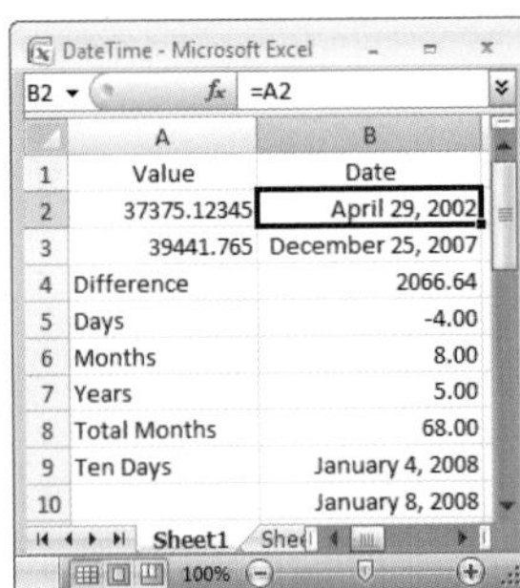

| | A | B |
|---|---|---|
| 1 | Value | Date |
| 2 | 37375.12345 | April 29, 2002 |
| 3 | 39441.765 | December 25, 2007 |
| 4 | Difference | 2066.64 |
| 5 | Days | -4.00 |
| 6 | Months | 8.00 |
| 7 | Years | 5.00 |
| 8 | Total Months | 68.00 |
| 9 | Ten Days | January 4, 2008 |
| 10 | | January 8, 2008 |

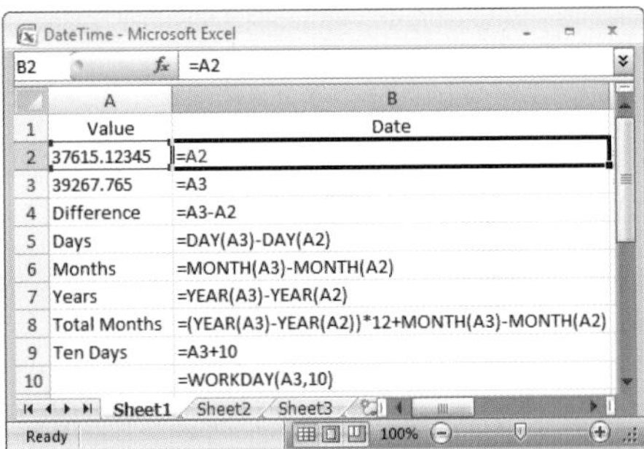

| | A | B |
|---|---|---|
| 1 | Value | Date |
| 2 | 37615.12345 | =A2 |
| 3 | 39267.765 | =A3 |
| 4 | Difference | =A3-A2 |
| 5 | Days | =DAY(A3)-DAY(A2) |
| 6 | Months | =MONTH(A3)-MONTH(A2) |
| 7 | Years | =YEAR(A3)-YEAR(A2) |
| 8 | Total Months | =(YEAR(A3)-YEAR(A2))*12+MONTH(A3)-MONTH(A2) |
| 9 | Ten Days | =A3+10 |
| 10 | | =WORKDAY(A3,10) |

| | |
|---|---|
| B4 | Difference in days |
| B5 | Subtracts calendar day numbers (may be minus) |
| B6 | Subtracts calendar months (may be minus) |
| B7 | Difference in years (ignores the part year) |
| B8 | Twelve months for every year +/- the difference in months |
| B9 | Adding ten days to A3 gives Jan 4, 2008 |
| B10 | Adding ten work days (to allow for weekends and holidays) gives the later date Jan 8, 2008 |

Beware

You can use date and time values in formulas, but because of the calendar effects the results may not always be what you'd expect.

There's a worksheet function called DateDif that's not listed in the Date & Time category, or shown in Excel Help. The syntax is:

=DATEDIF(StartDate,EndDate,Interval)

The Interval code controls the result that the function produces:

| Interval value | Calculates the number between the dates of |
|---|---|
| "y" | Whole years |
| "m" | Whole months |
| "d" | Days in total |
| "ym" | Whole months, ignoring the years |
| "yd" | Days, ignoring the years |
| "md" | Days, ignoring the months and years |

When entering the Interval code into DateDif as a constant, you enclose it in quotes. However, if your interval code is stored in a worksheet cell, it should not be enclosed in quotes in the cell.

1. Use the DateDif function with each of these codes in turn, to calculate the difference between the dates stored in cells B15 and B16.

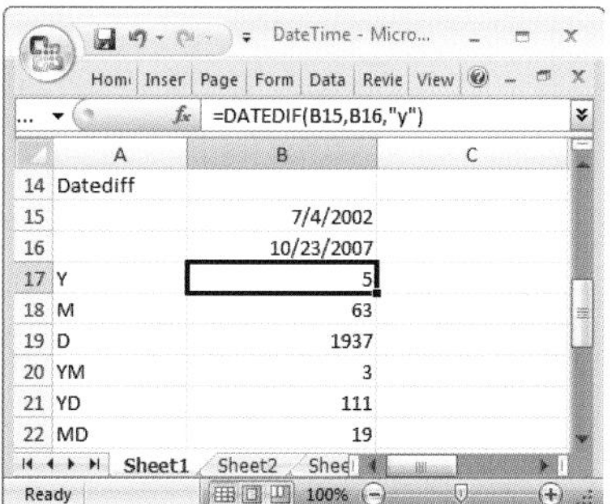


2. This function becomes useful when you need to calculate someone's exact age, in years, months and days. For example, DateDif applied to the date of birth and the current date gives the following:

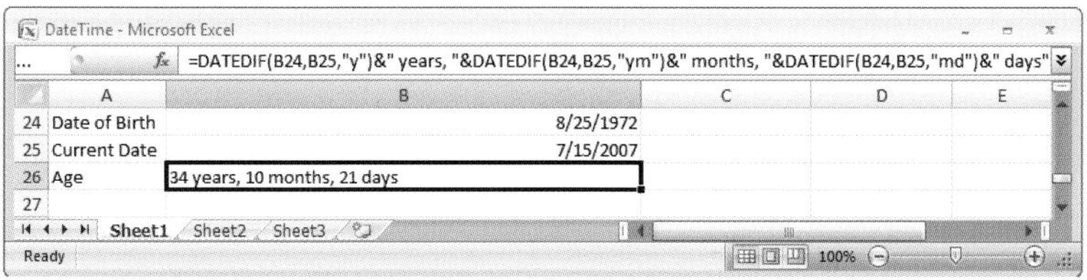


The & operators concatenate the results of the calculations with the literal text values " years ", " months " and " days".

**Hot tip**

Excel's Visual Basic for Applications (VBA) has a similar function called DateDiff, but without the "ym", "yd" and "md" Interval parameters.

**Hot tip**

DateDif is applied three times, to obtain the years, months and days, and the results are joined together into a single statement.

# Text Functions

Values can be presented in many different ways, even though they remain stored as numbers. Sometimes, however, you actually want to convert the values into text (enclosed in quotes), perhaps to include them in a specific format in a report or message.

This uses the Text function. Its syntax is =TEXT(value, format).

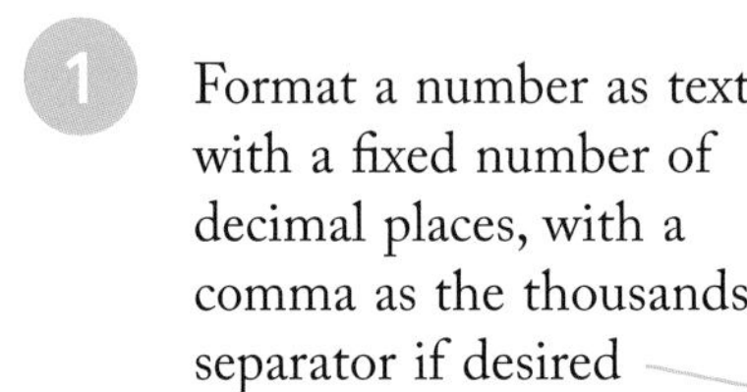

1. Format a number as text with a fixed number of decimal places, with a comma as the thousands separator if desired

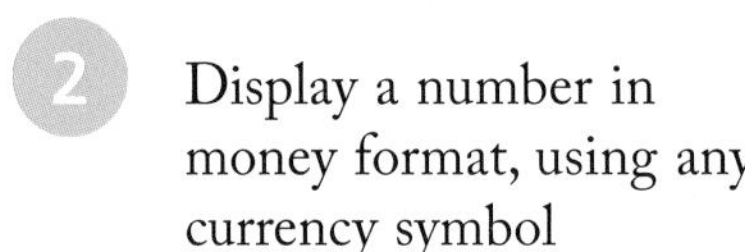

2. Display a number in money format, using any currency symbol

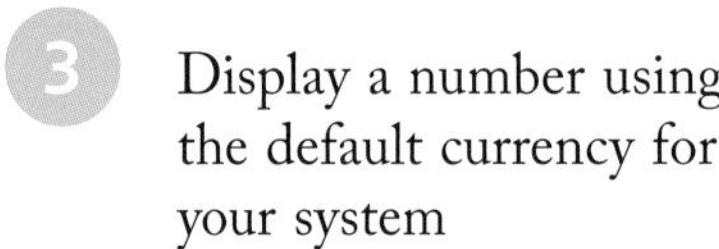

3. Display a number using the default currency for your system

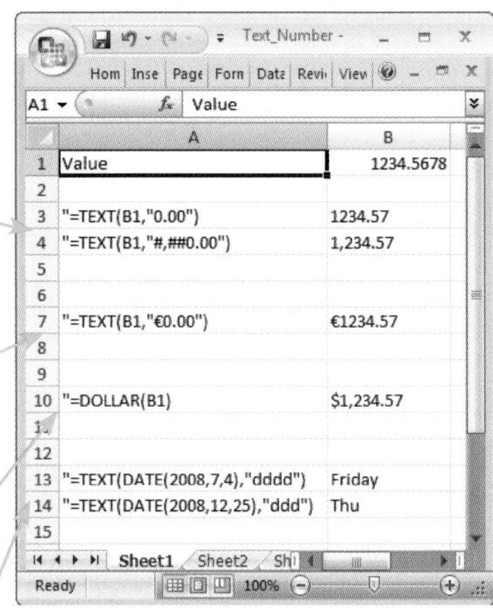


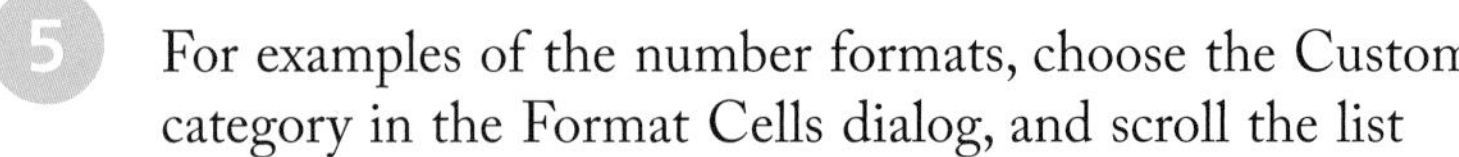

4. Show the day of the week for a date value, using the long or the short form of the day name

5. For examples of the number formats, choose the Custom category in the Format Cells dialog, and scroll the list

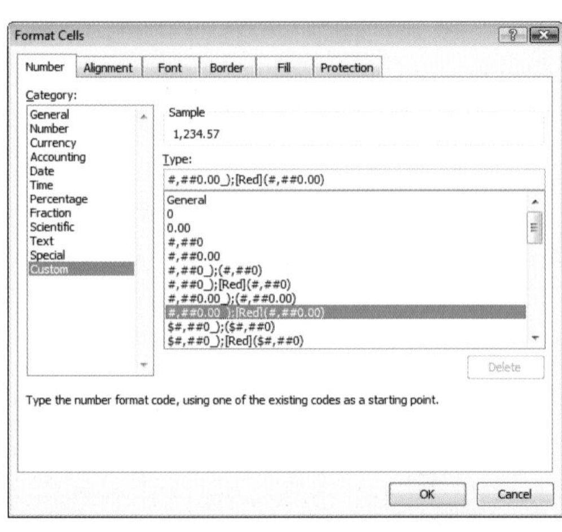


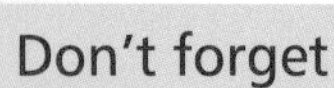
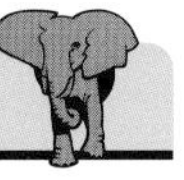

Don't forget

The Dollar function will display the value in the default currency format for your system, for example using the Sterling symbol (£) for UK systems.

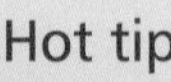

Hot tip

You can use any of the number formats shown in the Format Cells dialog (see page 58), other than General format.

There are several functions provided to help you manipulate a piece of text, to make it more suitable for presentation.

1. Remove all extraneous blanks, leaving a single space between words
2. Convert all the characters in the text into lower-case format

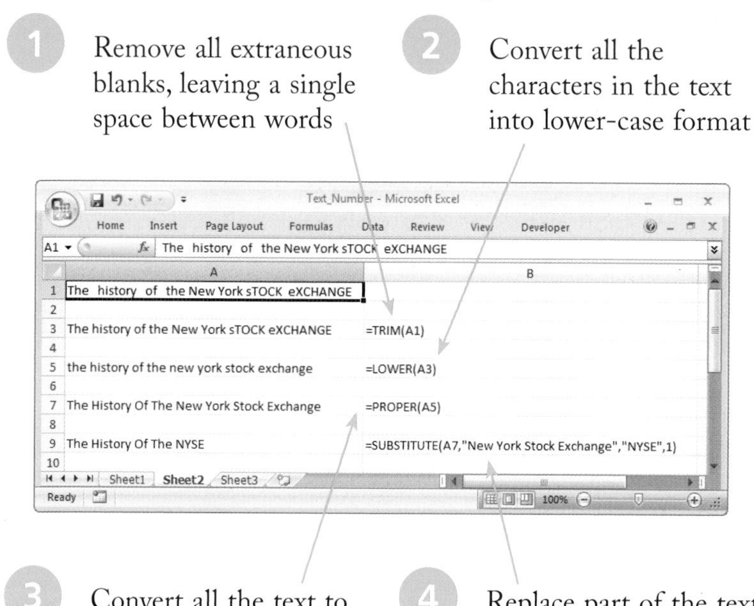


3. Convert all the text to proper case (title case)
4. Replace part of the text with different words

Excel does not have a Word Count function, but the text functions can be used in combination to find the number of words in a cell.

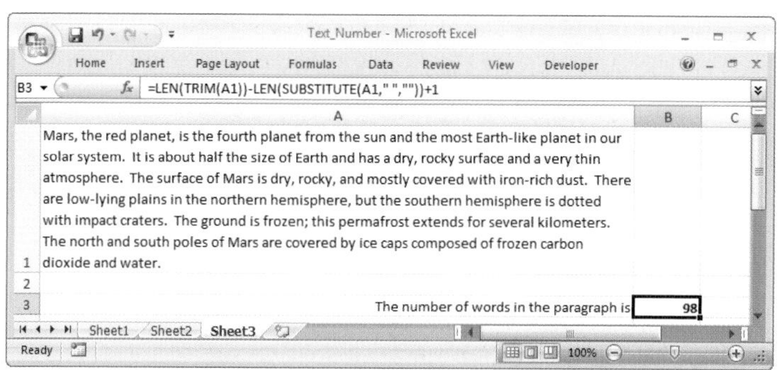


The Trim function removes multiple spaces from the text; then the first Len function counts all the characters including spaces. The Substitute function removes all spaces from the text; then the second Len function counts the remaining characters. The difference between the two lengths is the number of spaces between words. Add one, and you have the number of words.

### Hot tip

The text functions can help you tidy up text information that you import from an external source, especially if you repeat the import on a regular basis to update the information.

### Don't forget

The Substitute function replaces every instance of the text specified, unless you indicate the specific occurrence that you want to change.

### Hot tip

These functions don't change the text in cell A1. Only the working copies used during the calculation are modified.

# Math & Trig Functions

These functions allow you to carry out calculations using cell contents, computed values and constants.

**Don't forget**

With 60 functions this is the largest category in the Function Library.

For example:

1. The Product function multiplies price times (1 - discount) times quantity to get the cost of the item

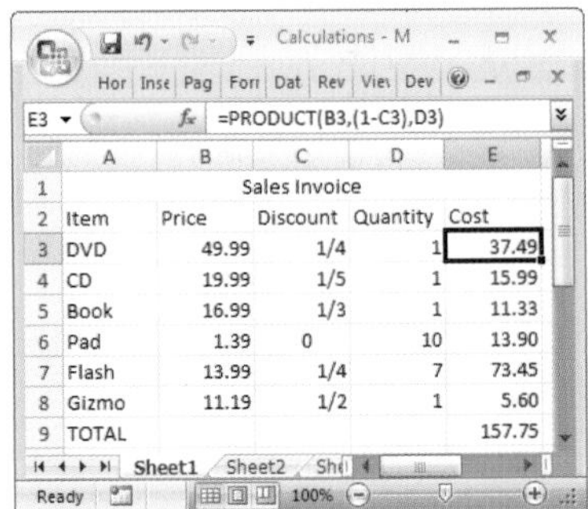


| | A | B | C | D | E |
|---|---|---|---|---|---|
| 1 | | | Sales Invoice | | |
| 2 | Item | Price | Discount | Quantity | Cost |
| 3 | DVD | 49.99 | 1/4 | 1 | 37.49 |
| 4 | CD | 19.99 | 1/5 | 1 | 15.99 |
| 5 | Book | 16.99 | 1/3 | 1 | 11.33 |
| 6 | Pad | 1.39 | 0 | 10 | 13.90 |
| 7 | Flash | 13.99 | 1/4 | 7 | 73.45 |
| 8 | Gizmo | 11.19 | 1/2 | 1 | 5.60 |
| 9 | TOTAL | | | | 157.75 |

2. Copy the formula to calculate the costs for the other items

3. The total cost is the sum of the individual item costs

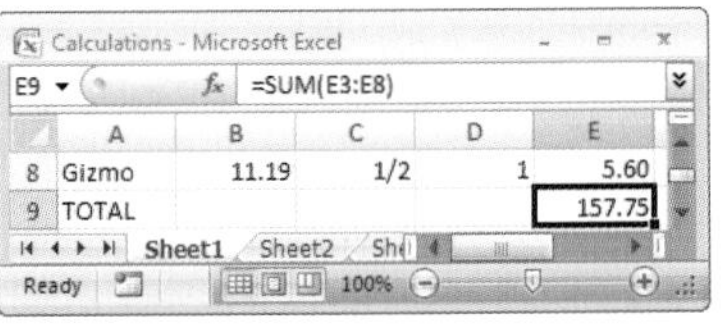


| | A | B | C | D | E |
|---|---|---|---|---|---|
| 8 | Gizmo | 11.19 | 1/2 | 1 | 5.60 |
| 9 | TOTAL | | | | 157.75 |

You may sometimes want to make calculations without showing all of the intermediate values.

For example:

1. The total cost (before discount) is the sum of the products of the item prices and item quantities, i.e. B3*D3 + B4*D4 + ...

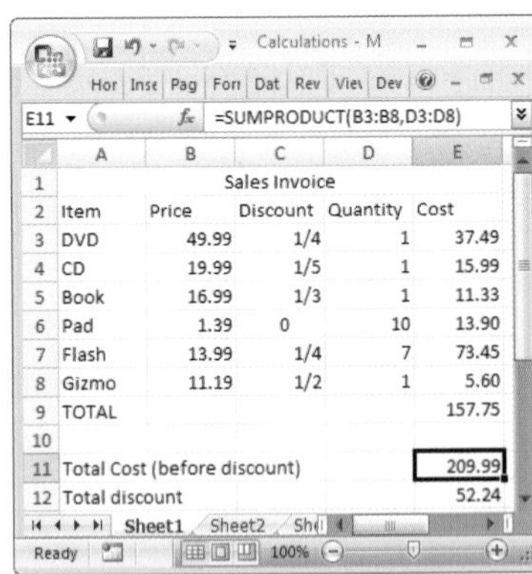


| | A | B | C | D | E |
|---|---|---|---|---|---|
| 1 | | | Sales Invoice | | |
| 2 | Item | Price | Discount | Quantity | Cost |
| 3 | DVD | 49.99 | 1/4 | 1 | 37.49 |
| 4 | CD | 19.99 | 1/5 | 1 | 15.99 |
| 5 | Book | 16.99 | 1/3 | 1 | 11.33 |
| 6 | Pad | 1.39 | 0 | 10 | 13.90 |
| 7 | Flash | 13.99 | 1/4 | 7 | 73.45 |
| 8 | Gizmo | 11.19 | 1/2 | 1 | 5.60 |
| 9 | TOTAL | | | | 157.75 |
| 10 | | | | | |
| 11 | Total Cost (before discount) | | | | 209.99 |
| 12 | Total discount | | | | 52.24 |

2. This value is calculated with the Sumproduct function, which multiplies the sets of cells and totals the results

Calculations - Microsoft Excel
E12 =E11-E9

| | A | B | C | D | E |
|---|---|---|---|---|---|
| 9 | TOTAL | | | | 157.75 |
| 10 | | | | | |
| 11 | Total Cost (before discount) | | | | 209.99 |
| 12 | Total discount | | | | 52.24 |

3. Rather than using the Sumproduct function to calculate the total discount, you can simply subtract actual cost from total cost. This avoids problems with rounding

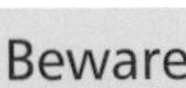

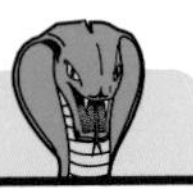

**Beware**

Since this is a single function, the detailed workings won't be revealed even when you use the Evaluate command (see page 104) to perform the calculations in single steps.

errors, which can show up even in straightforward functions such as Sum. To illustrate the type of problem that can arise, imagine placing an order for goods where there's a special gift for spending $140 or more.

1. A quick check seems to indicate that the total is just over the amount required

2. But the total that Excel actually calculates is just under that amount

Calculations - Microsoft Excel

E9 =SUM(E3:E8)

| | A | B | C | D | E | F |
|---|---|---|---|---|---|---|
| 1 | | | Sales Invoice | | | |
| 2 | Item | Price | Discount | Quantity | Cost | |
| 3 | DVD | 49.99 | 1/3 | 1 | 33.33 | |
| 4 | CD | 19.99 | 1/3 | 1 | 13.33 | |
| 5 | Book | 16.99 | 1/3 | 1 | 11.33 | 140.01 |
| 6 | Pad | 1.39 | 1/3 | 10 | 9.27 | |
| 7 | Flash | 13.99 | 1/3 | 7 | 65.29 | |
| 8 | Gizmo | 11.19 | 1/3 | 1 | 7.46 | |
| 9 | TOTAL | | | | 139.99 | |
| 10 | | Spend $140 to get that Special Gift | | | | |
| 11 | | | | | | |
| 12 | Total Cost | | | | 209.99 | |
| 13 | Total discount | | | | 70.00 | |

Excel hasn't got its sums wrong – the stored numbers that it totals aren't quite the same as those on display.

| |
|---|
| 33.326667 |
| 13.326667 |
| 11.326667 |
| 9.266667 |
| 65.286667 |
| 7.460000 |
| 139.993333 |

3. Change the cell format to show more decimal places, and you'll see they are slightly lower

4. Click cell E3 and add the Round function to the existing formula, to round the item cost to two places

5. Copy the formula into cells E4:E8, and you'll see that the total is now the expected amount

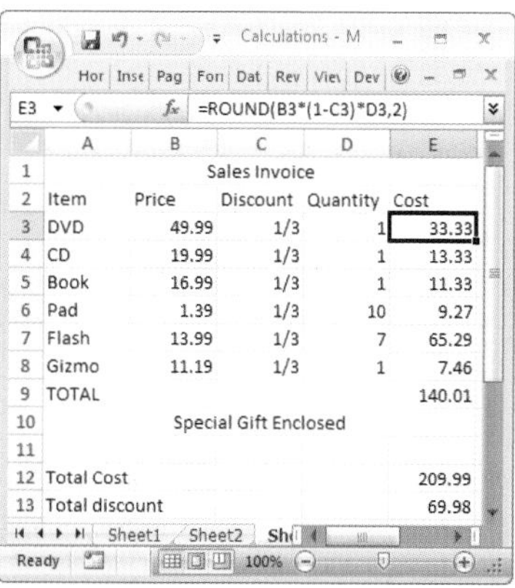

Calculations - M

E3 =ROUND(B3*(1-C3)*D3,2)

| | A | B | C | D | E |
|---|---|---|---|---|---|
| 1 | | | Sales Invoice | | |
| 2 | Item | Price | Discount | Quantity | Cost |
| 3 | DVD | 49.99 | 1/3 | 1 | 33.33 |
| 4 | CD | 19.99 | 1/3 | 1 | 13.33 |
| 5 | Book | 16.99 | 1/3 | 1 | 11.33 |
| 6 | Pad | 1.39 | 1/3 | 10 | 9.27 |
| 7 | Flash | 13.99 | 1/3 | 7 | 65.29 |
| 8 | Gizmo | 11.19 | 1/3 | 1 | 7.46 |
| 9 | TOTAL | | | | 140.01 |
| 10 | | | Special Gift Enclosed | | |
| 11 | | | | | |
| 12 | Total Cost | | | | 209.99 |
| 13 | Total discount | | | | 69.98 |

The Round function rounds up or down. So 1.234 becomes 1.23 while 1.236 becomes 1.24 (rounded to two decimal places). You can specify a negative number of places, and round values to the nearest multiple of ten (-1 places) or a hundred (-2 places), etc.

| |
|---|
| 33.330000 |
| 13.330000 |
| 11.330000 |
| 9.270000 |
| 65.290000 |
| 7.460000 |
| 140.010000 |

## Hot tip

Values may be displayed or converted to text with a fixed number of decimal digits, but the original value will still have the number of digits as originally typed or as calculated when the value was created.

## Beware

You will find that what you see on the worksheet isn't always what you get in the calculations.

## Don't forget

In some cases you may always want to round the values in the same direction. Excel provides the functions Roundup and Rounddown for those situations.

# Random Numbers

It is sometimes useful to produce sets of random numbers. This could be for sample data, when creating or testing worksheets. Another use might be to select a variety of tracks from your music library, to generate a play list.

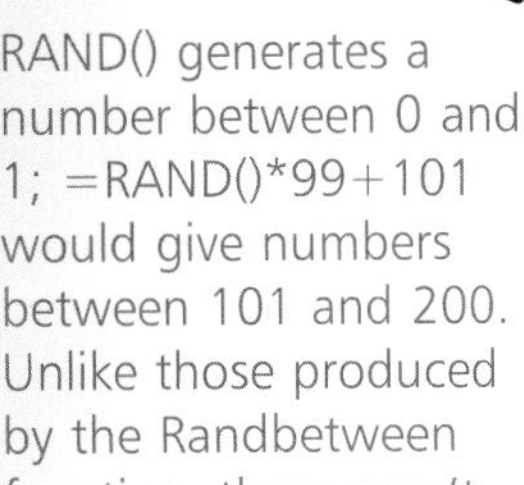

**Hot tip**

RAND() generates a number between 0 and 1; =RAND()*99+101 would give numbers between 101 and 200. Unlike those produced by the Randbetween function, these aren't whole numbers.

1. Click in A1 and enter the function =Rand() to generate a random number between 0 and 1

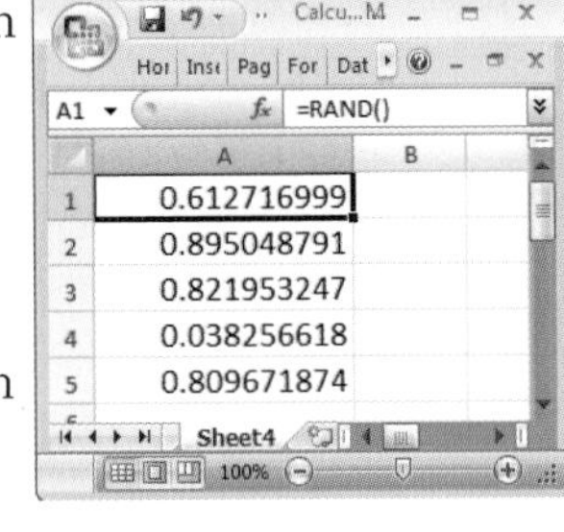


2. Copy A1 down into A2:A5, and a different number will be shown in each cell

3. Click C1 and enter the function =Randbetween(1,+10) to generate a whole number less than or equal to 10

4. Copy B1 down into B2:B5, and a number will be shown in each cell (with possible repeats since there are only ten possibilities)

5. You can generate negative numbers: for example, E1:E5 has numbers between -99 and +99

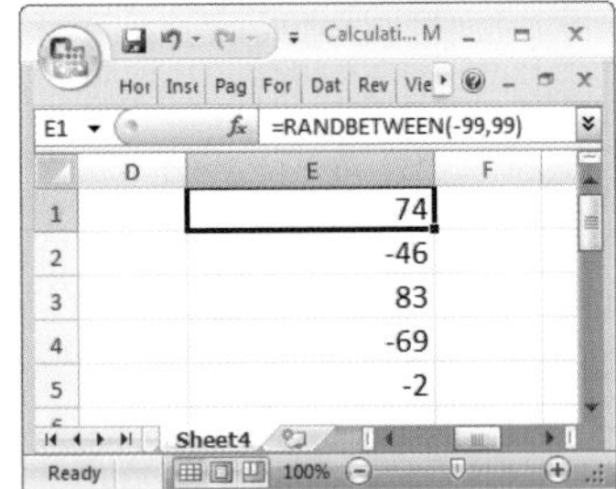


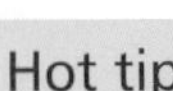

**Hot tip**

To generate a random number that doesn't change each time the worksheet is recalculated, type =RAND() on the formula bar and press F9. The generated number is placed into the cell as a literal value.

6. Select the Formulas tab, click Calculate Now in the Calculation group, and the numbers will change

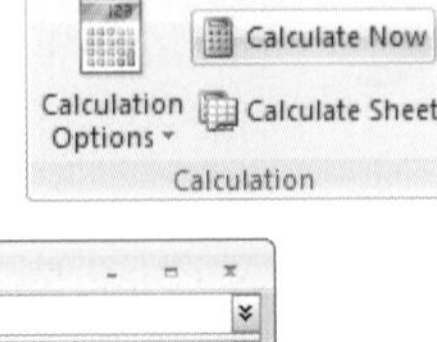


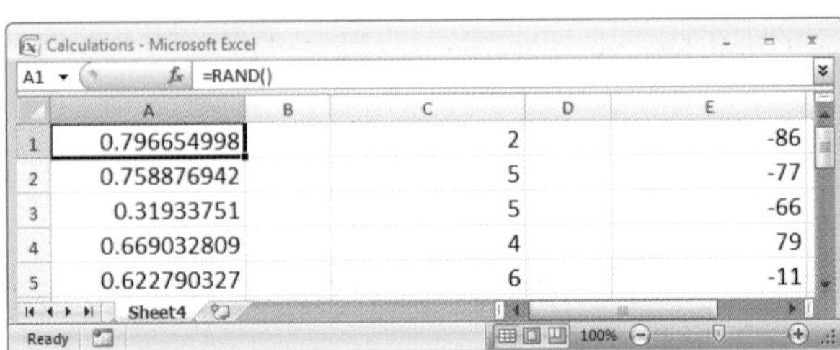

# Other Functions: Statistical

There's a large number of statistical functions, but the most likely one to be used is the Average function.

1. Create a block A1:E5 of random numbers between 101 and 200, to use as data for the functions

Stats - Microsoft Excel

A1 =RAND()

| | A | B | C | D | E |
|---|---|---|---|---|---|
| 1 | 135 | 124 | 110 | 196 | 111 |
| 2 | 192 | 131 | 179 | 127 | 119 |
| 3 | 184 | 149 | 178 | 136 | 195 |
| 4 | 134 | 102 | 107 | 182 | 194 |
| 5 | 184 | 165 | 161 | 115 | 186 |

Sheet1 Sheet2 She

Ready 100%

2. Define the name Sample for the range $A$1:$A$5

3. Select and Copy A1:E5; then select the Home tab, click the arrow on the Paste command and select Paste Values (to replace the formula with the literal value, in each cell)

Calculate some typical statistics.

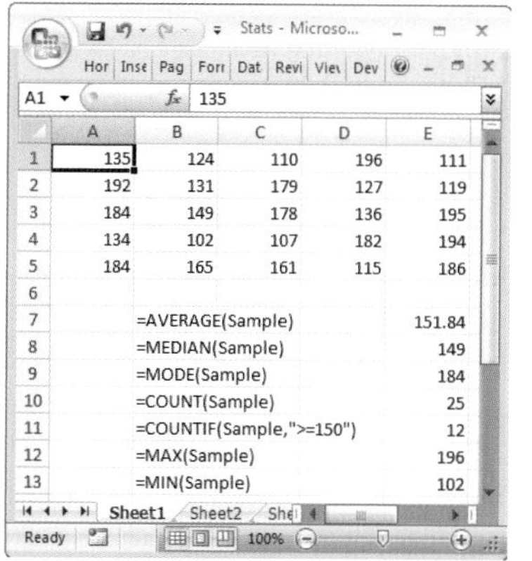

Stats - Microso...

Hor Inse Pag Forr Dat Revi Viev Dev

A1 135

| | A | B | C | D | E |
|---|---|---|---|---|---|
| 1 | 135 | 124 | 110 | 196 | 111 |
| 2 | 192 | 131 | 179 | 127 | 119 |
| 3 | 184 | 149 | 178 | 136 | 195 |
| 4 | 134 | 102 | 107 | 182 | 194 |
| 5 | 184 | 165 | 161 | 115 | 186 |
| 6 | | | | | |
| 7 | | =AVERAGE(Sample) | | | 151.84 |
| 8 | | =MEDIAN(Sample) | | | 149 |
| 9 | | =MODE(Sample) | | | 184 |
| 10 | | =COUNT(Sample) | | | 25 |
| 11 | | =COUNTIF(Sample,">=150") | | | 12 |
| 12 | | =MAX(Sample) | | | 196 |
| 13 | | =MIN(Sample) | | | 102 |

Sheet1 Sheet2 She

Ready 100%

1. The arithmetic mean is =Average(Sample)
2. The number in the middle of the sample is =Median(Sample)
3. The most frequently occurring value is =Mode(Sample)
4. The number of values in the sample is =Count(Sample)
5. The number of values in the sample that are greater than or equal to 150 is =Countif(Sample,“>=150”
6. The maximum value in the sample is =Max(Sample)
7. The minimum value in the sample is =Min(Sample)

**Hot tip**

Using Paste Values to replace the formula means that, once generated, the random numbers won't be affected by recalculation of the worksheet.

**Don't forget**

There are a number of different ways to interpret the term Average. Make sure that you use the function that's appropriate for your requirements.

# Other Functions: Engineering

## Hot tip

The Other Functions category also includes the Cube functions and the Information functions

There are some rather esoteric functions in the Engineering category, but some are quite generally applicable, for example:

1. Convert from one measurement system to another, using the function =Convert(value, from_unit, to_unit)

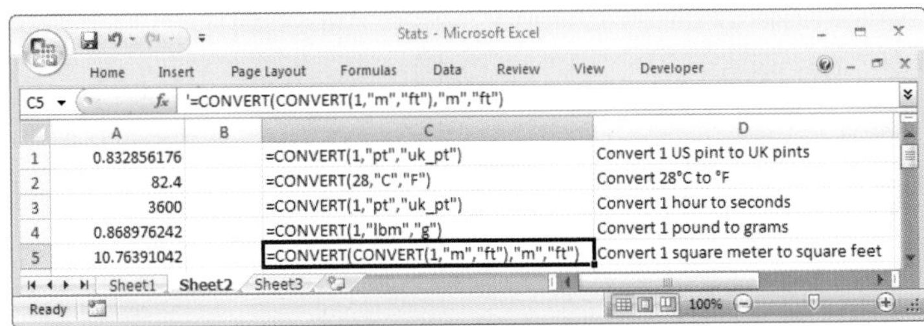

C5: '=CONVERT(CONVERT(1,"m","ft"),"m","ft")

| | A | B | C | D |
|---|---|---|---|---|
| 1 | 0.832856176 | | =CONVERT(1,"pt","uk_pt") | Convert 1 US pint to UK pints |
| 2 | 82.4 | | =CONVERT(28,"C","F") | Convert 28°C to °F |
| 3 | 3600 | | =CONVERT(1,"pt","uk_pt") | Convert 1 hour to seconds |
| 4 | 0.868976242 | | =CONVERT(1,"lbm","g") | Convert 1 pound to grams |
| 5 | 10.76391042 | | =CONVERT(CONVERT(1,"m","ft"),"m","ft") | Convert 1 square meter to square feet |

This function deals with units of weight and mass, distance, time, pressure, force, energy, power, magnetism, temperature and liquids

There are functions to convert between any two pairs of number systems, including binary, decimal, hexadecimal and octal.

2. Convert decimal values to binary, octal and hexadecimal

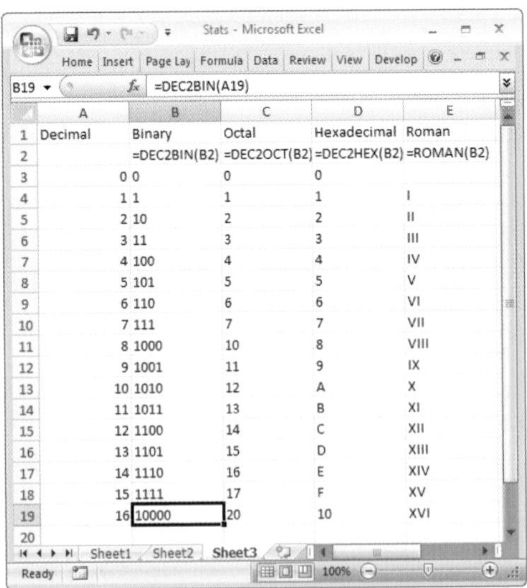

B19: =DEC2BIN(A19)

| | A | B | C | D | E |
|---|---|---|---|---|---|
| 1 | Decimal | Binary | Octal | Hexadecimal | Roman |
| 2 | | =DEC2BIN(B2) | =DEC2OCT(B2) | =DEC2HEX(B2) | =ROMAN(B2) |
| 3 | 0 | 0 | 0 | 0 | |
| 4 | 1 | 1 | 1 | 1 | I |
| 5 | 2 | 10 | 2 | 2 | II |
| 6 | 3 | 11 | 3 | 3 | III |
| 7 | 4 | 100 | 4 | 4 | IV |
| 8 | 5 | 101 | 5 | 5 | V |
| 9 | 6 | 110 | 6 | 6 | VI |
| 10 | 7 | 111 | 7 | 7 | VII |
| 11 | 8 | 1000 | 10 | 8 | VIII |
| 12 | 9 | 1001 | 11 | 9 | IX |
| 13 | 10 | 1010 | 12 | A | X |
| 14 | 11 | 1011 | 13 | B | XI |
| 15 | 12 | 1100 | 14 | C | XII |
| 16 | 13 | 1101 | 15 | D | XIII |
| 17 | 14 | 1110 | 16 | E | XIV |
| 18 | 15 | 1111 | 17 | F | XV |
| 19 | 16 | 10000 | 20 | 10 | XVI |
| 20 | | | | | |

## Don't forget

The function supports the classic Roman numeral style, plus some more concise styles.

| | |
|---|---|
| =ROMAN(1499,0) | MCDXCIX |
| =ROMAN(1499,1) | MLDVLIV |
| =ROMAN(1499,2) | MXDIX |
| =ROMAN(1499,3) | MVDIV |
| =ROMAN(1499,4) | MID |

There's also a Roman numeral conversion, but it's just a one-way conversion between Arabic numerals and Roman numerals (and it comes from the Math & Trig category, rather than Engineering).

# Excel Add-ins

There are Add-ins included with Excel, but they must be loaded before they can be used.

1. Click the Microsoft Office button, and then click Excel Options

2. Click the Add-Ins category, and in the Manage box, click Excel Add-ins, and then click Go

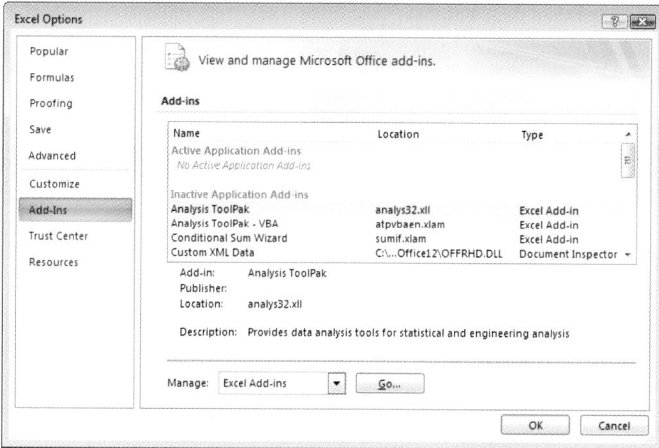


3. To load the Excel Add-in, select the associated check-box and then click OK

4. You may be required to install the selected programs

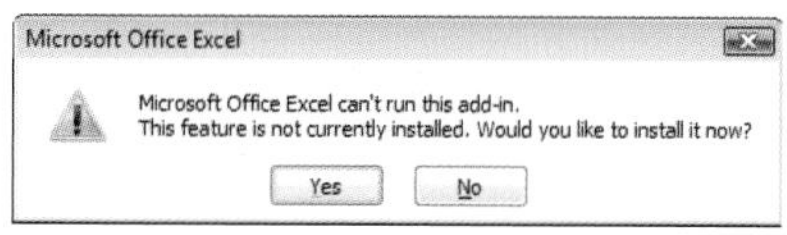


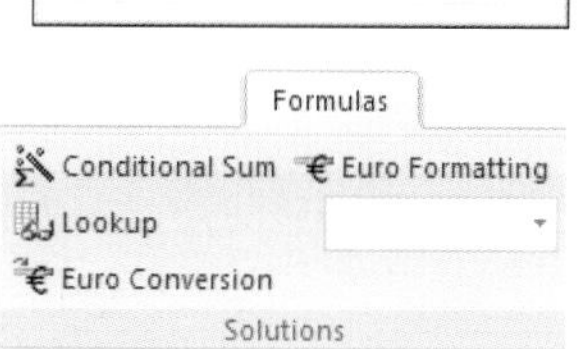


5. The new functions are included on the Formulas tab in the Solutions group, and on the Data tab in the Analysis group

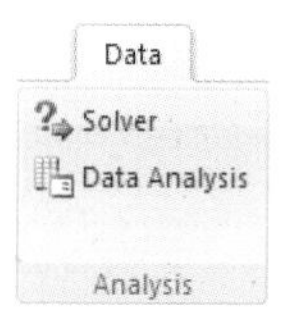

## Hot tip

If you are still looking for the functions you need, you may find them in an Excel Add-in such as the Analysis ToolPak or the Solver Add-in.

## Don't forget

To unload an Excel Add-in, clear the associated check-box and then click OK. This does not delete the Add-in from your computer.

# Evaluate Formula

If you are not sure exactly how a formula works, especially when there are nested functions, use the Evaluate command to run the formula a step at a time.

1. Select the cell with the formula you wish to investigate

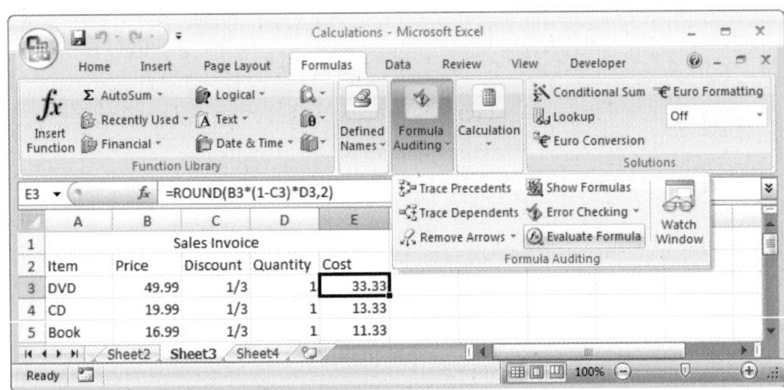

## Hot tip

This is the formula for rounding the item costs, as shown in step 4 on page 99.

2. Select the Formulas tab, click the Formula Auditing button and select the Evaluate Formula command

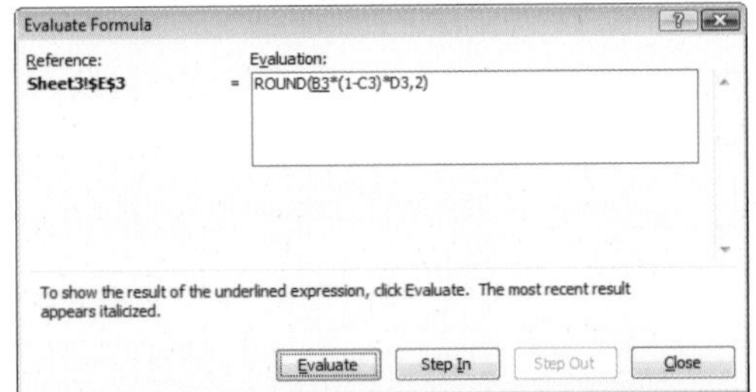

## Don't forget

Press the Step In button to check details such as the value of a constant or to see the expansion of a range name or table name. Click Step Out to continue the evaluation.

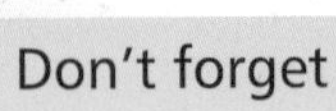

3. Press the Evaluate button to move the calculation on a step; then press again to move to the subsequent steps

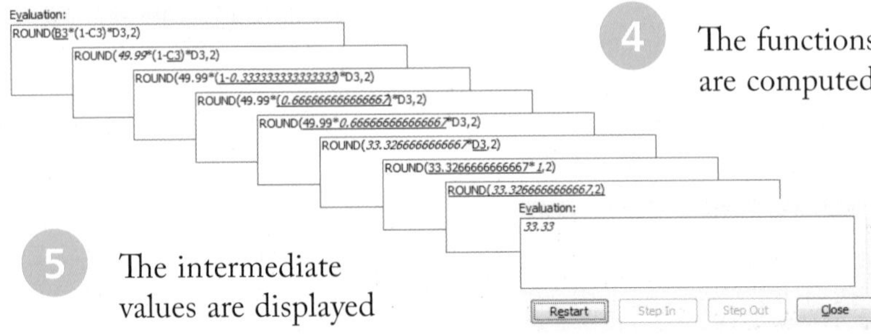

4. The functions are computed

5. The intermediate values are displayed

# 7 Control Excel

*To keep control of your worksheets, audit the formulas and check for errors. Make backup copies, and use the automatic save and recover capabilities. You can also control Excel through startup switches, shortcuts, KeyTips for the Ribbon commands, and the Quick Access and Mini toolbars.*

# Audit Formulas

## Hot tip

When you are reviewing a worksheet and the formulas it contains, use the tools in the Formula Auditing group.

1. Click the Formulas tab to see the Formula Auditing group

2. If the commands are grayed, click the Office button, select Excel Options and click Advanced

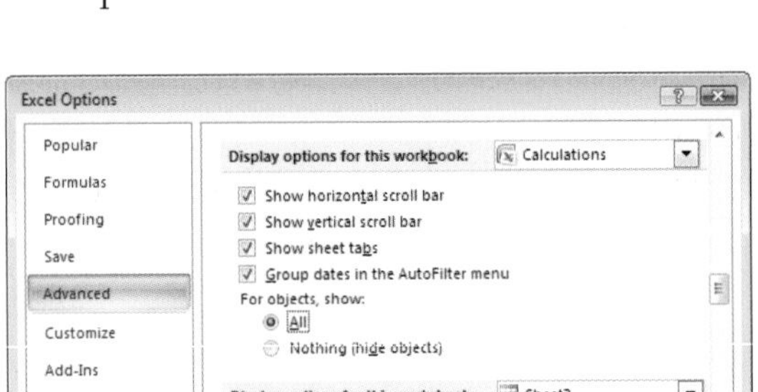




3. In the "Display options for this Workbook" section, make sure that the All option is selected

4. Select a cell and click the Trace Precedents button in the Formula Auditing group

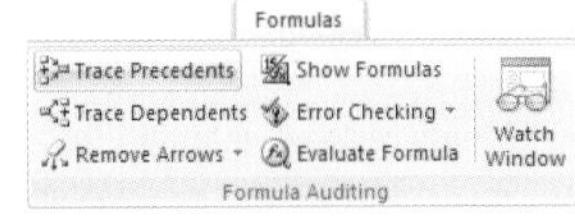


## Don't forget

Precedents are those cells that are referred to by the formula in the selected cell.

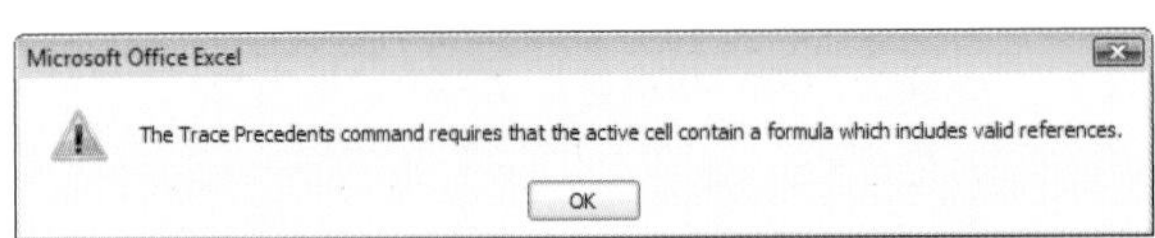


## Beware

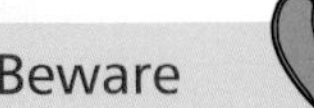

The cell you select must contain a formula for the Trace Precedents button to operate.

5. If there's no formula, you receive a message

6. With cells such as E9 that contain a formula, the arrow shows cells directly referred to by that formula

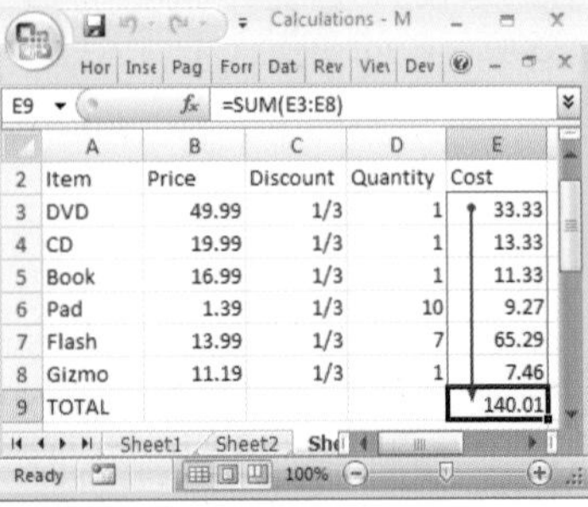


| | A | B | C | D | E |
|---|---|---|---|---|---|
| 2 | Item | Price | Discount | Quantity | Cost |
| 3 | DVD | 49.99 | 1/3 | 1 | 33.33 |
| 4 | CD | 19.99 | 1/3 | 1 | 13.33 |
| 5 | Book | 16.99 | 1/3 | 1 | 11.33 |
| 6 | Pad | 1.39 | 1/3 | 10 | 9.27 |
| 7 | Flash | 13.99 | 1/3 | 7 | 65.29 |
| 8 | Gizmo | 11.19 | 1/3 | 1 | 7.46 |
| 9 | TOTAL | | | | 140.01 |

7 Click Trace Precedents to see the next level of cells (if the first level of precedent cells refer to more cells)

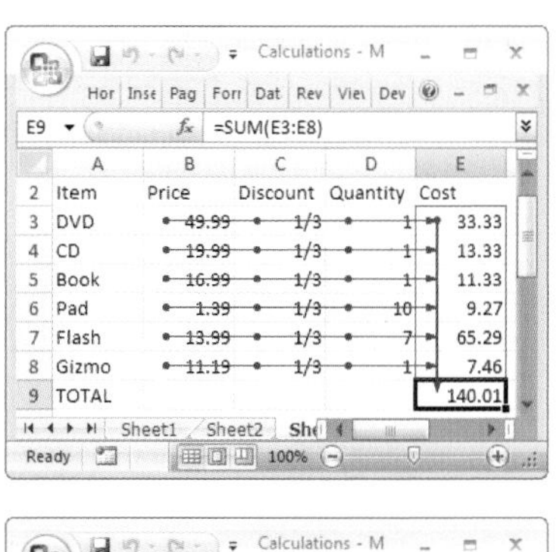

8 Click Trace Dependents to show the cells that rely on the value in the selected cell

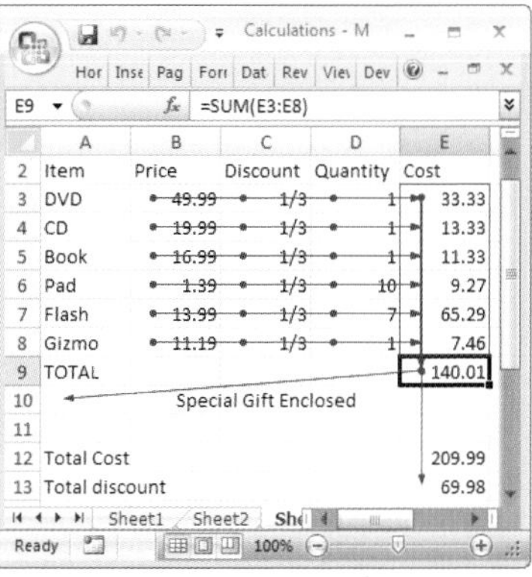

9 Click Remove Arrows in Formula Auditing

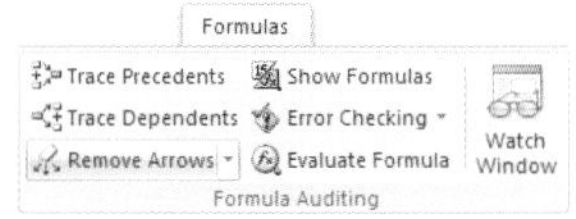

Dependents are those cells that contain formulas that refer to the selected cell.

You can analyze the role of cells that contain only literal values:

1 Click a cell, e.g. B3, that contains no formula, and then click the Trace Dependents button

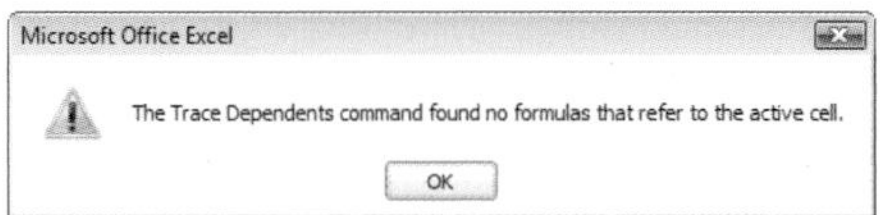


2 If the cell isn't referred to by any formulas, you receive a warning message.

3 Click Trace Dependents two more times to view the remaining levels of dependent cells

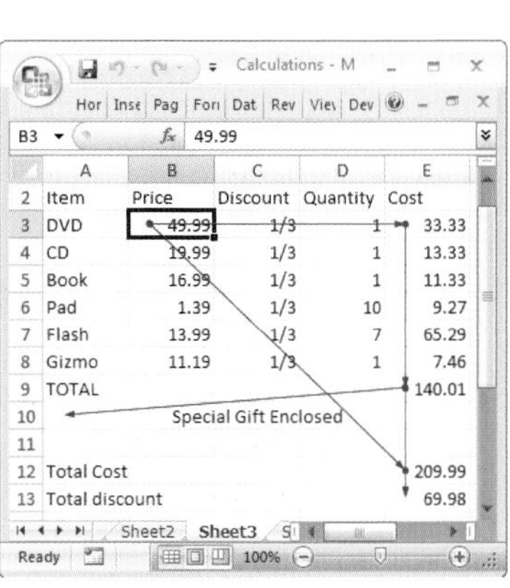

# Protect Formulas

This is the same action as performed by the keyboard shortcut Ctrl+` (the grave accent key).

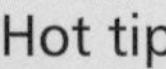

When you print the worksheet with the formulas revealed, make sure you include the column and row headings. Select the Page Layout tab and click Print Headings in the Sheet Options group.

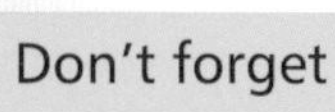

You can select ranges of cells, to protect multiple formulas at once.

1. Click the Formulas tab; then click Show Formulas to display the formulas in the worksheet

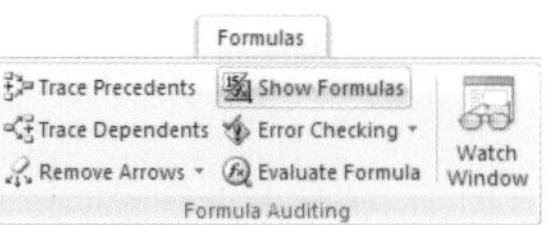


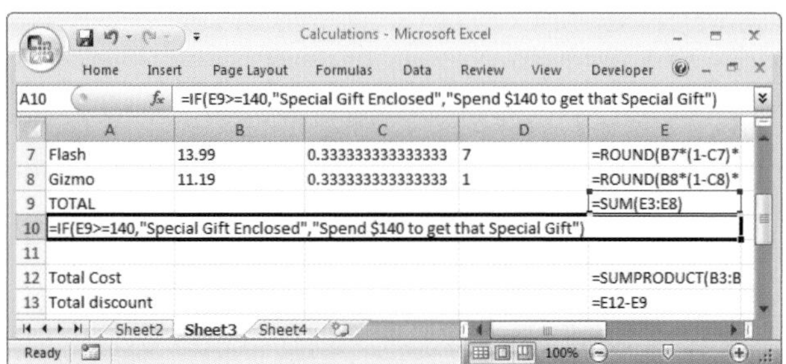


2. Click Show Formulas again to return to displaying the results of the formulas

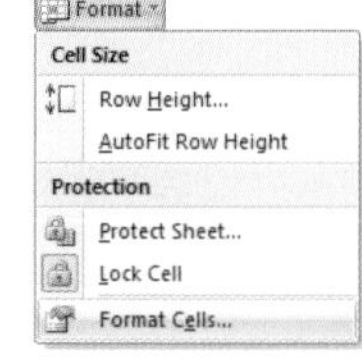


3. To hide a formula, select the cell; then click the Home tab, Format and then Format Cells

4. Click in the box labeled Hidden and click OK

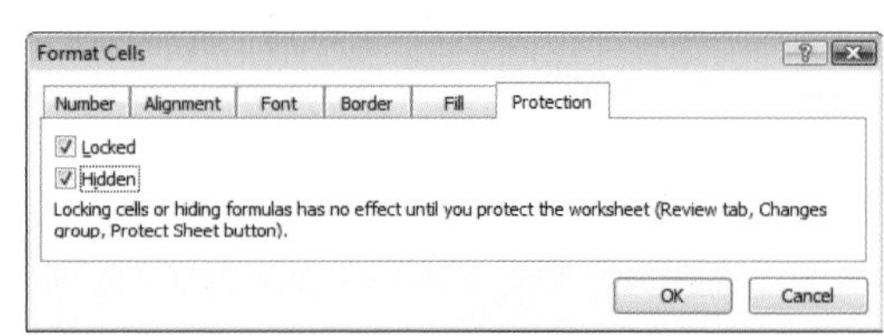


5. Click the Home tab, Format and select Protect Work Sheet

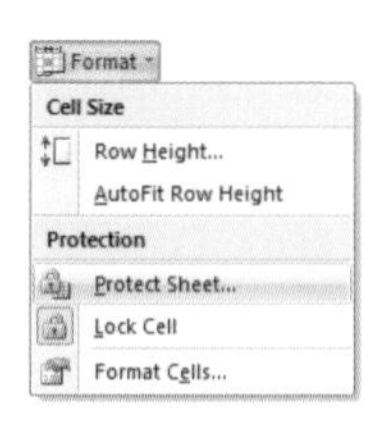


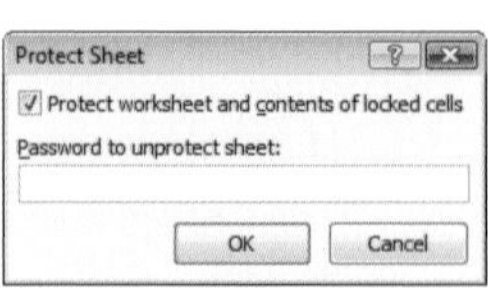

6. The formula will no longer display on the Formula bar or when you Show Formulas

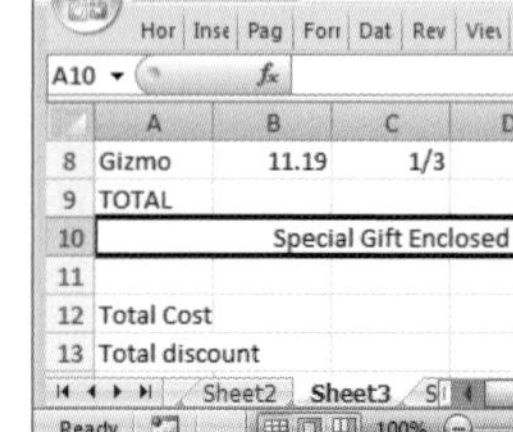

# Check for Errors

Excel applies rules to check for potential errors in formulas.

1. Click the Office button, select Excel Options and then click the Formulas category

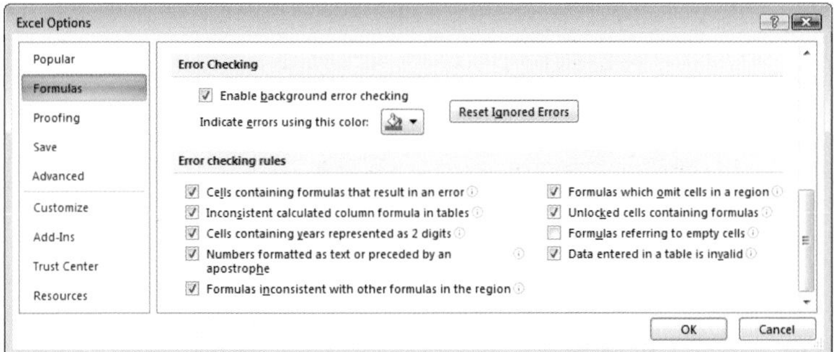


2. Select or clear the check-boxes to change the errors that Excel will detect

3. Select Formulas, and click the arrow next to Error Checking in the Formula Auditing group

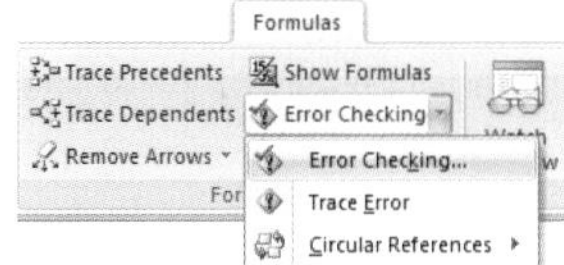


4. Click Error Checking to review errors one by one, making corrections on the Formula bar

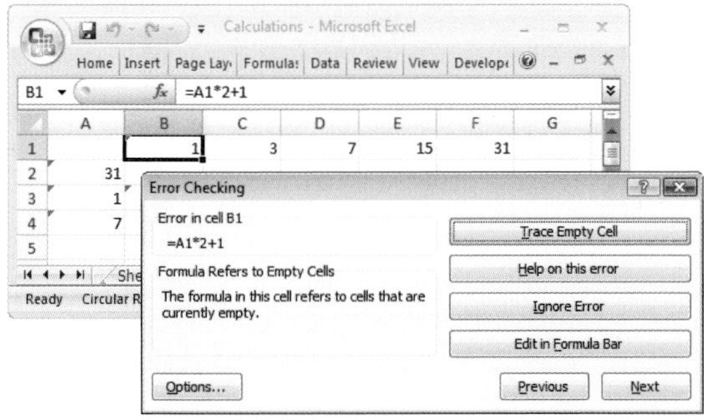


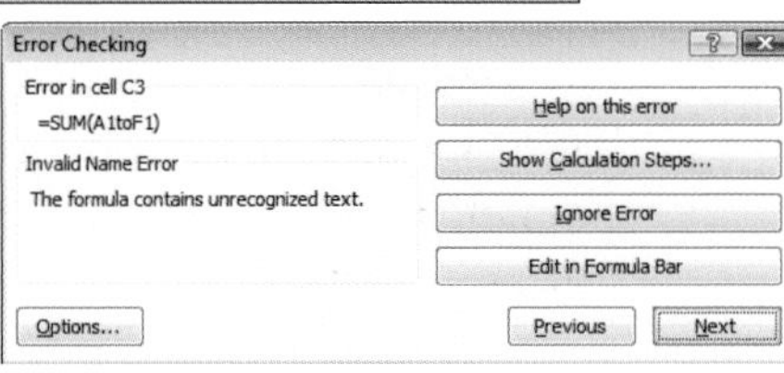


5. Click the Next button to review subsequent errors

**Hot tip**

Some errors will just be warnings, and some may be due to information not yet recorded.

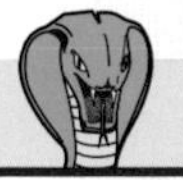

**Beware**

If the worksheet has previously been checked, any Ignored errors will not appear until you press the Reset Ignored Errors button in Excel Options.

**Don't forget**

You can select Circular References to see the cells that refer to their own contents, directly or indirectly.

## ...cont'd

You can also review individual errors on the worksheet.

1. Click an error and then select Trace Error from the Error Checking menu in Formula Auditing

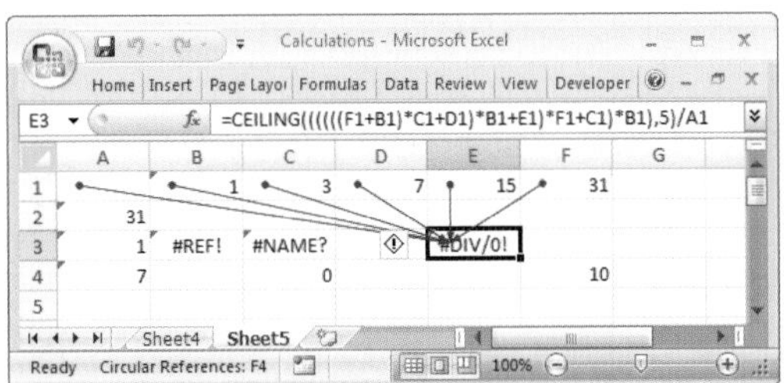


**Hot tip**

The Error Checking options become very useful when you have large worksheets, where errors and warnings are off screen, out of view.

2. You can select Circular References to see the cells that refer to their own contents, directly or indirectly

Error Checking
Error Checking...
Trace Error
Circular References
$C$7
$F$7
$F$4
$C$4

3. Click a cell from the list to navigate to that location

4. Press F9 to recalculate the worksheet, and the cells involved in circular references will be identified

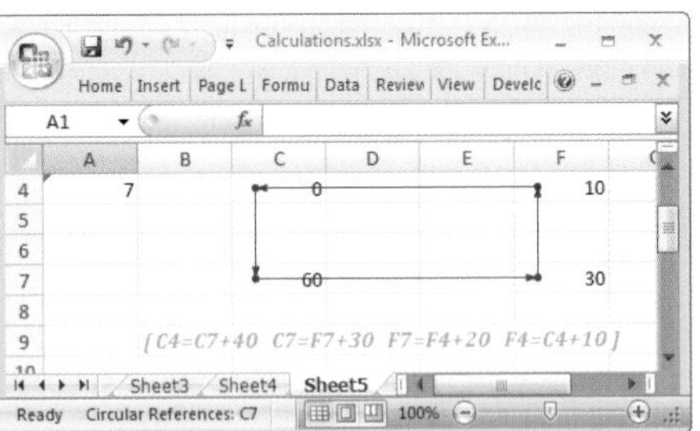


5. Click the Information button on an individual error to see more options, tailored to the particular error type

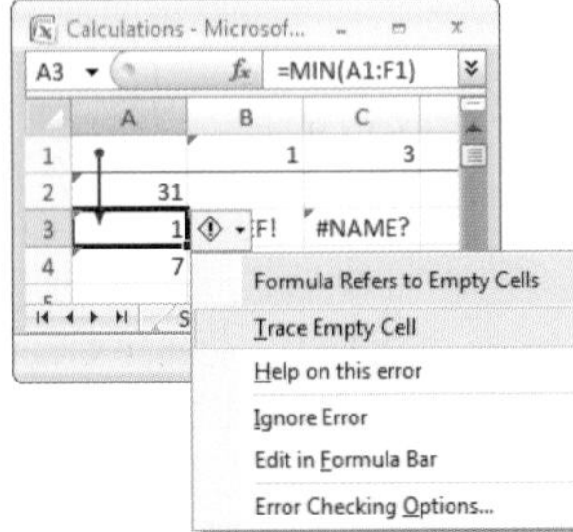


**Don't forget**

Click Trace Empty Cell to identify the empty cells referred to, directly or indirectly, by the selected formula.

# Backup

To make a copy of your workbook:

1. Click the Office button and select Open (or press the Ctrl+O shortcut key)

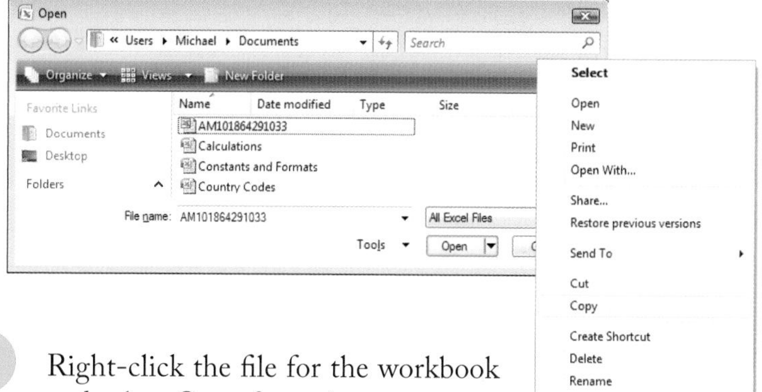


2. Right-click the file for the workbook and select Copy from the menu

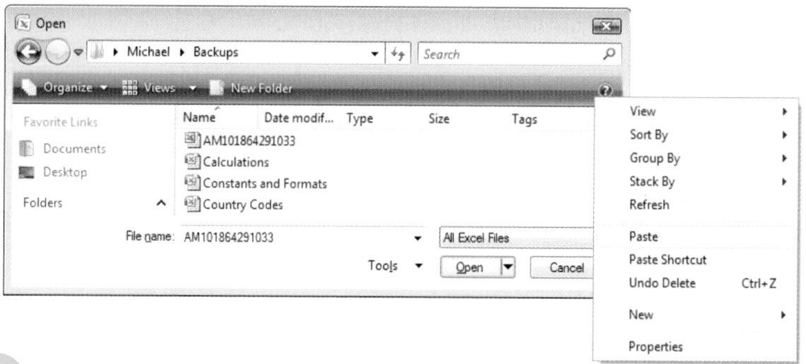


3. Switch to the backup folder, right-click an empty area and select Paste

4. The file is copied to the folder, unless there's an existing copy in the backup folder

## Hot tip

When you are working on a large worksheet, it is often helpful to make a copy before you apply significant changes, so that you can undo them if necessary.

## Don't forget

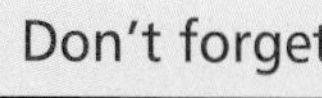

If there's already a copy, Windows compares the two versions, and lets you choose to replace the file, keep the two copies or skip copying the workbook.

# AutoSave and AutoRecovery

To review and adjust the AutoRecover and AutoSave settings:

1. Click the Office button; then click Excel Options and select the Save category

Excel Options

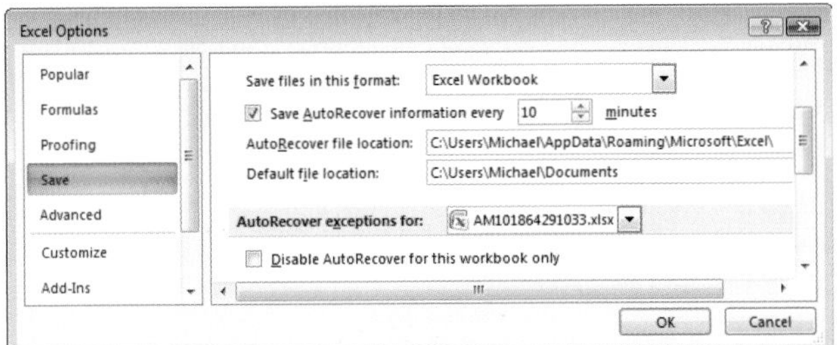


2. Make sure that the "Save AutoRecover information" box is checked and adjust the frequency if desired; then click OK

If your system shuts down without saving the current changes, the next time you start up Windows and Excel you'll be given the opportunity to recover your changes, as recorded up to the last AutoSave.

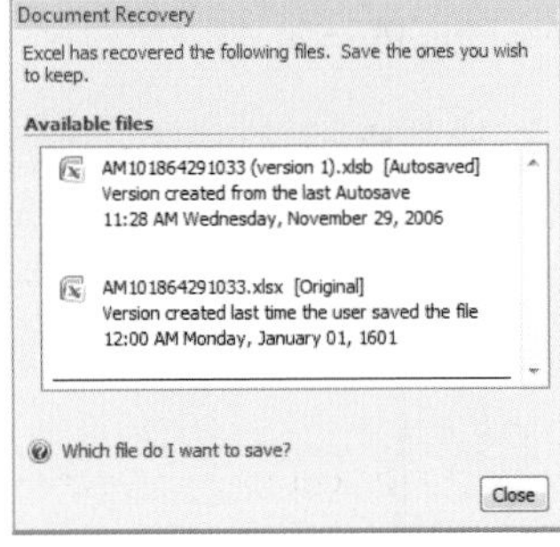


1. Click any of the entries to review the contents, and Save the version of the file that contains the information you need

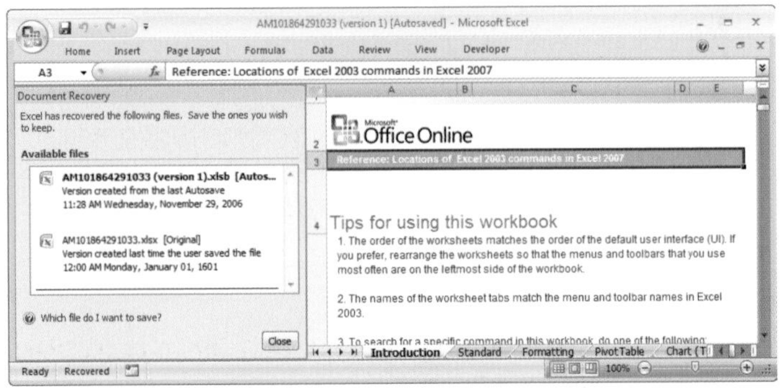


## Hot tip

Excel will automatically save your worksheet periodically, and can recover the file if your system shuts down in the middle of an update.

## Don't forget

You can also change the folder in which the recovery versions of your workbooks will be stored.

## Hot tip

The Document Recovery task pane displays up to three versions of your file, with the most recent at the top.

# Startup Switches

When you start Excel normally, it displays the Excel splash screen and then opens with a new blank workbook, e.g. Book1

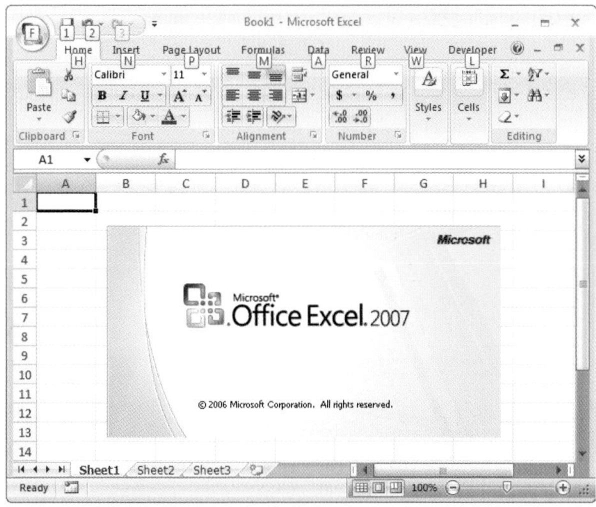


To start Excel without these items displaying:

1. Press the Windows Logo key + R, type excel.exe /e and then press Enter

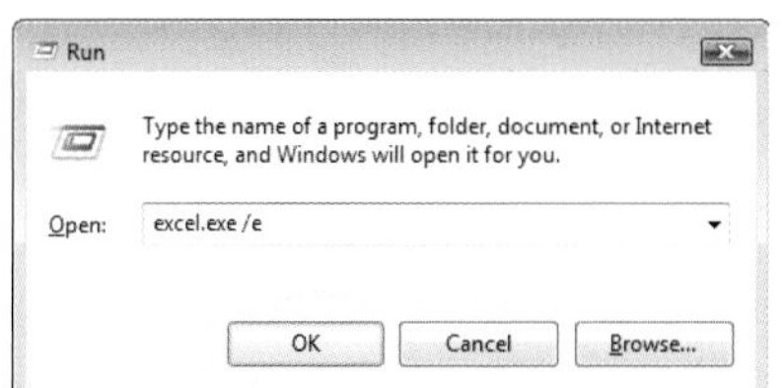


2. Excel opens without splash screen or workbook

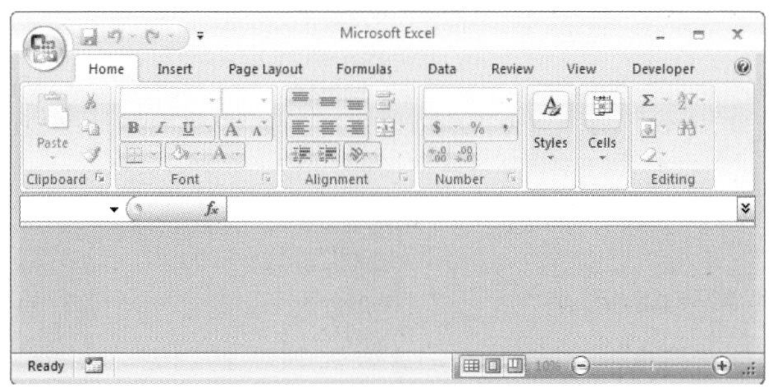


When you start Excel using the normal Start menu entry, these items will still be displayed.

You can use this method start Excel in safe mode by typing excel.exe /safe. This can be useful if you are having problems opening a particular workbook.

You can create a shortcut to Excel with your required parameters and place this on the Start menu.

# Create a Shortcut

To create a shortcut to Excel:

1. Locate the Excel.exe file on your hard drive, typically C:\Program Files\Microsoft Office\Office12\Excel.exe

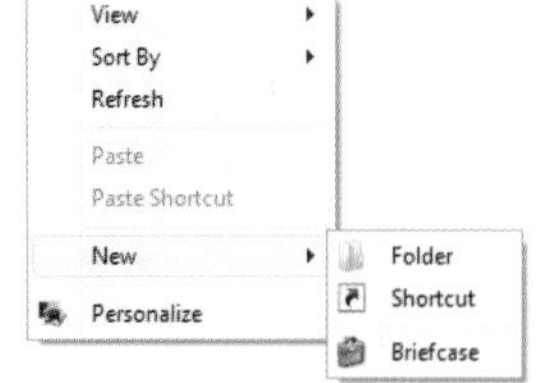


2. Right-click the desktop and select New, Shortcut

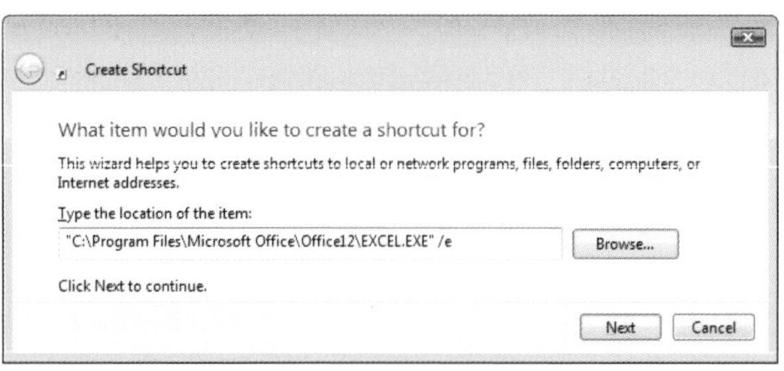


3. Browse to the Excel.exe file and select it; then add the required switch (e.g. /e or /safe) outside the quote marks

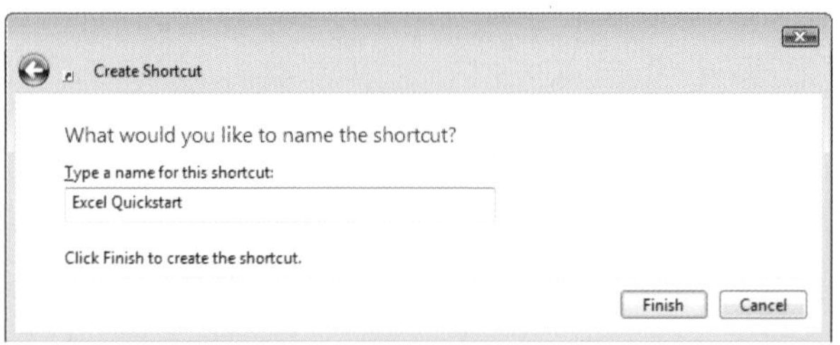


4. Name the shortcut and click Finish; then right-click the shortcut on the desktop and select Pin to Start Menu

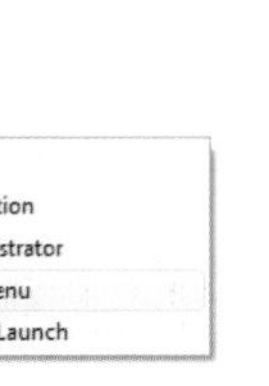


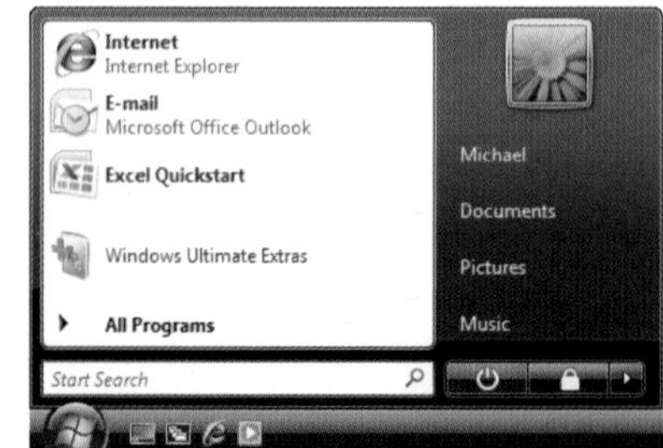

**Hot tip**

If necessary, use Windows Search to locate the Excel.exe program and note the location.



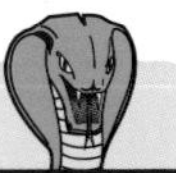

**Beware**

Make sure that you enter a space between the final quote mark and the command-line switch.

**Don't forget**

You could choose Add to Quick Launch to put the shortcut onto the Quick Launch bar.

# Ribbon KeyTips

Although the Ribbon is designed for mouse selection, it is still possible to carry out any task available on the Ribbon without moving your hands from the keyboard.

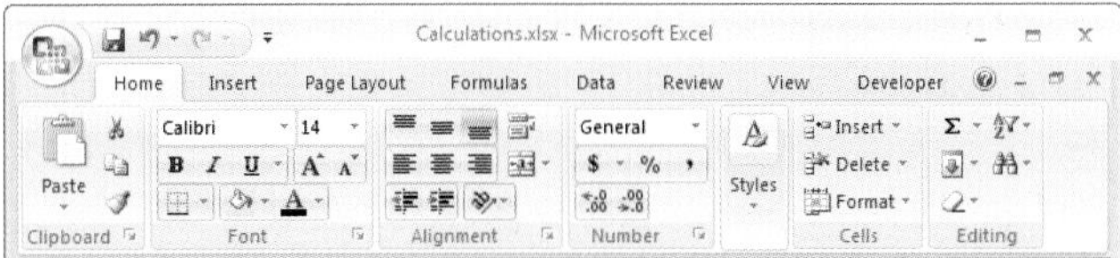


1. Press and release the Alt key (or press the F10 key) to show KeyTips (the keyboard shortcuts for the Ribbon)

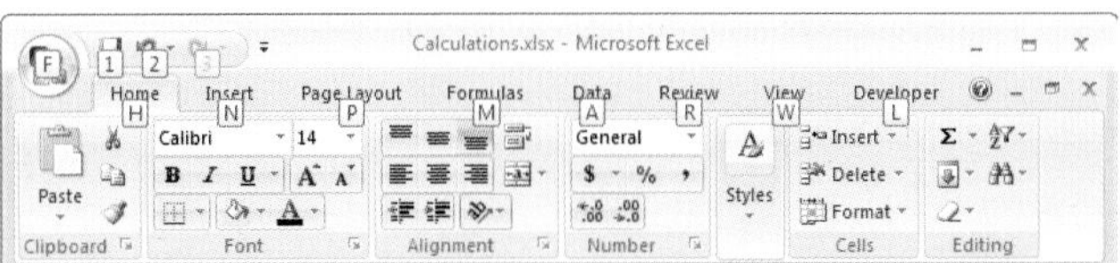


2. Press the letter for the command tab that you want to display; for example, press W for View

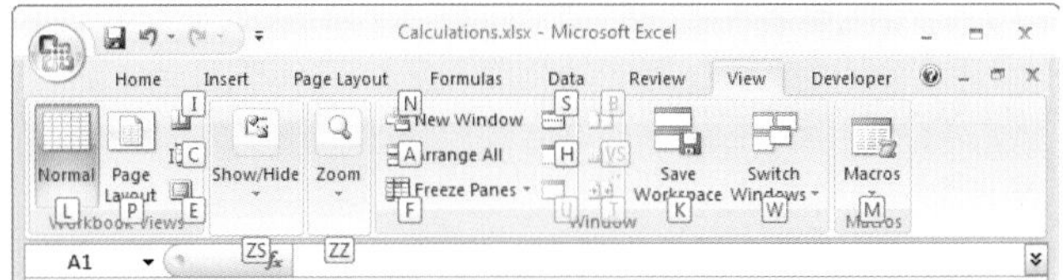


3. Press the letter(s) for the command or group that you want; for example, press ZS for Show/Hide

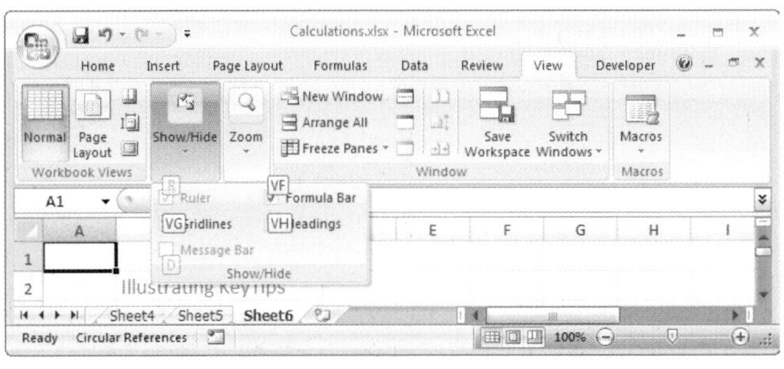

## Hot tip

If you hold down the Alt key for a couple of seconds, the KeyTips will display. Click F10 to hide them temporarily.

## Don't forget

The KeyTips change when you select a tab, and further KeyTips display when you select specific commands.

## Hot tip

It doesn't matter if Alt is pressed or not: the shortcut keys in the KeyTips will still operate.

# Using KeyTips

1 To go to a specific cell, for example C7, press these keys:

You can go to a cell using keystrokes only.

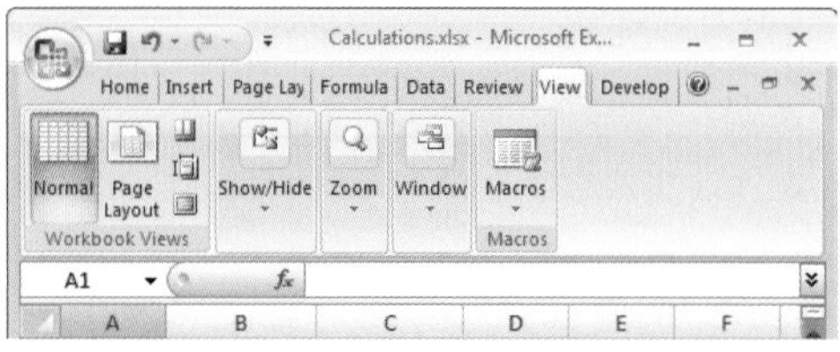


**Alt**

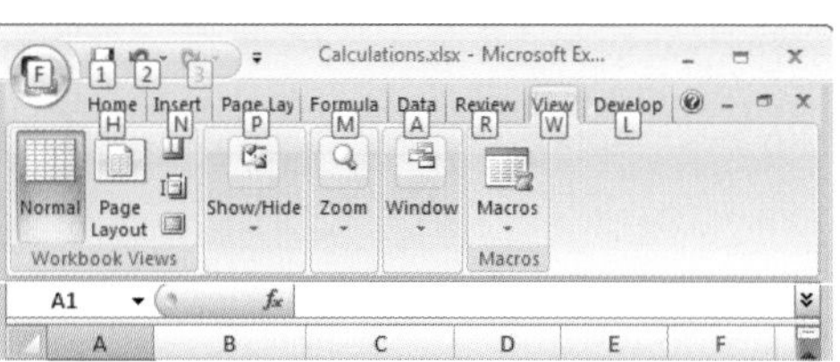


**H**

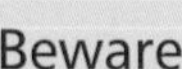


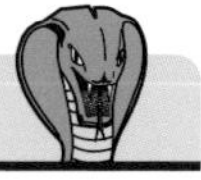

The action associated with a particular letter may change as you switch to another command tab or command group. For example, N can be the Insert tab, or New window in View.

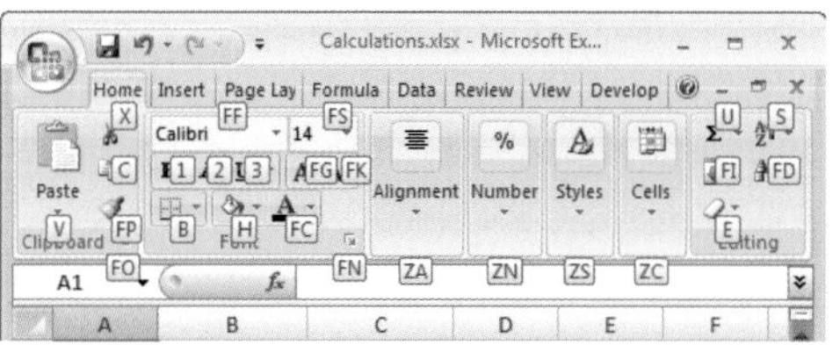


**FD**

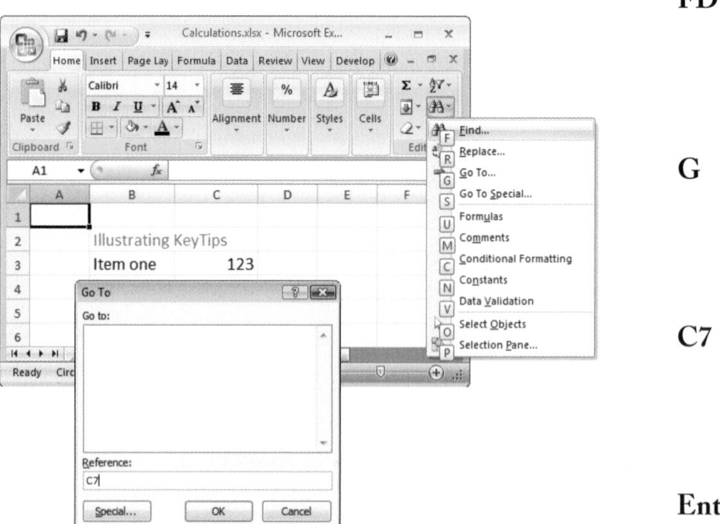


**G**

**C7**

**Enter**

2 The active cell changes to C7, the cell address specified

1. To select AutoSum, press these keys:

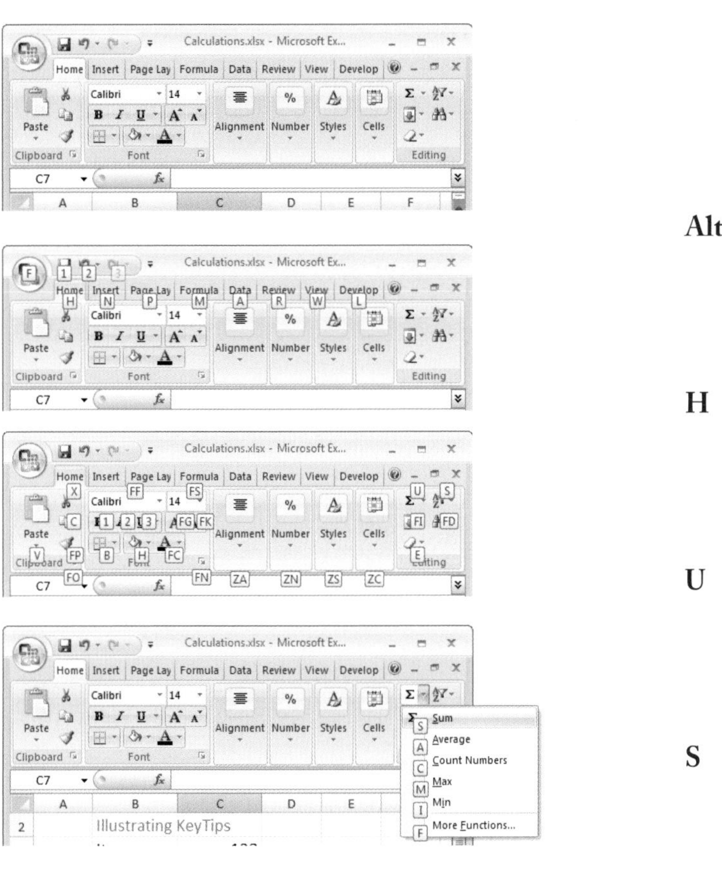

Alt

H

U

S

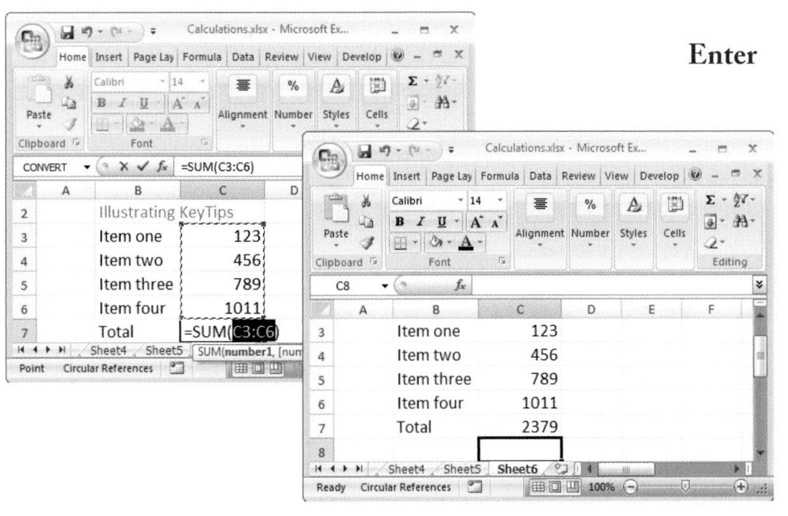

Enter

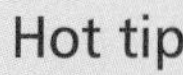

## Hot tip

You can insert the AutoSum function into the active cell using keystrokes only.

## Don't forget

For tasks that you perform often, the KeyTips option can become the quickest way to operate, as you become familiar with the keystrokes needed.

# Minimize the Ribbon

## Don't forget

Excel initially starts up with the Ribbon displayed, but you can minimize the Ribbon in several ways. To redisplay the Ribbon fully, repeat any of these actions.

1. Right-click the Command bar or the Quick Access bar and select Minimize the Ribbon, or double-click any of the command tabs on the Ribbon, or press keys Ctrl+F1

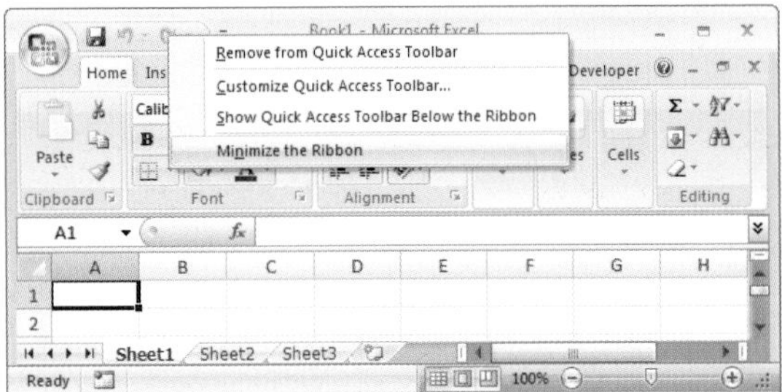


## Hot tip

When you close down Excel with the Ribbon minimized, it will still be minimized when Excel restarts. When the Ribbon is fully displayed at close down, it will be displayed on restart.

2. With the Ribbon minimized, single-click a tab to display the Ribbon temporarily, to select commands from that tab

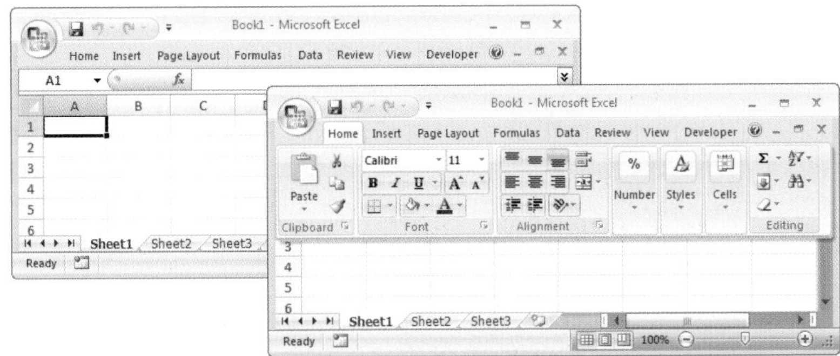


3. The Alt key and the KeyTips still operate, even when you have the Ribbon minimized

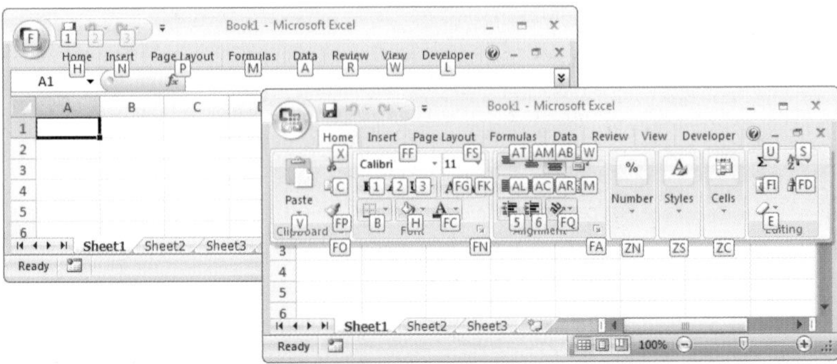

# Quick Access Toolbar

The Quick Access Toolbar contains a set of commands that are independent of the particular Command tab being displayed. There are initially three commands (Save, Undo and Redo) plus a Customize button, but you can add other commands. By default the Quick Access Toolbar is located next to the Office button, but you can move it below the Ribbon.

1. Right-click the Command tab bar, and select Show Quick Access Toolbar Below the Ribbon

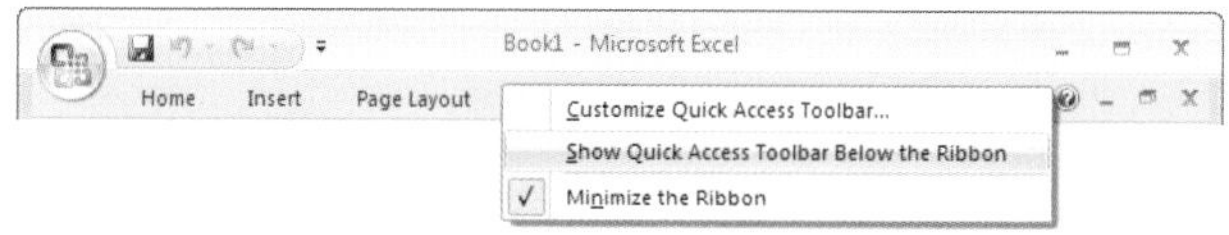


2. To restore the default, right-click the Command tab bar, and select Show Quick Access Toolbar Above the Ribbon

3. To add a command, click Customize Quick Access Toolbar

4. Choose a command from the list, or select More Commands

5. Choose a command category; select a command; click Add, and then OK

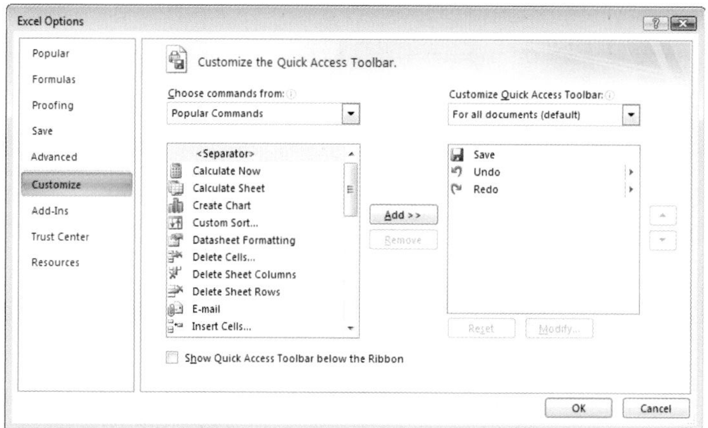


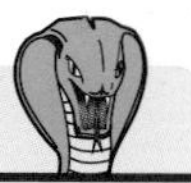

## Beware

If you position the Quick Access toolbar below the Ribbon and then minimize the Ribbon, you'll hide the Quick Access toolbar.

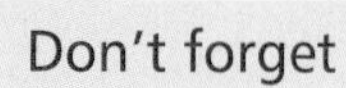

## Don't forget

You can also right-click any command on the Ribbon, and then select Add to Quick Access Toolbar from the menu.

# Mini Toolbar

The Mini toolbar appears when you select text, when editing the contents of a cell (and also when working with charts and text boxes). It offers quick access to the tools you need for text editing, such as font, size, style, alignment, color and bullets. To see the mini toolbar:

1. Choose a cell with text content, enter edit mode by pressing F2, and then select (highlight) part of the text

Don't forget

This is a rather transient feature in Excel, but may be rather more in evidence in the more text-oriented Word and PowerPoint applications.

2. The Mini toolbar appears very faintly, almost looking transparent

3. Move the mouse pointer towards the Mini toolbar, and the image strengthens

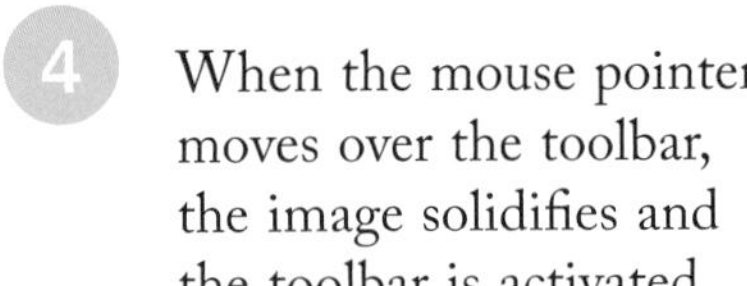

4. When the mouse pointer moves over the toolbar, the image solidifies and the toolbar is activated

5. Move the mouse pointer away from the toolbar, and the image fades out and may disappear

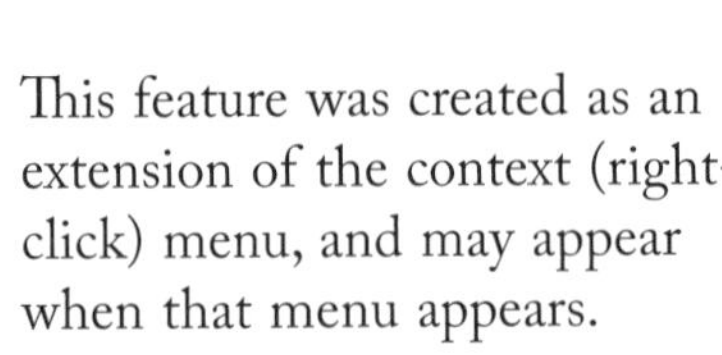

This feature was created as an extension of the context (right-click) menu, and may appear when that menu appears.

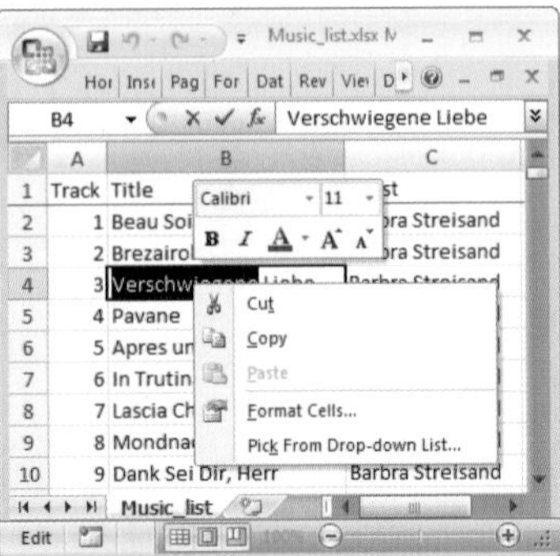


6. Right-click a selection of text, and observe the Mini toolbar above the context menu

# Print Worksheets

To preview printing for multiple worksheets:

1. Open the workbook, and click the tab for the first sheet

2. To select adjacent sheets, hold down the Shift key, and click the tab for the last sheet in the group

3. To add other non-adjacent sheets, hold down the Ctrl key and click the tabs for all of the other sheets required

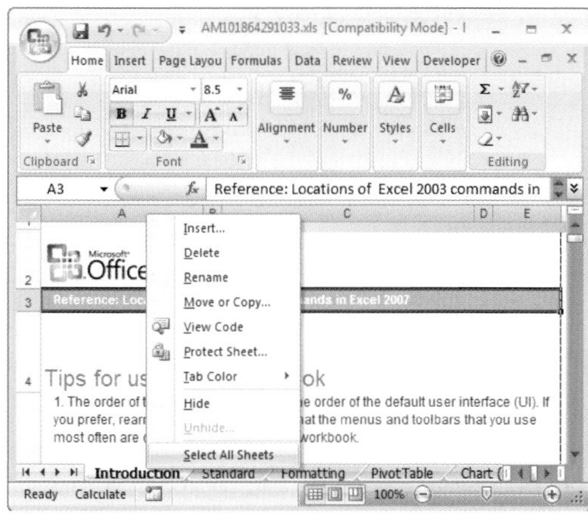


4. To select all the sheets, right-click any tab and click Select All Sheets

5. Click the Office button, click the arrow next to Print and select Print Preview (or press the keyboard shortcut Ctrl+F2)

   If you prefer to use KeyTips shortcuts, press Alt F W V

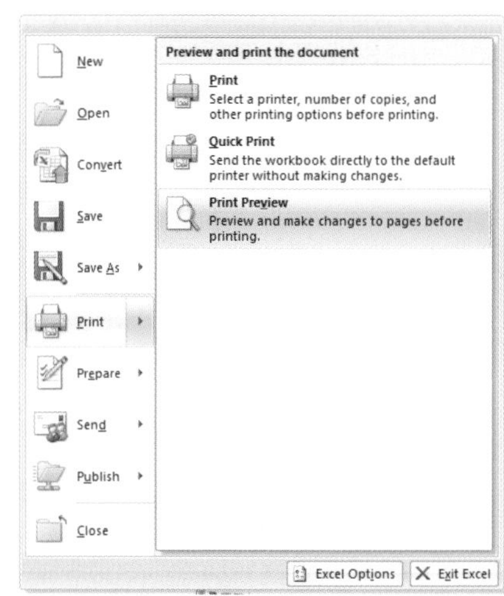


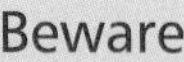

## Beware

If you change any cell while multiple sheets are selected, the change is automatically applied to all selected sheets.

## Don't forget

When multiple sheets are selected, the term [Group] appears on the Title bar.

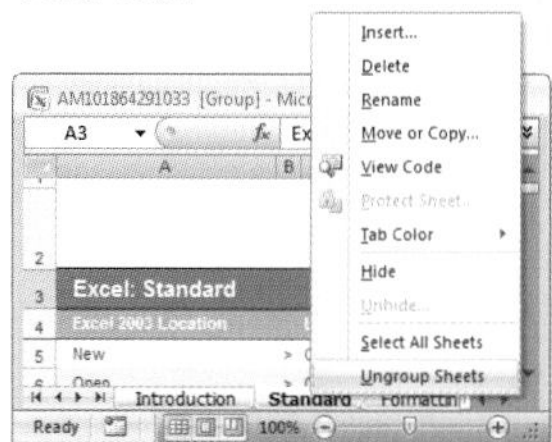


## Hot tip

To cancel the selection, click any unselected tab, or right-click any tab and click Ungroup Sheets.

## ...cont'd

The print previews for the selected sheets are displayed.

1. Click Next Page to go forward, or Previous Page to go backwards

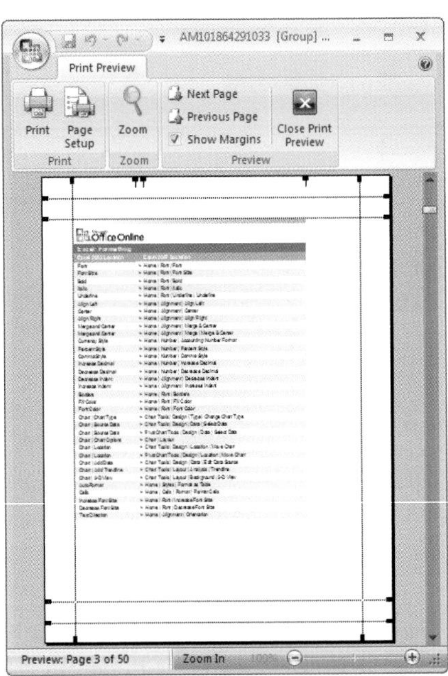


2. Click the box Show Margins to display the print margins

3. Click and drag the margins to adjust their positions

4. Click Page Setup to make changes to orientation, scaling and paper size

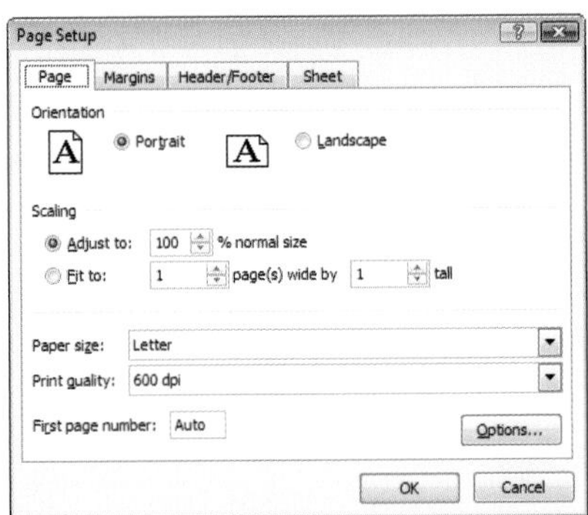


5. Click the tabs to change other print settings

6. Click Print on the Ribbon to start the actual printing

### Hot tip

If the Print Preview commands don't appear, right-click the Commands bar and click Minimize Ribbon.

Click Print on the Office button menu to go to Print without previewing.

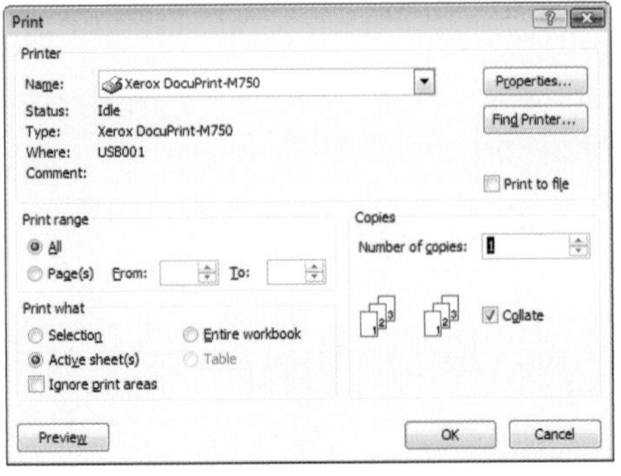

# 8 Charts

*Excel makes it easy to turn your worksheet data into a chart. You can apply formatting, change the type, reselect the data and add effects such as 3-D display. Special chart types allow you to display data for stocks and shares. You can print the completed charts, on their own or as part of the worksheet.*

# Create a Chart

The following information about share purchases and prices will be used for the purpose of illustrating the Excel charting features.

1. Total value of shares in portfolio at the start of each year (to be charted)

2. The individual prices of the shares on those dates (for calculations)

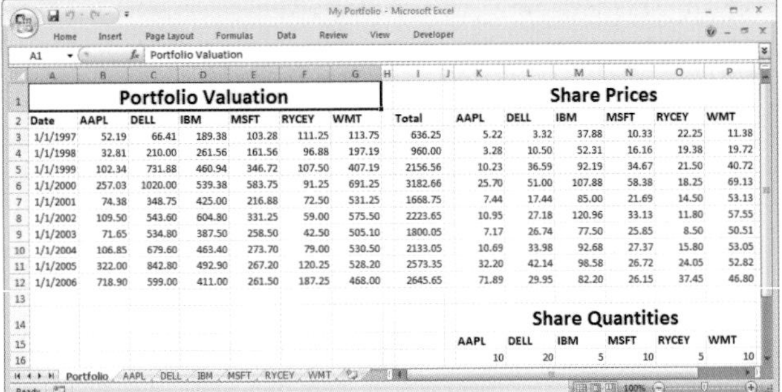

**Portfolio Valuation**

| Date | AAPL | DELL | IBM | MSFT | RYCEY | WMT | Total |
|---|---|---|---|---|---|---|---|
| 1/1/1997 | 52.19 | 66.41 | 189.38 | 103.28 | 111.25 | 113.75 | 636.25 |
| 1/1/1998 | 32.81 | 210.00 | 261.56 | 161.56 | 96.88 | 197.19 | 960.00 |
| 1/1/1999 | 102.34 | 731.88 | 460.94 | 346.72 | 107.50 | 407.19 | 2156.56 |
| 1/1/2000 | 257.03 | 1020.00 | 539.38 | 583.75 | 91.25 | 691.25 | 3182.66 |
| 1/1/2001 | 74.38 | 348.75 | 425.00 | 216.88 | 72.50 | 531.25 | 1668.75 |
| 1/1/2002 | 109.50 | 543.60 | 604.80 | 331.25 | 59.00 | 575.50 | 2223.65 |
| 1/1/2003 | 71.65 | 534.80 | 387.50 | 258.50 | 42.50 | 505.10 | 1800.05 |
| 1/1/2004 | 106.85 | 679.60 | 463.40 | 273.70 | 79.00 | 530.50 | 2133.05 |
| 1/1/2005 | 322.00 | 842.80 | 492.90 | 267.20 | 120.25 | 528.20 | 2573.35 |
| 1/1/2006 | 718.90 | 599.00 | 411.00 | 261.50 | 187.25 | 468.00 | 2645.65 |

**Share Prices**

| AAPL | DELL | IBM | MSFT | RYCEY | WMT |
|---|---|---|---|---|---|
| 5.22 | 3.32 | 37.88 | 10.33 | 22.25 | 11.38 |
| 3.28 | 10.50 | 52.31 | 16.16 | 19.38 | 19.72 |
| 10.23 | 36.59 | 92.19 | 34.67 | 21.50 | 40.72 |
| 25.70 | 51.00 | 107.88 | 58.38 | 18.25 | 69.13 |
| 7.44 | 17.44 | 85.00 | 21.69 | 14.50 | 53.13 |
| 10.95 | 27.18 | 120.96 | 33.13 | 11.80 | 57.55 |
| 7.17 | 26.74 | 77.50 | 25.85 | 8.50 | 50.51 |
| 10.69 | 33.98 | 92.68 | 27.37 | 15.80 | 53.05 |
| 32.20 | 42.14 | 98.58 | 26.72 | 24.05 | 52.82 |
| 71.89 | 29.95 | 82.20 | 26.15 | 37.45 | 46.80 |

**Share Quantities**

| AAPL | DELL | IBM | MSFT | RYCEY | WMT |
|---|---|---|---|---|---|
| 10 | 20 | 5 | 10 | 5 | 10 |

3. The total number of shares held (constants, for simplicity)

## Select the Data

Some chart types, such as pie and bubble charts, require a specific data arrangement. For most chart types, however, including line, column and bar charts, you can use the data as arranged in the rows or columns of the worksheet.

1. Select the cells that contain the data that you want to use for the chart (or select one cell, and Excel automatically selects all cells with data that directly surround that cell)

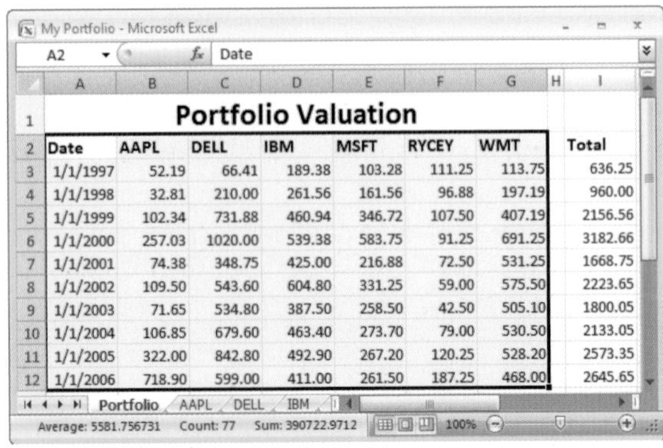

**Portfolio Valuation**

| Date | AAPL | DELL | IBM | MSFT | RYCEY | WMT | Total |
|---|---|---|---|---|---|---|---|
| 1/1/1997 | 52.19 | 66.41 | 189.38 | 103.28 | 111.25 | 113.75 | 636.25 |
| 1/1/1998 | 32.81 | 210.00 | 261.56 | 161.56 | 96.88 | 197.19 | 960.00 |
| 1/1/1999 | 102.34 | 731.88 | 460.94 | 346.72 | 107.50 | 407.19 | 2156.56 |
| 1/1/2000 | 257.03 | 1020.00 | 539.38 | 583.75 | 91.25 | 691.25 | 3182.66 |
| 1/1/2001 | 74.38 | 348.75 | 425.00 | 216.88 | 72.50 | 531.25 | 1668.75 |
| 1/1/2002 | 109.50 | 543.60 | 604.80 | 331.25 | 59.00 | 575.50 | 2223.65 |
| 1/1/2003 | 71.65 | 534.80 | 387.50 | 258.50 | 42.50 | 505.10 | 1800.05 |
| 1/1/2004 | 106.85 | 679.60 | 463.40 | 273.70 | 79.00 | 530.50 | 2133.05 |
| 1/1/2005 | 322.00 | 842.80 | 492.90 | 267.20 | 120.25 | 528.20 | 2573.35 |
| 1/1/2006 | 718.90 | 599.00 | 411.00 | 261.50 | 187.25 | 468.00 | 2645.65 |

Average: 5581.756731 Count: 77 Sum: 390722.9712

**Hot tip**

To create a chart that you can modify and format later, start by entering the data on a worksheet. Then select that data and choose the chart type that you want to use.

**Don't forget**

If the cells you want are not in a continuous range, you can select non-adjacent cells or ranges as long as the final selection forms a rectangle. You can also hide rows or columns that you don't need.

**Hot tip**

If you let Excel choose the data, make sure that there is a blank row and a blank column between the data you want to plot and other data on the worksheet.

2 Click the Insert tab and then select a chart type (for example Column) from the Charts group

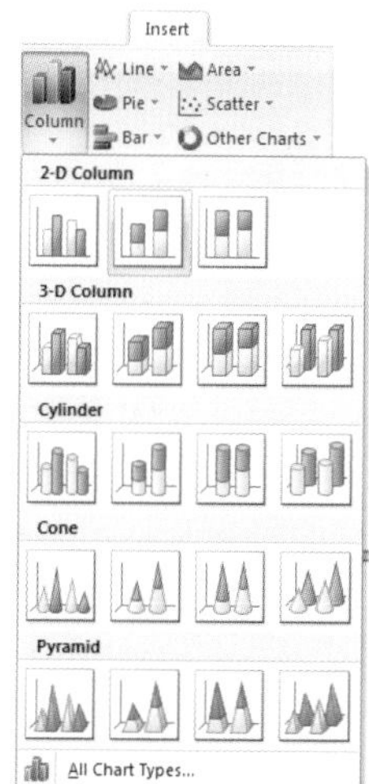


3 Choose the chart subtype, e.g. 2-D Stacked Column (to show how each share contributes to the total value)

4 The chart is superimposed over the data on the worksheet, and Chart Tools (Design, Layout and Format tabs) are added to the Ribbon

When you move the mouse pointer over one of the subtypes, you get a description and an indication of when that chart subtype might be useful.

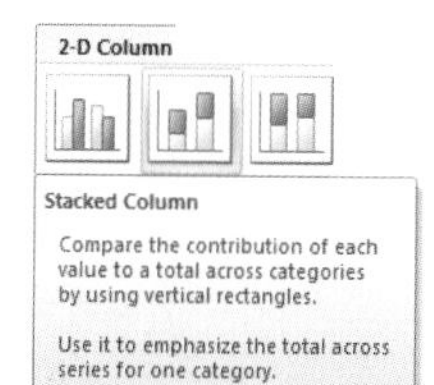


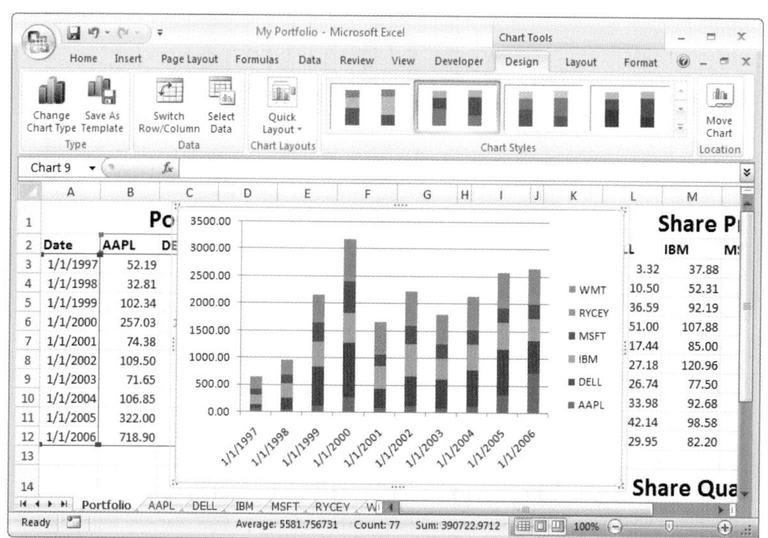


5 Click Move Chart, in the Location group on the Design tab, to choose where you want the chart to be placed, for example on a separate chart sheet

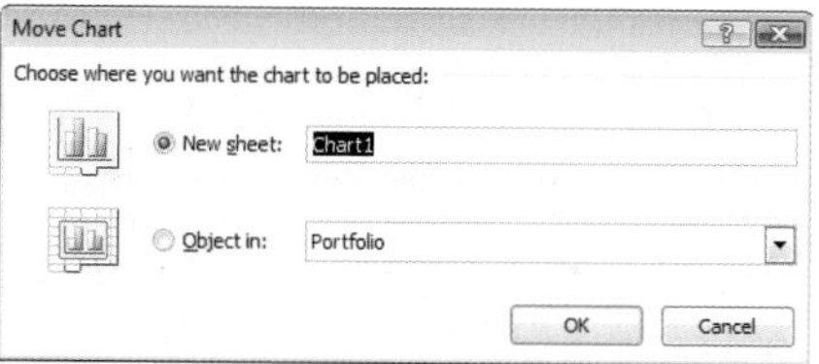

You can also move the chart on the worksheet, by clicking the border and dragging the chart to another part of the worksheet.

# Default Chart Type

To create a chart based on the default chart type, select the data that you want to use, and then press either ALT+F1 or F11.

1. When you press ALT+F1, the chart is embedded in the current worksheet (as shown on page 125)

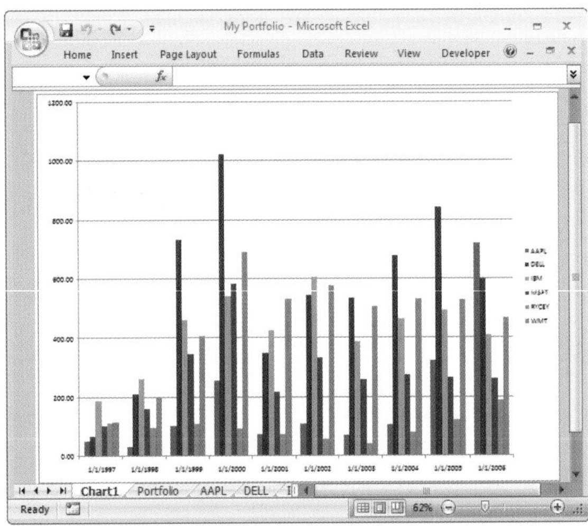


2. When you press F11, the chart is displayed on a separate chart sheet named Chart1 (or Chart2, etc)

You can set any chart type as the default:

1. Click the arrow next to the Charts group name (or click any chart button and select All Chart Types)

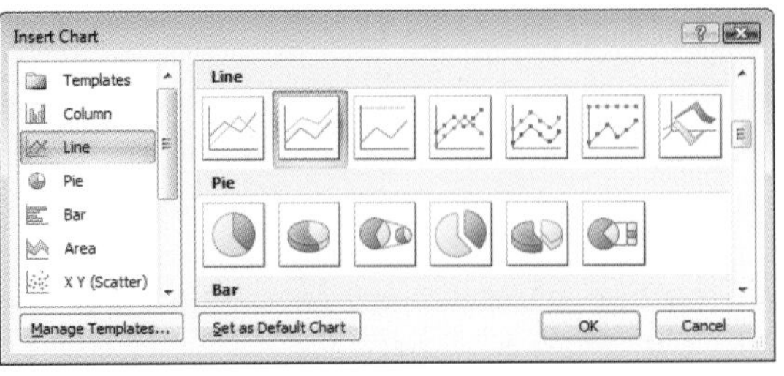


2. On the Insert Chart dialog, choose the chart type and subtype and click Set as Default Chart and then OK (or Cancel)

Hot tip

The default chart type is 2-D Clustered Column, which compares values across categories using vertical rectangles.

The 2-D Stacked Line chart shows the trend in the contribution from each of the categories.

# Change Chart Layout

1 Click the Chart Tools Layout tab to modify the chart

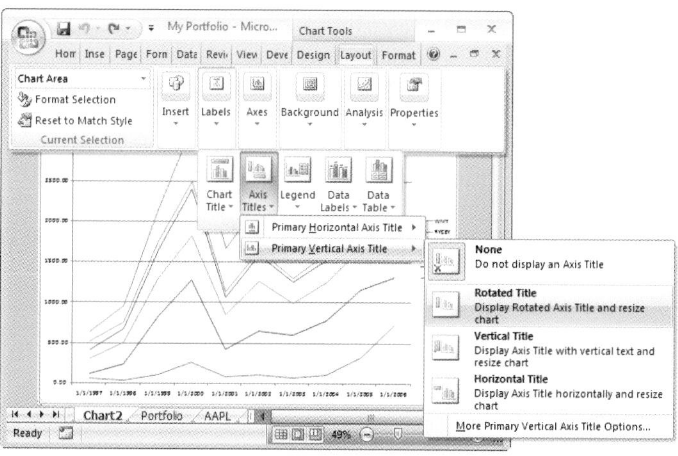


2 Click Labels, Axis Titles, Primary Vertical Axis Title; choose the position, and the words Axis Title are inserted

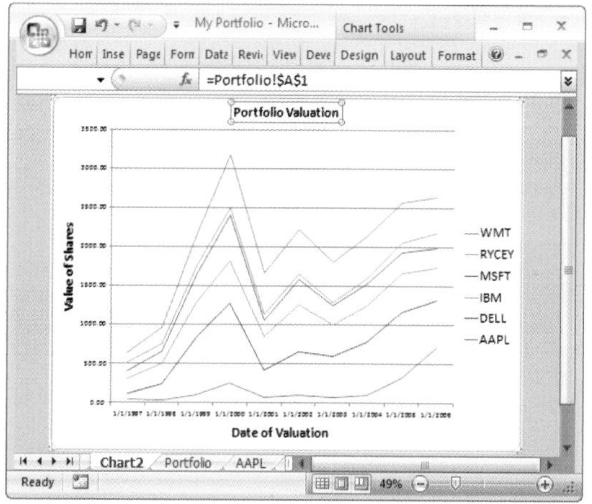


3 Edit the title. Then add the Horizontal Axis Title and the Chart Title, and edit these also

4 Right-click any of the text to change the font size or style on the Mini toolbar

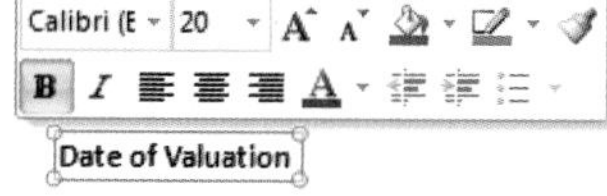


## Hot tip

Instead of typing the titles directly, link to a cell on the worksheet. Click in the title, type = on the Formula bar, select the cell with the text and then press Enter.

# Legend and Data Table

Hot tip

The Legend provides the key to the entries on the chart, in this case the stock symbols for all of the shares.

You can also display data labels, to show the data values at each point on the lines.

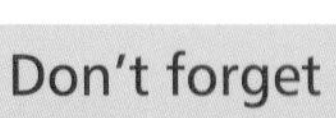

You can display the data for the chart in a table, and include legend keys as well (in which case, the legend itself can be turned off).

1. From the Layout tab, click Labels, Legend and choose the position and alignment on the chart

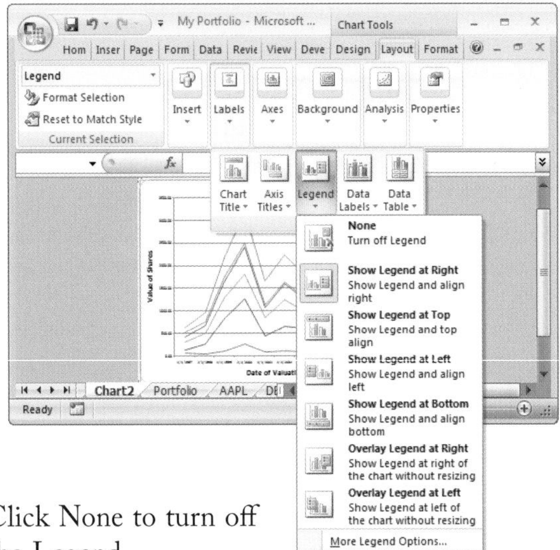


2. Click None to turn off the Legend

3. Click Data Table in the Labels group and choose where to position the table, and whether to display the key

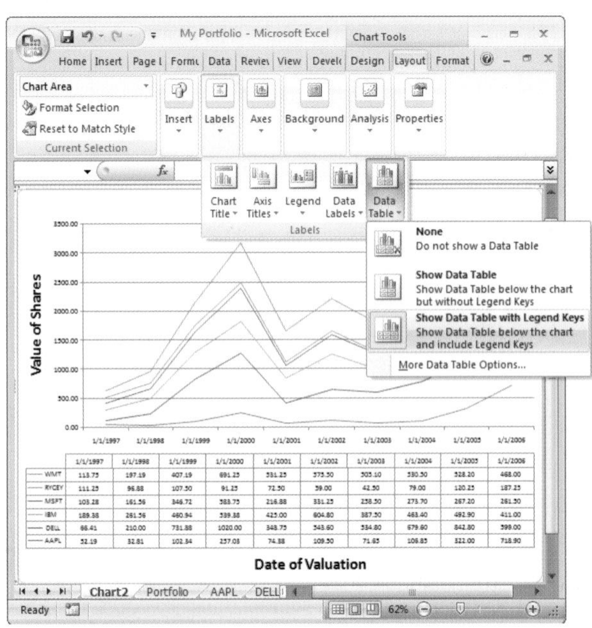

# Change Chart Type

1. Click the chart area to display Chart Tools

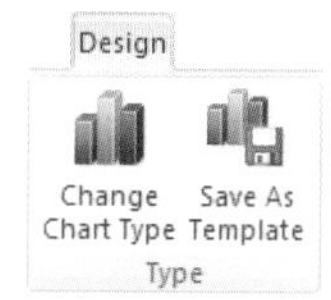


2. Select the Design tab and click Change Chart Type from the Type group

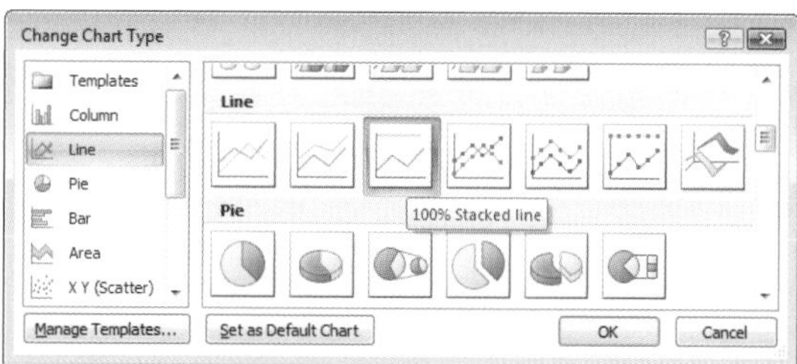


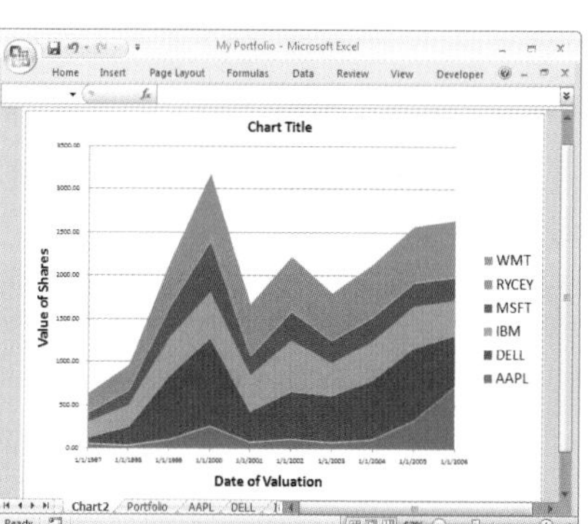


3. In the Change Chart Type dialog, select the chart type and subtype (for example, chart type Area and subtype Stacked Area) and click OK

4. Another way to compare the relative contributions of the shares is to use type Area and subtype 100% Stacked Area

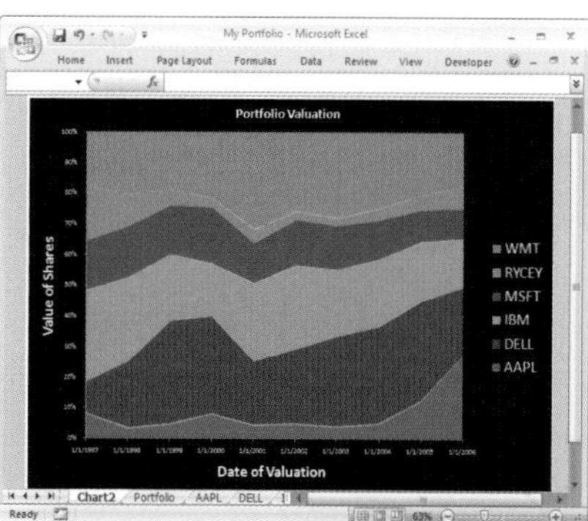


5. A new chart style has been selected from the Shape Styles group on the Format tab

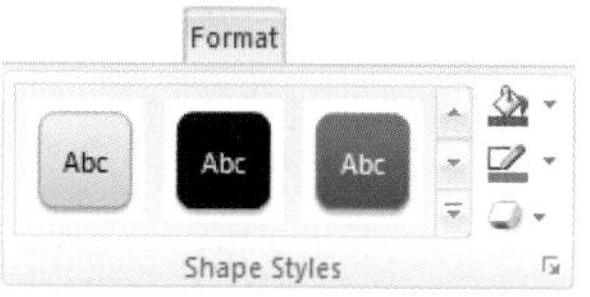


## Hot tip

As with the Insert Chart dialog, you can make your chosen chart type and subtype the default.

## Beware

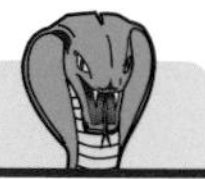

When you change the chart style, you may need to reapply other changes such as text font sizes.

# Pie Chart

Hot tip

The usual way to compare contributions of individual items to the total is with the Pie Chart. This is intended for a single set of data, for example one year's share values.

1. Select the data labels and one set of data, in an adjacent row (or hold down Ctrl to select non-adjacent cells)

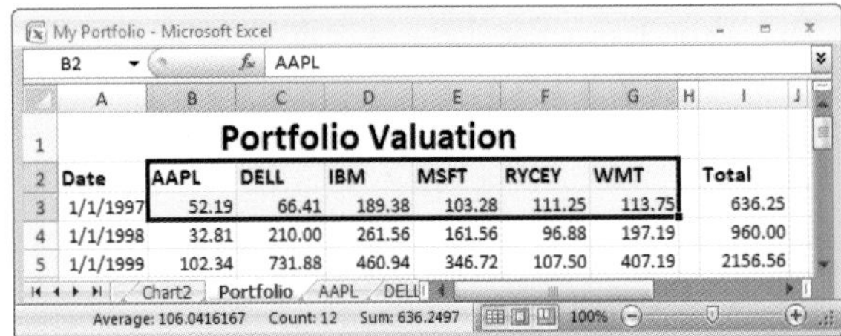


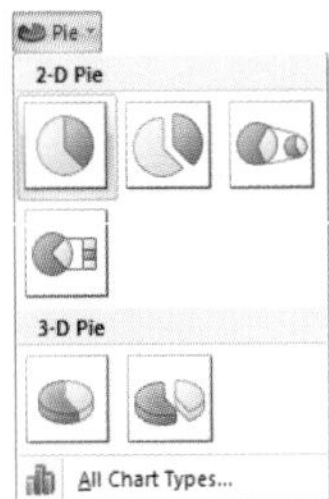


2. Click the Insert tab, select Pie from the Charts group, and choose the chart type, for example the standard 2-D Pie Chart

Don't forget

The layouts provide several ways to handle the data labels, legend and data table.

3. Click the Design tab and select Move Chart to create a chart sheet

4. Select Quick Layout in the Chart Layouts group, and choose the layout you prefer

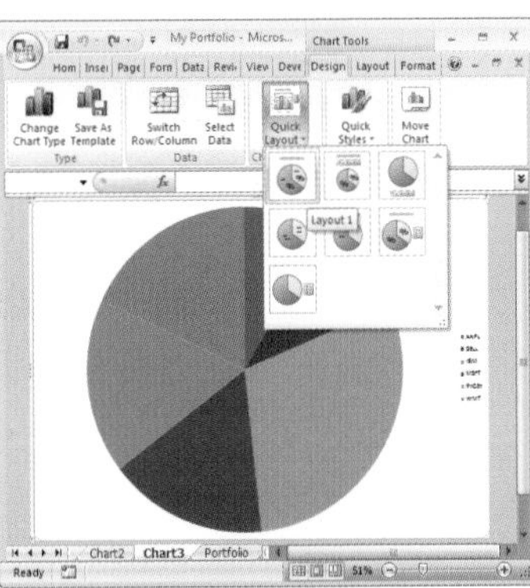


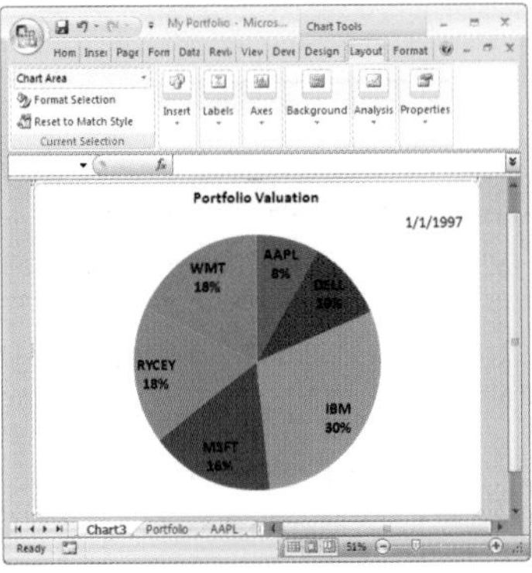


5. This layout shows the data labels and the relative percentage contributions to the total value, shown on the pie chart segments rather than using a separate legend box

You can change the data series selected for the pie chart.

1. Select the Chart Tools Design tab and then click Select Data, in the Data group

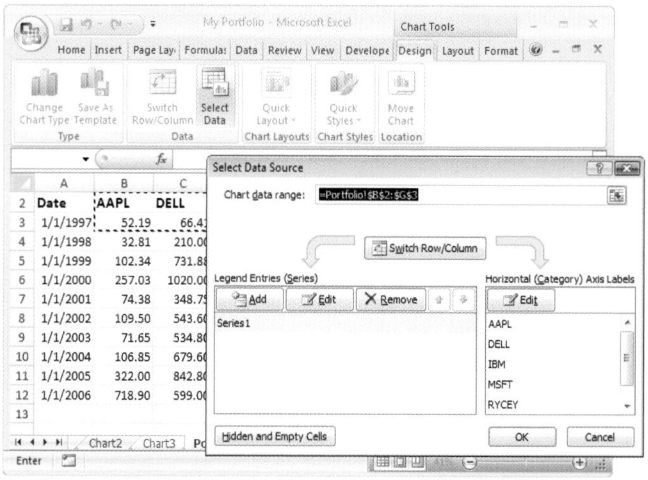

You can also right-click the chart and choose Select Data to modify the data source settings.

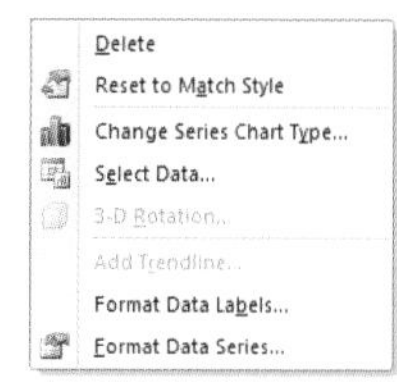


2. Click the data selection (usually Series1) and click the Edit button

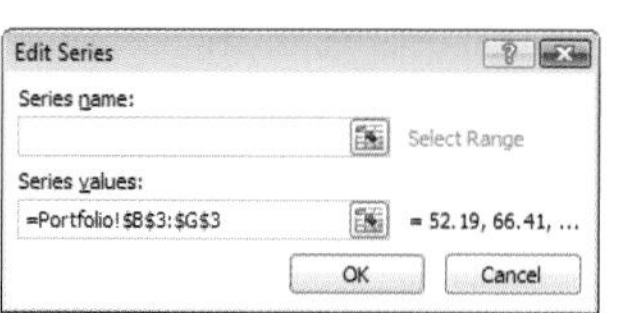


3. Click the Collapse button and select a new range of data such as the 2006 values; then click the Expand button

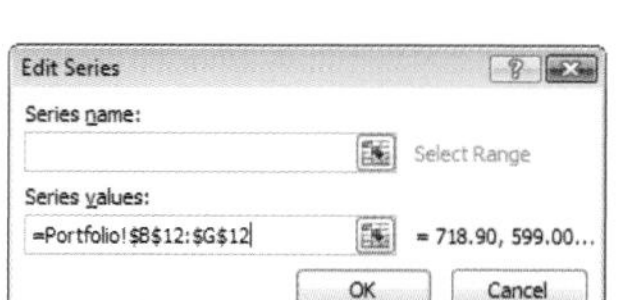

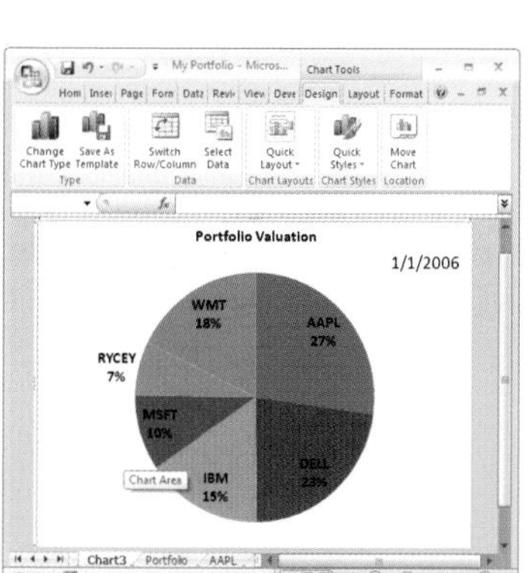


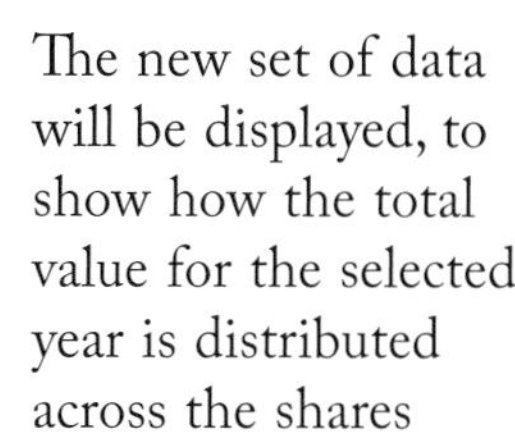

4. The new set of data will be displayed, to show how the total value for the selected year is distributed across the shares

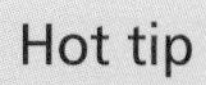

Note how Excel decides where to put the data label, moving it outside the segment if the text won't fit into the space available.

# 3-D Pie Chart

Some of the subtypes for the pie chart offer a 3-D view.

1. Select the Chart Tools Design tab, click Change Chart Type, select Pie, Exploded Pie in 3-D, and click OK

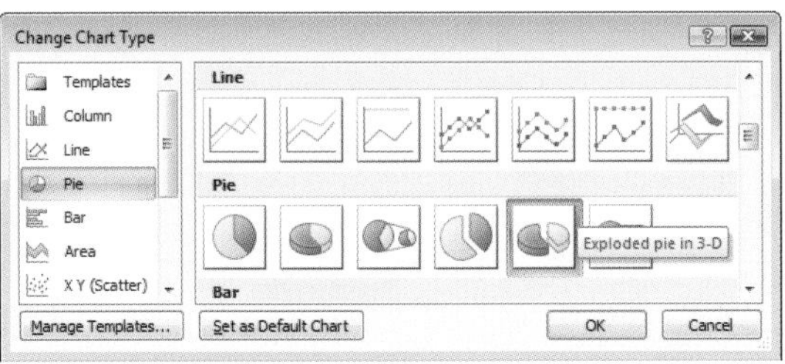


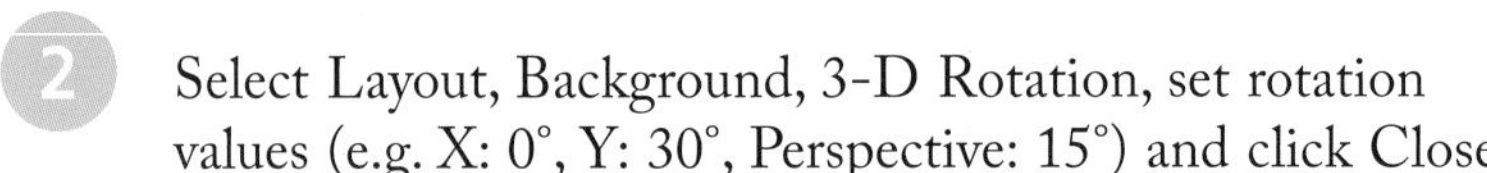

**Don't forget**

In a 3-D pie chart, it is the chart segments that are displayed in 3-D format, rather than the data itself (hence the grayed Z component).

2. Select Layout, Background, 3-D Rotation, set rotation values (e.g. X: 0°, Y: 30°, Perspective: 15°) and click Close

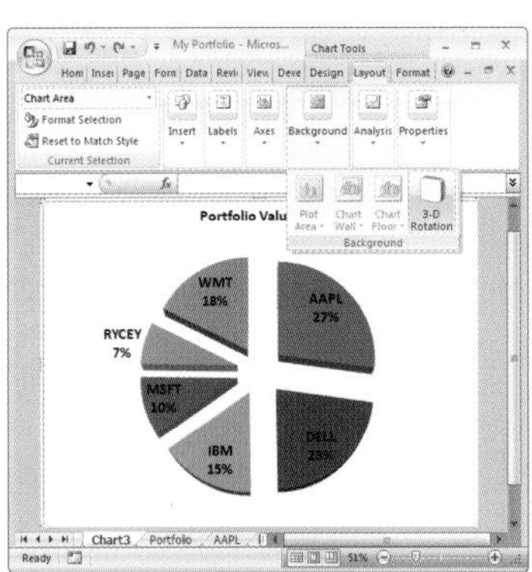


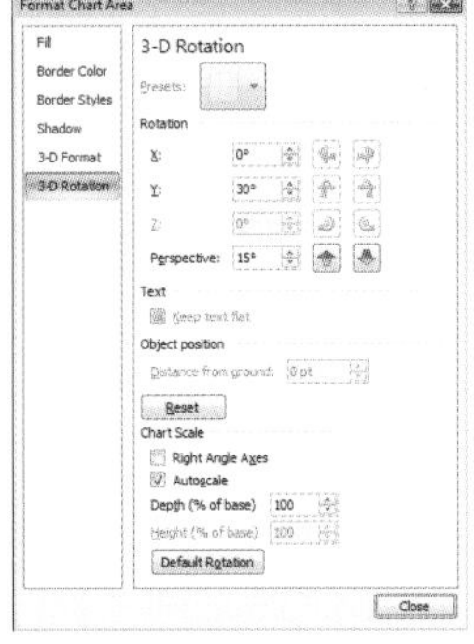


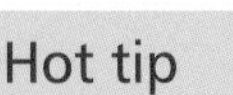

**Hot tip**

Experiment with the rotation and format options to find the most effective presentation form for your data.

3. The information is presented in 3-D display form. You can select Chart Tools Format to adjust the appearance, for example if you wish to add a background color

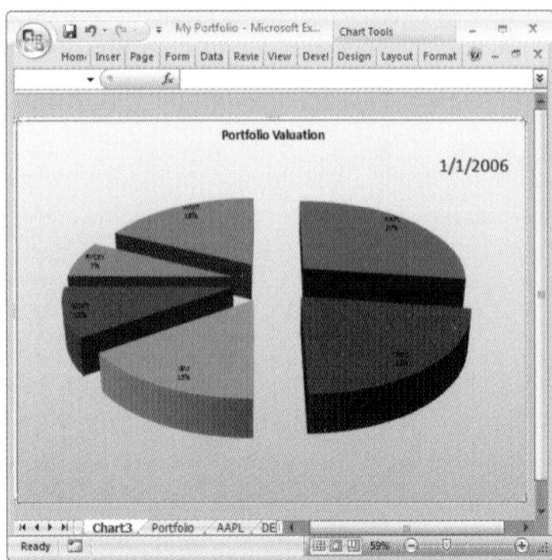

# 3-D Column Chart

A true 3-D chart has three sets of values to plot, giving three axes. In the example data, these would be Shares, Values and Dates.

1 Select the data, click Insert, Charts, Column and select the 3-D Column chart type

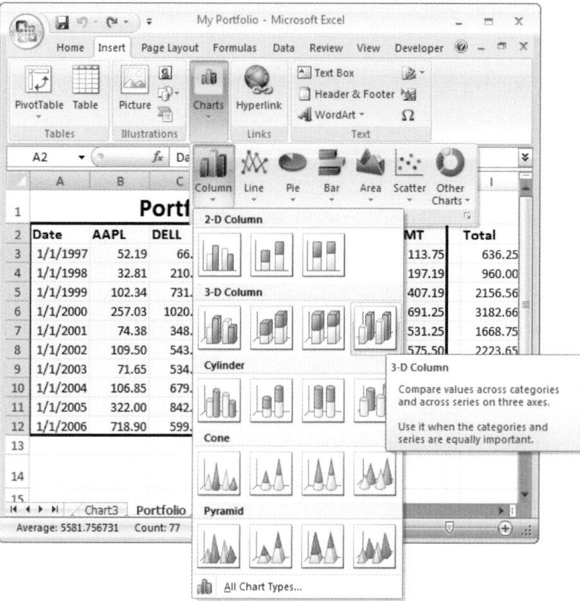


2 Select Chart Tools Design, Layout and Format to make desired adjustments to the appearance

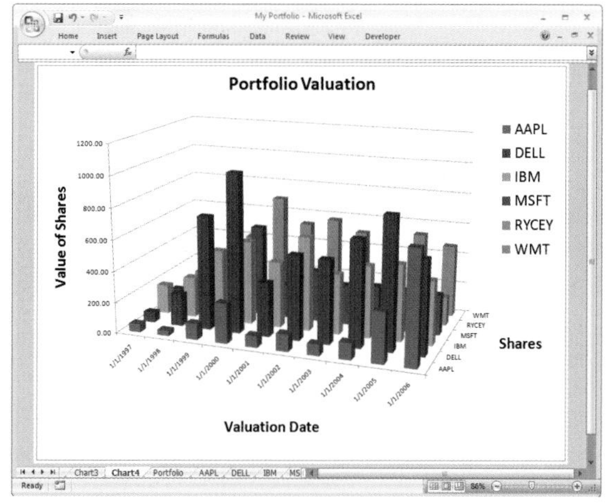

## Hot tip

The 3-D Area chart also presents data using three axes, to give a true 3-D representation.

## Don't forget

Click Chart Tools, Design, Select Data and click the Switch Row/Column button to exchange the horizontal and depth axes, to give a different view of the data.

# Share Data

The share prices in the portfolio worksheet were taken from price history tables downloaded from the MSN Money website.

The price history table at MSN Money provides information in reverse date sequence, on a weekly or daily basis depending on the length of period chosen.

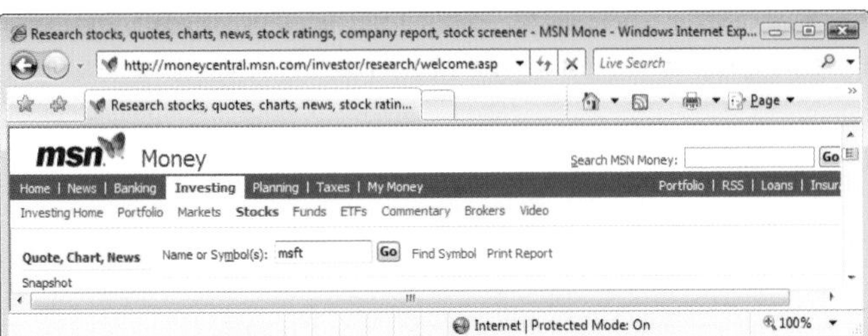


The table provides a comma-separated file, with date, prices (open, high, low and close) and volume of transfers for a specific share.

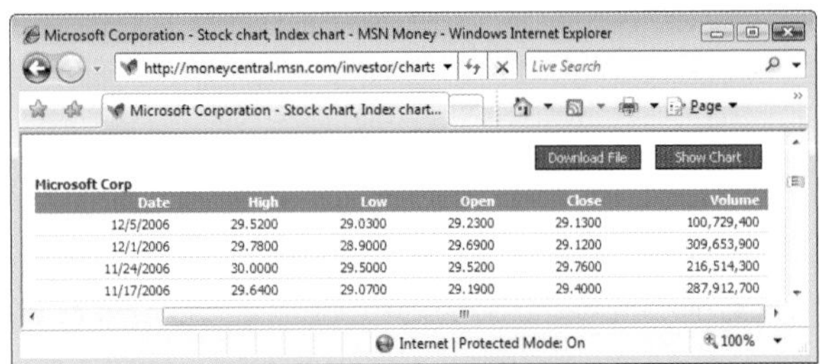


| Date | High | Low | Open | Close | Volume |
|---|---|---|---|---|---|
| 12/5/2006 | 29.5200 | 29.0300 | 29.2300 | 29.1300 | 100,729,400 |
| 12/1/2006 | 29.7800 | 28.9000 | 29.6900 | 29.1200 | 309,653,900 |
| 11/24/2006 | 30.0000 | 29.5000 | 29.5200 | 29.7600 | 216,514,300 |
| 11/17/2006 | 29.6400 | 29.0700 | 29.1900 | 29.4000 | 287,912,700 |

See page 72 for details of converting a range into an Excel table.

For the portfolio workbook, the information for each share was sorted into date order and converted into an Excel lookup table.

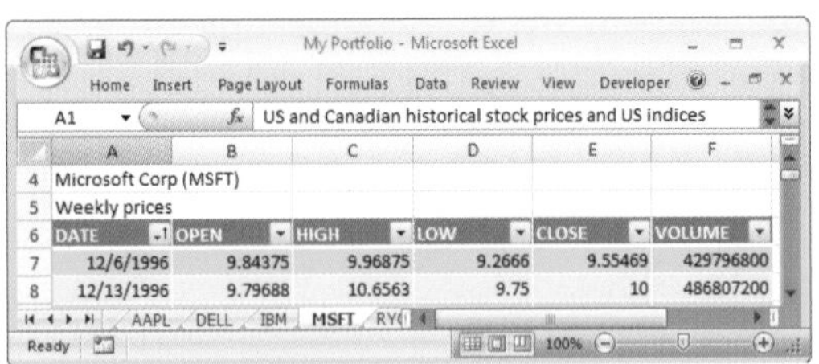


| | A | B | C | D | E | F |
|---|---|---|---|---|---|---|
| 6 | DATE | OPEN | HIGH | LOW | CLOSE | VOLUME |
| 7 | 12/6/1996 | 9.84375 | 9.96875 | 9.2666 | 9.55469 | 429796800 |
| 8 | 12/13/1996 | 9.79688 | 10.6563 | 9.75 | 10 | 486807200 |

The table is used to find the price of the share on a given day.

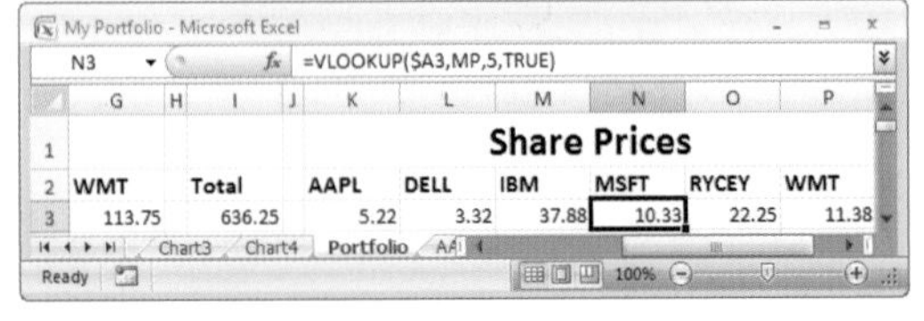


| | G | I | K | L | M | N | O | P |
|---|---|---|---|---|---|---|---|---|
| 2 | WMT | Total | AAPL | DELL | IBM | MSFT | RYCEY | WMT |
| 3 | 113.75 | 636.25 | 5.22 | 3.32 | 37.88 | 10.33 | 22.25 | 11.38 |

# Line Chart

The charts so far have used just a few dates from the tables. The complete tables, however, provide a continuous view of the data.

1. The Historical worksheet contains the date column and the closing price column for each of the shares

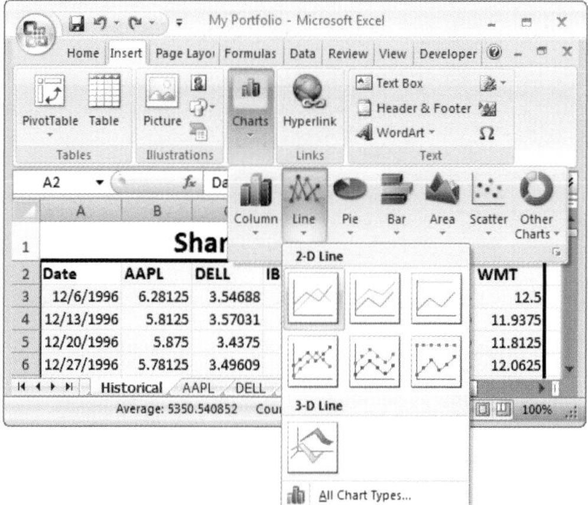


2. Select the data, click Insert, Chart and Line, and choose the 2-D Line chart subtype to get a plot for each share

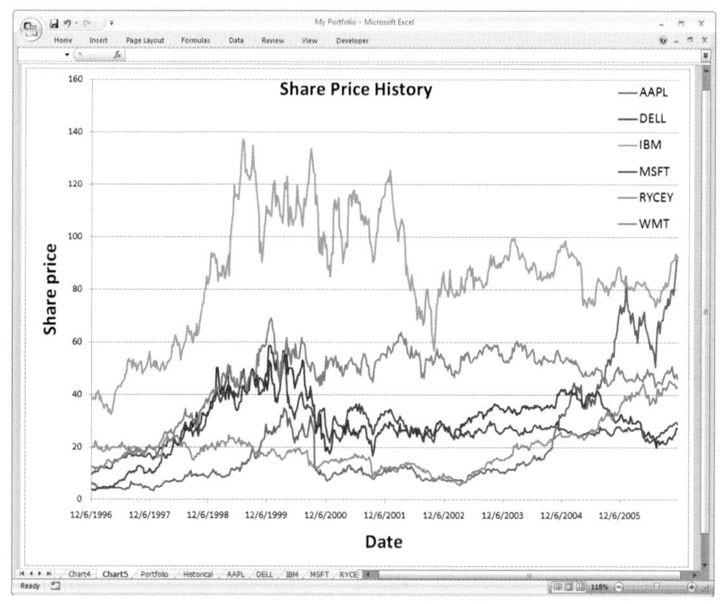


Hot tip

You can choose line, stacked line, or 100% stacked line (with or without markers). There's also a 3-D line, but this is just a perspective view, not three axes of data.

Don't forget

As with all the charts, you can move this chart to a separate chart sheet, and adjust position and styles for the titles and the legend.

# Stock Chart

The downloaded share data can also be used for a special type of chart known as the Stock Chart.

1. From the share table, filter the data (e.g. for 2002) and then select the columns for Date, High, Low and Close

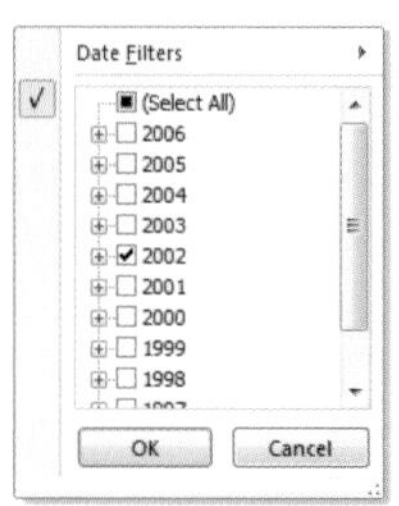


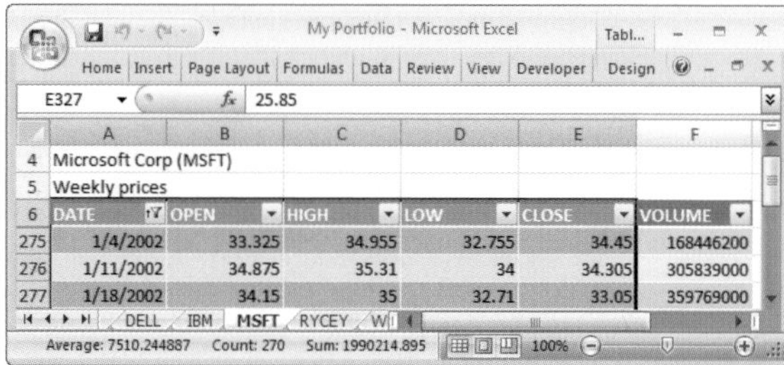

## Beware

This chart type requires data in a specific layout for the chart subtype, e.g.
High Low Close
Open High Low Close
(and the date values can be used as data labels).

2. Open the Insert Chart dialog (see page 126), select the Stock chart, select type Open-High-Low-Close, and then click OK

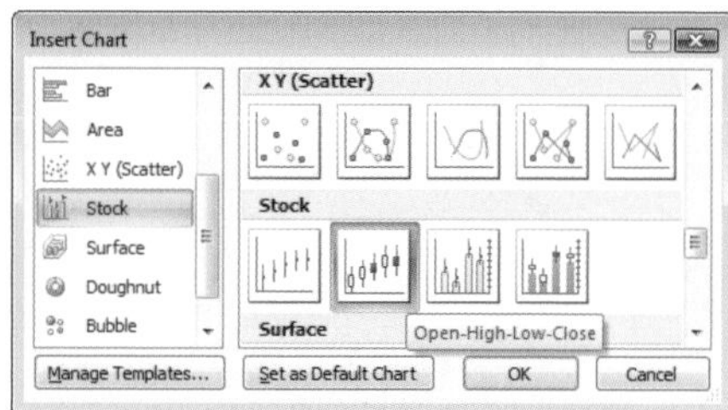


## Hot tip

Move the chart to a separate chart sheet, add titles and format the titles and the legend. Right-click the axis and select Format Axis to change the minimum and maximum to emphasize the price spreads.

3. The prices are plotted, with lines for high/low, hollow boxes for increases and solid boxes for decreases

# Mixed Types

You can have more than one type of chart displayed at the same time, as in the Volume subtypes of stock chart.

1. Insert a worksheet column after the Date column, and move the Volume column to that position

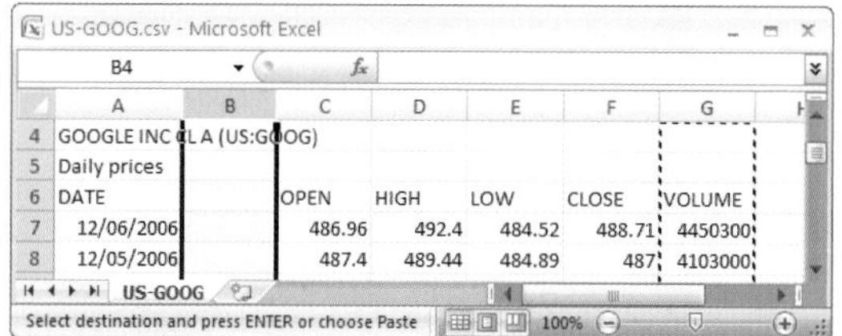


2. Select the data, including the headings, and Insert the Stock chart, choosing type Volume-Open-High-Low-Close

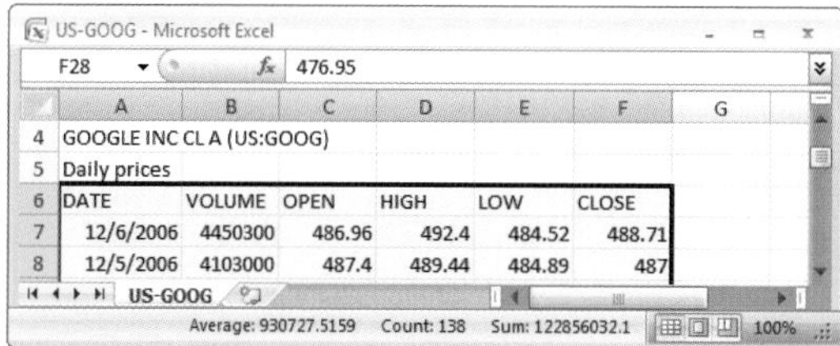


3. Two vertical axes are used, to show volumes and prices

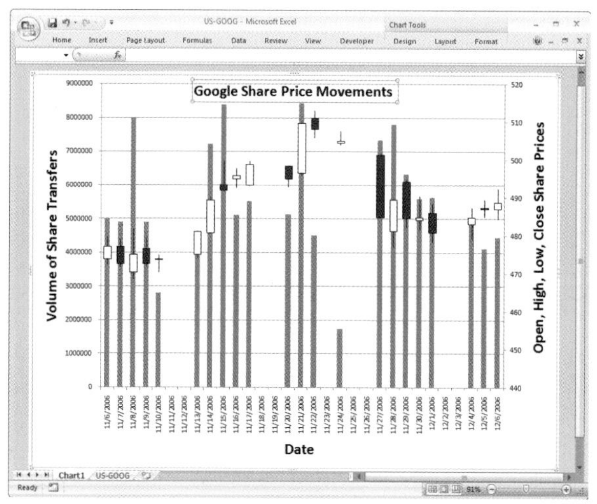


## Hot tip

You need to rearrange the data downloaded from MSN Money to create the volume stock charts, since volumes must be listed before prices.

## Don't forget

In this example, the two types of chart use the same horizontal values (dates). When necessary, however, Excel will specify a secondary horizontal axis.

# Print Charts

Beware

The chart may obscure part of the data. Switch to Page Break Preview and drag the chart to reposition it before printing the worksheet.

When you have an embedded chart in your worksheet, it will be printed, as positioned, along with the data when you select Print from the Office button.

To print the chart on its own:

1. Select the chart; then select Print from the Office button

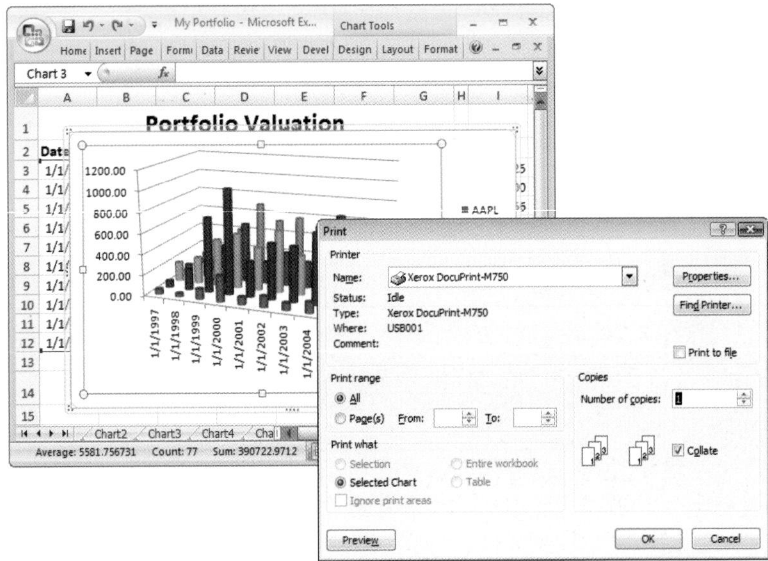

Hot tip

When the chart is in a separate chart sheet, you can print it on its own or as part of the workbook, just as you print a worksheet.

2. An extra "Print what" option (Selected Chart) appears and the other options are grayed, so only the chart will print

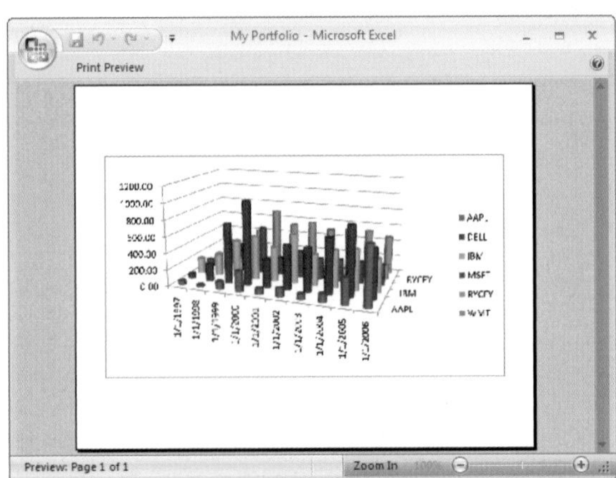

# 9 Macros in Excel

*If there are tasks that you carry out frequently, you can define the actions required as a macro. You can assign the macro to a key combination or to an icon on the toolbar to make it easy to reuse. However, you must make sure that security is in place to prevent abuse.*

# Macros

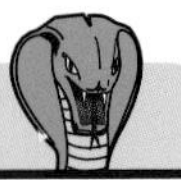

Beware

Because macros have such a wide range of capabilities, they can be subject to misuse. Microsoft has included security checks and limitations in Excel, to authenticate macros and help prevent them being introduced into your system and run without your knowledge.

Don't forget

To check which type of workbook you have open, tell Windows to reveal the file type (see page 37).



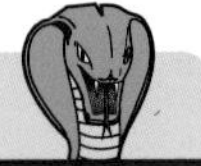

Beware

"Enable all macros" is not recommended as a permanent setting. Select a more restricted level as soon as you have finished creating or changing the macros stored in your active workbook.

Any task in Excel may be performed by a macro. Often, macros are used to carry out simple but repetitive tasks, such as entering your name and address, or inserting a standard piece of text. In other cases, macros may be used for complex and involved tasks, difficult to reproduce accurately without some kind of help.

To create a macro, you simply carry out an example of the actions, with Excel recording the keystrokes involved as you complete the task. The sequence is then stored as a macro, using the Visual Basic for Applications programming language. You can edit your recorded macros or create macros from scratch using the Visual Basic Editor.

Macros can be very powerful because they are able to run commands on your computer. For this reason, Microsoft Excel prevents the default Excel 2007 file format (file type .xlsx) from storing VBA macro code.

Therefore, the recommended place for storing the macros you create is in your hidden Personal Macro Workbook, and this is the method used for the examples in the following pages.

If you share macros, they need to be stored in the workbooks that use them. These workbooks must then be saved in the Excel 2007 macro-enabled file format (file type .xlsm). In such cases, you may need to reset the security level temporarily to enable all macros, so that you can work on macros in the active workbook:

1. Select the Developer tab (see page 141), click Macro Security, select "Enable all macros" and then click OK

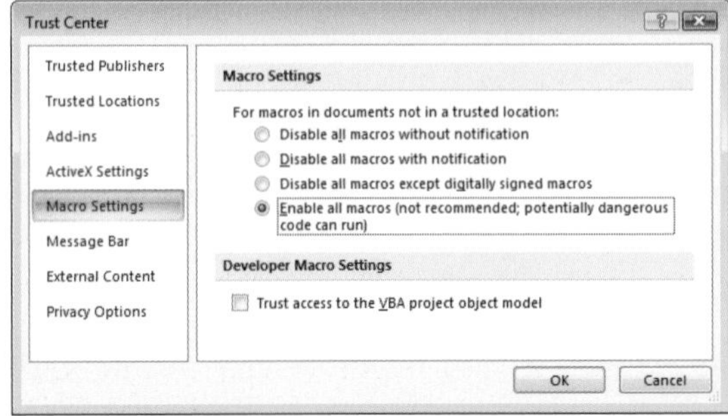

# Create Macros

To display the commands for recording and viewing macros:

1. Select the View tab and click the arrow below the Macros button in the Macros group

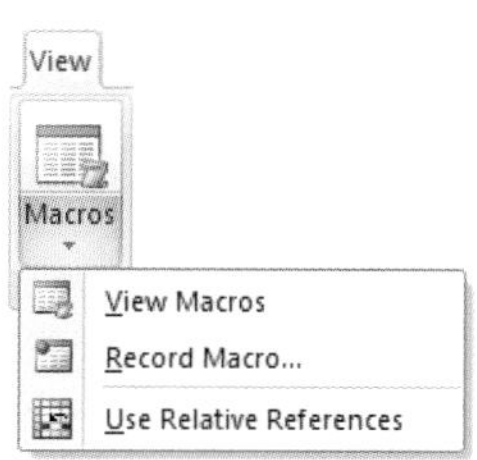


2. You can choose to view or record macros, and there's also a toggle to choose between relative or absolute cell references

These options are also available from the Developer tab along with the Macro Security and Visual Basic commands. By default, this tab is not displayed. To add the tab to the Ribbon:

1. Click the Office button, and then click the Excel Options button (or press the keys Alt F I)

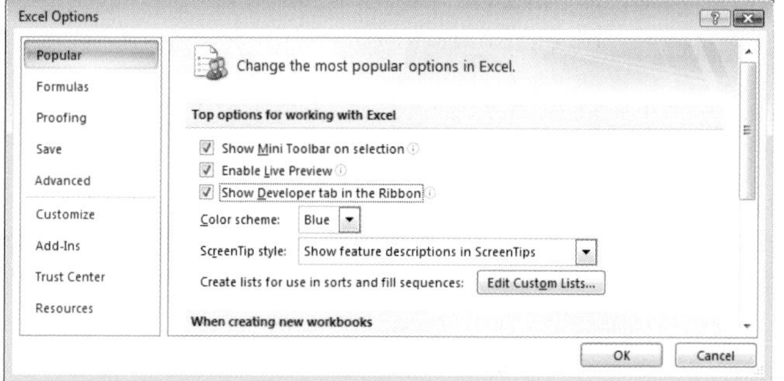


2. Select the Popular category, then click the box labeled Show Developer tab in the Ribbon, and then click OK

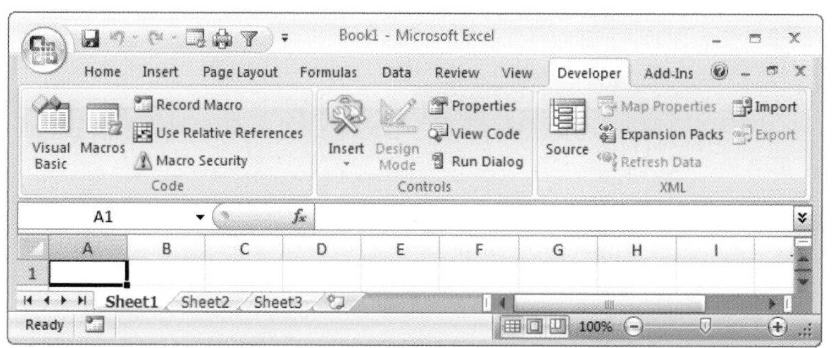


## Don't forget

Selecting the Macros button rather than the arrow has the same effect as selecting the View Macros entry.

## Hot tip

You can record, view and edit macros using commands from either the View tab or the Developer tab, but to create macros from scratch, or to change security settings, you will need to use the Developer tab.

# Record a Macro

Assume that you need to add some standard disclaimer text to a number of workbooks. To create a macro for this:

1. Open a blank workbook and click in cell A1

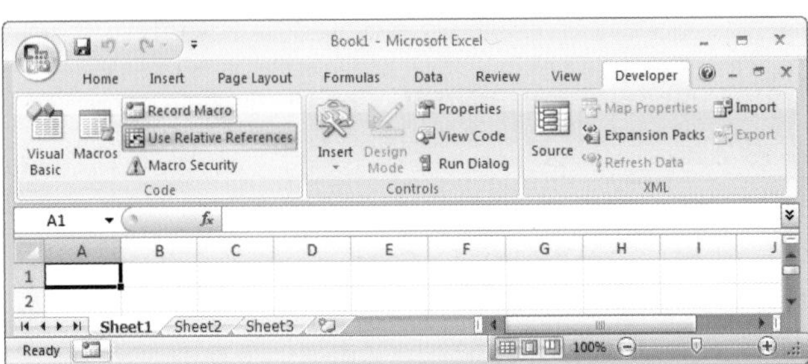


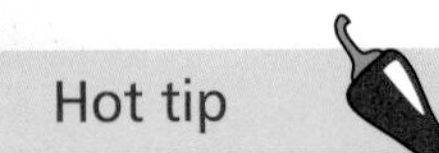


You can click the Record Macro button to the left of the status bar to start and stop macro recording.

2. Select the Developer tab; then from the Code group, click Use Relative References and click Record Macro

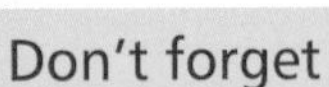

The first character of the macro name must be a letter, followed by letters, numbers or underscores. Spaces are not allowed.

3. Enter a name for the macro, and specify a shortcut key such as Shift+D (the Ctrl key is automatically added)

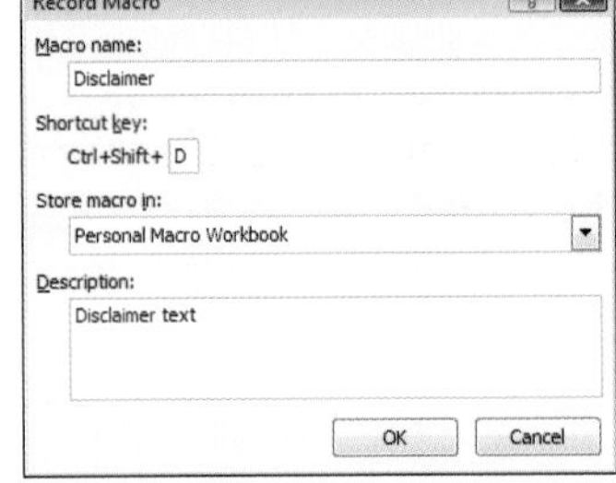


4. Select Personal Macro Workbook (the preferred location for storing macros), add a description if desired, and then click OK to start the recording

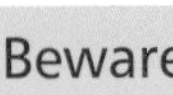

Excel shortcuts already use most Ctrl+lowercase letter key combinations, so it is better to use capitals for macro shortcuts.

5. Perform the actions that you want to record; then select the Developer tab, Code group and click Stop Recording

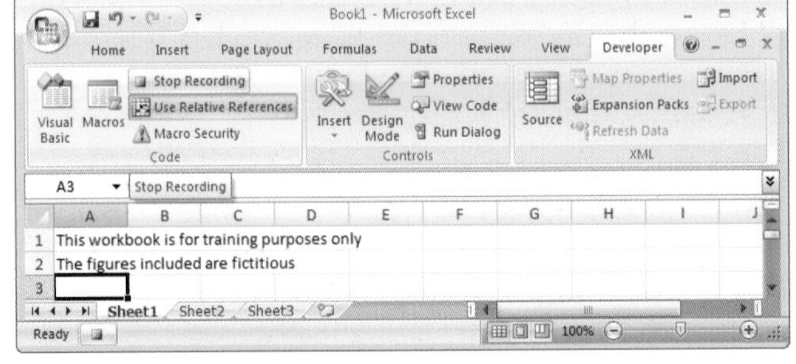

To check out the macro:

6. Click in a different cell, C5 for example, and press Shift+Ctrl+D to try out the macro

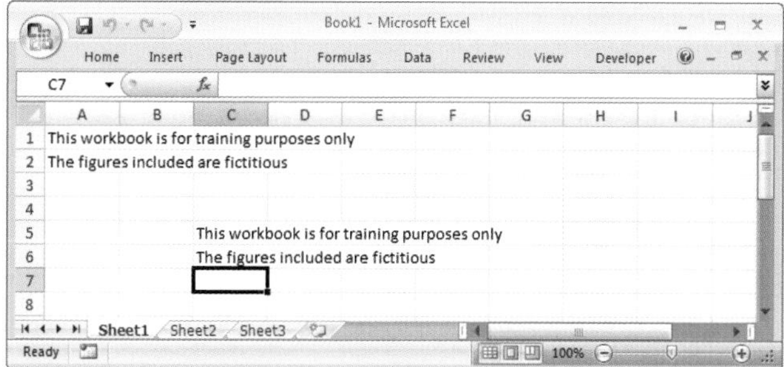


7. The text will be entered into the worksheet, starting from the active cell

The start location changes, because the macro was created with relative references. However, if you click in any specific cells while the macro is being recorded, those references will be honored.

When you have finished checking the macro, you can close the workbook. If you chose to store the macro in the Personal Macro Workbook:

1. Click the Office button and select Close

2. Select No when asked if you want to save changes

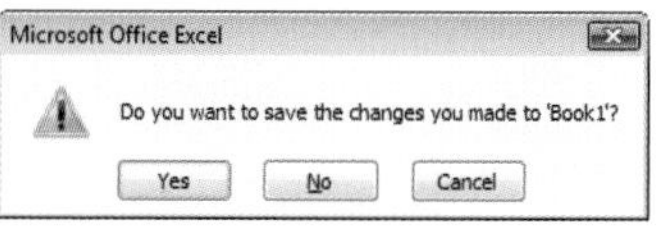


The macro itself will be retained in the Personal Macro Workbook. This will be saved at the end of the Excel session (see page 144).

## Active Workbooks Macros

If you selected to store the recorded macro in the active workbook, you must save that workbook as file type .xlsm. You will also need to reset the level of macro security (see page 140). When you close the active workbook, the macros it contains will no longer be available in that Excel session.

### Don't forget

If there are problems with the macro, you may be able to use the Visual Basic Editor to make the changes that are needed (see page 148).

### Beware

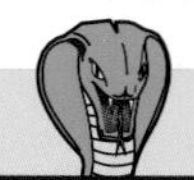

The relative reference applies to the macro as the cell was selected before the macro recording was started.

# Apply the Macro

Don't forget

The macro remains available throughout the Excel session if you stored it in the Personal Macro Workbook, and you can apply it to any Excel workbook (.xlsm, .xlsx, or .xls types). Once saved, it will be available in future sessions.

1. Open a workbook that requires the disclaimer text, and select the location (e.g. My Personal Budget, cell A16)

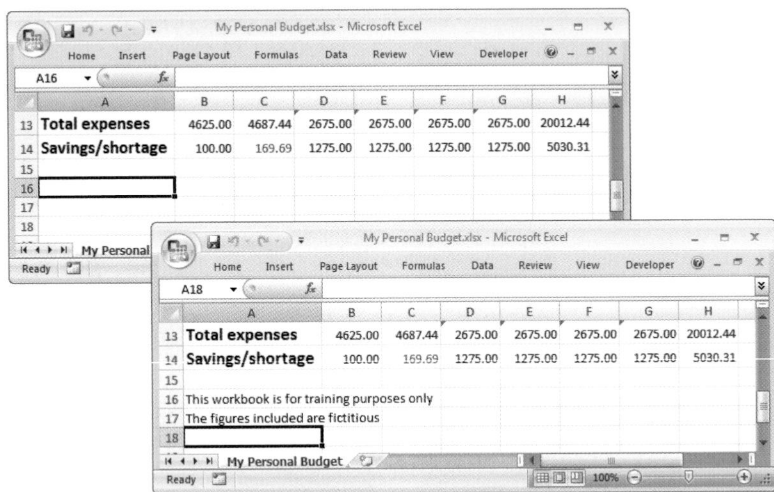


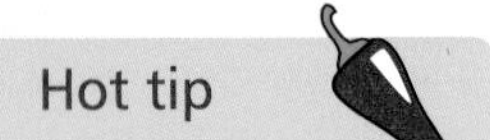


The workbook type does not need to be changed to .xlsm, since you are adding text to it, not the actual macro code.

2. Press the shortcut key Shift+Ctrl+D

3. Save the worksheet (no need to change the file type)

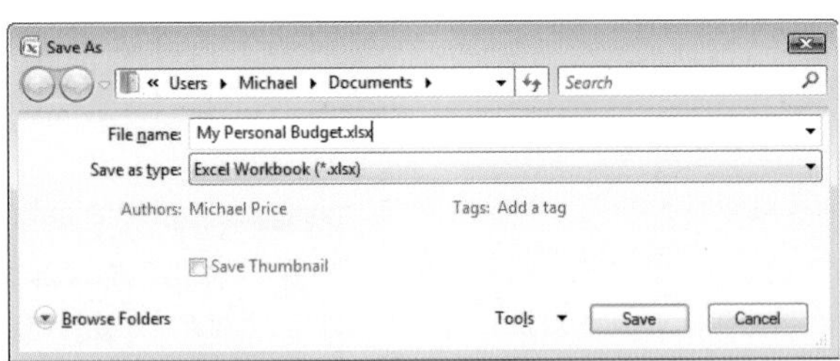

If you choose not to save the Personal Macro Workbook, any macros created during this Excel session will be lost. This can be a useful way of trying out new ideas, without commitment.

4. When you end the Excel session, you can save your Personal Macro Workbook, and with it any macros that you have created during the session

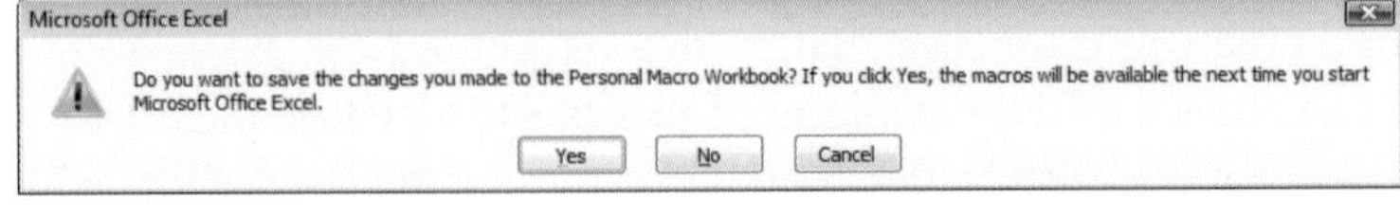

# View the Macro

1 Select the View tab; then from the Window group click Unhide

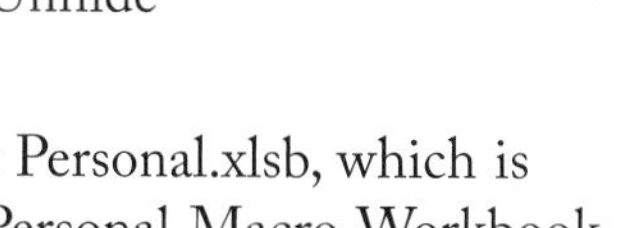

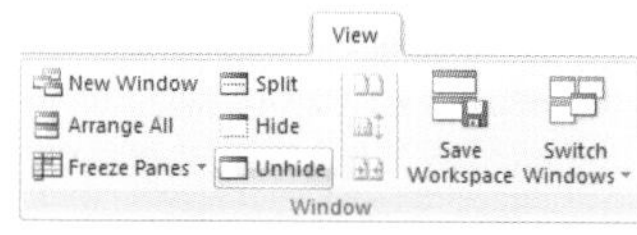


2 Select Personal.xlsb, which is your Personal Macro Workbook, and click OK

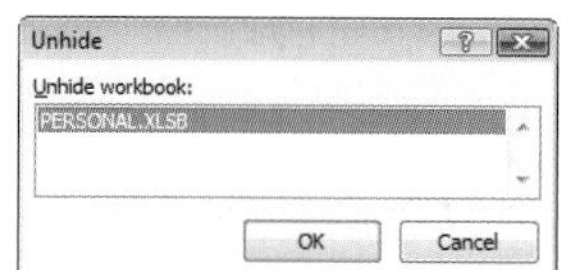


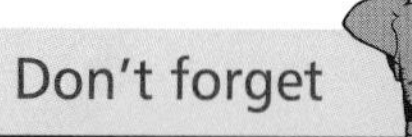

## Don't forget

You can view and edit the macro. However, since it is stored in a hidden workbook, you must start by making the workbook visible.

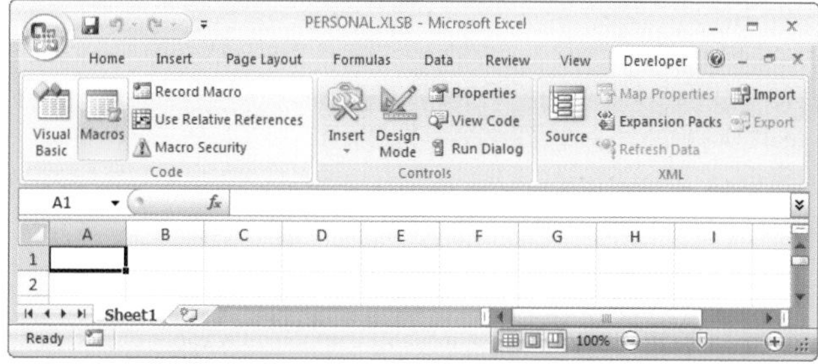


3 From the Developer tab, and the Code group, select Macros

4 Select the macro and click Edit, to display the code in the VB Editor

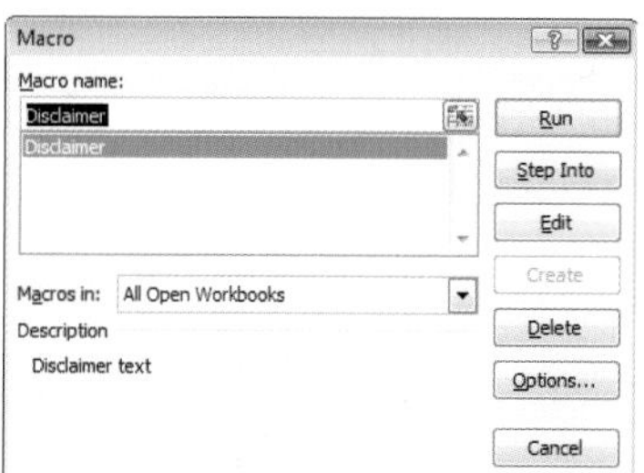


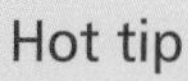

## Hot tip

You can make changes to the macro, e.g. revise the text that is entered into the cells, even if you don't know the VBA language.

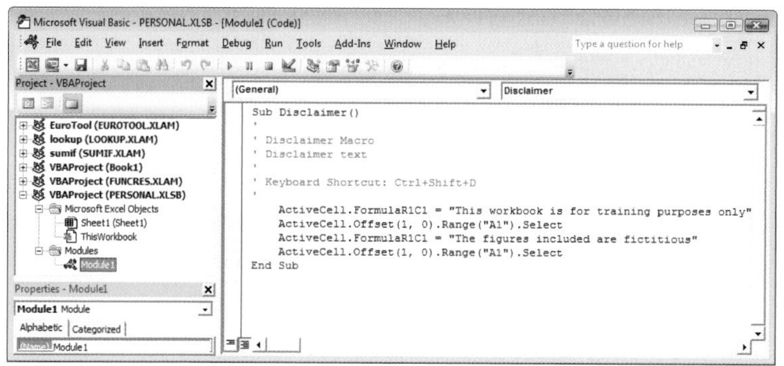

## Beware

When you've finished viewing or changing your macros, select View, Hide to hide the Personal Macro Workbook.

5 Select File, Close and Return to Microsoft Excel

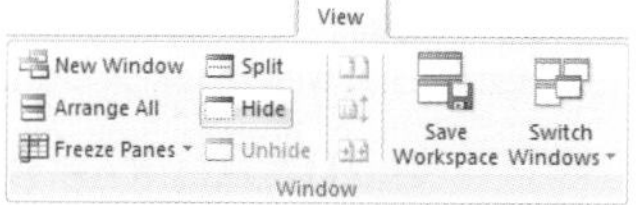

# Create a Table

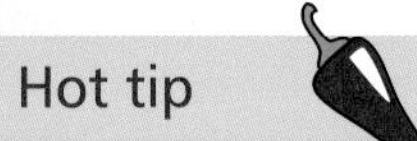

Hot tip

You can record a macro that carries out a more complex task, for example creating an Excel table from a share history file.

1. Open a share history file, for example YHOO.csv

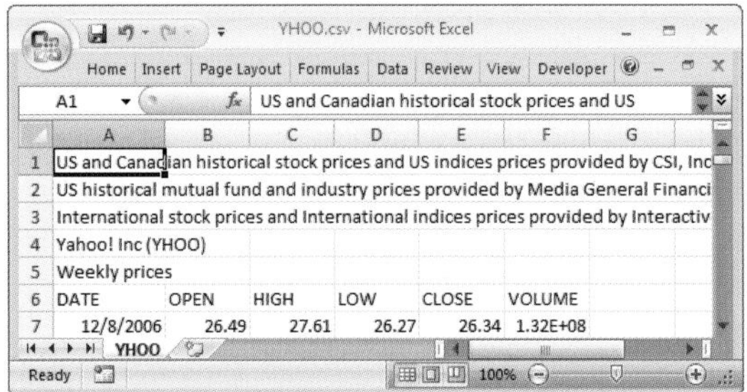


2. Select Developer, Use Relative References, and then click Record Macro

3. Specify the macro name, shortcut and description and click OK to start recording

Hot tip

You may find that it is better to use keystrokes rather than mouse selections when creating a macro. It is also useful to carry out a practice run, noting the keystrokes required, and then record the macro.

The steps in the process are as follows:

1. Go to cell A6 (the start of the data range)

**Alt H FD G A6 Enter**

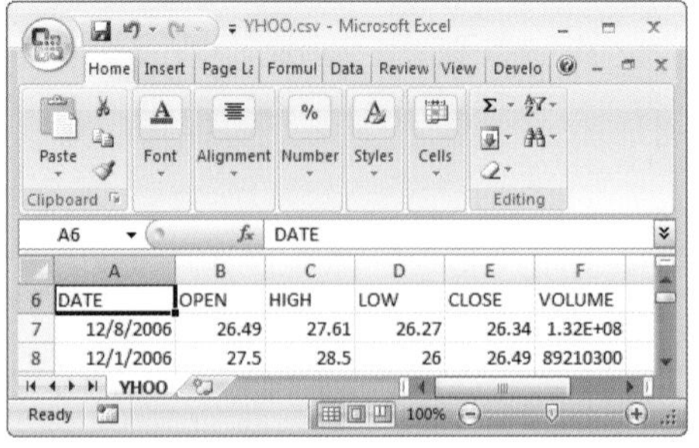


2. Select the data range (A6:F533) using End and Arrows

**ShiftDown End RightArrow End DownArrow ShiftUp**

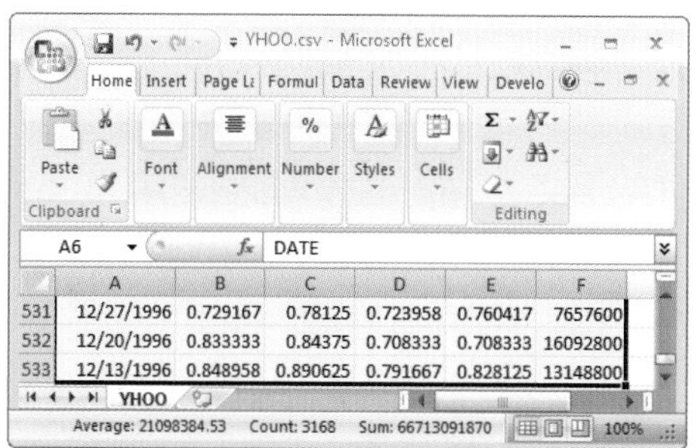


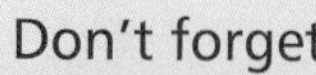

Don't forget

This shows the data range selected ready for creating the Excel table.

3 Create Excel Table from the selection

Create Table
Where is the data for your table?
=$A$6:$F$533
My table has headers
OK Cancel

**Alt N T Enter**

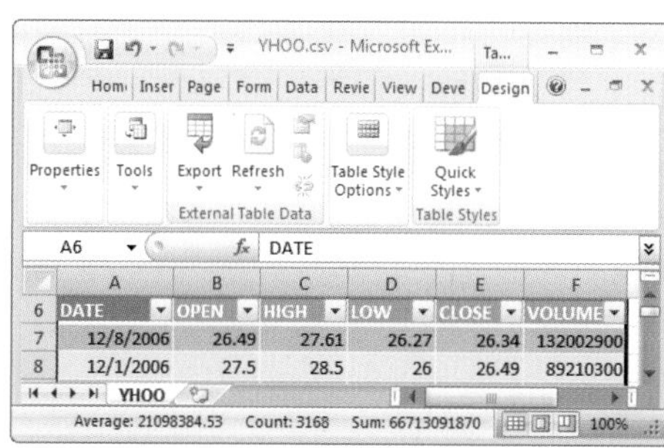

Don't forget

The table is created, but the date column is in descending order (unsuitable for a lookup table).

4 Go to cell A6 (the top of the Date column)

**Alt H FD G A6 Enter**

5 Sort the column in ascending date sequence

**Alt A A**

6 Click Stop Recording

7 The macro is stored in the Personal Macro Workbook

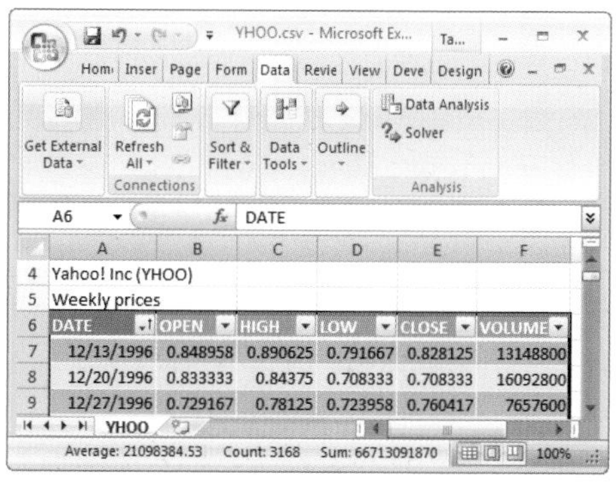


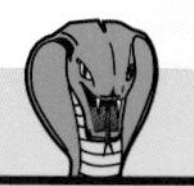

Beware

If you create an Excel table in a .csv file, you must Save As Excel Workbook (.xlsx format) to retain the table.

# Edit the Macro

**Hot tip**

Check the recorded macro to see if any changes are needed.

1. Unhide the Personal Macro Workbook (see page 145)

2. Select Developer and then Macros from the Code group

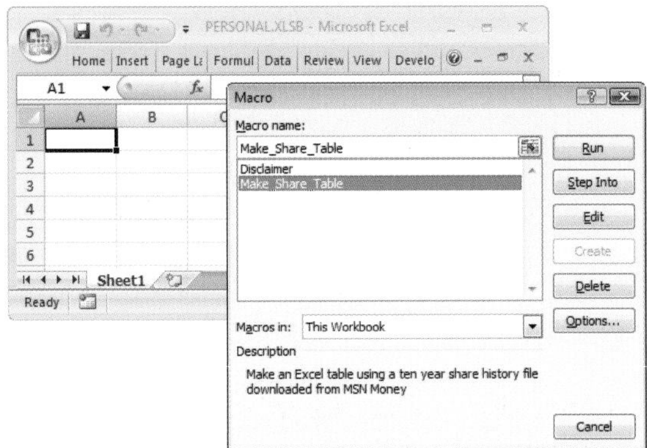


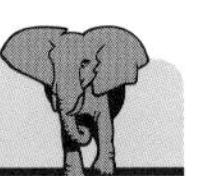

**Don't forget**

Sections of the macro may be specific to the original workbook. In this case there are references to the worksheet name. These can be replaced by the generic reference to ActiveSheet.

3. Select the Make_Share_Table macro and click Edit, to display the code in the Visual Basic Editor

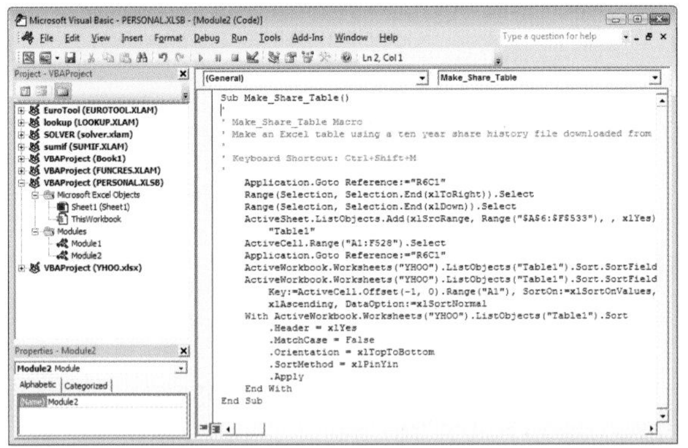

**Beware**

You should hide the Personal Macro Workbook when you have finished making changes to the macro.

4. Select Edit, Replace to replace Worksheets("YHOO") by ActiveSheet, and click the Replace All button

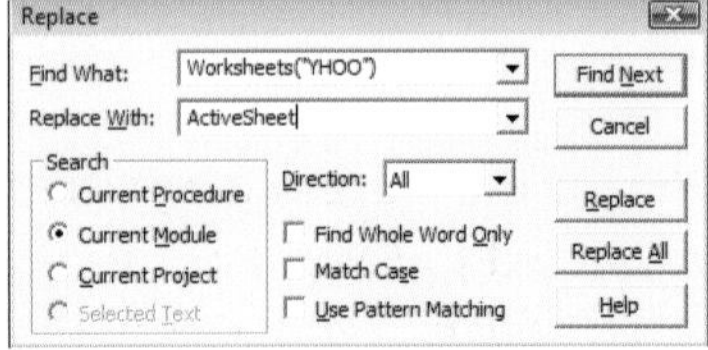


5. Select File, Save and Return to Microsoft Excel (or press Alt+Q)

# Use the Macro

1. Open another share history file (for example ibm.csv) that needs to be changed to an Excel table

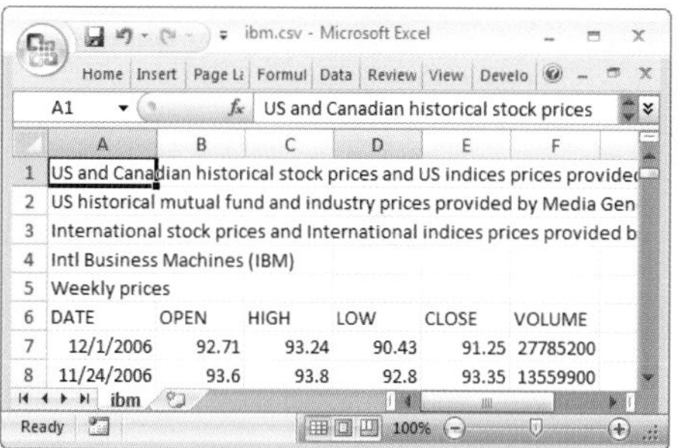


2. Press the macro shortcut key Shift+Ctrl+M, and the data range is immediately converted to Excel table format

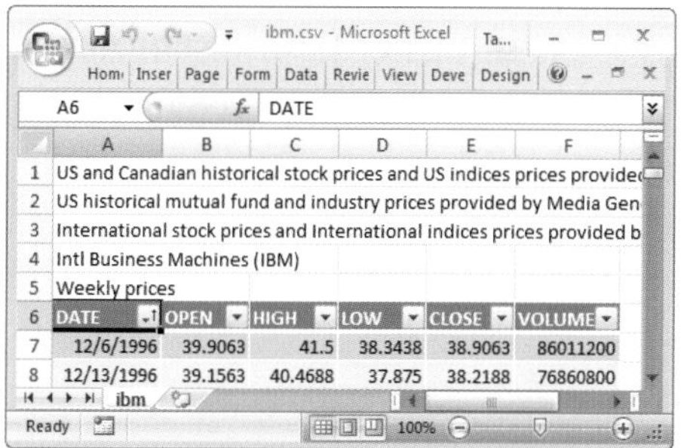


3. Save the worksheet as file type Excel Workbook (.xlsx)

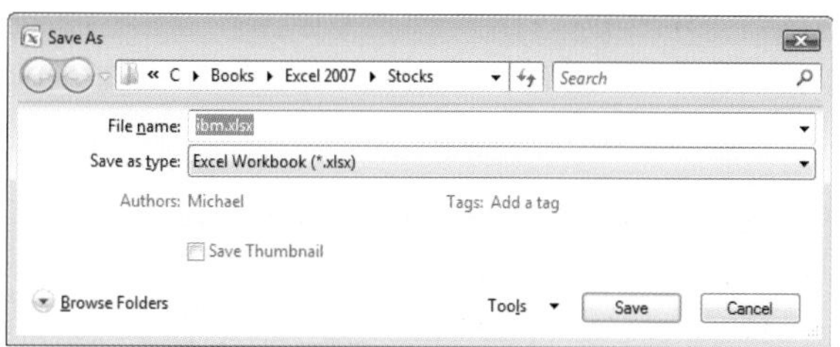


Repeat this for any other share history files, which can each be converted to Excel table format with a single click of the Make_Share_Table macro shortcut key.

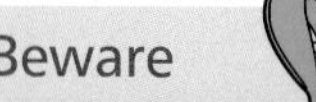

**Beware**

As written, the macro assumes that the worksheet will have data in rows 6 to 533 (ten years). If there are fewer actual rows, the remainder will appear as empty table rows.

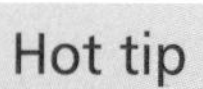

**Hot tip**

Since the macro now refers to the ActiveSheet, it converts the data range in the current worksheet without regard to its name.

**Don't forget**

The macro remains in the Personal Macro Workbook, so the share workbooks do not need to be macro-enabled.

# Create Macros with VBA

**Hot tip**

The Music List from Chapter 3 is used here to illustrate the use of Visual Basic to create a macro, in this case to insert page breaks after each album.

1. Display the Developer tab on the Ribbon (see page 141)

2. Select the Developer tab and then from the Code group select Visual Basic

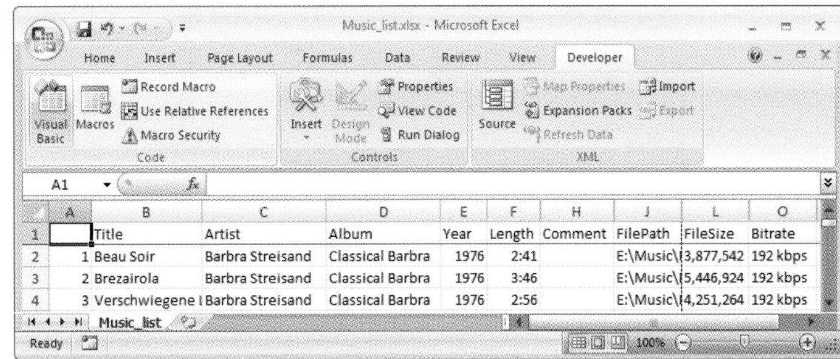


3. Click the VBAProject (in this case Personal.xlsb) and select Insert, Module

Insert
Procedure...
UserForm
Module
Class Module
File...

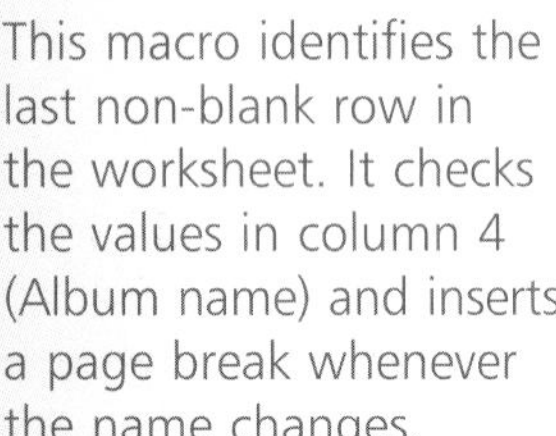

**Don't forget**

This macro identifies the last non-blank row in the worksheet. It checks the values in column 4 (Album name) and inserts a page break whenever the name changes.

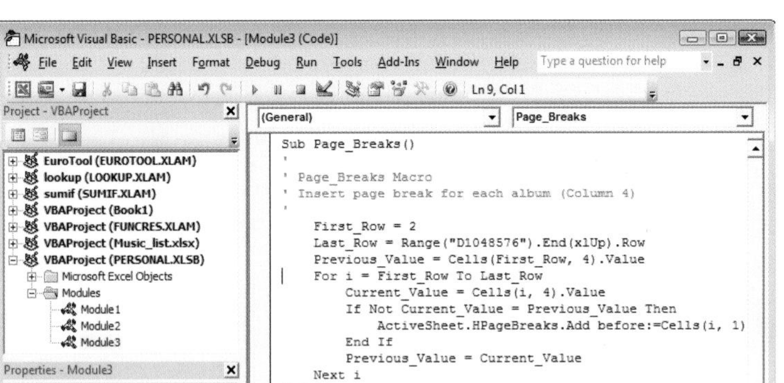

**Hot tip**

You'll find sample code for macros on the Internet at, for example, MSDN2.microsoft.com/library.

4. In the code window for the module, type (or paste) the code for your macro

5. Select File, Save and Return to Microsoft Excel

6 In the Music_list worksheet, click the Page Break Preview button on the status bar to see the page setup

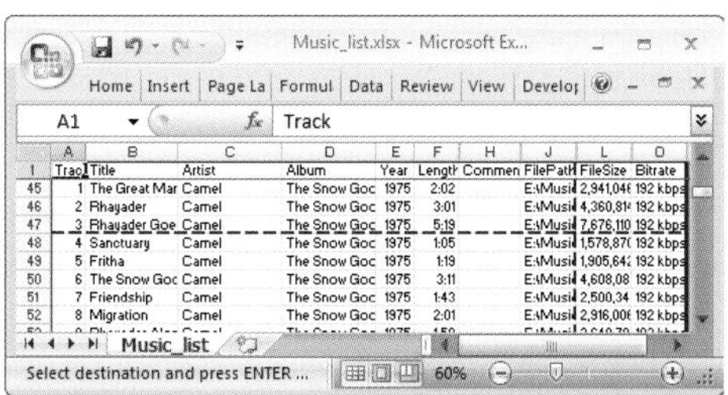

7 Select the Developer tab and click the Macros button

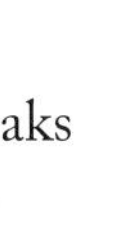

8 Select the Page_Breaks macro and click the Run button

9 Manual page breaks are inserted at every change of album in the worksheet data range

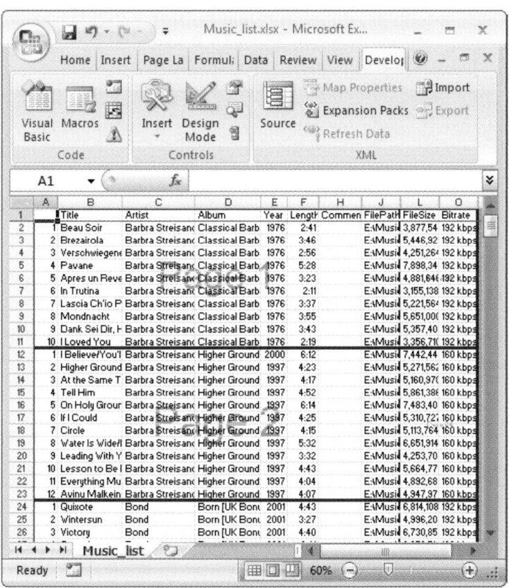

## Hot tip

The Page_Breaks macro is now stored in the Personal Macro Workbook, ready for use.

## Don't forget

Save the workbook to retain the new page breaks, or just print the pages required and close it without saving. The page breaks can be reinserted at any time by rerunning the macro.

# Add Macros to the Toolbar

Don't forget

The Customize option is explicitly for modifying the Quick Access Toolbar contents.

If you specified a Ctrl or Shift+Ctrl shortcut when you created your macro, you can run the macro by pressing the appropriate key combination. You can also run the macro by clicking the Macros button from the View tab or the Developer tab. To make macros more accessible, you can add the View Macros option to the Quick Access Toolbar.

1. Select the Office button and click Excel Options; then click Customize and select Popular Commands

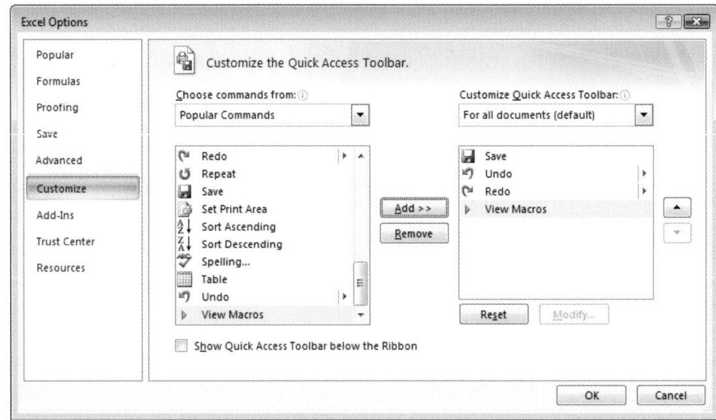




2. Click View Macros, click Add and click OK, and View Macros appears on the Quick Access Toolbar

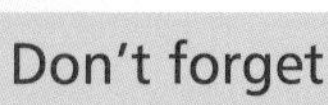

If you want to add or change the shortcut key for a macro, select it using the Macros button and then click the Options button.

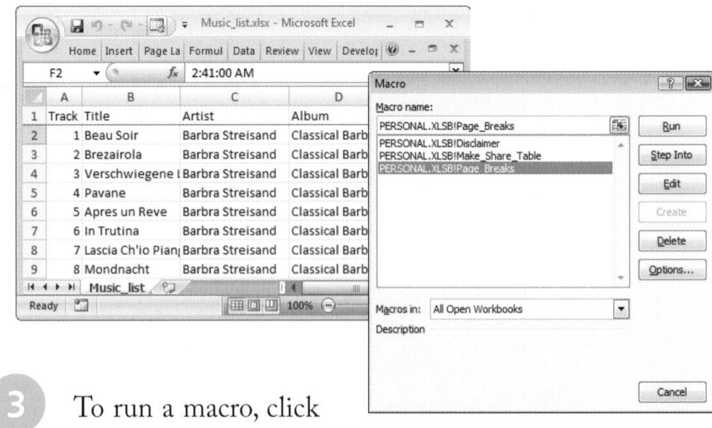


3. To run a macro, click the View Macros button on the toolbar, select the macro and click Run

Alternatively, you can add macros as individual icons on the Quick Access Toolbar.

1. Open Excel Options, select Customize and select Macros

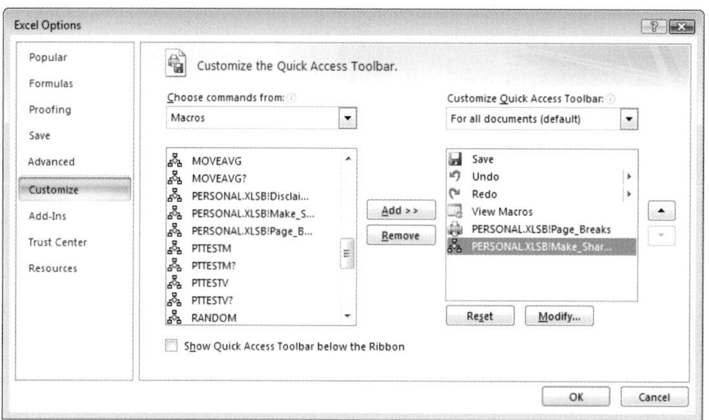


2. Scroll down to the particular macros, select each one in turn and click Add

3. Each macro will have the same icon. You can click Modify and select a different icon

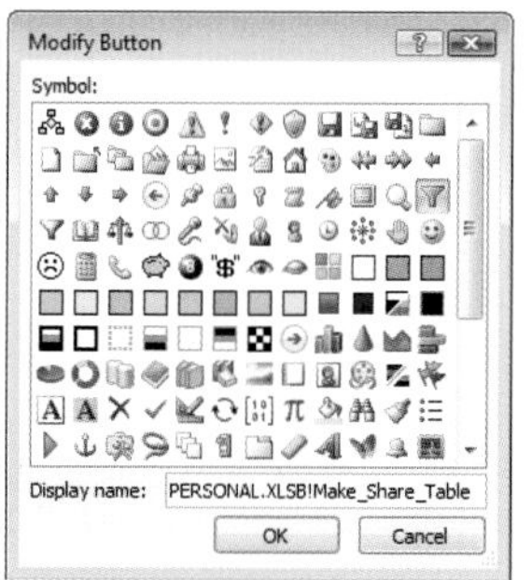
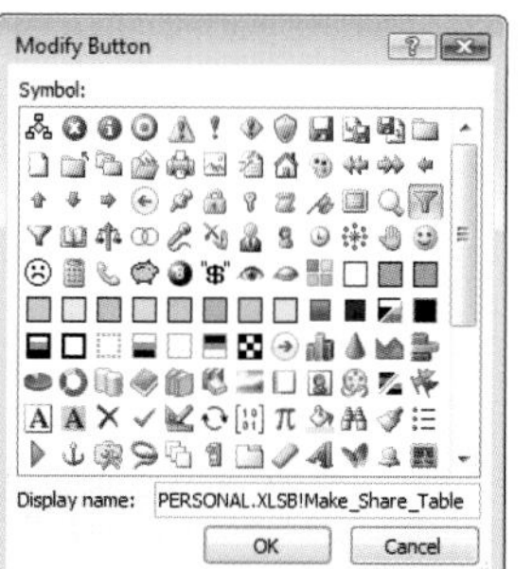


4. The icons for the macros are added to the Quick Access toolbar

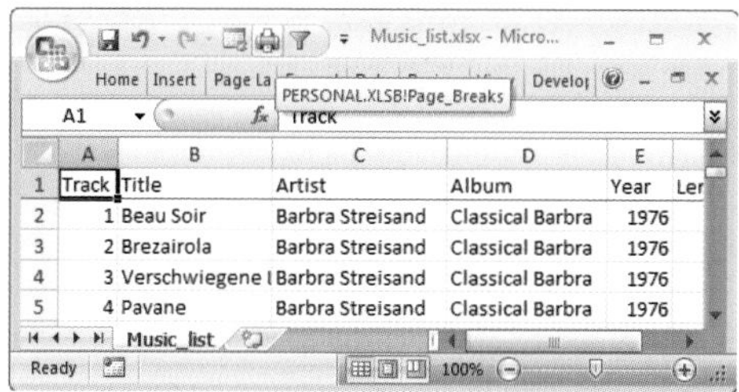


5. The tooltip shows the name of the macro, which runs immediately when you select its icon

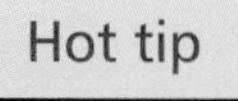

## Hot tip

Macros can also be associated with graphics or hot spots on the worksheet.

# Debug Macros

If you are having a problem with a macro, or if you are just curious to see how it works, you can run it a step at a time.

1. Select Macros from Developer (or from View), choose the macro you want to run, and click Step Into

2. Press F8 repeatedly to run through the code, one step at a time

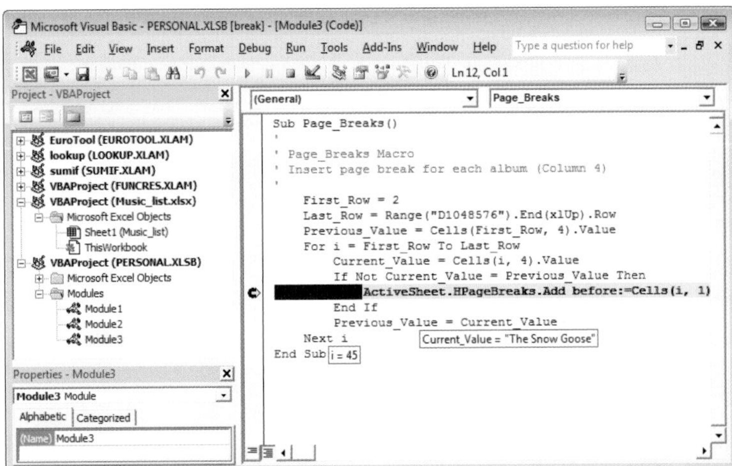


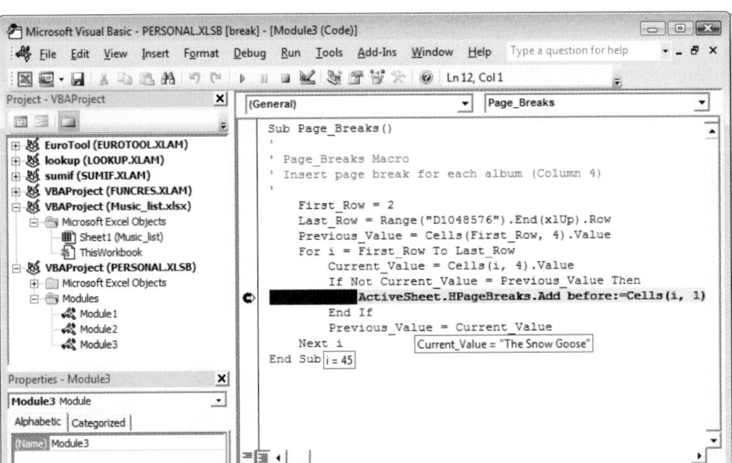

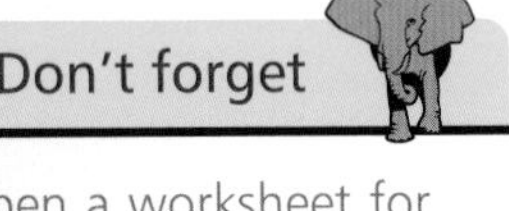

**Don't forget**

Open a worksheet for which the macro was written, before selecting the Step In option.

3. Hold the mouse over a variable to see its current value

4. Select Debug to see the other testing options available, such as setting breakpoints

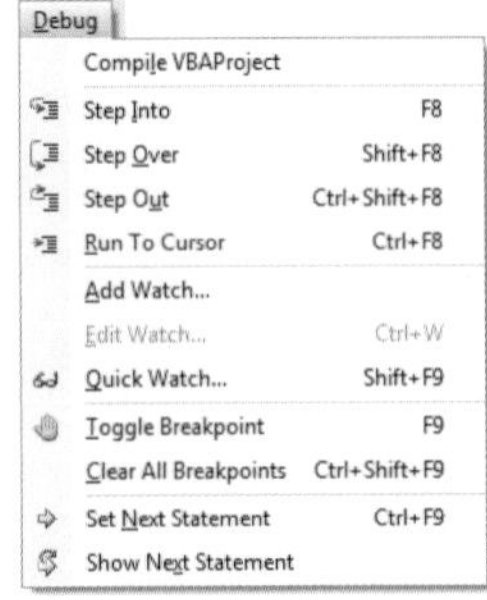


5. Press F5 to continue to the next breakpoint (or to complete the macro, if no breakpoints are set)

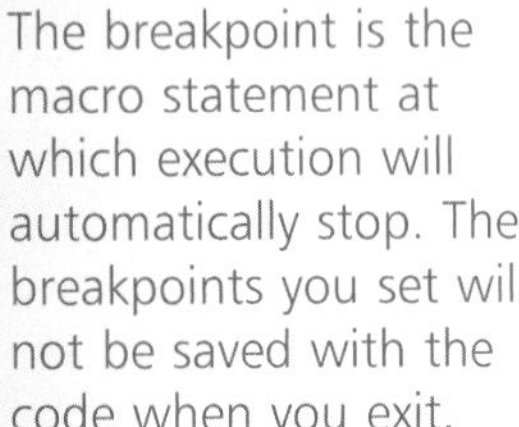

**Hot tip**

The breakpoint is the macro statement at which execution will automatically stop. The breakpoints you set will not be saved with the code when you exit.

# 10 Templates and Scenarios

*For the most frequent uses of Excel you'll usually find ready-made templates to give you a head start. There are other Excel resources at the Microsoft Office website. Excel also has special problem-solving tools.*

# Templates

Hot tip

You can create your own templates, which will be listed under My Templates. You can also create new workbooks from existing workbooks.

You can save effort, and you may discover new aspects of Excel, if you base your new workbooks on available templates.

1. Click the Office button and then click New (or press Ctrl+N) to see the blank workbook and recently used templates

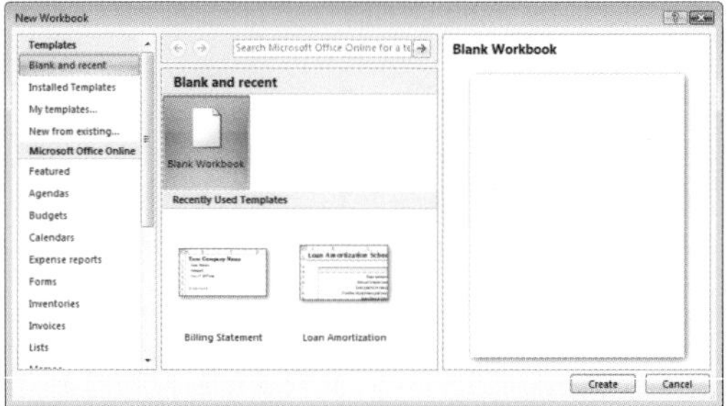


2. Click Installed Templates and select any template to see a preview in the pane on the right

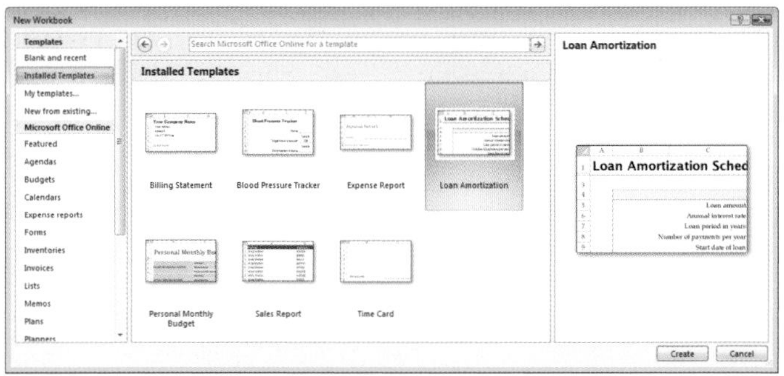


3. Select the template you want to use, for example the Loan Amortization Schedule template, and click Create

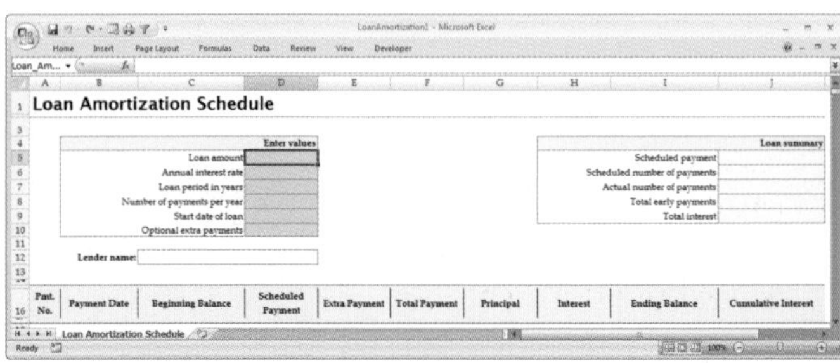


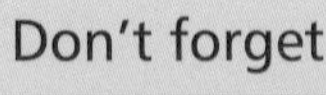

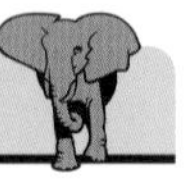

Don't forget

The workbook will be immediately usable, though of course you can make any changes you wish if it isn't exactly to your requirements.

4 Enter data in the input boxes, so that you can check out the way the workbook operates

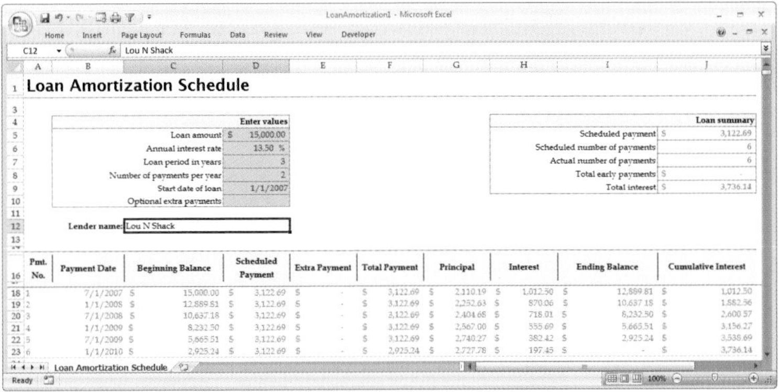


## Hot tip

Enter data and then make changes to the values, to see the effect. For example, specify 12 payments per annum, and then change to 2 payments.

5 The worksheet is extended by the number of payments, and displays the calculated amounts

6 To view the formulas behind the calculations, press Ctrl+` (or select the Formulas tab and click Show Formulas)

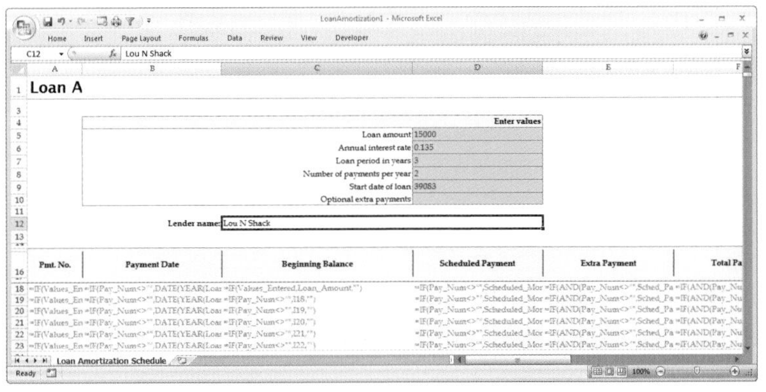


## Beware

You'll find the worksheet is designed for periods of up to 40 years.

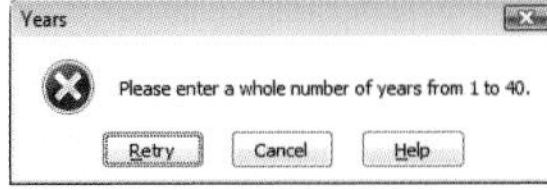


7 Select the Formulas tab and click the Name Manager button (or press Ctrl+F3) to see the names defined in the workbook, with values and references

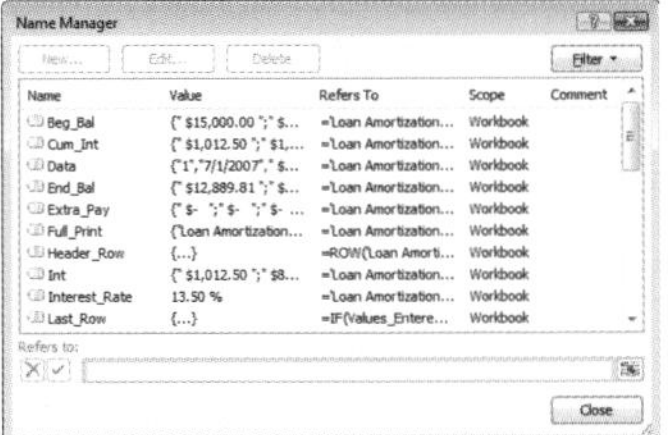


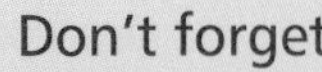

## Don't forget

You need to save the workbook – the default name is the template name with a number appended.

# Online Templates

To obtain more workbook templates, you can download them from the Microsoft Office Online website.

## Don't forget

There are over 40 categories, some with just a few templates and others with 20 or more, giving an overall total of more than 500 templates.

1. Select Office, New and click a category in the Office Online section; then select a template to see a preview

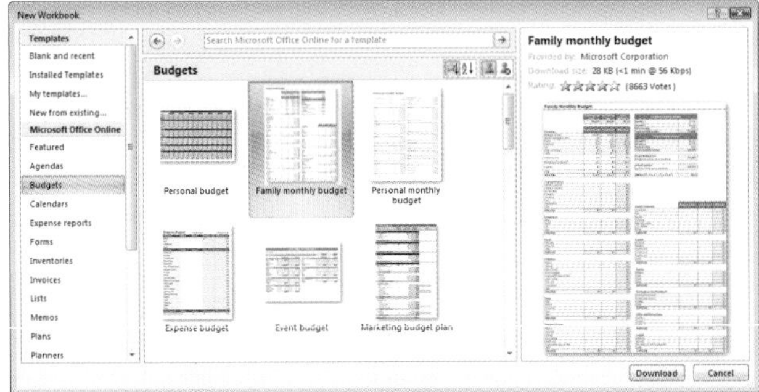


2. Click the Download button to retrieve the selected template from the website

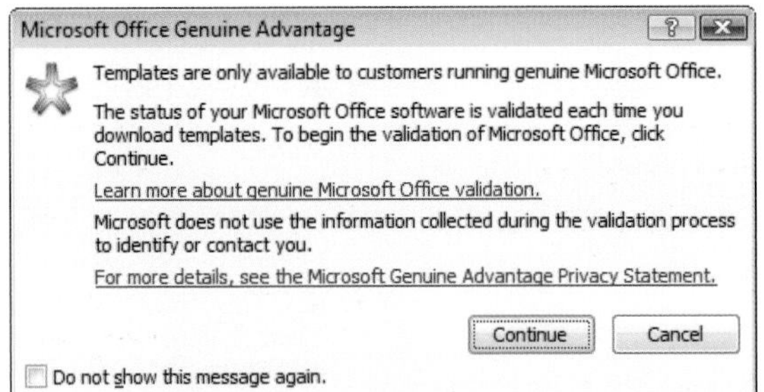


## Hot tip

Validation matches your PC hardware profile against your Office product key, but no other information is collected.

3. Click Continue to validate your copy of Windows and initiate the transfer of the template file

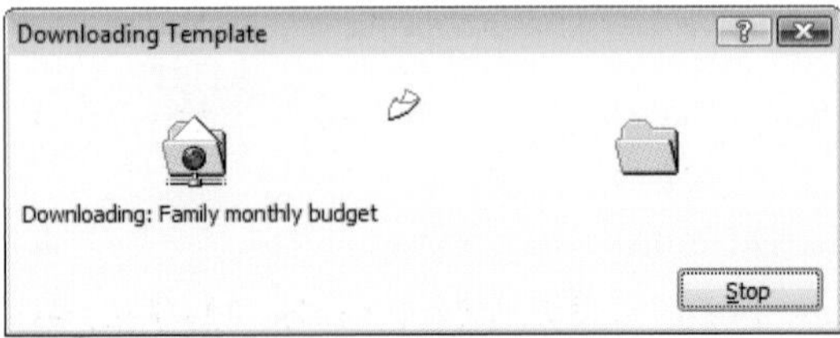

4. A new workbook (based on the downloaded template) will be displayed ready for updating

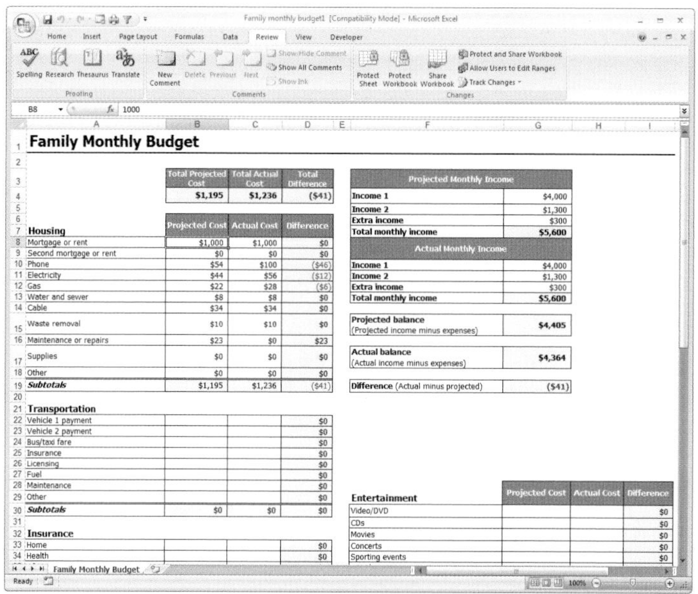


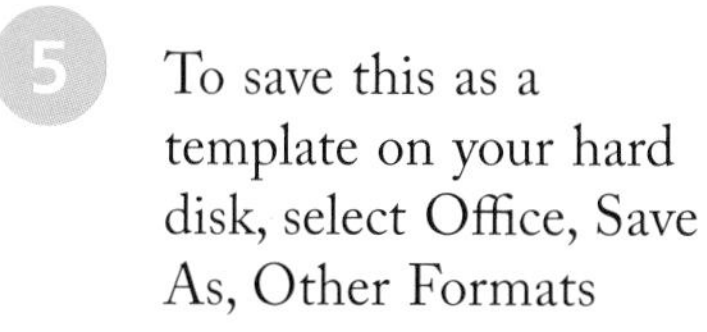

5. To save this as a template on your hard disk, select Office, Save As, Other Formats

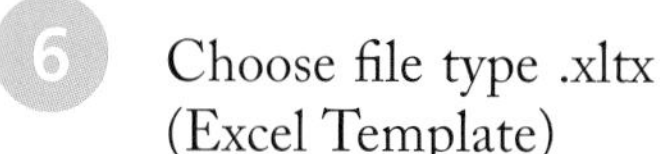

6. Choose file type .xltx (Excel Template)

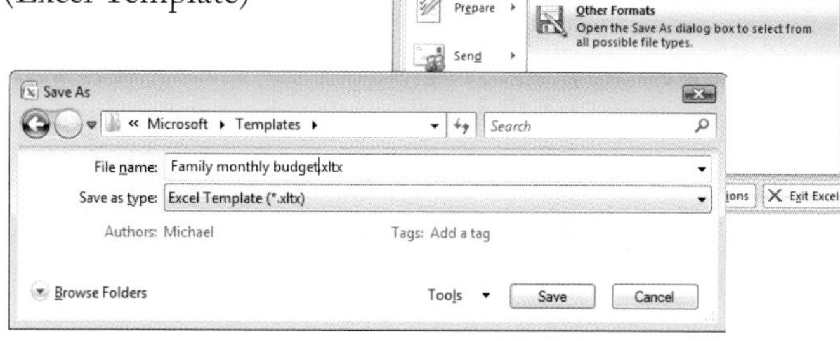


7. The template will be added to the My Templates section of the New Workbook dialog

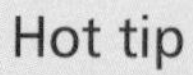

**Hot tip**

The template will be added to the Recently Used Templates list, but with the website address. However, you can save the new workbook as a local Excel template if you wish.

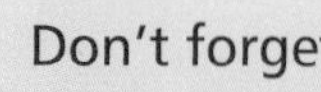

**Don't forget**

You can if you prefer remove the appended digit (1 or whatever) from the file name.

# More Excel Resources

The Internet is a prolific source of advice and guidance for Excel users at all levels. Here are some websites that may prove useful:

Hot tip 

A search on Google.com with Excel-related search terms will result in millions of matches, so it may be easier to start from a more focused website such as Microsoft Office.

1. Go to office.microsoft.com and select the Products tab

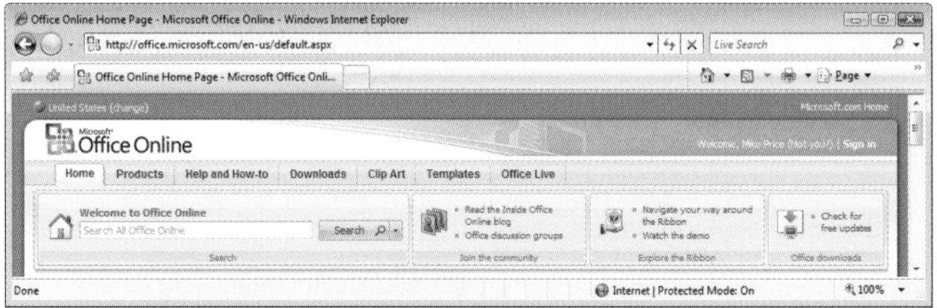


2. Select the Excel link to show associated links and details

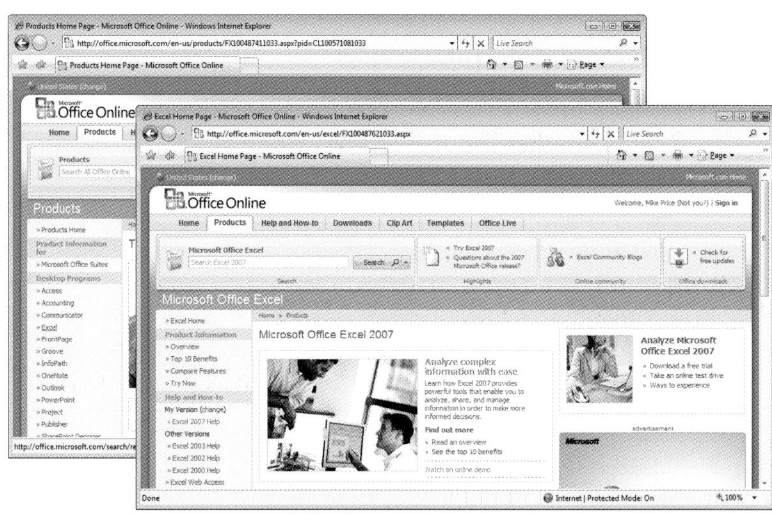


Beware 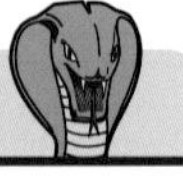

The actual links and content for these web pages change continually but you should normally expect to find links such as these.

3. For more detailed information about Excel, scroll down for links to Technical Resources and Additional Resources

4. If you are interested in creating Excel functions and macros, click the Developer Center link

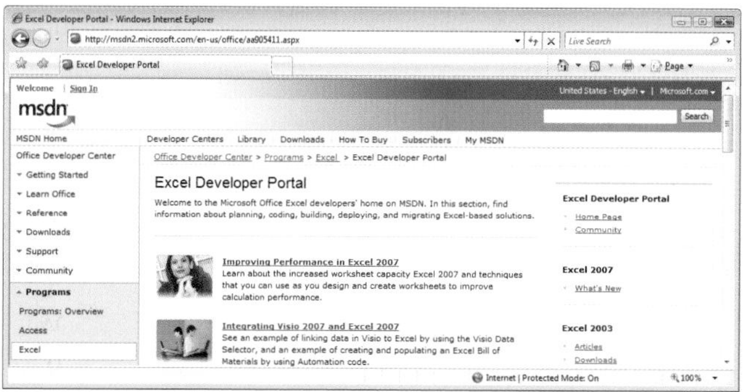

The Excel Developer Portal offers information about planning, coding, building, deploying and migrating Excel solutions.

5. Click the Excel MVPs link for a list of the Microsoft Most Valued Specialists who deal particularly with Excel

6. There's another list of Excel MVPs on the mvps.org website, at location www.mvps.org/links.html#Excel

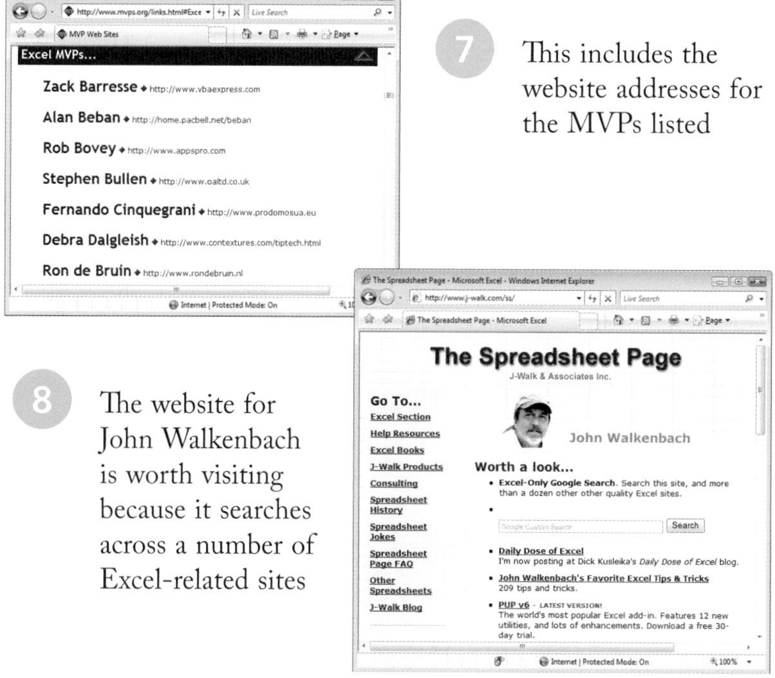


7. This includes the website addresses for the MVPs listed

8. The website for John Walkenbach is worth visiting because it searches across a number of Excel-related sites

You'll find that many references relate to Excel 2003 or older versions. These will often be just as applicable when you are running Excel 2007.

# What-If Analysis

## Don't forget

Sometimes you can set up your worksheet so that several outcomes are visible at once (as in the PMT example on page 93). You can achieve a similar effect by using What-If analysis and defining scenarios.

What-If analysis involves the process of changing values in cells to see how those changes affect the outcome on the worksheet. A set of values that represents a particular outcome is known as a scenario. To create a scenario:

1. Open the worksheet and enter details for a loan, for example a 25-year mortgage

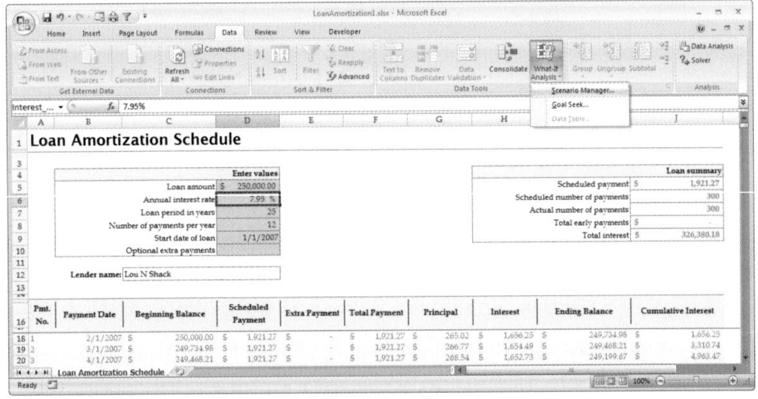




## Hot tip

In this case, the scenarios explore the effects of making extra payments, with the first scenario having an extra payment of zero.

2. Select the Data tab, and from the Data Tools group click What-If Analysis, Scenario Manager

3. Click Add, type a scenario name (e.g. X000), enter the references for cells that you want to change, and click OK

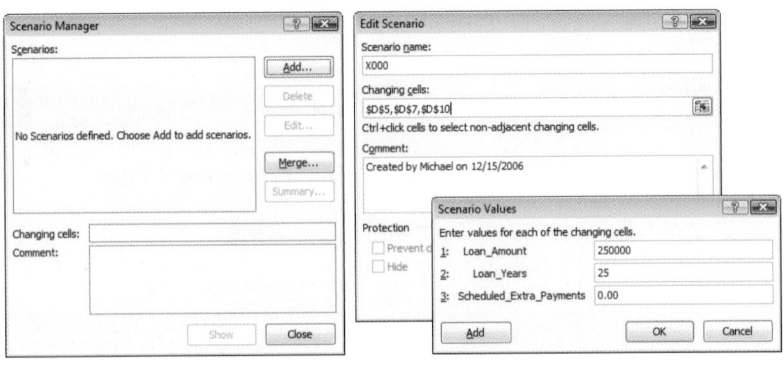


4. Change cells from their initial values as required, in this case adjusting the value of Scheduled_Extra_Payments

5. Repeat steps 3 & 4 for each scenario, incrementing by 50 (i.e. X050, X100,... X300) and clicking OK for the last one

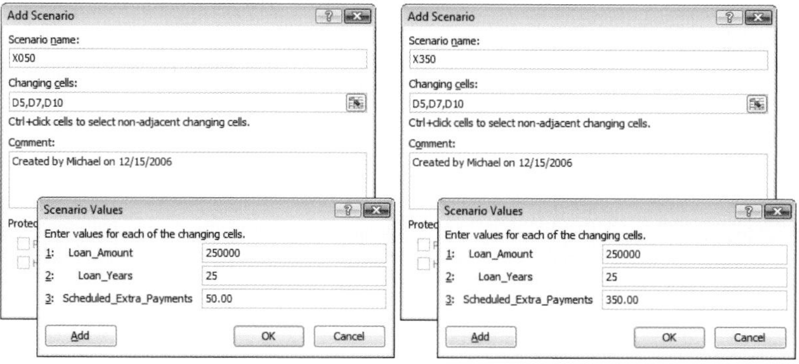

## Hot tip

Additional input cells (Loan_Amount and Loan_Years) have been selected. They have been left unchanged for these scenarios, but give the option for other scenarios in a future analysis.

6. Select a scenario and click Show to display any of the results on the worksheet

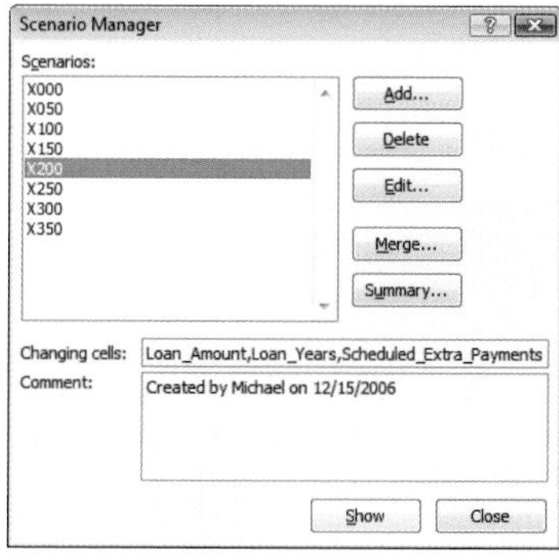

7. Select Close to end the Scenario Manager and return to the worksheet

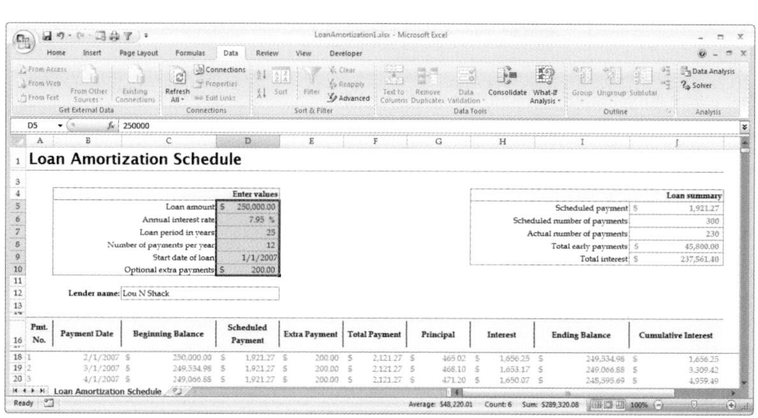

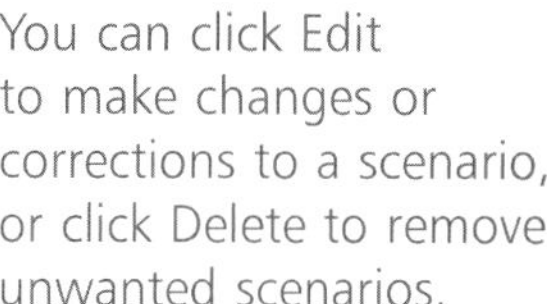

## Don't forget

You can click Edit to make changes or corrections to a scenario, or click Delete to remove unwanted scenarios.

The results from the scenario that was last shown will be displayed. If no scenario was left selected in the Scenario Manager, the original worksheet values will be shown.

# Summary Reports

To create a scenario summary report, showing all the possible outcomes on one worksheet:

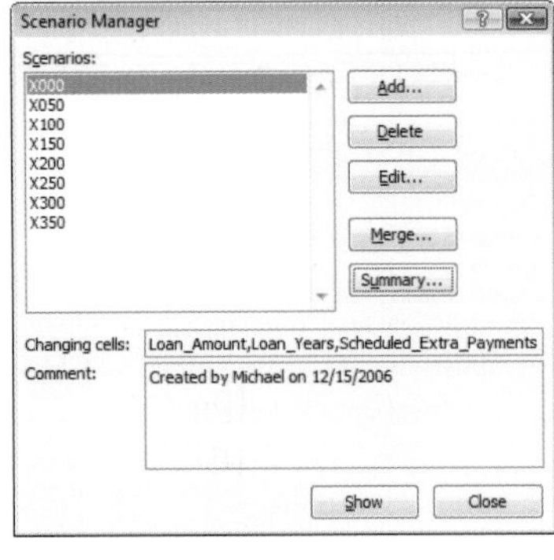


1. On the Data tab, in the Data Tools group, click What-If Analysis, click Scenario Manager and then click Summary

2. Choose "Scenario summary" report type

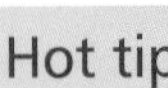

Hot tip

It isn't essential to select result cells to generate a scenario summary report, though you would normally want to include values that reflect outcomes.

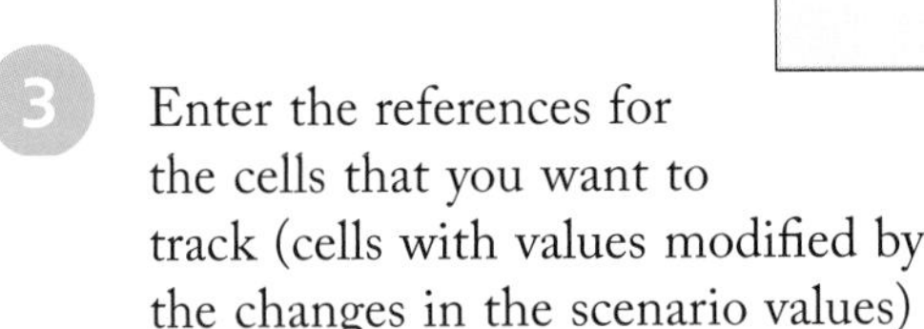

3. Enter the references for the cells that you want to track (cells with values modified by the changes in the scenario values)

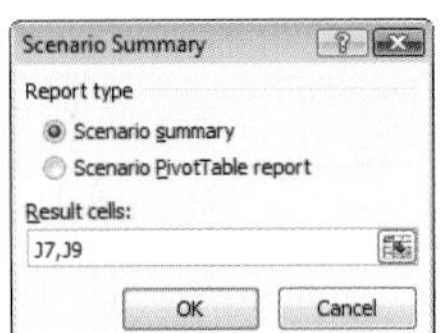


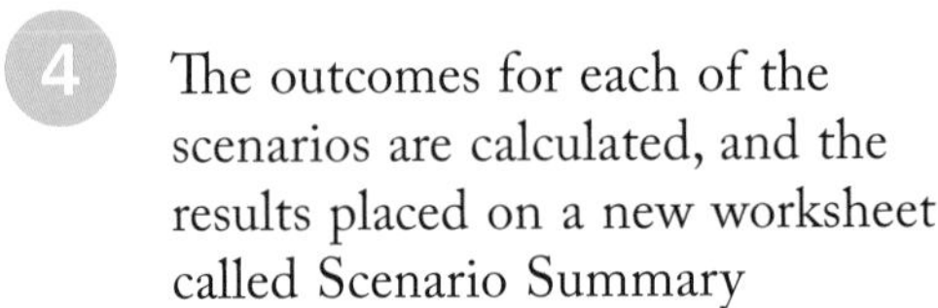

4. The outcomes for each of the scenarios are calculated, and the results placed on a new worksheet called Scenario Summary



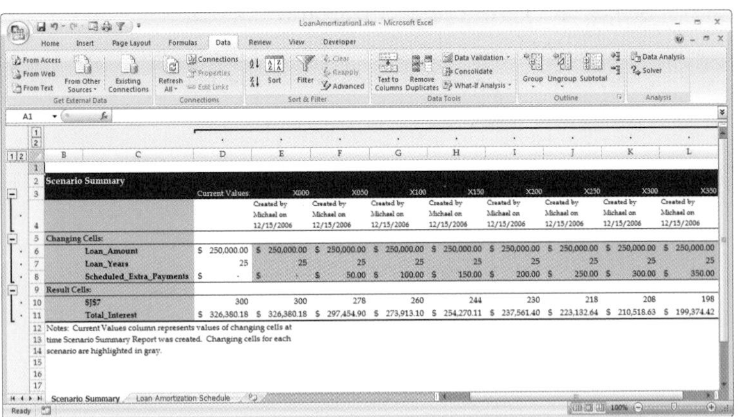

| Scenario Summary | Current Values: | X000 | X050 | X100 | X150 | X200 | X250 | X300 | X350 |
|---|---|---|---|---|---|---|---|---|---|
| | | Created by Michael on 12/15/2006 | Created by Michael on 12/15/2006 | Created by Michael on 12/15/2006 | Created by Michael on 12/15/2006 | Created by Michael on 12/15/2006 | Created by Michael on 12/15/2006 | Created by Michael on 12/15/2006 | Created by Michael on 12/15/2006 |
| Changing Cells: | | | | | | | | | |
| Loan_Amount | $ 250,000.00 | $ 250,000.00 | $ 250,000.00 | $ 250,000.00 | $ 250,000.00 | $ 250,000.00 | $ 250,000.00 | $ 250,000.00 | $ 250,000.00 |
| Loan_Years | 25 | 25 | 25 | 25 | 25 | 25 | 25 | 25 | 25 |
| Scheduled_Extra_Payments | $ - | $ - | $ 50.00 | $ 100.00 | $ 150.00 | $ 200.00 | $ 250.00 | $ 300.00 | $ 350.00 |
| Result Cells: | | | | | | | | | |
| $J$7 | 300 | 300 | 278 | 260 | 244 | 230 | 218 | 208 | 198 |
| Total_Interest | $ 326,380.18 | $ 326,380.18 | $ 297,454.90 | $ 273,913.10 | $ 254,270.11 | $ 237,561.40 | $ 223,132.64 | $ 210,518.63 | $ 199,374.42 |

Notes: Current Values column represents values of changing cells at time Scenario Summary Report was created. Changing cells for each scenario are highlighted in gray.

The Changing Cells section displays the values for each scenario of the cells that were selected when the scenarios were created. The Result Cells section shows the values of the cells specified when the summary report was created. The Current Values column shows the original values, before the scenarios were defined.

The results can also be presented as a Scenario PivotTable report:

1. Open the Scenario Manager, click Summary, choose Scenario PivotTable report and enter the references for the result cells

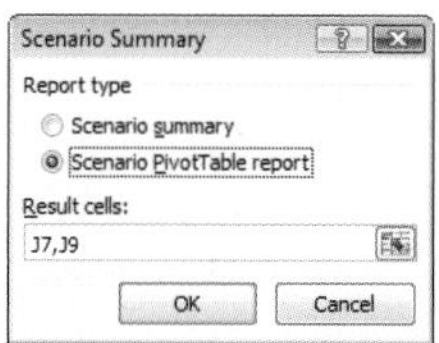


2. The results are shown in a table on a separate worksheet

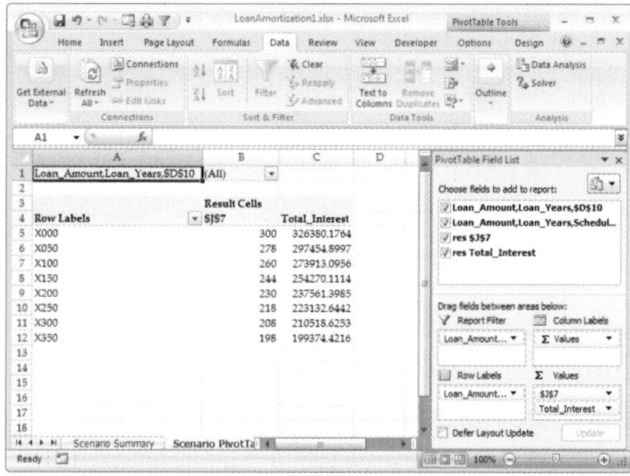


3. Select the PivotTable Tools Options tab; then select PivotChart from the Tools group, choose the type of chart, for example Line Chart, and click OK

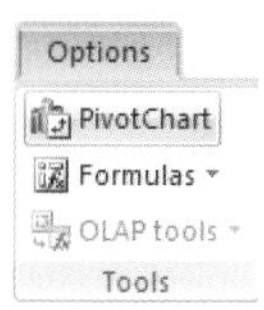


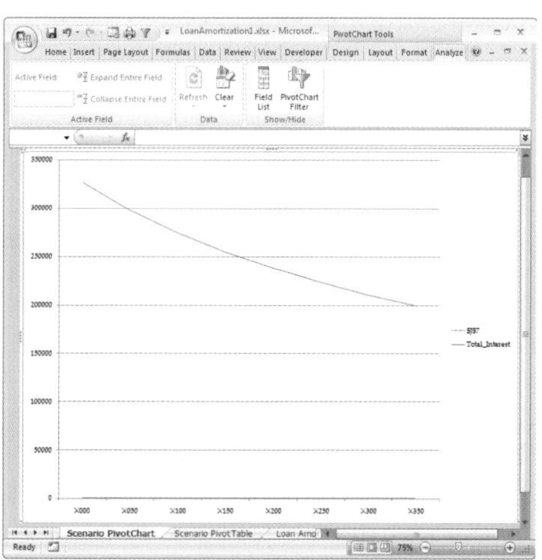


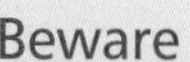


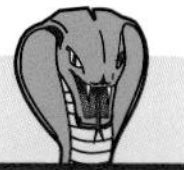

You must switch back to the Loan Amortization Schedule worksheet before opening the Scenario Manager.

## Hot tip

To generate a Scenario PivotTable report, it is always necessary to specify the relevant result cells.

# Goal Seek

If you know the result that you want from an analysis, but not the input values the worksheet needs to get that result, you can use the Goal Seek feature. For example, you can use Goal Seek in the Loan Amortization worksheet to determine the extra payment required to keep total interest below $150,000.

**Hot tip**

Start off with the original data scenario, and the extra payment value will be incremented until the target interest level has been achieved.

1. Select Data, Data Tools, What-If Analysis, and Goal Seek

2. For Set cell, enter the reference for the cell with the target value (cell J9).

3. In the To value box, type the result you want (150000)

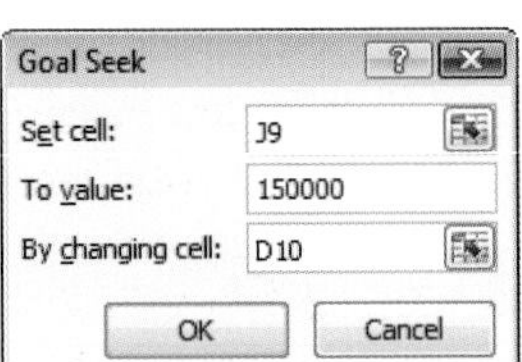


4. In the "By changing cell" box, enter the reference for the cell that contains the value you want to adjust (D10)

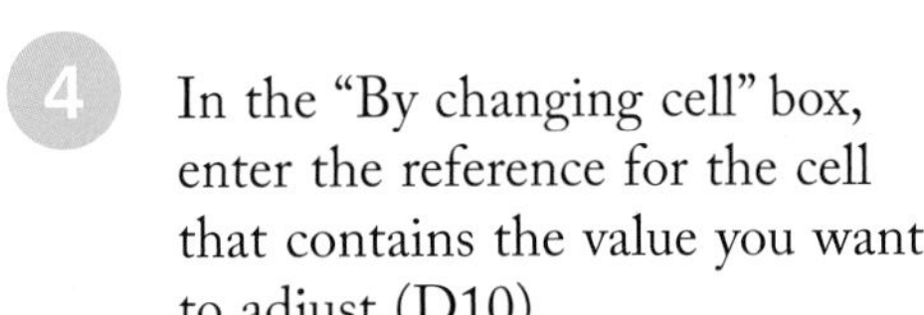

**Don't forget**

The "By changing" cell must be referred to by the formula in the Set cell, where the changes should be reflected.



5. The value in D10 is rapidly varied, and the worksheet continually recalculated, until the target value of interest is reached

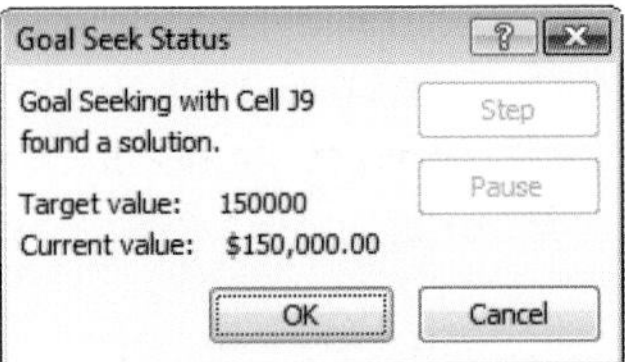


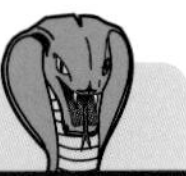

**Beware**

The references for the Set cell and for the "By changing" cell must be to single cells only.

6. Click OK to return to the worksheet with the computed result (and save it as a scenario if desired)

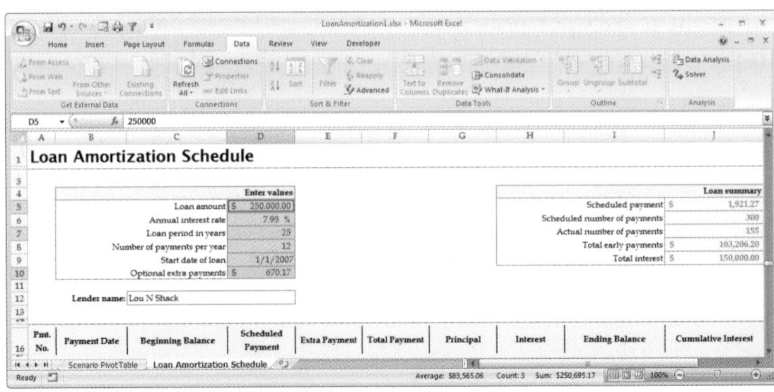

# Optimization

Goal Seek allows you to solve problems where you want to find the value of a single input to generate the desired result. It is of no help when you need to find the best values for several inputs. For this you require an optimizer, a software tool that helps you find the best way to allocate resources. These could be raw materials, machine time, people time, money or anything that is in limited supply. The best or optimal solution will perhaps be the one that maximizes profit, or minimizes cost, or meets some other requirement. All kinds of situations can be tackled this way, including allocating finance, scheduling production, blending raw materials, routing goods and loading transportation.

Excel includes an add-in optimizer called Solver. You may need to install this (see page 103) if it doesn't appear on your system. To illustrate the use of Solver, we'll examine a product mix problem.

## Sample Solver Problem

Imagine that your hobby is textiles, and you produce craft goods (ponchos, scarves and gloves). There's a craft fair coming up, and you plan to use your existing inventory of materials (warp, weft and braid) and your available time (for the loom and to finish goods). You want to know the mix of products that will maximize profits, given the inventory and time available. These include 800 hanks of warp, 600 hanks of weft, 50 lengths of braid, 300 hours of loom time and 200 hours of finishing time.

To produce a poncho, you will need 8 units of warp, 7 of weft, 1 of braid, 6 for loom and 2 for finish. For a scarf, the values are 3 warp, 2 weft, 0 braid, 1 loom and 1 finish. For a pair of gloves, they are 1 warp, 0 weft, 0 braid, 0 loom and 4 finish.

You make the assumption that your profit is $25 per poncho, $10 per scarf and $8 per pair of gloves.

You remember that you need four of each item as samples to show the visitors to the fair. Also you recall that usually half the scarves are sold in sets with gloves.

Hot tip

Relationships between the objective, constraints and decision variables are analyzed to decide the best solution to satisfy the requirements.

Don't forget

The problem description must be in sufficient detail to establish the relationships and identify the constraints.

# Project Worksheet

The craft fair optimization information (see page 167) can be expressed in a worksheet as follows:

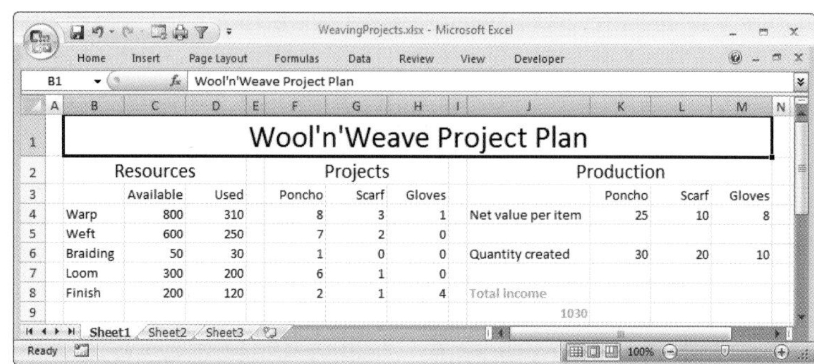

WeavingProjects.xlsx - Microsoft Excel

| | B | C | D | F | G | H | J | K | L | M |
|---|---|---|---|---|---|---|---|---|---|---|
| 1 | Wool'n'Weave Project Plan | | | | | | | | | |
| 2 | Resources | | | Projects | | | Production | | | |
| 3 | | Available | Used | Poncho | Scarf | Gloves | | Poncho | Scarf | Gloves |
| 4 | Warp | 800 | 310 | 8 | 3 | 1 | Net value per item | 25 | 10 | 8 |
| 5 | Weft | 600 | 250 | 7 | 2 | 0 | | | | |
| 6 | Braiding | 50 | 30 | 1 | 0 | 0 | Quantity created | 30 | 20 | 10 |
| 7 | Loom | 300 | 200 | 6 | 1 | 0 | | | | |
| 8 | Finish | 200 | 120 | 2 | 1 | 4 | Total income | | | |
| 9 | | | | | | | 1030 | | | |

The formulas that are included in the spreadsheet are:

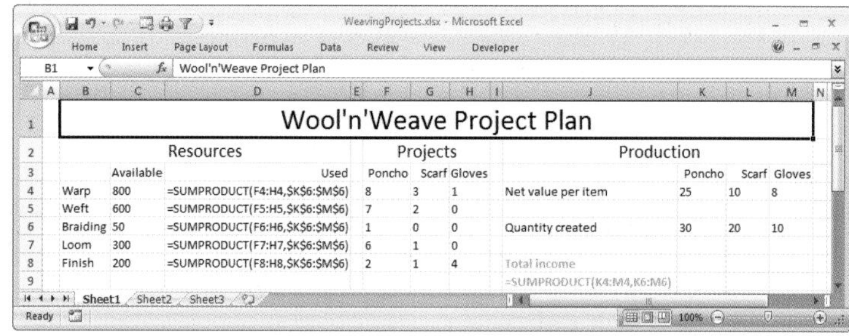

WeavingProjects.xlsx - Microsoft Excel

| | B | C | D | F | G | H | J | K | L | M |
|---|---|---|---|---|---|---|---|---|---|---|
| 1 | Wool'n'Weave Project Plan | | | | | | | | | |
| 2 | Resources | | | Projects | | | Production | | | |
| 3 | | Available | Used | Poncho | Scarf | Gloves | | Poncho | Scarf | Gloves |
| 4 | Warp | 800 | =SUMPRODUCT(F4:H4,$K$6:$M$6) | 8 | 3 | 1 | Net value per item | 25 | 10 | 8 |
| 5 | Weft | 600 | =SUMPRODUCT(F5:H5,$K$6:$M$6) | 7 | 2 | 0 | | | | |
| 6 | Braiding | 50 | =SUMPRODUCT(F6:H6,$K$6:$M$6) | 1 | 0 | 0 | Quantity created | 30 | 20 | 10 |
| 7 | Loom | 300 | =SUMPRODUCT(F7:H7,$K$6:$M$6) | 6 | 1 | 0 | | | | |
| 8 | Finish | 200 | =SUMPRODUCT(F8:H8,$K$6:$M$6) | 2 | 1 | 4 | Total income | | | |
| 9 | | | | | | | =SUMPRODUCT(K4:M4,K6:M6) | | | |

The worksheet captures the information about resources available and the amounts needed for any specified level of production.

Sample values for the production quantities have been inserted, just to check that the worksheet operates as expected. Excel Solver will be used to compute the optimum quantities.

There are some limitations or constraints that must be taken into account. These are:

1. You cannot exceed the available resources
2. There must be at least 4 of each product (samples for the craft show)
3. There must be whole numbers of products (integers)
4. There must be a pair of gloves each for at least half the scarves (so that sets can be offered for sale)

Don't forget

Some constraints are specified in the problem description, while others may be implicit (e.g. the requirement for integer (and positive) values of production).

# Solver

To calculate the optimum solution for the craft fair problem:

1. Click the cell J9 that contains the target value Total Income; then select the Data tab and click Solver in the Analysis group

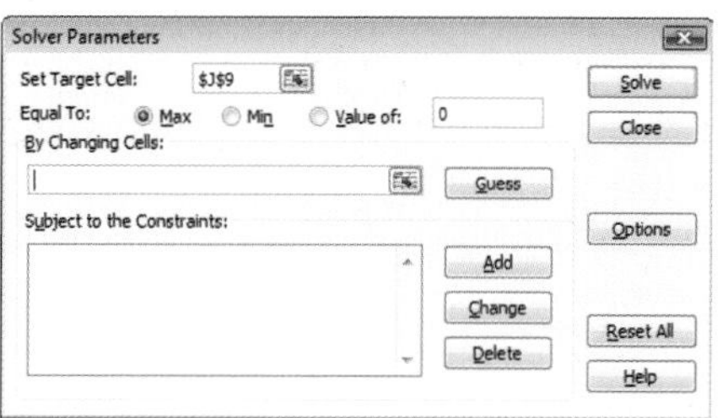


2. Choose the Max option. Then click the By Changing Cells box, and use the Collapse and Expand buttons to select the product quantities cells (K6:M6)

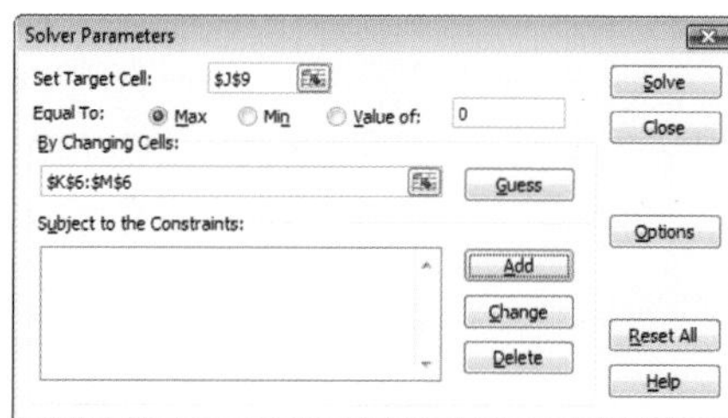


3. Click the Add button and select cells to specify that resources used must be less than or equal to those available

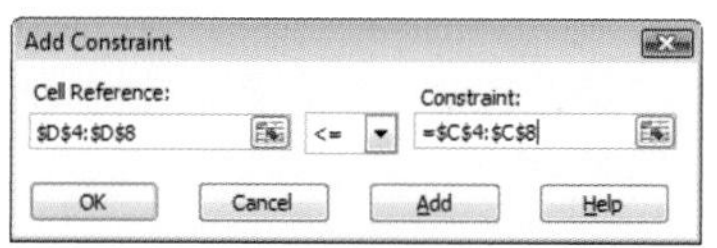


4. Click Add and select cells to specify that quantities produced must be greater than or equal to 4

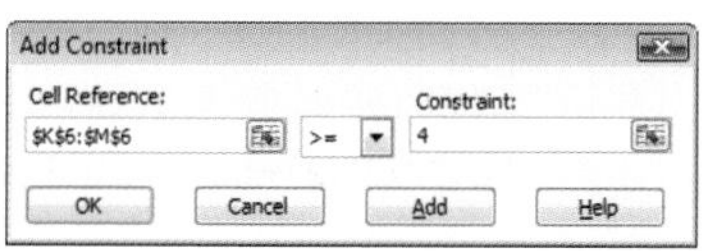


5. Add a constraint that quantities must be integers

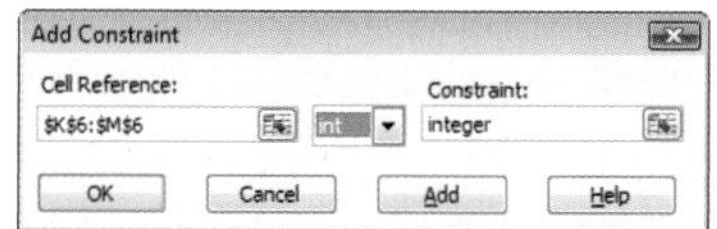

Solver will use the currently selected cell as the target, unless you replace this reference with another cell.

Click Add to define the next constraint, or click OK to return to the Solver Parameters panel.

...cont'd

6 Specify that the quantity of gloves must be at least half the quantity of scarves, and click OK

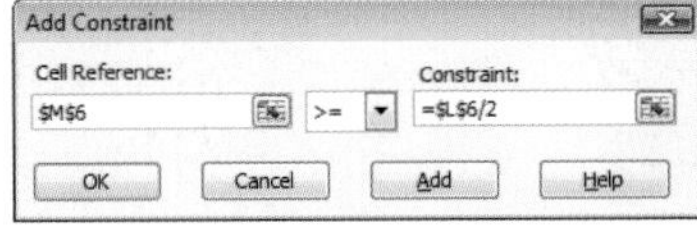

The Solver now has all the information required to get the answer.

The Guess button allows Solver to make its own choice of Changing Cells. If you use this, check that the cells selected are appropriate for your purposes.

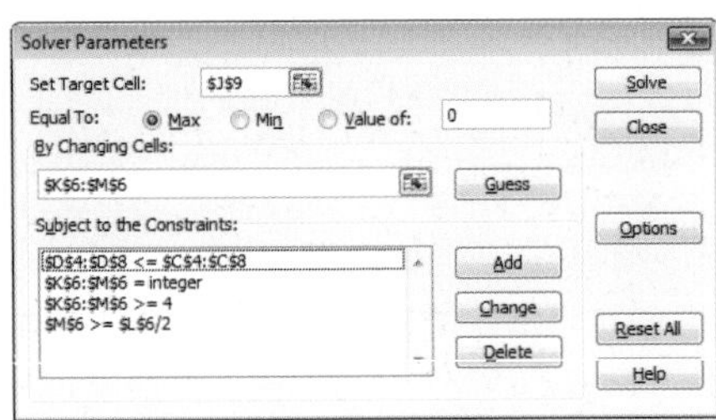

## Solution

1 Click Solve, and the results are calculated and displayed

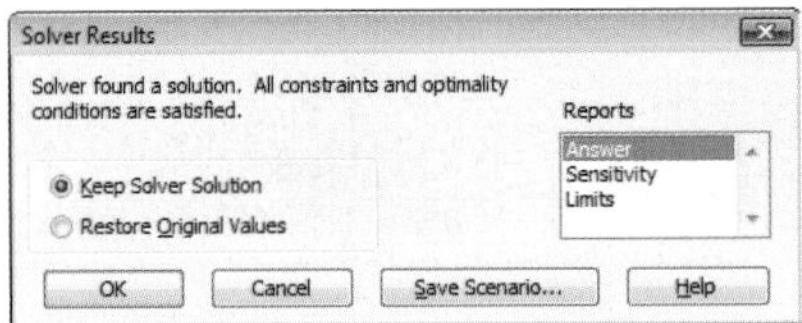

2 If Solver found a solution, choose Answer (to save the statistical report), click Keep the solution, and then click OK

The Answer worksheet will list the results and the constraints applied. Sensitivity and Limits reports are also available, but will not be meaningful for problems with integer constraints.

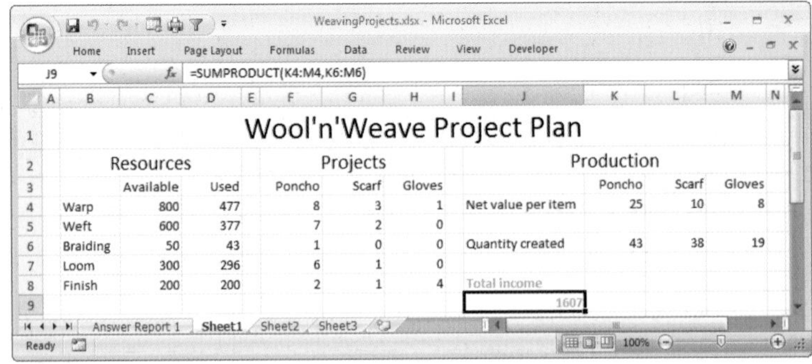

3 This shows the product mix required for maximum profit

# 11 Links and Connections

*Excel lets you make external references to other workbooks or to web pages that contain data needed for your active worksheet. Your worksheet is updated automatically if the source data changes. You can also share your data as an Office document or as a PDF.*

# Link to Workbooks

**Hot tip**

Workbook links are very useful when you need to combine information from several workbooks that may be created in different locations or on different systems.

Sometimes you may want to refer to the data in one workbook from another, separate workbook. You may for example want to provide an alternative view of the data in a worksheet, or to merge data from individual workbooks to create a summary workbook. You can refer to the contents of cells in another workbook by creating external references (also known as links).

References may be to a cell or a range, though it is usually better to refer to a defined name in the other workbook.

To establish defined names in a source workbook:

1. Open a source workbook, for example North.xlsx

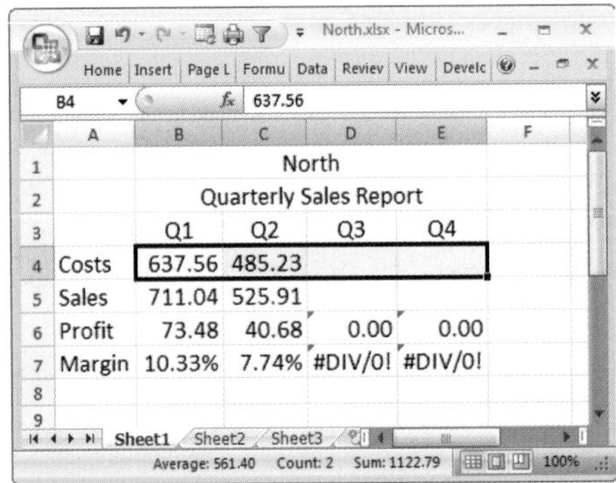

| | A | B | C | D | E | F |
|---|---|---|---|---|---|---|
| 1 | | | North | | | |
| 2 | | | Quarterly Sales Report | | | |
| 3 | | Q1 | Q2 | Q3 | Q4 | |
| 4 | Costs | 637.56 | 485.23 | | | |
| 5 | Sales | 711.04 | 525.91 | | | |
| 6 | Profit | 73.48 | 40.68 | 0.00 | 0.00 | |
| 7 | Margin | 10.33% | 7.74% | #DIV/0! | #DIV/0! | |
| 8 | | | | | | |
| 9 | | | | | | |



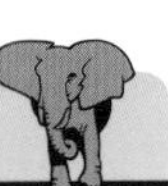

**Don't forget**

This shows the sales by quarter for one region, with the first two quarters entered. The calculations for margin (profit/sales) for the remaining quarters show zero divide errors, since the associated sales values are zero.

2. Select a range of cells, for example B4:E4 (the costs)

3. Select the Formulas tab and click Define Name in the Defined Names group

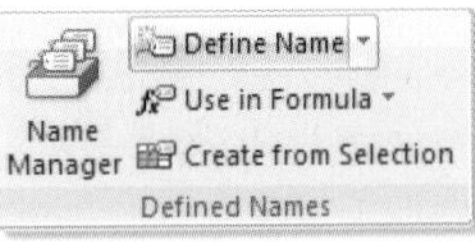



4. Specify the name (or accept the suggested name, e.g. Costs) and then click OK

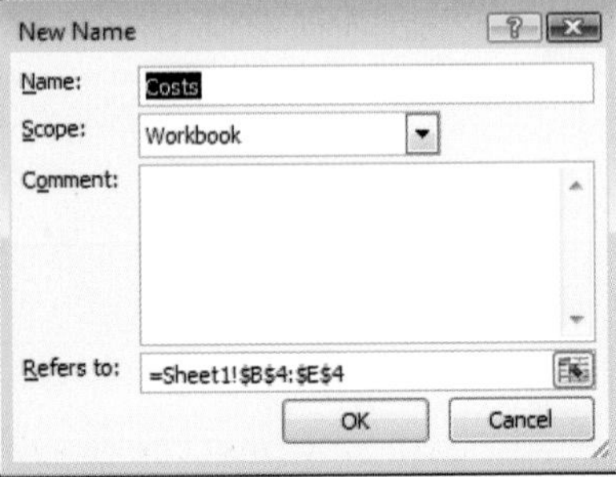



5. Repeat the Define Name process for names Sales (B5:E5) and Profit (B6:E6)

6 Select the Formulas tab and click Name Manager in the Defined Names group, to see all the name definitions

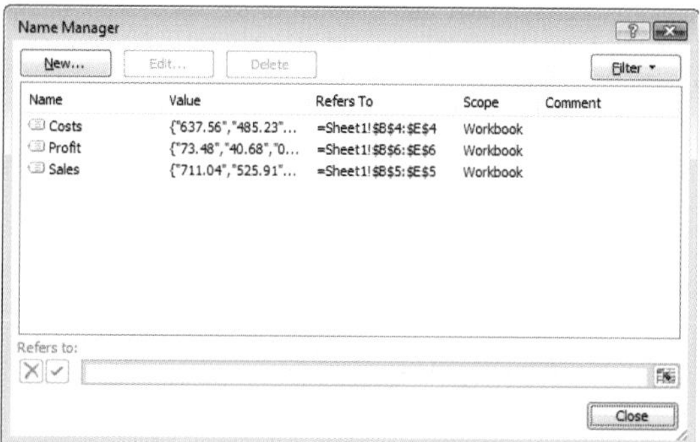

7 Save and close the North workbook

Repeat this for the other source workbooks (in this example they are South, East and West), to define range names Costs, Sales and Profit for each of them.

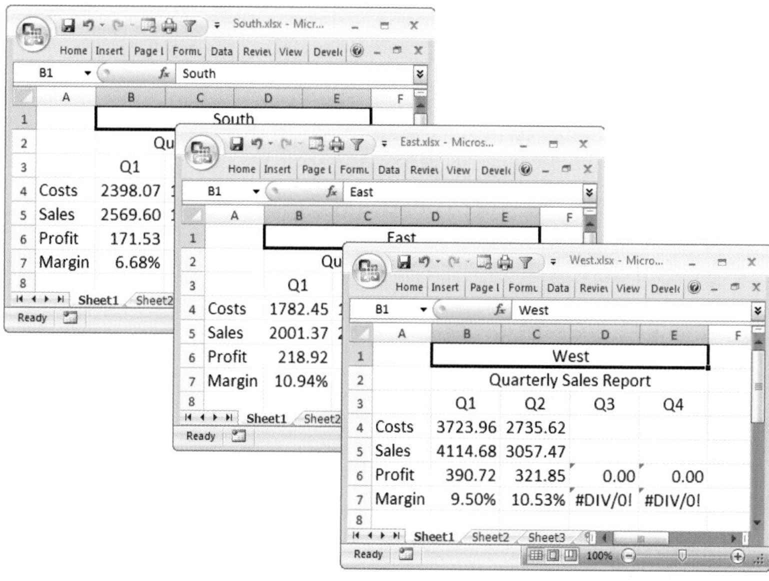

8 Save and close the South, East and West workbooks

Hot tip

The names will have the same cell references for the associated ranges as those shown for the North workbook.

Don't forget

The benefit of links is that when source workbooks change you won't have to change the destination workbooks that refer to those sources manually.

# Create External References

1. Open the source workbooks that contain the cells you want to refer to (e.g. North, South, East and West)

2. Open the workbook that will contain the external references (in the example it is called Overall.xlsx)

You can incorporate the external reference into a function or formula, as you might with any cell reference.

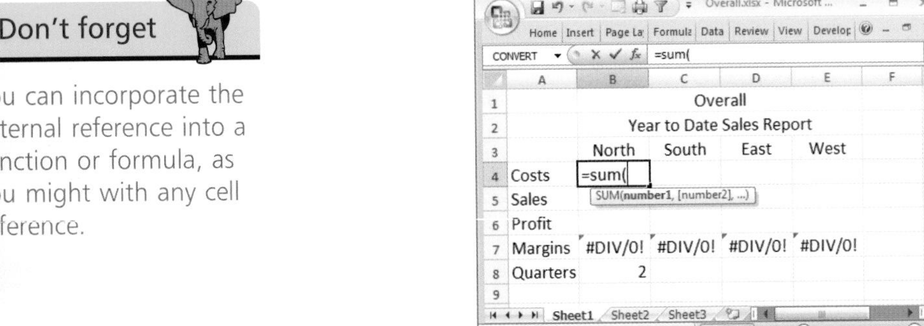
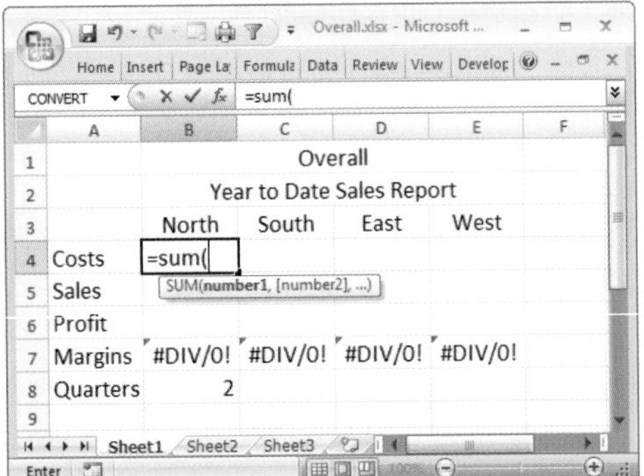


3. Select the cell in which you want to create the first of the external references (e.g. B4) and type (for example) =sum(

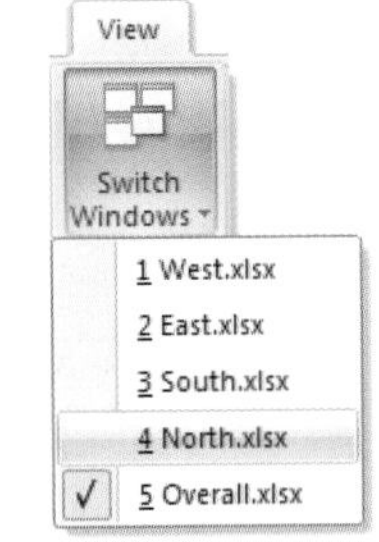


4. Select the View tab, and in the Windows group click Switch Windows, click the source workbook, and if necessary select the worksheet that contains the cells that you want to link to

5. Press F3, and select the defined name for the range of cells, e.g. Costs, click OK and then press Enter

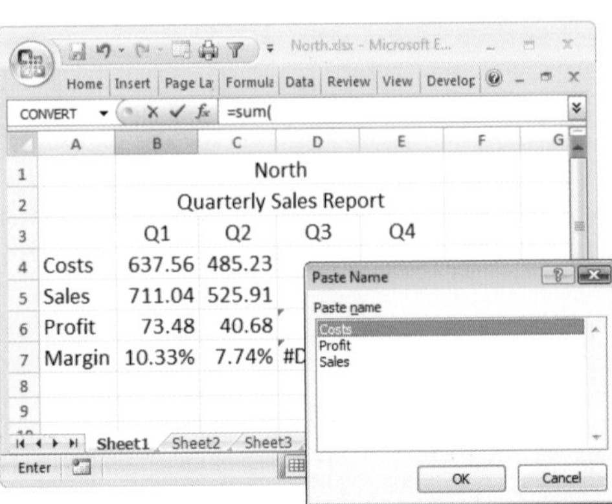

6. Similarly, enter a formula in B5 to sum Sales, and enter a formula in B6 to sum Profit

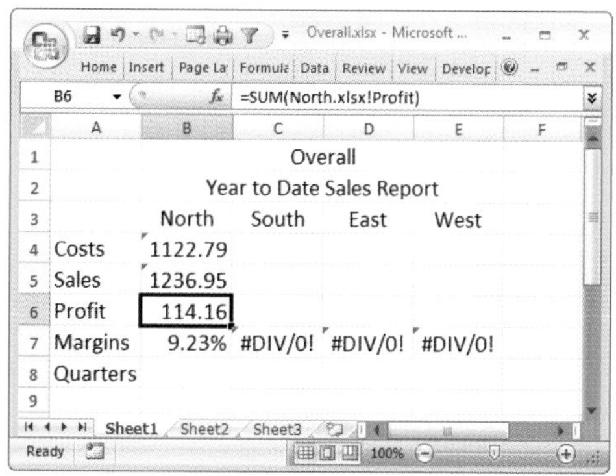

## Hot tip

You can copy the formula for Costs and then change the defined name to Sales or Profit.

You could refer to source workbook cells directly:

1. Click in cell B8 and type =count(

2. Switch to North and select the cell range B7:E7

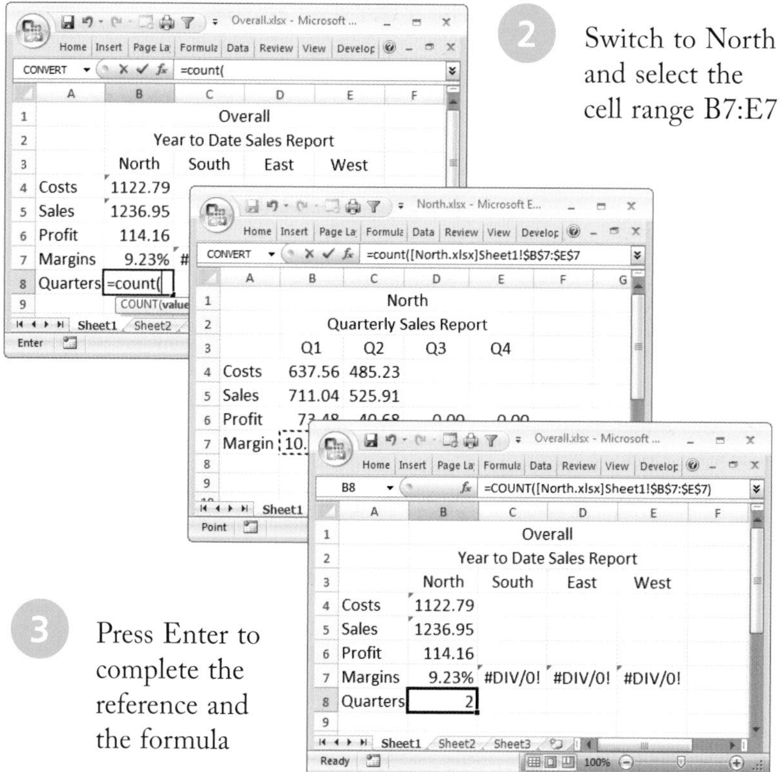


3. Press Enter to complete the reference and the formula

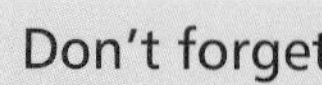

## Don't forget

This function counts the number of cells containing numbers (thus ignoring the incomplete quarters where the Margin shows Divide by Zero).

# Styles of Reference

While the source workbooks are open, the links to defined names take the form:

**North.xlsx!Costs**

Where you refer to cells directly, the links take the form:

**[North.xlsx]Sheet1!$B$7:$E$7**

Note that the cell references could be relative or mixed as well as absolute as shown.

Close the source workbook, and you'll find that the external references are immediately expanded to include a fully qualified link to the source workbook file.

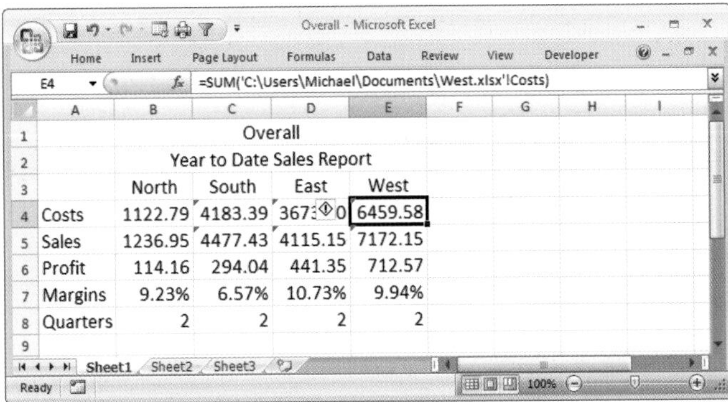

Overall - Microsoft Excel

E4 =SUM('C:\Users\Michael\Documents\West.xlsx'!Costs)

| | North | South | East | West |
|---|---|---|---|---|
| Costs | 1122.79 | 4183.39 | 367[illegible]0 | 6459.58 |
| Sales | 1236.95 | 4477.43 | 4115.15 | 7172.15 |
| Profit | 114.16 | 294.04 | 441.35 | 712.57 |
| Margins | 9.23% | 6.57% | 10.73% | 9.94% |
| Quarters | 2 | 2 | 2 | 2 |

Links with direct cell references also show the file path and name:

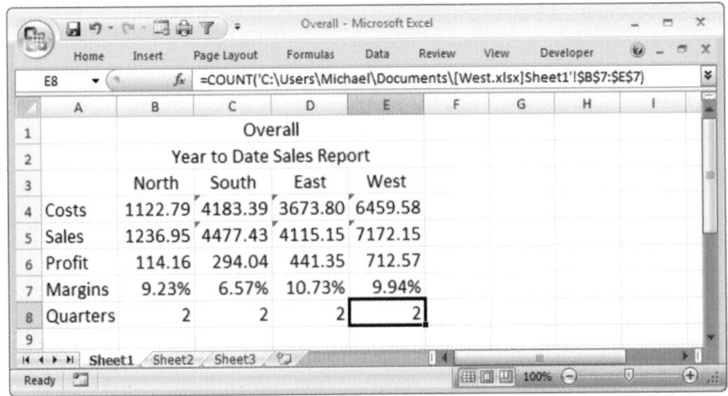

Overall - Microsoft Excel

E8 =COUNT('C:\Users\Michael\Documents\[West.xlsx]Sheet1'!$B$7:$E$7)

| | North | South | East | West |
|---|---|---|---|---|
| Costs | 1122.79 | 4183.39 | 3673.80 | 6459.58 |
| Sales | 1236.95 | 4477.43 | 4115.15 | 7172.15 |
| Profit | 114.16 | 294.04 | 441.35 | 712.57 |
| Margins | 9.23% | 6.57% | 10.73% | 9.94% |
| Quarters | 2 | 2 | 2 | 2 |

In each case, the path and file name will be enclosed in quotation marks, whether or not there are spaces included.

**Don't forget**

Quotation marks will be applied to the workbook name if it contains any spaces, e.g. 'Sales North.xlsx'!Costs

**Hot tip**

The references for South, East and West have been incorporated. You can do this by selection as with North, or you can just copy the formulas for North and change the name appropriately.

# Source Workbook Changes

Assume that you receive new versions of the source workbooks (with the next quarter's data). You can control how these changes affect the destination workbook.

When the source and destination workbooks are open on the same computer, links will be updated automatically.

1. Open the destination workbook (leaving all of the source workbooks closed)

2. The security warning says that automatic updating has been disabled

3. Click the Options button

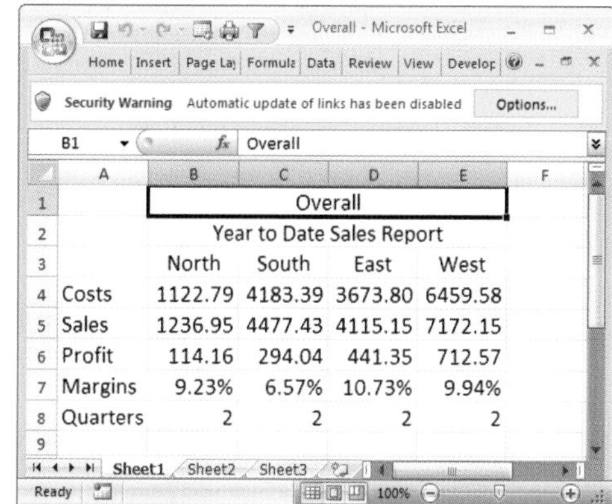


| | A | B | C | D | E | F |
|---|---|---|---|---|---|---|
| 1 | | Overall | | | | |
| 2 | | Year to Date Sales Report | | | | |
| 3 | | North | South | East | West | |
| 4 | Costs | 1122.79 | 4183.39 | 3673.80 | 6459.58 | |
| 5 | Sales | 1236.95 | 4477.43 | 4115.15 | 7172.15 | |
| 6 | Profit | 114.16 | 294.04 | 441.35 | 712.57 | |
| 7 | Margins | 9.23% | 6.57% | 10.73% | 9.94% | |
| 8 | Quarters | 2 | 2 | 2 | 2 | |
| 9 | | | | | | |

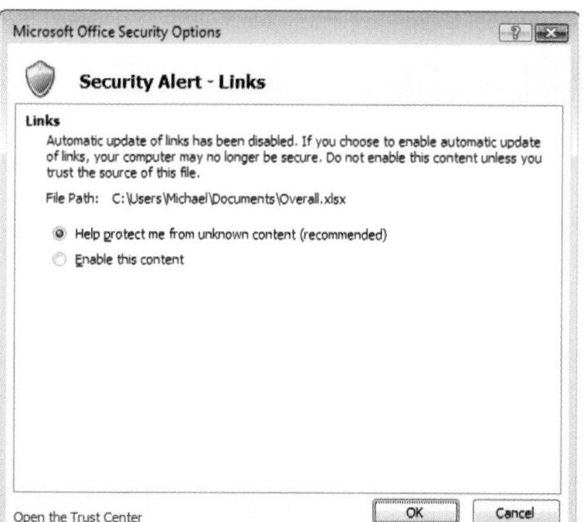


4. Leave the choice as "Help protect me", and click the OK button

This is the normal default setting, but you can change it to allow updating always (see page 179).

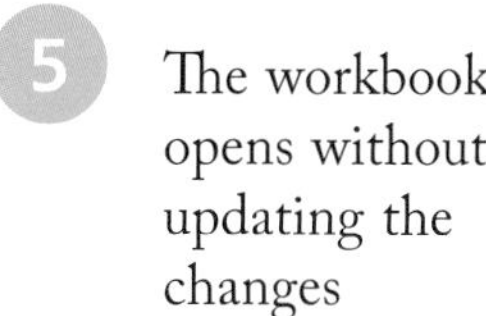

5. The workbook opens without updating the changes

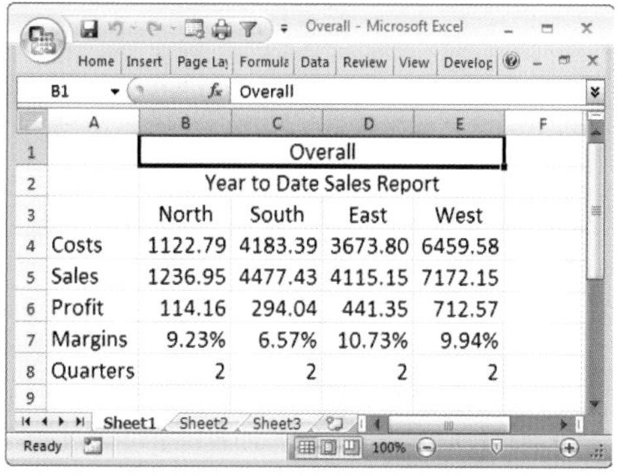


| | A | B | C | D | E | F |
|---|---|---|---|---|---|---|
| 1 | | Overall | | | | |
| 2 | | Year to Date Sales Report | | | | |
| 3 | | North | South | East | West | |
| 4 | Costs | 1122.79 | 4183.39 | 3673.80 | 6459.58 | |
| 5 | Sales | 1236.95 | 4477.43 | 4115.15 | 7172.15 | |
| 6 | Profit | 114.16 | 294.04 | 441.35 | 712.57 | |
| 7 | Margins | 9.23% | 6.57% | 10.73% | 9.94% | |
| 8 | Quarters | 2 | 2 | 2 | 2 | |
| 9 | | | | | | |

# Apply the Updates

1. Select the Data tab; then in the Connections group choose Edit Links

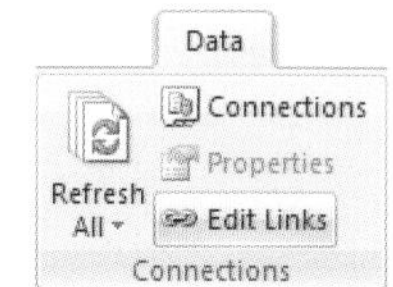


2. Select the entries you want to refresh and click the Update Values button

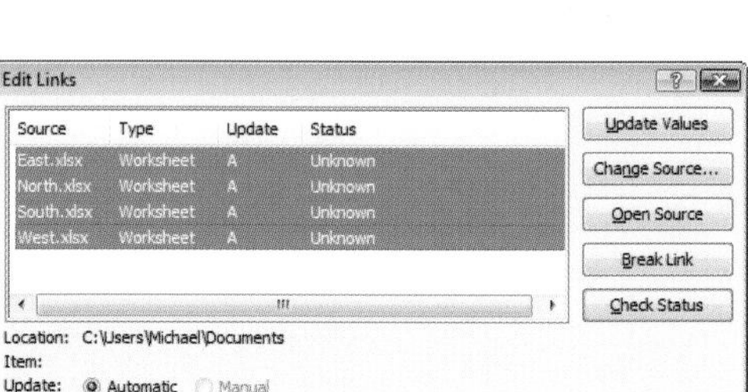

## Don't forget

You can update only selected entries if you wish, and you can use the Check Status button to see which entries still need to be applied.

3. Data changes are applied and worksheet status is updated

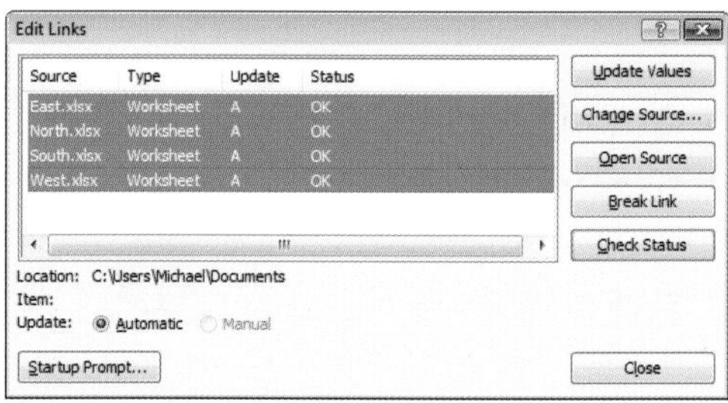




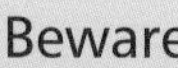

## Beware

Do not apply updates where you are unsure of the origin of the changes, or if you want to retain the current values.

4. The updated information is added to the destination workbook, which now displays the data for three quarters

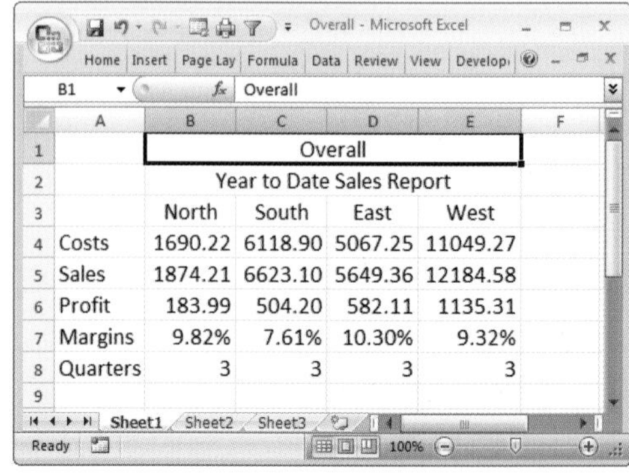


| | A | B | C | D | E |
|---|---|---|---|---|---|
| 1 | | Overall | | | |
| 2 | | Year to Date Sales Report | | | |
| 3 | | North | South | East | West |
| 4 | Costs | 1690.22 | 6118.90 | 5067.25 | 11049.27 |
| 5 | Sales | 1874.21 | 6623.10 | 5649.36 | 12184.58 |
| 6 | Profit | 183.99 | 504.20 | 582.11 | 1135.31 |
| 7 | Margins | 9.82% | 7.61% | 10.30% | 9.32% |
| 8 | Quarters | 3 | 3 | 3 | 3 |

# Turn Off the Prompt

You can turn off the update prompt for a specific workbook.

1. Open the workbook, select the Data tab, and click Edit Links in the Connections group

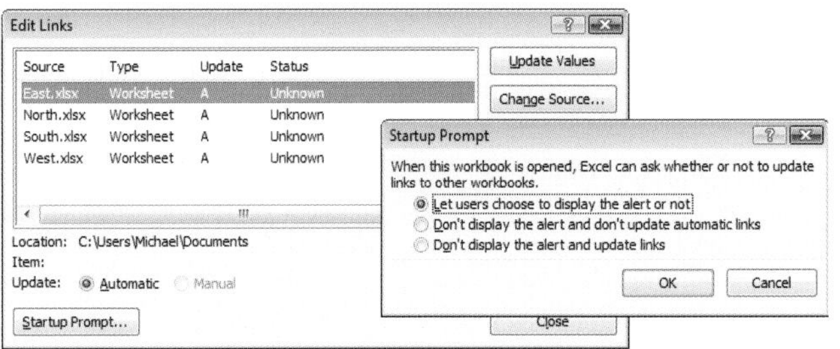


2. Click the Startup Prompt button and choose “Don’t display the alert”, with or without updating as desired

There is an Excel option to turn off all update prompts. To review this setting:

1. Select the Office button, click Excel Options and choose the Advanced category
2. There is an option called “Ask to update automatic links”, which is normally selected
3. Do not clear this option: this would cause automatic updates to be applied to all workbooks with no prompt

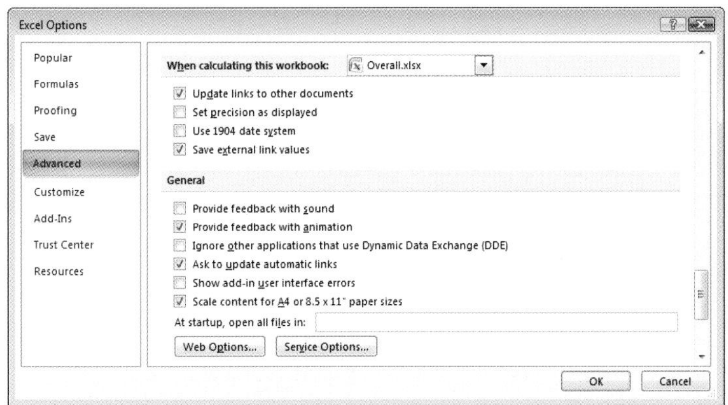

If you turn off the alert and disallow updates, users of the workbook won’t know that the data is out of date.

Beware

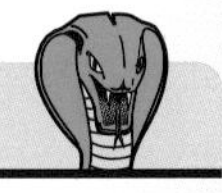

Do not use this option to turn off the prompt, or you will not be aware when workbooks get updated. Use the workbook-specific method only.

# Excel in Word

Hot tip

When you've completed your worksheet, you can present the information in a Microsoft Office Word document (as illustrated here) or in a PowerPoint presentation.

To add data from an Excel worksheet to your Word document:

1. In Excel, select the worksheet data and press Ctrl+C (or select Home and click Copy from the Clipboard group)

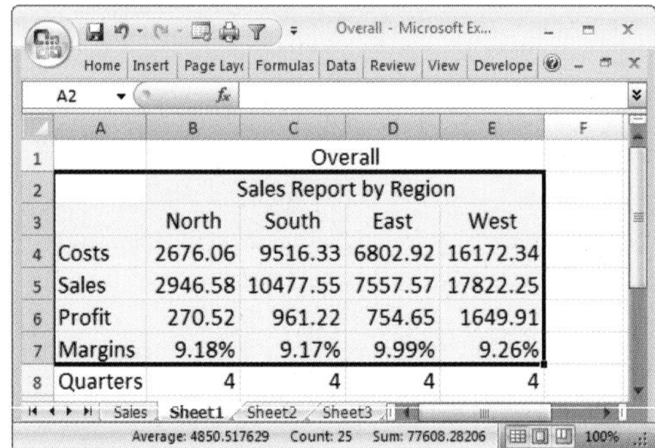


2. Click in the Word document and press Ctrl+V (or select Home and click Paste from the Clipboard group)

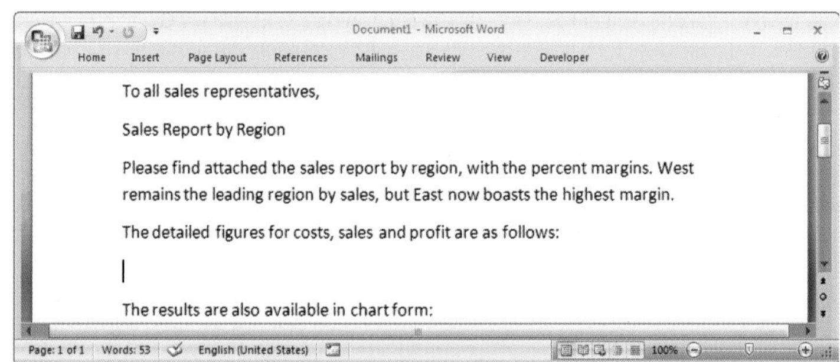


3. Click Paste Options and select the type of paste you want

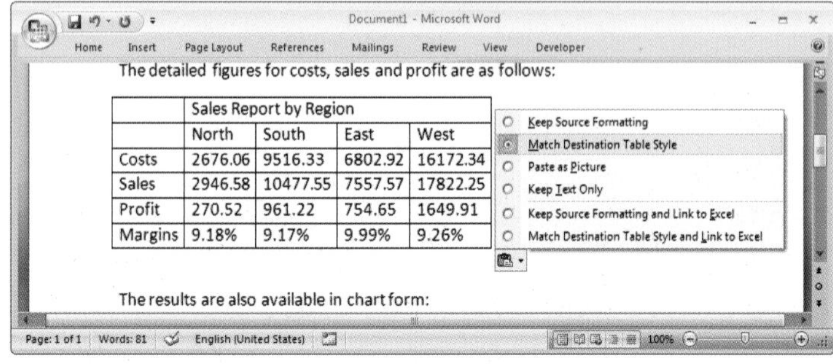


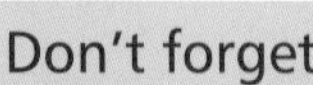

You can paste the data as a table, retaining the original formatting or using styles from the Word document. Alternatively, paste the data as a picture or as tab-separated text. There are also options to maintain a link with the original worksheet.

To copy an Excel chart to your Word document:

1. In Excel, select the chart on the worksheet or chart sheet and press Ctrl+C (or select Home, Clipboard, Copy)

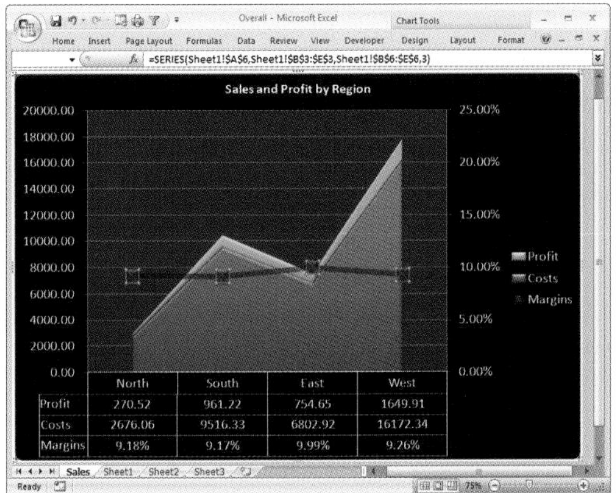


2. In the Word document, click where you want the chart and press Ctrl+V (or select Home, Clipboard, Paste)

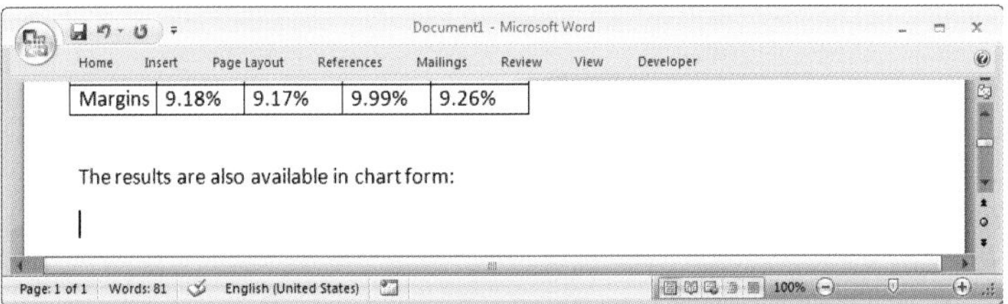


3. Click Paste Options and select the type you want

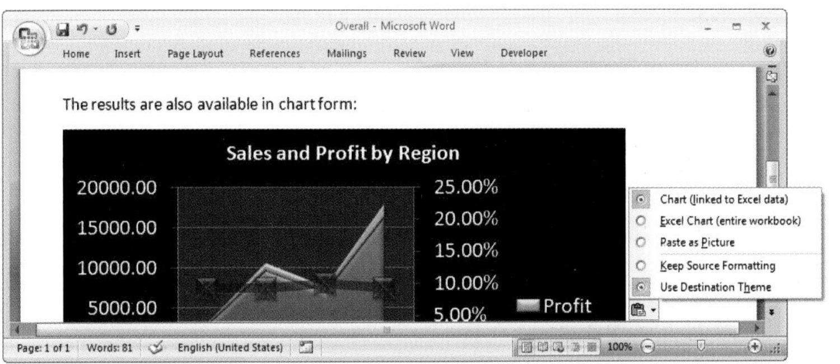

**Hot tip**

Apply any text styles or chart formatting required before you copy the chart to the clipboard.

**Don't forget**

You can choose Chart (linked to Excel data), Excel Chart (entire workbook), Paste as Picture, Keep Source Formatting or Use Destination Theme.

# Publish as PDF

Hot tip

This requires the PDF Add-in available from the Microsoft website www.microsoft.com/downloads.

Hot tip

You can save your workbook as a PDF file and be sure that the files you share retain exactly the data and format you intended.

Don't forget

You can publish the entire workbook, the active worksheet or the ranges of cells selected within the worksheet.

To send information to others who do not have Excel or Word, you can publish the workbook in the Adobe Acrobat PDF format, which requires only the Adobe Reader, available for no charge from www.adobe.com.

1. Open the workbook in Excel, click the Office button and click the arrow next to Save As

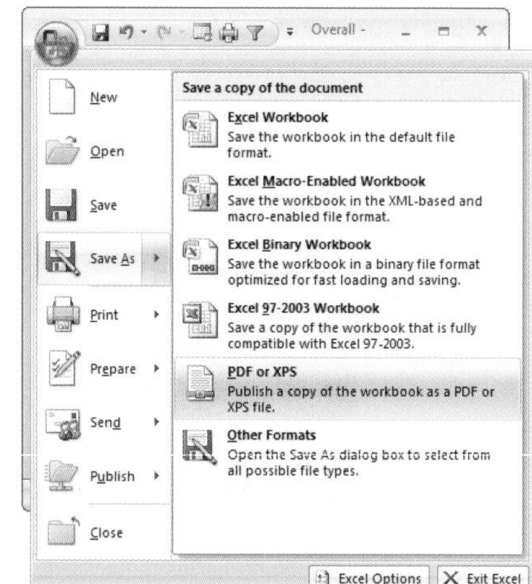


2. Click the entry for PDF or XPS publishing

3. Click the Options button to set the scope

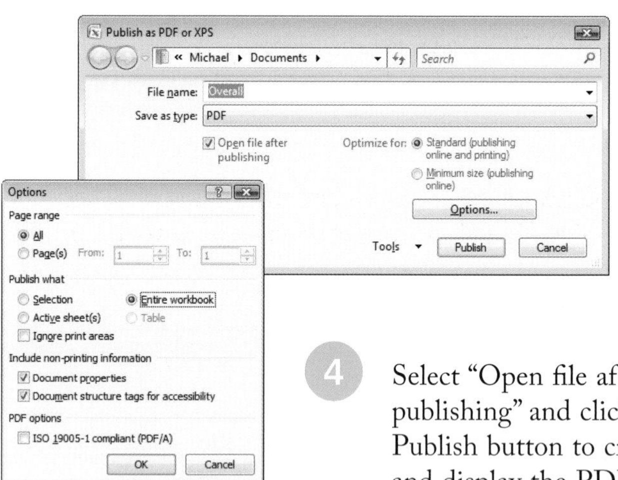


4. Select "Open file after publishing" and click the Publish button to create and display the PDF file

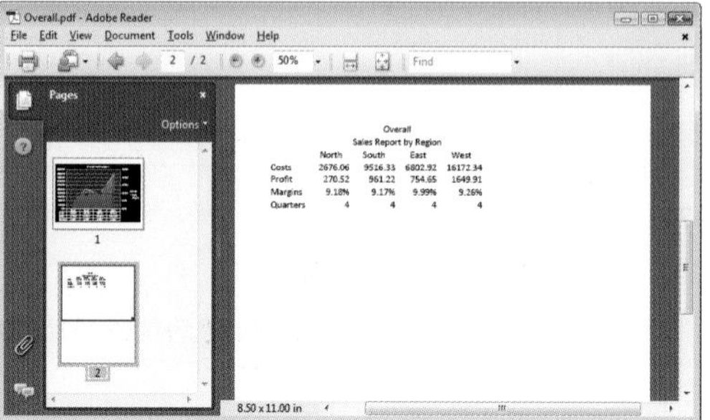

# Exchange Data with the Web

If you have access to Excel Services, you can publish a workbook to that server so that other users can access it via their browsers by using Microsoft Office Excel Web Access.

You don't need Excel Services in order to receive data from the Internet, though you may need to install additional software. For example, you can receive dynamic share price updates from the MSN Money website if you install the Stock Quotes add-in.

1. Go to www.microsoft.com/downloads, search for Stock Quotes and click MSN Money Stock Quotes Add-in

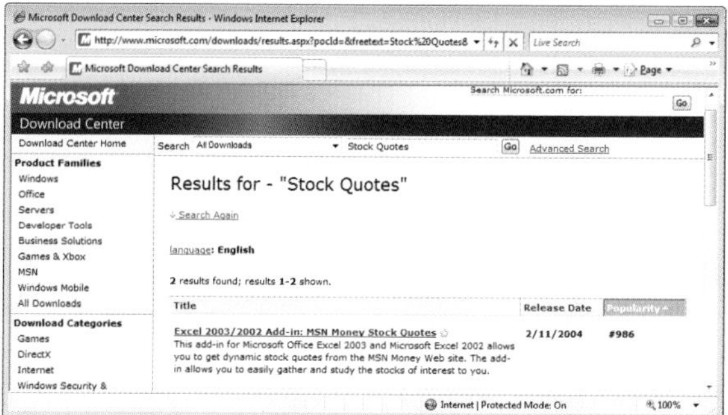


2. Click Continue to validate your version of Office; then click Download to save msnsq.exe to your hard disk

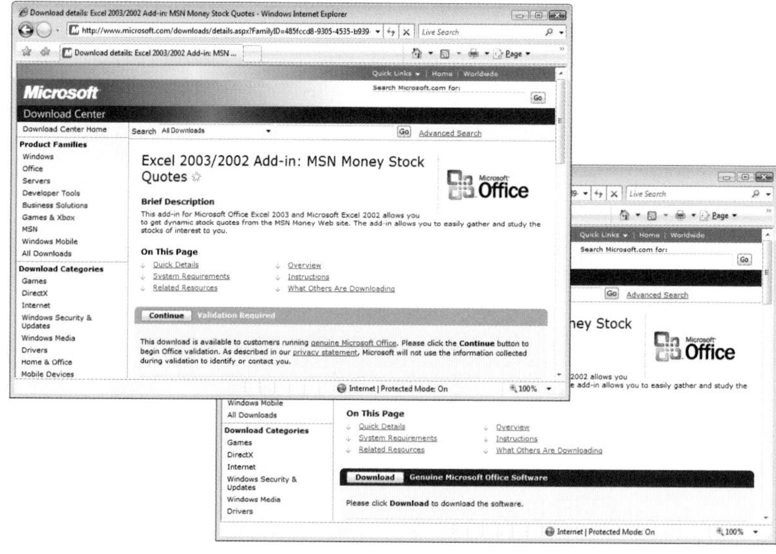

**Hot tip**

Excel Services is a server running Microsoft Office SharePoint Server 2007 that is capable of running Excel Calculation Services, which include many Excel features.

**Don't forget**

This is described as an Excel 2002/2003 add-in, but it also works with Excel 2007.

# Install and Use Stock Quotes

1. Run the downloaded installation file application (see page 183) to start the installation wizard for the Stock Quotes add-in

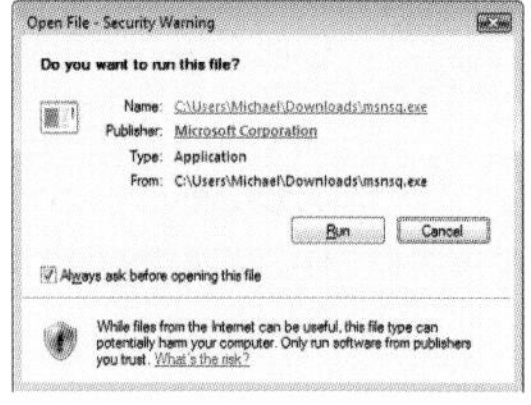


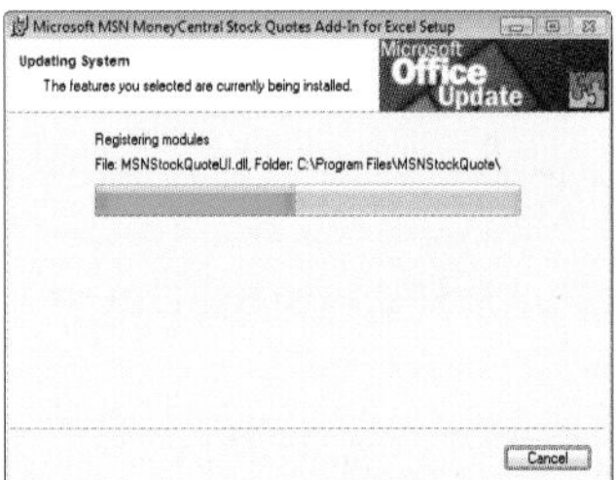


2. Follow the prompts to complete the installation

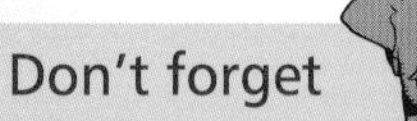


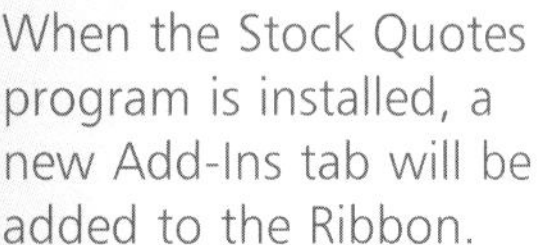

When the Stock Quotes program is installed, a new Add-Ins tab will be added to the Ribbon.

3. To set up the add-in, open Excel while your system is connected to the Internet

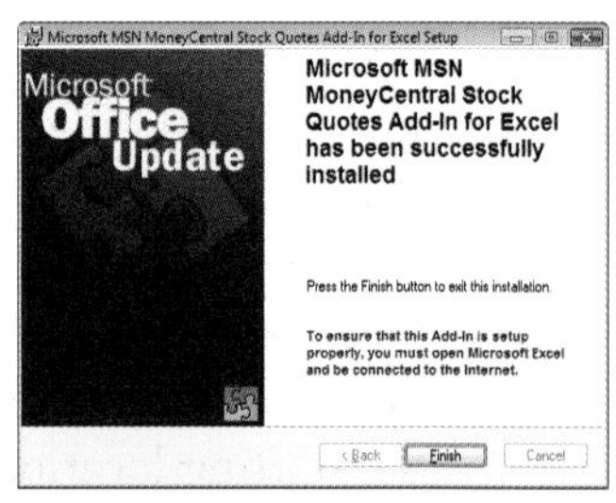


Use the add-in to insert prices and other share-related information:

1. Open a new workbook, and click the Add-Ins tab to display the MSN Money Central Stock Quotes toolbar

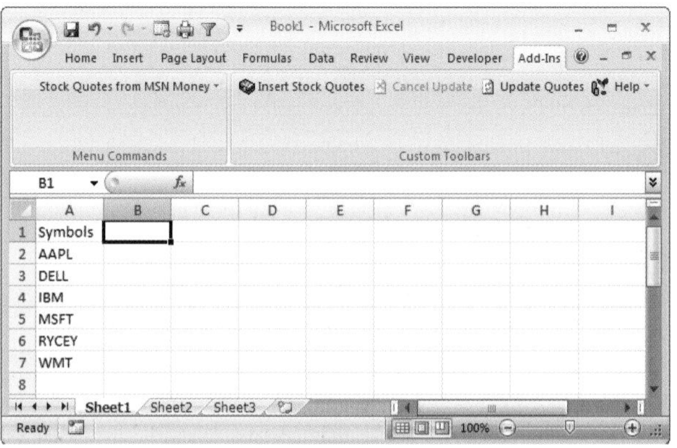


2. Type the heading Symbols, and enter a list of stock symbols such as AAPL, DELL, IBM, MSFT, RYCEY and WMT below the heading

3. Click in cell B1 and then click Insert Stock Quotes to download the dialog

MSN Money Stock Quotes

Loading dialog...

Cancel

4. Type the range that contains the stock symbols

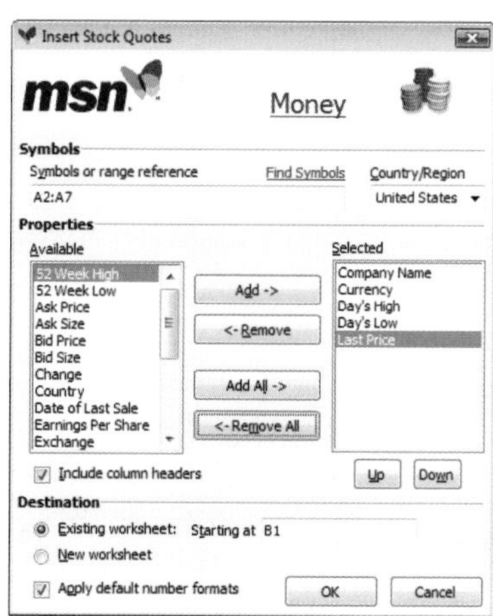


5. Add the properties you want to insert (e.g. company name, currency and various prices)

6. Choose to include column headers; then click Existing Worksheet and check the starting location

7. Click OK to insert the data at that location (which should allow for headers and/or stock symbols)

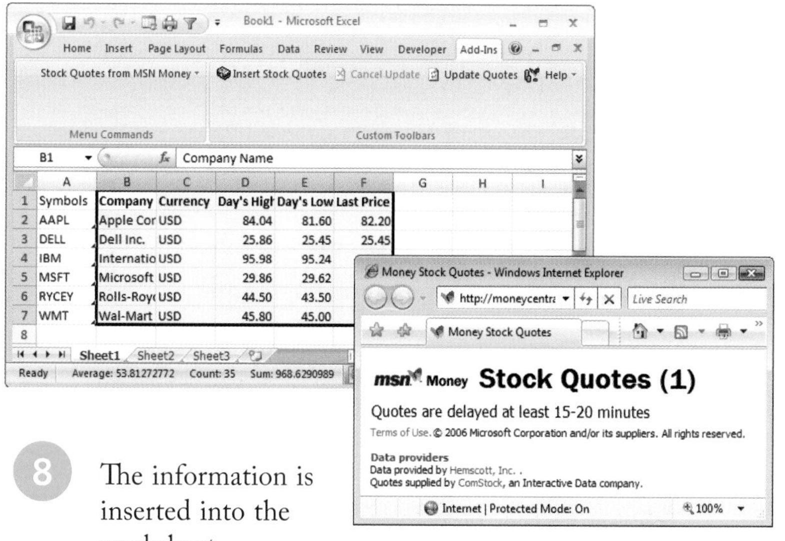


8. The information is inserted into the worksheet

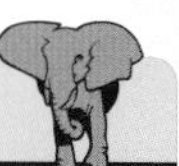

## Don't forget

You can type the stock symbols directly in the box, separating multiple entries by commas, spaces or semicolons. If you are unsure of the symbol, click the Find Symbols link.

## Hot tip

Click Update Quotes on the toolbar to refresh the information. As the Internet Explorer note indicates, the quotes will be delayed by at least 15–20 minutes.

# Currency Rate Calculator

A different approach to Internet access is taken with the Currency Rate calculator, which incorporates a web query. There is no need to install software – you just open the template.

1. Open a new workbook using the Currency rate calculator online template (from Other Categories, see page 158)

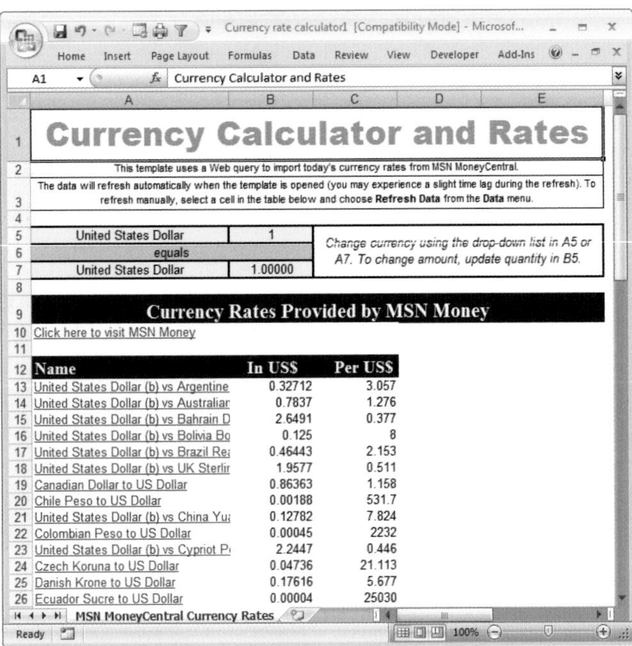


2. The data will be updated when the workbook is opened (if you allow the data connection)

3. Select Data, Connections, Refresh All to insert the latest currency rates into the workbook, during the Excel session

4. Respond OK to the external data sources security message to apply the updates

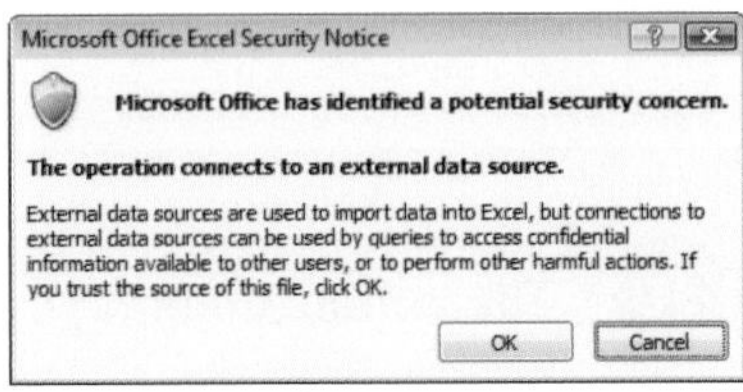


**Don't forget**

To convert between currencies, choose the initial currency (A5) and the final currency (A7); enter the initial amount (B5), and the final value appears in B7.

| UK Sterling Spot | 100 |
|---|---|
| equals | |
| Canadian Dollar | 226.68272 |

## A



## B



## C



## D

## E



## F



## G

## H



## I



## J



## K



## L



## M

## S



## T

## U



## V



## W



## X

## Y



## Z